UNDERSTANDING HUMAN COMM

► Speech is civilization itself. The word, even the most contradictory word, preserves contact—it is silence which isolates.

—Thomas Mann
The Magic Mountain

UNDERSTANDING HUMAN COMMUNICATION

▶ **THIRD EDITION**

Ronald B. Adler
Santa Barbara City College

George Rodman
Brooklyn College,
The City University of New York

HOLT, RINEHART AND WINSTON, INC.

Fort Worth   Chicago   San Francisco   Philadelphia   Montreal   Toronto   London   Sydney   Tokyo

LIBRARY OF CONGRESS CATALOGING-IN-PUBLICATION DATA

Adler, Ronald B. (Ronald Brian), date.
  Understanding human communication.

  Includes bibliographies and index.
  I. Communication.   I.   Rodman, George R., date.
II. Title.
P90.A32 1988   001.51   87–17719

ISBN 0-03-013363-7

Printed in the United States of America
       9   0   1   039   9   8   7   6   5

Holt, Rinehart and Winston, Inc.
The Dryden Press
Saunders College Publishing

► PREFACE

Despite two successful editions, we're beginning to have doubts about whether *Understanding Human Communication* is the right title for the book you're about to read. *Understanding* the complexities of face-to-face human interaction is certainly important, but intellectual awareness by itself isn't enough to satisfy most instructors or students who devote an entire semester or quarter to studying the subject. In addition to expanding their knowledge, most people want to improve their communication *behavior.* They want to speak and listen better in the multitude of one-to-one, group, and public situations they face in everyday life.

Like its predecessors, this edition of *Understanding Human Communication* recognizes the importance of both intellectual understanding and behavior change. Rather than take sides in the "theory vs. skills" debate, the book shows how theories and research on face-to-face communication translate into skills that students can use to communicate more effectively in their everyday lives. Thus, students can expect to finish the basic course well equipped both to talk *about* communication and to talk *with* the people who are important to them.

A number of changes distinguish this edition from its prececessors. At the request of many users, several key topics are expanded and clarified. These include a nonideological treatment of empathy, the power of language, types of listening, and the relationship between verbal and nonverbal communication. Two chapters are now devoted to interpersonal communication. Besides describing the communication dynamics of one-to-one relationships, the information in these chapters will also prove valuable for improving the quality of communication in other contexts. The treatment of critical thinking and group problem solving in Chapter 10 has been expanded, both to clarify that important topic and to reflect its importance. The chapters on public speaking have also been improved. They contain new information on visual aids, constructive speech criticism, ethics, persuasive strategies, and building credibility. The principles of public speaking in these chapters are illustrated by many excerpts from student speeches, as well as by the complete annotated texts of several outstanding student presentations.

Several instructional aids in this edition promise to make student learning easier and more effective. Key vocabulary terms are introduced in the opening of each chapter and highlighted when they first appear in the text. A comprehensive glossary provides definitions for these terms in a clear, accessible way. Finally, an expanded Instructor's Manual by Mary Bozik of the University of Northern Iowa will help instructors design and teach their courses in ways that boost both the quality and enjoyment of learning.

Despite these changes, *Understanding Human Communication* still follows the same approach that instructors and students have appreciated in previous editions. The text aims to present ideas in a readable manner, based on the belief that important ideas needn't be obscure or tedious. Every chapter contains a wide variety of epigrams, photos, brief readings, sophisticated cartoons, and individual exercises that present key ideas in an interesting and useful manner.

The success of *Understanding Human Commmunication* is due in great part to the contributions of the reviewers who offered their constructive suggestions: Richard Arthur, Montana State University; Ruth Aurelius, Des Moines Area Community College; Ann E. Busse, Northern Illinois University; Daniel Canary, Portland Community College; Robert T. Dixon, St. Louis Community College; Carley Dodd, Abeline Christian University; Diane M. Harney, Florida State University; David Hough, Vincennes University; Albert Katz, University of Wisconsin–Superior; Melba Kop, Chaminade University of Honolulu; Paul D. Krivonos, California State University–Northridge; Judith Litterst, St. Cloud State University; Don Morlan, University of Dayton; Kaye J. Nubel, Saddleback College; Gwenn D. Schultz, Portland State University; John P. Sprowl, University of Connecticut; Charlotte Toguchi, Kapiolani Community College; and Barbara Willard, Florida State University.

We wish to extend thanks to the following members of our focus group from St. Louis Community College at Meramec: Alice Bante, Linda Bianca, Dianne Breitwieser, Chris Carenza, Marilyn Davis, Bob Dixon, Jim Greer, Phil Hanson, Jan Mirikitani, Ray Sikes, and Sue Stanton.

We are also grateful for the contributions of the many professionals who worked so hard to make *Understanding Human Communication* a success. The talent of our designer, Janet Bollow, is apparent. Less obvious but equally valuable has been the support of the people at Holt, Rinehart and Winston, especially Debra Rapaport, Lucy Rosendahl, Lester A. Sheinis, Nancy Myers, and Louis Scardino.

Finally, we want to offer our thanks and love to the most important communicators in our lives: our wives and children.

Ronald B. Adler
George Rodman

▶ CONTENTS

▶ **CHAPTER 3**

LANGUAGE 48

▶ **CHAPTER 4**

LISTENING 72

▶ **CHAPTER 10**   **SOLVING PROBLEMS IN GROUPS   234**

▶ **PART FOUR**   **PUBLIC COMMUNICATION   261**

▶ **CHAPTER 11**   **CHOOSING AND DEVELOPING A TOPIC   262**

▶ **CHAPTER 12**   **ORGANIZATION AND SUPPORT   290**

▶ **CHAPTER 13**   **PRESENTING YOUR MESSAGE   330**

► **CHAPTER 14**

► **CHAPTER 15**

UNDERSTANDING HUMAN COMMUNICATION

►CHAPTER I

KEY TERMS

affection
channel
communication
control
decoding
encoding
environment
external noise
feedback

inclusion
interactive communication
   model
linear communication model
message
model
noise
physical need
physiological noise

psychological noise
receiver
safety need
self-actualization need
self-esteem need
social need
symbol
transactional communication
   model

HUMAN COMMUNICATION: WHAT AND WHY

After reading this chapter, you should understand the following:

1. The working definition of communication used in *Understanding Human Communication.*

2. The needs satisfied by communication.

3. The value of a communication model.

4. The elements of the transactional communication model introduced in this chapter.

5. Five common misconceptions about communication.

You should be able to do the following:

1. Give specific examples of the various types of needs you attempt to satisfy by communicating.

2. Identify the elements of the communication model in this chapter as they apply to an incident in your life.

3. Identify the misconceptions about communication you have held and suggest a more accurate belief for each.

Because this is a book about communication, it makes sense to begin by defining that term. This is not as simple as it might seem, for people use the word in a variety of ways that are only vaguely related:

▶ Family members, co-workers, and friends make such statements about their relationships as "We just can't communicate" or "We communicate perfectly."

▶ Business people talk about "office communications systems" consisting of computers, telephones, printers, and so on.

▶ Scientists study and describe communication among ants, dolphins, and other animals.

▶ Certain organizations label themselves "communications conglomerates," publishing newspapers, books, and magazines and owning radio and television stations.

There is clearly some relationship among uses such as these, but we need to narrow our focus before going on. A look at the Table of Contents of this book shows that it obviously doesn't deal with animals, computers, or newspapers. Neither is it about Holy Communion, the bestowing of a material thing, or many of the other subjects mentioned in the *Oxford English Dictionary*'s 1,200-word definition of communication.

What, then, *are* we talking about when we use the term *communication*? A survey of the ways in which scholars use the word will show that there is no single, universally accepted usage. Some definitions are long and complex whereas others are brief and simple. This isn't the place to explore the differences between these conceptions or to defend one against the others. What we need

© 1976 by Sidney Harris—American Scientist Magazine.

"Although humans make sounds with their mouths and occasionally look at each other, there is no solid evidence that they actually communicate with each other."

is a working definition that will help us in our study. For our purposes we will say that **communication** refers to *the process of human beings responding to the face-to-face symbolic behavior of other persons.*

A point-by-point examination of this definition reveals some important characteristics of communication as we will be studying it.

Communication Is Human

In this book we'll be discussing communication between human beings. Animals clearly do communicate: Bees instruct their hive-mates about the location of food by a meaning-laden dance. Chimpanzees have been taught to express themselves with the same sign language used by deaf humans, and a few have developed impressive vocabularies. And on a more commonplace level, pet owners can testify to the variety of messages their animals can express. Although this subject of animal communication is a fascinating and an important one, it goes beyond the scope of this book.

Communication Is a Face-to-Face Activity

Written messages, like books and letters, do not require face-to-face interaction; neither do mass media messages delivered by radio, television, or film. These types of communication are certainly important—so important that they deserve full treatment elsewhere. In this book we will focus on communication between persons who are in each other's presence.

Communication Is a Process

We often talk about communication as if it occurred in discrete, individual acts. In fact, communication is truly a continuous, ongoing process. Consider, for example, a friend's compliment about your appearance. Your interpretation of those words will depend on a long series of experiences stretching far back in time: How have others judged your appearance? How do you feel about your looks? How honest has your friend been in the past? How have you been feeling about one another recently? All this history will help shape your response to the other person's remark. In turn, the words you speak and the way you say them will shape the way your friend behaves toward you and others—both in this situation and in the future.

This simple example shows that it's inaccurate to talk about "acts" of communication as if they occurred in isolation. To put it differently, communication isn't a series of incidents pasted together like photographs in a scrapbook; instead, it is more like a motion picture in which the meaning comes from the unfolding of an interrelated series of images.

Communication Is Symbolic

Symbols are signs used to represent things, processes, ideas, or events in ways that make communication possible. Chapter 3 discusses the nature of symbols in detail, but this idea is so important that it needs an introduction now. The most significant feature of symbols is their *arbitrary* nature. For example, there's no logical reason why the letters in *book* should stand for the object you're reading now. Speakers of Spanish would call it a *libro* whereas Germans would label it a *Buch*. Even in English, another term would work just as well as long as everyone agreed to use it in the same way. We overcome the arbitrary nature of symbols by linguistic rules and customs. Effective communication depends on agreement among people about these rules. This is easiest to see when we observe people who don't follow linguistic conventions. For example, recall how unusual the speech of children and nonnative speakers of a language often sounds.

We've already talked about words as one type of symbol. In addition, nonverbal behavior can have symbolic meaning. As with words, some nonverbal behaviors, though arbitrary, have clearly agreed-upon meanings: For example, to most North Americans, placement of a thumb and first finger together while facing the palm of the hand outward stands for the idea of something being "OK." But even more than words, nonverbal behaviors are ambiguous. Does a frown signify anger or unhappiness? Does a hug stand for a friendly greeting or a symbol of the hugger's romantic interest in you? One can't always be sure. We'll discuss the nature of nonverbal communication in Chapter 5.

Communication Requires the Response of a Receiver

Sending by itself isn't sufficient to create an act of communication: There needs to be some response to a message as well. To understand this point, think of a radio station broadcasting late at night without a single listener tuned in. One needn't argue about trees falling in an unpopulated forest to agree that no communication has occurred here. In the same way, a speaker talking at one or more people who aren't listening isn't communicating—at least by our definition.

Ideally we hope that others receive and understand our messages exactly as we intend them; but for our purposes we'll say that this doesn't have to occur for communication to take place. There are many other types of receiver response that qualify as part of the communication process. Sometimes a person who isn't your target receives a message, as when a bystander overhears you muttering about matters that weren't intended for others' ears. In other cases, the intended receiver does, in fact, pick up a message but interprets it incorrectly, as when an overly sensitive friend takes your joking insults seriously. Finally, there are cases where no one seems to have received your message, but where your behavior has created an internal, unobservable response in someone else. We have known students who appeared to be daydreaming through our lecture but who, when questioned, prove to have been listening carefully.

▶ FUNCTIONS OF COMMUNICATION

Now that we have a working understanding of the term *communication,* it is important to discuss why we will spend so much time exploring this subject. Perhaps the strongest argument for studying communication is its central role in our lives. The amount of time we spend communicating is staggering. In one study, researchers measured the amount of time a sample group of college students spent on various activities.[1] They found that the subjects spent an average of over 61 percent of their waking hours engaged in some form of communication. Whatever one's occupation, the results of such a study would not be too different. Most of us are surrounded by others, trying to understand them and hoping that they understand us: family, friends, co-workers, teachers, and strangers.

There's a good reason why we speak, listen, read, and write so much: Communication satisfies most of our needs.

Physical Needs

Communication is so important that it is necessary for physical health. In fact, evidence suggests that an absence of satisfying communication can even jeopardize life itself. Medical researchers have identified a wide range of hazards that result from a lack of close relationships. For instance:

1. Socially isolated people are two to three times more likely to die prematurely than are those with strong social ties. The type of relationship doesn't seem to matter: Marriages, friendship, religious and community ties all seem to increase longevity.[2]

2. Divorced men (before age seventy) die from heart disease, cancer, and strokes at double the rate of married men. Three times as many die from hypertension; five times as many commit suicide; seven times as many die from cirrhosis of the liver; and ten times as many die from tuberculosis.[3]

3. The rate of all types of cancer is as much as five times higher for divorced men and women, compared to their single counterparts.[4]

4. Poor communication can contribute to coronary disease. One Swedish study examined thirty-two pairs of identical twins. One sibling in each pair had heart disease whereas the other was healthy. The researchers found that the obesity, smoking habits, and cholesterol levels of the healthy and sick twins did not differ significantly. Among the significant differences, however, were "poor childhood and adult interpersonal relationships": the ability to resolve conflicts and the degree of emotional support given by others.[5]

5. The likelihood of death increases when a close relative dies. In one Welsh village, citizens who had lost a close relative died within one year at a rate more than five times greater than those who had not suffered from a relative's death.[6]

Research like this demonstrates the importance of satisfying personal relationships. Remember: Not everyone needs the same amount of contact, and the quality of communication is almost certainly as important as the quantity. The important point here is that personal communication is essential for our well-being. In other words, "people who need people" aren't "the luckiest people in the world"... they're the *only* people!

Ego Needs

Communication does more than enable us to survive. It is the way—indeed, the *only* way we learn who we are. As you'll read in Chapter 2, our sense of identity comes from the way we interact with other people. Are we smart or stupid, attractive or ugly, skillful or inept? The answers to these questions don't come from looking in the mirror. We decide who we are based on how others react to us.

Deprived of communication with others, we would have no sense of identity. In his book *Bridges, Not Walls,* John Stewart dramatically illustrates this fact by citing the case of the famous "Wild Boy of Aveyron," who spent his early childhood without any apparent human contact. The boy was discovered in January 1800 while digging for vegetables in a French village garden. He showed no behaviors one would expect in a social human. The boy could not speak but uttered only weird cries. More significant than this absence of social skills was his lack of any identity as a human being. As author Roger Shattuck put it, "The boy had no human sense of being in the world. He had no sense of himself as a person related to other persons."[7] Only after the influence of a loving "mother" did the boy begin to behave—and, we can imagine, think of himself as a human.

Like the boy of Aveyron, each of us enters the world with little or no sense of identity. We gain an idea of who we are from the way others define us. As Chapter 2 explains, the messages we receive in early childhood are the strongest, but the influence of others continues throughout life.

Social Needs

Besides helping define who we are, communication is the way we relate socially with others. Psychologist William Schutz describes three types of social needs we strive to fulfill by communicating.[8] The first is **inclusion,** the need to feel a sense of belonging to some personal relationship. Inclusion needs are sometimes satisfied by informal alliances: the friends who study together, a group of runners, or neighbors who help one another with yard work. In other cases, we get a sense of belonging from formal relationships: everything from religious congregations to a job to marriage.

A second type of social need is the desire for **control**—the desire each of us has to influence others, to feel some sense of power over our world. Some types of control are obvious, such as the boss or team captain whose directions make things happen. Much control, however, is more subtle. Experts in child development tell us that preschoolers who insist on staying up past bedtime or having a treat in the supermarket may be less concerned with the issue at hand than with knowing that they have at least some ability to make things happen.[9] In this case, even driving a parent crazy can satisfy the need for control. This answers the parent's question "Why are you being so stubborn?"

The third social need is **affection**—a desire to care for others and know that they care for us. Affection, of course, is critical for most of us. Being included and having power aren't very satisfying if the important people in our lives don't care for us.

Practical Needs

We shouldn't overlook the everyday, important functions communication serves. Communication is the tool that lets us tell the hair stylist to take just a little off the sides, the doctor where it hurts, and the plumber that the broken pipe needs attention *now!* Communication is the means of learning important information in school. It is the method you use to convince a prospective employer that you're the best candidate for a job, and it is the way to persuade the boss you deserve a raise. The list of common but critical jobs performed by communicating goes on and on, and it's worth noticing that the inability to express yourself clearly and effectively in every one of the preceding examples can prevent you from achieving your goal.

Psychologist Abraham Maslow suggested that human needs such as the preceding ones fall into five categories, each of which must be satisfied before we concern ourselves with the following ones.[10] As you read on, think about the ways in which communication is often necessary to satisfy each need. The most basic of these needs are **physical:** sufficient air, water, food, and rest and the ability to reproduce as a species. The second of Maslow's needs involves **safety:** protection from threats to our well-being. Beyond physical and safety concerns are the **social** needs we have mentioned already. Even beyond these, Maslow suggests that each of us has **self-esteem** needs: the desire to believe that we are worthwhile, valuable people. The final category of needs described by Maslow involves **self-actualization:** the desire to develop our potential to the maximum, to become the best person we can be.

▶ People don't get along because they fear each other. People fear each other because they don't know each other.
They don't know each other because they have not properly communicated with each other.

Martin Luther King, Jr.

▶ *See that man over there?*
Yes.
Well, I hate him.
But you don't know him.
That's why I hate him.

Gordon Allport
The Nature of Prejudice

So far we have introduced a basic definition of communication and seen the functions communication performs. This information is useful, but it only begins to describe the subject. One way to understand more about communication is to examine a model of that process.

Why Use Models?

A **model** is a simplified representation of some process. For instance, consider what a model of "digestion" might look like. At one end of a page we could draw a mouth with food going into it, followed by tubes running into a baglike object representing the stomach. To represent the intestines, we could draw a coiled hose connected at the top end to the stomach.

Whereas this representation may begin to tell us something about digestion, it also tells us a great deal about the following characteristics of models:

1. *Models can represent the relevant elements of a process.* Even though our diagram is crude, it does provide a good introduction to the basic parts of the digestive tract.
2. *Models organize the parts of a process and indicate how they are related to each other.* For example, an uninformed viewer would learn from our drawing that the stomach is below the esophagus and above the intestines.
3. *Models simplify a complex event.* This simplification helps promote understanding. It's certainly easier for an uninitiated learner to start exploring the digestion process with a simple model than by looking into the entire process in all its complexity.
4. *Models provide an opportunity to look at a familiar process in a new way.* By doing so, models sometimes make us aware that we've been operating on misconceptions. For instance, adding an explanation of what goes on in each part of our digestion model makes clear how little digestion actually goes on in the stomach, contrary to the belief of many people.

Whereas models clearly offer several advantages, they also suffer from a number of potential drawbacks. First, in an attempt to make a complex event simple, a model may oversimplify and lead viewers into thinking that the event itself is simple. This mistaken assumption has the highest probability of occurring if a learner has little information on what the event is really like. For instance, someone not versed in physics might actually believe that an atom is quite similar in form and motion to marbles spinning around a grapefruit.

It's also important to remember that a model is an analogy, nothing more. The danger of confusing the map with the territory is illustrated by the story of an elementary school child who, having studied geography by using the classroom map, was surprised to discover that Spain was not a pink country, France green, and so on.

Finally, a model can cause us to stop thinking about the process that it represents and can cause us to conclude that we know everything significant about the subject. This mistake is termed *premature closure* and, of course, should be avoided.

A Communication Model

Keeping the advantages and dangers of models in mind, we can begin to build a representation of what goes on in the process of communication. Because we need to begin somewhere, let's start with your wanting to express an idea (see Figure 1–1). If you think about it for a moment, you'll realize that most ideas you have don't come to you already put into words. Rather, they're more like mental images, often consisting of unverbalized feelings (anger, excitement, and the like), intentions (wants, desires, needs), or even mental pictures (such as how you want a job to look when it is finished). We can represent your mental image in Figure 1–1 like this:

FIGURE 1–1

Sender

Because people aren't mind readers, you have to translate this mental image into symbols (usually words) that others can understand. No doubt you can recall times when you actually shuffled through a mental list of words to pick exactly the right ones to explain an idea. This process, called **encoding,** goes on every time we speak (see Figure 1–2). Chapter 3 will deal in some detail with the problems and skills of being an effective encoder.

FIGURE 1–2

Sender Encodes

Once you have encoded an idea, the next step is to send it. We call this step the **message** phase of our model. The message includes both the speaker's planned words and actions and the unplanned, sometimes unconscious signals sent. There are a number of ways a message can be delivered. For instance, you might express yourself in a letter, over the telephone or in a face-to-face conversation. In this sense, writing, telecommunication, and speaking are three of the **channels** through which we send messages (see Figure 1–3). In addition to these channels, we transfer our thoughts and feelings by touch, posture, gestures, distance, clothing, and many other ways described in Chapter 5.

FIGURE 1–3

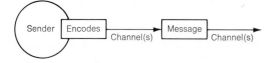

Sender Encodes Channel(s) Message Channel(s)

All communication channels aren't equal: The method of communication often influences the type of interaction that occurs between people. For instance, one study revealed that students were more likely to ask questions of professors through computer networks than in person.[11] Another showed that some discussions carried on by computer hookups are more argumentative than face-to-face sessions, but also more equal in terms of shared discussion time and decision making.[12]

When your message reaches another person, much the same process we described earlier occurs in reverse (see Figure 1–4). The **receiver** must make some sense out of the symbols you've sent by **decoding** them back into feelings, intentions, or thoughts that mean something.

FIGURE 1–4

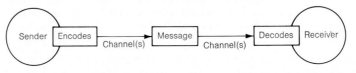

A **linear communication model** characterizes communication as a one-way activity in which information flows from sender to receiver. In a linear model, communication seems like something that an active sender "does" to a passive receiver. A linear model suggests that messages exist in a sender and that conveying meaning is the sender's role alone. As some scholars metaphorically suggest, a linear model implies that communication is like giving or getting an inoculation: Ideas and feelings are prepared in some form of message and then injected in a straight line into a receiver. Although some types of messages (print and broadcast media, for example) appear to flow in a one-way manner, a linear model is not a complete or accurate representation of any type of communication, especially the interpersonal variety. What's missing? The model we've just examined ignores the fact that receivers *react* to messages.

Consider, for instance, the significance of a friend's yawn as you describe your vacation exploits. Imagine the blush you might see as a listener's response to one of your raunchier jokes. Nonverbal behaviors like these show that most communication—especially in interpersonal situations—is two-way. The discernible response of a receiver to a sender's message is called **feedback.** Not all feedback is nonverbal, of course. Sometimes it is oral, as when you ask questions to clarify a speaker's remarks. In other cases, it can be written, as when you demonstrate your knowledge of this material to your instructor on an examination. When we add the element of feedback, we have an image of communication as pictured in the **interactive communication model** in Figure 1–5. A sender formulates and transmits a message to a receiver, who, in turn, formulates and sends a response.

FIGURE 1–5

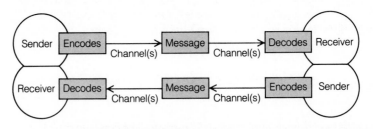

The interactive model suggests that, after a period of interaction, the mental images of the sender and receiver ought to match. If this happens, we can say that an act of successful communication has occurred. However, as you know from your own experience, things often go wrong somewhere between the sender and the receiver. For instance,

Your constructive suggestion is taken as criticism.

Your carefully phrased question is misunderstood.

Your friendly joke is taken as an insult.

Your hinted request is missed entirely.

And so it often goes. Why do such misunderstandings occur? To answer this question, we need to add more details to our model. We recognize that, without several more crucial elements, our model would not represent the world.

First, it's important to recognize that communication always takes place in an **environment.** By this term we do not mean simply a physical location but also the personal history that each person brings to a conversation. The problem here is that each of us has a different environment because of our differing backgrounds. Although we certainly have some experiences in common, we also see each situation in a unique way. For instance, consider how two individuals' environments would differ if

A were well rested and B were exhausted;

A were rich and B were poor;

A were rushed and B had nowhere special to go;

A had lived a long, eventful life and B were young and inexperienced; or

A were passionately concerned with the subject and B were indifferent to it.

Obviously this list could go on and on. The problem of differing environments is critical to effective communication. Even now, though, you can see from just these few items that the world is a different place for sender and receiver. We can represent this idea in Figure 1–6 with a revised model:

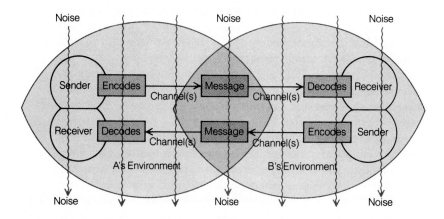

FIGURE 1–6

Notice that the environments of A and B overlap. This overlapping represents those things that our communicators have in common. This point is important because it is through our shared knowledge and experiences that we are able to communicate. For example, you are able at least partially to understand the messages we are writing on these pages because we share the same language, however imprecise it often may be.

Different environments aren't the only cause of ineffective communication. Social scientists use the term **noise** to label other forces that interfere with the process and point out that it can occur in every stage. There are three types of noise that can block communication—external, physiological, and psychological. **External noise** includes those factors outside the receiver that make it difficult to hear, as well as many other kinds of distractions. For instance, too much cigarette smoke in a crowded room might make it hard for you to pay attention to another person, and sitting in the rear of an auditorium might make a speaker's remarks unclear. External noise can disrupt communication almost anywhere in our model—in the sender, channel, message, or receiver. **Physiological noise** involves biological factors in the receiver that interfere with accurate reception: hearing loss, illness, and so on.

Psychological noise refers to forces within a communicator that interfere with the ability to express or understand a message accurately. For instance, an outdoor person might exaggerate the size and number of the fish he caught in order to convince himself and others of his talents. In the same way, a student might become so upset upon learning that she failed a test that she would be unable (perhaps *unwilling* is a better word) to understand clearly where she went wrong. Psychological noise is such an important communication problem that we have devoted much of Chapter 10 to investigating its most common form, defensiveness.

Even with the addition of these new elements our model isn't completely satisfactory. Notice that the preceding discussion portrays communication as a static activity. It suggests that there are discrete "acts" of communication that begin and end in identifiable places and that a sender's message "causes" some "effect" in a receiver. Furthermore, it suggests that at any given moment a person is either sending or receiving.

In fact, none of these characterizations is valid for interpersonal communication. The activity of communicating is usually not interactive but transactional. A **transactional communication model** differs from the more simplistic ones we've already discussed in several ways.

First, a transactional model reveals that communicators usually send and receive messages simultaneously, so that the images of sender and receiver should not be separated as if a person were doing only one or the other, but rather, superimposed and redefined as "participants."[13] At a given moment, we are capable of receiving, decoding, and responding to another person's behavior while at the same time that other person is receiving and responding to ours. Consider, for example, what might occur when you and a housemate negotiate household chores. As soon as you begin to hear (receive) the words sent by your partner, "I want to talk about cleaning the bathroom..." you grimace and clench your jaw (sending a nonverbal message of your own while receiving the verbal one). This reaction causes your partner to interrupt himself, defensively sending a new message: "Now wait a minute...."

Besides illustrating the simultaneous nature of face-to-face interaction, this example reminds us that it's difficult to isolate a single discrete "act" of communication from the events that precede and follow it. Your partner's comment about cleaning the bathroom (and the way it was presented) probably grew

FIGURE 1–7

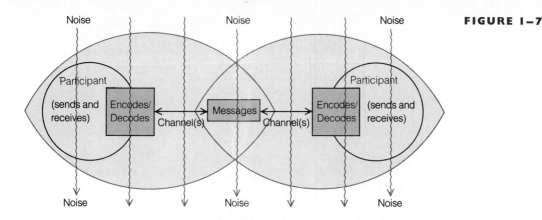

from exchanges you had in the past. Likewise, the way you'll act toward one another in the future depends on the outcome of this conversation. Although Figure 1–7 does a fair job of picturing the phenomenon we call communication, an animated version, in which the environments, communicators, and messages constantly changed, would be an even better way of capturing the process. You can also see that communication is not something that people do *to* one another but a process in which they create a relationship by interacting *with* each other.

CLARIFYING MISCONCEPTIONS ABOUT COMMUNICATION ◄

Having spent time talking about what communication is, we ought also identify some things it is not.[14] Recognizing these misconceptions is important, not only because they ought to be avoided by anyone knowledgeable about the subject, but also because following them can get you into personal trouble.

Communication Is Not Always a Good Thing

For most people, belief in the value of communication rates somewhere close to motherhood in their hierarchy of important values. In truth, communication is neither good nor bad in itself. Rather, its value comes from the way it is used. In this sense, communication is similar to fire: Flames in the fireplace on a cold night keep you warm and create a cozy atmosphere, but the same flames can kill if they spread to the surrounding room. Communication can be a tool for expressing warm feelings and useful facts, but under different circumstances the same words and actions can cause both physical and emotional pain.

Communication Will Not Solve All Problems

"If I could just communicate better . . ." is the sad refrain of many unhappy people who believe that if they could just express themselves better, their relationships would improve. Though this is sometimes true, it's an exaggeration to say that communicating—even communicating clearly—is a guaranteed panacea.

"I'm so glad we've had this little talk, Earl!"

Drawing by Gahan Wilson; © 1986 The New Yorker Magazine, Inc.

More Communication Is Not Always Better

Although it's certainly true that not communicating enough is a mistake, there are also situations when *too much* communication is a mistake. Sometimes excessive communication simply is unproductive, as when we "talk a problem to death," going over the same ground again and again without making any headway. And there are times when communicating too much can actually aggravate a problem. We've all had the experience of "talking ourselves into a hole"— making a bad situation worse by pursuing it too far. As McCroskey and Wheeless put it, "More and more negative communication merely leads to more and more negative results."[15]

There are even times when *no* communication is the best course. Any good salesperson will tell you that it's often best to stop talking and let the customer think about the product. And when two people are angry and hurt, they may say things they don't mean and will later regret. At times like these it's probably best to spend a little time cooling off, thinking about what to say and how to say it.

One key to successful communication, then, is to share an *adequate* amount of information in a *skillful* manner. Teaching you how to decide what information is adequate and what constitutes skillful behavior is one major goal of this book.

Meanings Rest in People, Not Words

We already hinted that meanings rest in people, not in words, when we said earlier that the symbols we use to communicate are arbitrary. It's a mistake to think that, just because you use a word in one way, others will do so too. Sometimes differing interpretations of symbols are easily caught, as when we might first take the statement "He's gay" to mean the subject has homosexual preferences, only to find out that he is cheerful—and straight. In other cases, however, the ambiguity of words and nonverbal behaviors isn't so apparent . . . and thus has more far-reaching consequences. Remember, for instance, a time when someone said to you, "I'll be honest . . . ," and only later did you learn that those words hid precisely the opposite fact. In Chapter 3 you'll read a great deal more about the problems that come from mistakenly assuming that meanings rest in words.

Communication Is Not Simple

Most people assume that communication is an aptitude that people develop without the need for training—rather like breathing. After all, we've been swapping ideas with one another since early childhood, and there are lots of people who communicate pretty well without ever having had a class on the subject. Though this picture of communication as a natural ability seems accurate, it's actually a gross oversimplification.

Throughout history there have been cases of infants raised without human contact. In all these instances the children were initially unable to communicate with others when brought into society. Only after extensive teaching (and not even then in some cases) were they able to speak and understand language in ways we take for granted. But what about the more common cases of effective communicators who have had no formal training yet are skillful at creating and understanding messages? The answer to this question lies in the fact that not all education occurs in a classroom: Many people learn to communicate skillfully because they have been exposed to models of such behavior by those around them. This principle of modeling explains why children who grow up in homes with stable relationships between family members have a greater chance of developing such relationships themselves. They know how to do so because they've seen effective communication in action.

Does the existence of these good communicators mean that certain people don't need courses like the one you're taking? Hardly. Even the best communicators aren't perfect: They often suffer the frustration of being unable to get a message across effectively, and they frequently misunderstand others. Furthermore, even the most successful people you know can probably identify ways in which their relationships could profit by better communication. These facts show that communication skills are rather like athletic ability: Even the most inept of us can learn to be more effective with training and practice, and those who are talented can always become better.

This chapter introduced some key concepts that provide a foundation for the material that follows in the rest of the book. It explained the nature of communication as it will be studied here: a face-to-face symbolic process between human beings, in which the receiver is involved. The chapter described several types of needs communication satisfies: physical, ego, social, and practical.

The chapter explained the value of models as a way of understanding any process and introduced a model of human communication. It also introduced several misconceptions about communication.

► **ACTIVITIES**

1. List the needs you have attempted to satisfy by communicating during a recent twenty-four-hour period. Because describing every need-satisfying act would call for writing a small book, choose a sample of incidents representing each of the categories described in the text.

2. Describe three incidents in which you communicated to satisfy each of the following social needs:
   a. inclusion
   b. control
   c. affection

3. Identify an important message that you would like to communicate within the next week. Describe
   a. The idea you want to send and the various ways you could encode it.
   b. The channels by which you could send it.
   c. The ways in which your receiver might decode it.
   d. Possible differences between your environment and that of the receiver that might make it difficult for your message to be accurately understood.
   e. Likely sources of external, physiological, and psychological noise that might interfere with the communication transaction.
   f. Types of feedback you can utilize to see whether or not you have succeeded in having your message understood.
   Based on your answers to these questions, describe the steps you can take to construct and deliver your message in a way that gives it the greatest chance of being accurately received.

4. To recognize that communication can be either good or bad, recall three incidents in which communication improved a situation and three in which acts of communication made matters worse.

5. What evidence can you provide to show that effective communication is not a natural ability? Include in your answer instances when people communicated poorly owing to
   a. lack of training
   b. exposure to ineffective models
   c. reinforcement of poor behavior
   d. punishment for effective behavior

Although the last two categories might seem unlikely, a bit of reflection will show you that many people do get social or material payoffs for communicating in ways that would generally be defined as unacceptable whereas others are punished for acting in a manner that would be regarded positively by most people.

NOTES ◄

1. Rudolph Verderber, Ann Elder, and Ernest Weiler, "A Study of Communication Time Usage Among College Students," unpublished study, University of Cincinnati, 1976.
2. R. Narem, "Try a Little TLC," research reported in *Science 80*: 1 (1980):15.
3. J. Lynch, *The Broken Heart: The Medical Consequences of Loneliness* (New York: Basic Books, 1977), pp. 239–242.
4. Ibid.
5. E. A. Liljefors and R. H. Rahe, "Psychosocial Characteristics of Subjects with Myocardial Infarction in Stockholm," in E. K. Gunderson and R. H. Rahe (eds.), *Life Stress Illness* (Springfield, Ill.: Charles C. Thomas, 1974), pp. 90–104.
6. W. D. Rees and S. G. Lutkins, "Mortality of Bereavement," *British Medical Journal* 4 (1967):13.
7. R. Shattuck, *The Forbidden Experiment: The Story of the Wild Boy of Aveyron* (New York: Farrar, Straus & Giroux, 1980), p. 37.
8. W. Schutz, *The Interpersonal Underworld* (Palo Alto, Calif.: Science and Behavior Books, 1966).
9. E. H. Erikson, *Childhood and Society* (New York: Norton, 1963).
10. A. H. Maslow, *Toward a Psychology of Being* (New York: Van Nostrand Reinhold, 1968).
11. D. Goleman, "The Electronic Rorschach," *Psychology Today* 17:2 (February 1983):42.
12. Ibid., p. 41.
13. E. M. Rogers and D. L. Kincaid, *Communication Networks: Toward a New Paradigm for Research* (New York: Free Press, 1981), pp. 43–48, 63–66.
14. Adapted from J. C. McCroskey and L. R. Wheeless, *Introduction to Human Communication* (Boston: Allyn and Bacon, 1976), pp. 3–10.
15. Ibid., p. 5.

►CHAPTER 2

KEY TERMS

empathy   selection
interpretation   self-concept
organization   self-fulfilling prophecy
perception checking   significant other
reflected appraisal

PERCEPTION AND THE SELF

After reading this chapter, you should understand the following:

1. The communicative influences that shape the self-concept.

2. The three elements of the perception process.

3. The perceptual errors that distort perception of others.

4. The importance of empathy in improving communication.

5. How self-fulfilling prophecies can influence behavior.

6. The requirements for changing one's self-concept.

You should be able to do the following:

1. Identify the ways you influence the self-concept of others and the way significant others influence your self-concept.

2. Describe the different ways that you and at least one other person perceive an event, showing how selection, organization, and interpretation lead to the differing perceptions.

3. Identify the errors listed in this chapter that have led you to develop distorted perceptions of others.

4. Use perception checking to become more accurate in your perceptions of others' behavior.

5. Identify communication-related self-fulfilling prophecies that you have imposed on yourself, that others have imposed on you, and that you have imposed on others.

6. List the steps you could take to change an important part of your self-concept that affects your communication.

A student is practicing his first assigned speech with several friends.

"This is a stupid topic," he laments. The other students sincerely assure him that the topic is an interesting one and that the speech sounds good.

Despite these reassurances, the student remains unconvinced. Later in class he becomes flustered because he believes that his speech is no good. As a result of his unenthusiastic delivery, the student receives a low grade on the assignment.

Despite her nervousness, a job candidate does her best in a job interview. She leaves the session convinced that she botched her big chance. A few days later she is surprised to receive a job offer.

At a party several guests have been emptying a keg of beer with great gusto. They are now engaged in conversation that they think is witty, but that a sober observer would find foolish. However, as there are no sober observers present, the reality of the situation is lost on the participants.

Stories like these are probably familiar to you. Yet behind this familiarity lie principles that are perhaps the most important ones in this book:

1. Two or more people often perceive an event in radically different ways.
2. The beliefs each of us holds about ourselves—our self-concept—have a powerful effect on our behavior, even when these beliefs are inaccurate.

These simple truths play a role in virtually all the important messages we send and receive. The goal of this chapter is to demonstrate the significance of these principles by describing the nature of perception and showing how it influences the way we view ourselves and how we relate to others.

▶ UNDERSTANDING THE SELF-CONCEPT

We will begin our study by examining the nature of the self-concept. We will first define that term and next go on to explore how the self-concept develops. Then after looking at the role of perception in human interaction, we will discuss how the self-concept affects communication.

Self-concept Defined

The **self-concept** is a set of relatively stable perceptions each of us holds about ourselves. The self-concept includes our conception about what is unique about us and what makes us both similar to, and different from, others.[1] To put it differently, the self-concept is rather like a mental mirror that reflects how we view ourselves: not only physical features, but also emotional states, talents, likes and dislikes, values, and roles.

We will have more to say about the nature of the self-concept shortly, but first you will find it valuable to gain a personal understanding of how this theoretical construct applies to you. You can do so by answering a simple question: "Who are you?"

How do you define yourself? As a student? A man or woman? By your age? Your religion? Occupation?

There are many ways of identifying yourself. Take a few more moments, and list as many ways as you can to identify who you are. You'll need this list later in this chapter, so be sure to complete it now. Try to include all the characteristics that describe you:

your moods or feelings	your intellectual capacity
your appearance and physical condition	your strong beliefs
your social traits	your social roles
talents you possess or lack	

Even a list of twenty or thirty terms would be only a partial description. To make this written self-portrait complete, your list would have to be hundreds— or even thousands—of words long.

Of course, not every item on such a list would be equally important. For example, the most significant part of one person's self-concept might consist of social roles whereas for another it could consist of physical appearance, health, friendships, accomplishments, or skills.

You can begin to see how important these elements are by continuing this personal experiment. Pick the ten items from your list that describe the most fundamental aspects of who you are. Rank these ten items so that the most fundamental one is in first place, with the others following in order of declining importance. Now, beginning with the tenth item, imagine what would happen if each characteristic in turn disappeared from your makeup. How would you be different? How would you feel?

For most people, this exercise dramatically illustrates just how fundamental the self-concept is. Even when the item being abandoned is an unpleasant one, it's often hard to give it up. And when they are asked to let go of their most central feelings or thoughts, most people balk. "I wouldn't be *me* without that," they insist. Of course, this proves our point: The self-concept is perhaps our most fundamental possession. Knowing who we are is essential, for without a self-concept it would be impossible to relate to the world.

▶ Retrospectively, one can ask "Who am I?" But in practice, the answer has come before the question.

J. M. Yinger

Communication and Development of the Self

So far we've talked about what the self-concept is; but at this point you may be asking what it has to do with the study of human communication. We can begin to answer this question by looking at how you came to possess your own self-concept.

Newborn babies come into the world with very little sense of self.[2] In the first months of life infants have no awareness of their bodies as being separate from the rest of the environment. At eight months of age, for example, a child will be surprised when a toy grabbed from the grip of another child "resists." Not until somewhere between their first and second birthday children are most able to recognize their own reflections in a mirror.[3]

How does this rudimentary sense of identity grow into the rich, multidimensional self-concept you identified in the preceding section? It develops almost exclusively from communication with others. As psychologists Arthur Combs and Donald Snygg put it:

> The self is essentially a social product arising out of experience with people.... We learn the most significant and fundamental facts about ourselves from ... "reflected appraisals," inferences about ourselves made as a consequence of the ways we perceive others behaving toward us.[4]

The term **reflected appraisal**, coined by Harry Stack Sullivan,[5] is a good one, for it metaphorically describes the fact that we develop an image of ourselves from the way we think others view us. This notion of the "looking-glass self" was first introduced in 1902 by Charles H. Cooley, who suggested that we put ourselves in the position of other people and then, in our mind's eye, view ourselves as we imagine they see us.[6] In other words, we interpret (or "decode," to use the terminology of our communication model) the behavior of others, assuming that this interpretation is an accurate representation of how they view us.

The stream of messages about who we are begins early in life, long before we have developed sufficiently to think about them in any systematic way. During this prelinguistic stage the messages are nonverbal. The amount of time parents allow their infant to cry before responding can, over time, communicate how important the child is to them. Their method of handling the baby also speaks volumes: Do they affectionately play with it, joggling it gently and holding it close, or do they treat it like so much baggage, changing diapers and feeding and

"Guess who Miss Price picked to play poison ivy in the class play."

bathing it in a brusque, impersonal manner? Does the tone of voice they use express love and enjoyment or disappointment and irritation?

As the youngster learns to speak and understand language, verbal messages—both positive and negative—also contribute to the developing self-concept. These messages continue later in life, especially when they come from what social scientists term **significant others**—people whose opinions we especially value. A teacher from long ago, a special friend or relative, or perhaps a barely known acquaintance whom you respected can all leave an imprint on how you view yourself. To see the importance of significant others, ask yourself how you arrived at your opinion of you as a student . . . as a person attractive to the opposite sex . . . as a competent worker . . . and you will see that these self-evaluations were probably influenced by the way others regarded you.

Research supports the importance of reflected appraisals. One study identified the relationship between adult attitudes toward children and the children's self-concepts.[7] The researcher first established that parents and teachers expect children from higher socioeconomic backgrounds to do better academically than socioeconomically disadvantaged youngsters. In other words, parents and teachers have higher expectations for socioeconomically advantaged students. Interestingly, when children from a higher socioeconomic class performed poorly in school their self-esteem dropped; but children from less advantaged backgrounds did not lose self-esteem. Why was there this difference? Because the parents and teachers sent messages about their disappointment to the higher status children whereas no such messages went to their less-advantaged counterparts. The relationship between others' evaluations of an individual and his or her self-concept persists into adulthood. Researchers conducted a study using several groups—fraternities, sororities, and sociology classes.[8] Each student rated himself or herself on a five-point scale for intelligence, self-confidence, physical attractiveness, and likableness. Next the subjects rated the other members of their group in terms of the same characteristics. The researchers found that the students whom others regarded highly also viewed themselves positively whereas those with lower peer ratings had less self-esteem.

You might argue that not every part of one's self-concept is shaped by others, insisting there are certain objective facts that are recognizable by self-observation. After all, nobody needs to tell you that you are taller than others, speak with an accent, can run quickly, and so on. These facts are obvious.

Though it's true that some features of the self are immediately apparent, the *significance* we attach to them—the rank we assign them in the hierarchy of our list and the interpretation we give them—depends greatly on the opinions of others. After all, there are many of your features that are readily observable, yet you don't find them important at all because nobody has regarded them as significant.

Recently we heard a woman in her eighties describing her youth. "When I was a girl," she declared, "we didn't worry about weight. Some people were skinny and others were plump, and we pretty much accepted the bodies God gave us." Compare this attitude with what you find today: It's seldom that you pick up a popular magazine or visit a bookstore without reading about the latest diet fads, and television ads are filled with scenes of slender, happy people. As a result, you'll find many people who complain about their need to "lose a few

▶ **Premier Artiste**

Watch me perform!
I walk a tightrope of unique
   design.
I teeter, falter, recover
   And bow.
      You applaud.
I run forward, backward,
   hesitate
   And bow.
      You applaud.
If you don't applaud
   I'll fall.
Cheer me! Hurray me!
Or you push me
Down.

Lenni Shender Goldstein

▶ I am not what I think I am.
I am not what you think I am.
I am what I think you think I
   am.

Aaron Bleiberg and Harry
Leubling

**PERCEPTION AND
THE SELF**

pounds." The reason for such concern has more to do with the attention paid to slimness these days than with any increase in the number of people in the population who are overweight. Furthermore, the interpretation of characteristics such as weight depends on the way people important to us regard them. We generally see fat as undesirable because others tell us it is. In a society where obesity is the ideal (and there are such societies), a heavy person would feel beautiful. In the same way, the fact that one is single or married, solitary or sociable, aggressive or passive, takes on meaning depending on the interpretation society attaches to those traits. Thus, the importance of a given characteristic in your self-concept has as much to do with the significance you and others attach to it as with the existence of the characteristic.

▶ PERCEPTION AND COMMUNICATION

By now it should be clear that the self-concept is not an objective characteristic, like height or hair color. Sometimes an individual's self-evaluation is unrealistically high. You might, for instance, see yourself as a witty joke teller when others can barely tolerate your attempts at humor; or you might consider yourself an excellent worker, in contrast to the employer who is thinking about firing you. In other cases, people view themelves more harshly than objective facts suggest. You may have known people, for instance, who insist they are unattractive or incompetent in spite of your honest insistence to the contrary.

Because we react to ourselves and others according to the perceptions we hold rather than objective events themselves, it is important to take a look at the process of perception and see how it influences communication.

The Perception Process

We need to begin our discussion of perception by talking about the gap between "what is" and what we know. Our idea of reality is only a partial one: The world contains far more than we are able to experience with our limited senses. Infrared photos, electron microscopes, and other technological tools reveal a world our ancestors never imagined. Certain animals can hear sounds and detect scents not apparent to humans.

Even within the realm of our senses we are only aware of a small part of what is going on around us. For instance, most people who live in large cities find that the noises of traffic, people, and construction soon fade out of awareness. Others can take a walk through the forest without distinguishing one bird's call from another or noticing the differences between various types of vegetation. On a personal level we have all had the experience of failing to notice something unusual about a friend—perhaps a new hairstyle or a sad expression—until it's called to our attention.

Sometimes our failure to recognize some events while noticing others comes from not paying attention to important information. But in other cases it simply isn't possible to be aware of everything, no matter how attentive we might be: There is just too much going on.

William James said that "to the infant the world is just a big, blooming, buzzing confusion." One reason for this is the fact that infants are not yet able to sort out the myriad impressions with which we're all bombarded. As we grow, we learn to manage all this information, and as we do so, we begin to make sense out of the world.

Because this ability to organize our perceptions in a useful way is such a critical factor in our ability to function, we need to begin our study of perception by taking a closer look at this process. We can do so by examining the three steps by which we attach meaning to our experiences.[9]

SELECTION As we are exposed to more input than we can possibly manage, the first step in perceiving is **selection,** the act of attending to certain stimuli in the environment. There are several factors that cause us to notice some messages and ignore others.

Stimuli that are *intense* often attract our attention. Something that is louder, larger, or brighter stands out. This explains why—other things being equal— we're more likely to remember extremely tall or short people and why someone who laughs or talks loudly at a party attracts more attention (not always favorable) than do more quiet guests.

Repetitious stimuli, repetitious stimuli, repetitious stimuli, repetitious stimuli, repetitious stimuli, repetitious stimuli also attract attention.* Just as a quiet but steadily dripping faucet can come to dominate our awareness, people to whom we're frequently exposed become noticeable.

ATTENTION IS ALSO FREQUENTLY RELATED TO contrast OR change IN STIMULATION. Put differently, unchanging people or things become less noticeable. This principle gives an explanation (excuse?) for why we come to take wonderful people for granted when we interact with them frequently. It's only when they stop being so wonderful or go away that we appreciate them.

Motives also determine what information we select from our environment. If you're anxious about being late for a date, you'll notice whatever clocks may be around you; and if you're hungry, you'll become aware of any restaurants, markets, and billboards advertising food in your path. Motives also determine how we perceive people. For example, someone on the lookout for a romantic adventure will be especially aware of attractive potential partners whereas the same person at a different time might be oblivious to anyone but police or medical personnel in an emergency.

ORGANIZATION After selecting information from the environment, we must **organize** it by arranging those data in some meaningful way. Many messages are ambiguous and can be organized in more than one manner. For example, consider Figure 2–1. How many ways can you view the boxes? Most people have a hard time finding more than one perspective. (There are four.) If you can't find all of them, turn to Figure 2–2 for some help.

We can see the principle of alternative organizing patterns in human interaction. Young children usually don't classify people according to their skin color.

*We borrowed the graphic demonstrations in this and the following paragraph from Dennis Coon's *Introduction to Psychology,* 2d ed. (St. Paul: West Publishing, 1981).

▶ For the most part we do not see first and then define; we define first and then see.

Walter Lippmann

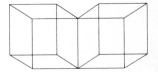

FIGURE 2–1

PERCEPTION AND THE SELF

FIGURE 2–2

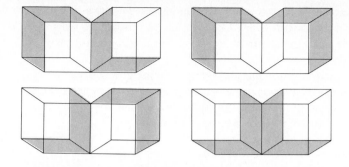

They are just as likely to identify a black person, for example, as being tall, wearing glasses, or being a certain age. As they become more socialized, however, they learn that one common organizing principle in today's society is race, and then their perceptions of others change. Figure 2–3 shows how different linguistic categories alter perception.[10] In the same way, it's possible to classify people or behaviors according to many schemes, each of which will result in different consequences. Do you organize according to age, education, occupation, physical attractiveness, astrological sign, or some other scheme? Imagine how different your relationships would be if you used different criteria for organizing.

INTERPRETATION   Having organized data, we give them meaning in the process of **interpretation.** There are many ways to interpret a single event. Is the person who smiles at you across a crowded room interested in romance or simply being polite? Is a friend's kidding a sign of affection or an indication of irritation? Should you take an invitation to "Drop by any time" literally or not?

There are several factors that cause us to interpret an event in one way or another:

1. **Past Experience.** What meanings have similar events held? If, for example, you've been gouged by landlords in the past, you might be skeptical about an apartment manager's assurances that careful housekeeping will ensure the refund of your cleaning deposit.

2. **Assumptions About Human Behavior.** "People generally do as little work as possible to get by." "In spite of their mistakes, people are doing the best they can." Beliefs like these will shape the way we interpret another's actions.

3. **Expectations.** Anticipation shapes interpretations. If you imagine that your boss is unhappy with your work, you'll probably feel threatened by a request to "see me in my office first thing Monday morning." On the other hand, if you imagine that your work will be rewarded, your weekend will probably be a pleasant one as you anticipate a reward from the boss.

4. **Knowledge.** If you know that a friend has just been jilted by a lover or been fired from a job, you'll interpret her aloof behavior differently than if you were unaware of what had happened. If you know that an instructor speaks sarcastically to all students, then you won't be as likely to take any such remarks personally.

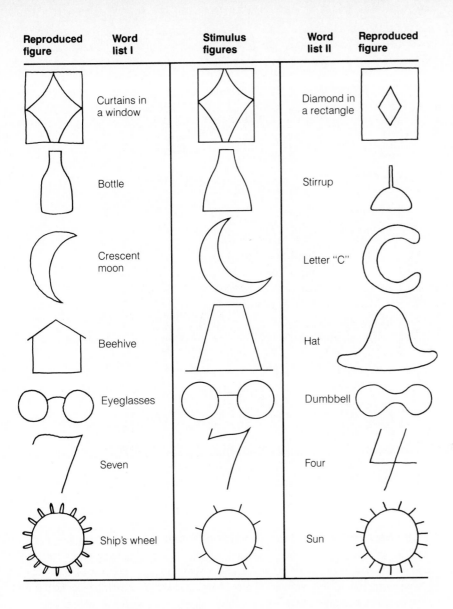

Reproduced figure	Word list I	Stimulus figures	Word list II	Reproduced figure
	Curtains in a window		Diamond in a rectangle	
	Bottle		Stirrup	
	Crescent moon		Letter "C"	
	Beehive		Hat	
	Eyeglasses		Dumbbell	
	Seven		Four	
	Ship's wheel		Sun	

FIGURE 2—3

An illustration of the way in which labels shape organization and interpretation of events. Subjects were presented with stimulus figures along with the descriptions in either Word list I or Word list II. Notice how the subjects' belief about what the stimulus figure represented shaped their perception and subsequent drawings. Think of several everyday examples in which the label given to people, objects, or events shapes the way in which they are perceived. (Carmichael, Hogan, and Walter, 1932)

5. **Personal Moods.** When you're feeling insecure, the world is a very different place from what it is when you're confident. The same goes for happiness and sadness or any other opposing emotions. The way we feel determines how we interpret events.

Accuracy and Inaccuracy in Person Perception

Not all interpretations are accurate. Research has uncovered several common perceptual errors we need to guard against if we are to gain a clear understanding of ourselves and others.[11]

THE INVESTIGATION

HE WAS A REAL TALL GUY DRESSED NORMALLY, WITH LIGHT, DRY HAIR.

HE WAS A HEALTHY, GOOD LOOKING YOUNG KID... BUT DRESSED RATHER SHABBILY.

HE WAS REAL BIG AND REAL OLD.

HE WAS A WELL-DRESSED SORT, A LITTLE OVERWEIGHT AND WITH A LOT OF HAIR.

I REMEMBER HE HAD A LARGE HEAD AND HE SMELLED FUNNY.

HE WAS SURELY A WESTERNER.

HE WAS A SCRAWNY LITTLE SHORT-HAIRED TWERP FROM BACK EAST.

HE HAD DARK HAIR AND A CUTE NOSE. A REAL DOLL.

HE WAS A ROUGH, FURRY GUY WITH LITTLE BEADY EYES. PROBABLY INEDIBLE.

JONIK

WE ARE INFLUENCED BY WHAT IS MOST OBVIOUS The error of being influenced by what is most obvious is understandable. As you read earlier, we select stimuli from our environment that are noticeable: intense, repetitive, unusual, or otherwise attention-grabbing. The problem is that the most obvious factor is not necessarily the only cause—or the most significant one for an event. For example:

▶ When two children (or adults, for that matter) fight, it may be a mistake to blame the one who lashes out first. Perhaps the other one was at least equally responsible, teasing or refusing to cooperate.

▶ You might complain about an acquaintance whose malicious gossiping or arguing has become a bother, forgetting that, by putting up with that kind of behavior, you have been at least partially responsible.

▶ You might blame an unhappy working situation on the boss, overlooking other factors beyond her control such as a change in the economy, the policy of higher management, or demands of customers or other workers.

WE CLING TO FIRST IMPRESSIONS, EVEN IF WRONG Labeling people according to our first impressions is an inevitable part of the perception process.
These labels are a way of making interpretations. "She seems cheerful." "He
seems sincere." "They sound awfully conceited."

If they're accurate, impressions like these can be useful ways of deciding how
to respond best to people in the future. Problems arise, however, when the
labels we attach are inaccurate; for once we form an opinion of someone, we
tend to hang onto it and make any conflicting information fit our image.

Suppose, for instance, you mention the name of your new neighbor to a
friend. "Oh, I know him," your friend replies. "He seems nice at first, but it's
all an act." Perhaps this appraisal is off-base. The neighbor may have changed
since your friend knew him, or perhaps your friend's judgment is simply unfair.
Whether the judgment is accurate or not, once you accept your friend's evaluation, it will probably influence the way you respond to the neighbor. You'll look
for examples of the insincerity you've heard about . . . and you'll probably find
them. Even if the neighbor were a saint, you would be likely to interpret his
behavior in ways that fit your expectations. "Sure he *seems* nice," you might
think, "but it's probably just a front." Of course, this sort of suspicion can create
a self-fulfilling prophecy, transforming a genuinely nice person into someone who
truly becomes an undesirable neighbor.

Given the almost unavoidable tendency to form first impressions, the best
advice we can offer is to keep an open mind and be willing to change your opinion as events prove that the first impressions were mistaken.

WE TEND TO ASSUME OTHERS ARE SIMILAR TO US People commonly imagine others possess the same attitudes and motives that they do. For example,
research shows that people with low self-esteem imagine that others view them
unfavorably whereas people who like themselves imagine that others like them
too.[12] The frequently mistaken assumption that others' views are similar to our
own applies in a wide range of situations. For example:

▶ You've heard a raunchy joke that you found funny. You might assume that it
won't offend a somewhat straight friend. It does.
▶ You've been bothered by an instructor's tendency to get off the subject during lectures. If you were a professor, you'd want to know if anything you
were doing was creating problems for your students, so you decide that
your instructor will probably be grateful for some constructive criticism.
Unfortunately, you're wrong.
▶ You lost your temper with a friend a week ago and said some things you
regret. In fact, if someone said those things to you, you would consider the
relationship was finished. Imagining that your friend feels the same way, you
avoid making contact. In fact, your friend feels that he was partly responsible
and has avoided you because he thinks you're the one who wants to end
things.

Examples like these show that others don't always think or feel the way we
do and that assuming similarities exist can lead to problems. How can you find
out the other person's real position? Sometimes by asking directly, sometimes

"The truth is, Cauldwell, we never
see ourselves as others see us."

by checking with others, and sometimes by making an educated guess after
you've thought the matter out. All these alternatives are better than simply
assuming everyone would react the way you do.

WE TEND TO FAVOR NEGATIVE IMPRESSIONS OVER POSITIVE ONES What
do you think about Harvey? He's handsome, hardworking, intelligent, and honest. He's also very conceited.

Did the last quality make a difference in your evaluation? If it did, you're not
alone. Research shows that when people are aware of both the positive and
negative characteristics of another, they tend to be more influenced by the
undesirable traits. In one study, for example, researchers found that job interviewers were likely to reject candidates who revealed negative information even
when the total amount of information was highly positive.[13]

Sometimes this attitude makes sense. If the negative quality clearly outweighs
any positive ones, you'd be foolish to ignore it. A surgeon with shaky hands and
a teacher who hates children, for example, would be unsuitable for their jobs
whatever their other virtues. But much of the time it's a bad idea to pay excessive attention to negative qualities and overlook good ones. This is the mistake

some people make when screening potential friends or dates. They find some who are too outgoing or too reserved, others who aren't intelligent enough, and still others who have the wrong sense of humor. Of course, it's important to find people you truly enjoy, but expecting perfection can lead to much unnecessary loneliness.

WE BLAME INNOCENT VICTIMS FOR THEIR MISFORTUNES The blame we assign for misfortune depends on who the victim is. When others suffer, we often blame the problem on their personal qualities. On the other hand, when we're the victims, we find explanations outside ourselves. Consider a few examples:

▶ When *they* botch a job, we might think they weren't listening well or trying hard enough; when *we* make the mistake, the problem was unclear directions or not enough time.
▶ When *he* lashes out angrily, we say he's being moody or too sensitive; when *we* blow off steam, it's because of the pressure we've been under.
▶ When *she* gets caught speeding, we say she should have been more careful; when *we* get the ticket, we deny we were driving too fast or say, "Everybody does it."

There are at least two explanations for this kind of behavior. As most of us want other people to approve of us, we defend ourselves by finding explanations for our own problems that make us look good. Basically what we're doing here is saying, "It's not *my* fault." And because looking good is so often a personal goal, putting others down can be a cheap way to boost our own self-esteem, stating in effect, "I'm better than he is."

Don't misunderstand: We don't always commit the kind of perceptual errors described in this section. Sometimes, for instance, people *are* responsible for their misfortunes, and our problems are not our fault. Likewise, the most obvious interpretation of a situation may be the correct one. Nonetheless, a large amount of research has proved again and again that our perceptions of others are often distorted in the ways listed here. The moral, then, is clear: Don't assume that your first judgment of a person is accurate.

Empathy: The Road to Understanding

After reading the preceding list of perceptual errors, you can see that we do indeed select, organize, and interpret the behaviors of others in ways that are often inaccurate. What we clearly need to do, then, is improve our ability to understand others from their point of view as well as from our own. This ability to put ourselves into another person's shoes—view an experience from the other's perspective—is called *empathy*.

EMPATHY DEFINED **Empathy** is the ability to project oneself into another person's point of view so as momentarily to think the same thoughts and feel the same emotions as the other person. The word *empathy* is derived from two Greek words (ἐν + πάθος) that mean "feeling in(side)."[14] These words suggest that empathy involves more than just intellectually understanding another person: It requires you to *experience* the other's perception.*

Empathy is quite different from sympathy. The roots for sympathy (σύν + πάθος) mean "feeling with." As this definition implies, when you feel sympathetic, you stand beside the other person, feeling compassion. But despite your concern, sympathy doesn't involve the degree of understanding that empathy does. When you sympathize, it is still the other's confusion, joy, or pain. When you empathize, the experience becomes your own, at least for the moment.

How important is empathy in interpersonal relationships? One simple experiment suggests the answer.[15] In this study, college students were asked to list their impression of people either shown in a videotaped discussion or described in a short story. Half the students were instructed to empathize with the person as much as possible, and the other half were not given any instructions about empathizing. The results were impressive: The students who did not practice empathy were prone to explain the person's behavior in terms of personality characteristics. For example, they might have explained a cruel statement by saying that the speaker was mean, or they might have attributed a divorce to the

*Technically speaking, *empathy* is the ability to experience *emotions* similar to another person's whereas *decentering* or *role taking* is the ability to experience the other's thoughts as well. In practice, however, *empathy* is used as the global, all-purpose term.

partners' lack of understanding. The empathic students, on the other hand, were more aware of possible elements in the situation that might have contributed to the reaction. For instance, they might have explained a person's unkind behavior in terms of job pressures or personal difficulties. In other words, practicing empathy seems to make people more tolerant.

You might argue here, "Why should I be more tolerant? Maybe behavior I disapprove of *is* due to the other person's personality defects and not just a result of outside factors. Maybe people are selfish, lazy, or stupid much of the time." Perhaps so, but research clearly shows that we are much more charitable when finding explanations for our own behavior.[16] When explaining our actions, we are quick to suggest situational causes: "I was tired." "She started it." "The instructions weren't clear." In other words, we often excuse ourselves by saying, "It wasn't my fault!" As we've already said, we're less forgiving when we judge others. Perhaps becoming more empathetic can help even the score a bit, enabling us to treat others at least as kindly as we treat ourselves.

REQUIREMENTS FOR EMPATHY   Empathy may be valuable, but it isn't always easy. In fact, research shows that it's hardest to empathize with people who are different from us radically: in age, sex, socioeconomic status, intelligence, and so forth.[17] In order to make the kind of perceptual leaps we are talking about, you need to develop several skills and attitudes.

Open-mindedness   Perhaps the most important ingredient of empathy is the ability and disposition to be open-minded—to set aside for the moment your own beliefs, attitudes, and values and consider those of the other person. This is especially difficult when the other person's position is radically different from your own. The temptation is to think (and sometimes say), "That's crazy!" "How can you believe that?" or "I'd do it this way. . . ." Of course, attitudes like these aren't helpful even if your position is correct.

Being open-minded is frequently difficult because people confuse *understanding* another's position with *accepting* it. These are quite different matters. To understand why a friend might disagree with you, for example, doesn't mean you have to give up your position and accept hers.

Imagination   Being open-minded often isn't enough to allow empathy. You also need enough imagination to be able to picture another person's background and thoughts. A happily married or single person needs imagination to empathize with the problems of a friend considering divorce. A young person needs it to empathize with a parent facing retirement. A teacher needs it to understand fully the problems facing students, just as those students can't be empathetic without having enough imagination to understand how their instructor feels.

Commitment   Because empathizing is often difficult, a third necessary quality is the sincere desire to understand the other person. Listening to unfamiliar, often confusing information takes time and isn't always fun. If you aim to be empathetic, it's realistic to be willing to face the challenge.

So far in this chapter we've talked about two important factors that influence communication: the self-concept and the perception process. Now we are ready to look at how these two factors influence each other.

How the Self-concept Influences Perception

You have already seen that we learn about ourselves through the reflected appraisal of others. But *what* others? And *what* appraisals? Every day we are bombarded with information about ourselves that is often contradictory. A letter from your family says, "We're proud of your work at school" whereas an instructor's comments suggest you're doing poorly. An old friend's phone call implies that you're important and valued, but a potential date's rejection of your invitation suggests the opposite.

Although it would be theoretically possible to incorporate contradictory messages like these into a single self-concept, in reality this usually doesn't happen. Rather than juggle conflicting messages, we strive for *simplicity* and *consistency* in our self-perception.[18]

You can verify the drive for consistency in your own life by looking at the self-concept list you developed on page 23. You will almost certainly find that it describes you in relatively simple, consistent terms: either intelligent or unintelligent, attractive or ugly, industrious or lazy, and so on.

Because messages about ourselves aren't consistent, we build and maintain a self-concept by creating perceptual filters that allow us to view the world in a way that fits our beliefs. We said earlier that perception is selective; now we see that our selection is guided by this desire for consistency.

Our perceptual filters maintain a consistent self-concept in two ways: by selecting and by distorting information. To see how the process of *selection* operates, imagine that the person with whom you live accuses you of being a slob and not doing your share of the housework. Unless your self-concept fits this description, you might defend yourself by pointing out all the neat, helpful things you've done while forgetting to remember the chores you've left unfinished. It's important to realize that in cases like this you probably wouldn't be lying, but rather remembering selectively.

Because your housemate's perceptions aren't limited by the need to maintain an image of you as conscientious and tidy, your selective memory would probably be met with a reminder of all the unfinished and sloppy housekeeping you forgot to mention. At this point the second perceptual filter, namely *distortion,* might come into play. You could protest that it really wasn't your fault that you failed to do your share of the work; that illness, schoolwork . . . anything but your unwanted habits were responsible for the undone chores. Although distortions like these probably wouldn't impress your housemate, they would serve the purpose of maintaining your self-image as a responsible, reasonably neat person. Distortions like these often take the form of defense mechanisms; as you can imagine, they can lead to troublesome conflicts.

The egocentric tendency to rate ourselves more favorably than others see us

PERCEPTION AND THE SELF

▶ It has become something of a cliché to observe that if we do not love ourselves, we cannot love anyone else. This is true enough, but it is only part of the picture. If we do not love ourselves, it is almost impossible to believe fully that we *are loved* by someone else. It is almost impossible to *accept* love. It is almost impossible to *receive* love. No matter what our partner does to show that he or she cares, we do not experience the devotion as convincing because we do not feel lovable to ourselves.

Nathaniel Branden
The Psychology of Romantic Love

---

has been demonstrated experimentally.[19] In one study, a random sample of men were asked to rank themselves on their ability to get along with others.[20] Defying mathematical laws, all subjects—every last one—put themselves in the top half of the population. Sixty percent rated themselves in the top 10 percent of the population, and an amazing 25 percent believed they were in the top 1 percent. In the same study, 70 percent of the men ranked their leadership in the top quarter of the population whereas only 2 percent thought they were below average. Sixty percent said they were in the top quarter in athletic abilities whereas only 6 percent viewed themselves as below average.

Distortions like these usually revolve around the desire to maintain a self-concept that has been threatened. The desire to maintain a favorable presenting image is often strong. If you want to view yourself as a good student or musician, for example, an instructor who gives you a poor grade or a critic who doesn't appreciate your music *must* be wrong, and you'll find evidence to show it. If you want to think of yourself as a good worker or parent, you'll find explanations for the problems in your job or family that shift the responsibility away from you. Of course, the same principle works for people with excessively negative self-images: They'll go out of the way to explain any information that's favorable to them in terms that show they really are incompetent or undesirable.

The self-concept not only influences our perceptions of ourselves. It also affects the way we judge others (see Table 2–1). Extensive research shows that a person with high self-esteem is more likely to think well of others whereas someone with low self-esteem is likely to have a poor opinion of others.[21] Your own experience may bear this out: Persons with low self-esteem are often cynical and quick to ascribe the worst possible motives to others whereas those who feel good about themselves are disposed to think favorably about the people they encounter. As one writer put it, "What we find 'out there' is what we put there with our unconscious projections. When we think we are looking out a window, it may be, more often than we realize, that we are really gazing into a looking glass."[22]

Perception Checking to Prevent Misunderstandings

By now it is apparent that our perceptions of others are often distorted. The problems that can arise when we act on these distorted perceptions are

TABLE 2–1 Self-esteem Affects Perceptions of Others

PERSONS WITH HIGH SELF-ESTEEM	PERSONS WITH LOW SELF-ESTEEM
1. Likely to think well of others.	1. Likely to disapprove of others.
2. Expect to be accepted by others.	2. Expect to be rejected by others.
3. Evaluate their own performance more favorably than people with low self-esteem.	3. Evaluate their own performance less favorably than people with high self-esteem.
4. Perform well when being watched: not afraid of other's reactions.	4. Perform poorly when being watched: sensitive to possible negative reaction.
5. Work harder for people who demand high standards of performance.	5. Work harder for undemanding, less critical people.
6. Inclined to feel comfortable with others they view as superior in some way.	6. Feel threatened by people they view as superior in some way.
7. Able to defend themselves against negative comments of others.	7. Have difficulty defending themselves against others' negative comments: more easily influenced.

Reported in D. E. Hamachek, *Encounters with Others: Interpersonal Relationships and You* (New York: Holt, Rinehart and Winston, 1982), pp. 3–5.

obvious. Like most people, you probably resent others' jumping to conclusions about the reasons for your behavior:

"Why are you mad at me?" (Who said you were?)

"What's the matter with you?" (Who said anything was the matter?)

"Come on now. Tell the truth." (Who said you were lying?)

Even if your interpretation is correct, a dogmatic, mind-reading statement is likely to generate defensiveness.

The skill of **perception checking** provides a better way to handle your interpretations. A perception check has three parts:

A description of the behavior you have noticed.
At least two possible interpretations of the behavior.
A request for feedback about how to interpret the behavior correctly.

Perception checks for the preceding three examples would look like this:

"When you stomped out of the room and slammed the door, I wasn't sure whether you were mad at me, or whether you were just in a hurry. How *did* you feel?"

"You haven't laughed much in the last couple of days. It makes me wonder whether something's bothering you or whether you're just feeling quiet. What's up?"

"You said you really liked the job I did, but there was something about your voice that made me think you may not like it. How do you really feel?"

Perception checking statements like these will keep you from jumping to false conclusions. Not only will they prevent the hard feelings that come from misinterpreting others' actions and motives; they can also help bring your self-concept more in line with reality. Exercise 4 at the end of this chapter will give you practice in developing perception checking statements.

The Self-fulfilling Prophecy

The self-concept is such a powerful force on the personality that it not only determines how we communicate in the present, but it can actually influence our future behavior and that of others. Such occurrences come about through a phenomenon called the self-fulfilling prophecy.

A **self-fulfilling prophecy** occurs when a person's expectation of an event makes the outcome more likely to occur than would otherwise have been true. Self-fulfilling prophecies occur all the time although you might never have given them that label. For example, think of some instances you may have known:

You expected to become nervous and botch a job interview and later did so.

You anticipated having a good (or terrible) time at a social affair and found your expectations being met.

A teacher or boss explained a new task to you, saying that you probably wouldn't do well at first. You did not do well.

A friend described someone you were about to meet, saying that you wouldn't like the person. The prediction turned out to be correct—you didn't like the new acquaintance.

In each of these cases, there is a good chance that the event happened because it was predicted to occur. You needn't have botched the interview, the party might have been boring only because you helped make it so, you might have done better on the job if your boss hadn't spoken up, and you might have liked the new acquaintance if your friend hadn't given you preconceptions. In other words, what helped make each event occur was the expectation that it would happen.

There are two types of self-fulfilling prophecies. The first occurs when your own expectations influence your behavior. Like the job interview and the party described earlier, there are many times when an event that needn't have occurred does happen because you expect it to. In sports you have probably psyched yourself into playing either better or worse than usual, so that the only explanation for your unusual performance was your attitude that you would behave differently. Similarly, you have probably faced an audience at one time or another with a fearful attitude and forgotten your remarks, not because you were unprepared, but because you said to yourself, "I know I'll blow it." (We'll offer advice on overcoming this kind of stage fright in Chapter 15.)

A second type of self-fulfilling prophecy occurs when the expectations of one person govern another's actions. The classic example was demonstrated by Robert Rosenthal and Lenore Jacobson:

> Twenty percent of the children in a certain elementary school were reported to their teachers as showing unusual potential for intellectual growth. The names of these 20 percent were drawn by means of a table of random numbers, which is to say that the names were drawn out of a hat. Eight months later these unusual or "magic" children showed significantly greater gains in IQ than did the remaining children who had not been singled out for the teachers' attention. The change in the teachers' expectations regarding the intellectual performance of these allegedly "special" children had led to an actual change in the intellectual performance of these randomly selected children.[23]

In other words, some children may do better in school, not because they are any more intelligent than their classmates, but because they learn that their teacher, a significant other, believes they can achieve.

To put this phenomenon in context with the self-concept, we can say that when a teacher communicates to students the message, "I think you're bright," they accept that evaluation and change their self-concepts to include that evaluation. Unfortunately, we can assume that the same principle holds for those students whose teachers send the message, "I think you're stupid."

This type of self-fulfilling prophecy has been shown to be a powerful force for shaping the self-concept and thus the behavior of people in a wide range of settings outside the schools. In medicine, patients who unknowingly use placebos—substances such as injections of sterile water or doses of sugar pills that have no curative value—often respond just as favorably to treatment as people who actually received a drug. The patients believe they have taken a substance that will help them feel better, and this belief actually brings about a "cure." In psychotherapy, Rosenthal and Jacobson describe several studies that suggest that patients who believe they will benefit from treatment do so, regardless of the type of treatment they receive. In the same vein, when a doctor believes a patient will improve, the patient may do so precisely because of this expectation whereas another person for whom the physician has little hope often fails to recover. Apparently the patient's self-concept as sick or well—as shaped by the doctor—plays an important role in determining the actual state of health.

The self-fulfilling prophecy operates in families as well. If parents tell their children long enough that they can't do anything right, the children's self-concepts will soon incorporate this idea, and they will fail at many or most of the tasks they attempt. On the other hand, if children are told they are capable or lovable or kind persons, there is a much greater chance of their behaving accordingly.

The self-fulfilling prophecy is an important force in communication, but it doesn't explain all behavior. There are certainly times when the expectation of an event's outcome won't bring about that occurrence. Your hope of drawing an ace in a card game won't in any way affect the chance of that card's turning up in an already shuffled deck, and your belief that good weather is coming won't stop the rain from falling. In the same way, believing you'll do well in a job interview when you're clearly not qualified for the position is unrealistic. Similarly, there will probably be people you don't like and occasions you won't enjoy, no

There is an old joke about a man who was asked if he could play a violin and answered, "I don't know. I've never tried." This is psychologically a very wise reply. Those who have never tried to play a violin really do not know whether they can or not. Those who say too early in life and too firmly, "No, I'm not at all musical," shut themselves off prematurely from whole areas of life that might have proved rewarding. In each of us there are unknown possibilities, undiscovered potentialities—and one big advantage of having an open self-concept rather than a rigid one is that we shall continue to expose ourselves to new experiences and therefore we shall continue to discover more and more about ourselves as we grow older.

S. I. Hayakawa

matter what your attitude. To connect the self-fulfilling prophecy with the "power of positive thinking" is an oversimplification.

In other cases, your expectations will be borne out because you are a good predictor and not because of the self-fulfilling prophecy. For example, children are not equally well equipped to do well in school, and in such cases it would be wrong to say that a child's performance was shaped by a parent or teacher even though the behavior did match what was expected. In the same way, some workers excel and others fail, some patients recover and others don't—all according to our predictions but not because of them.

As we keep these qualifications in mind, it's important to recognize the tremendous influence that self-fulfilling prophecies play in our lives. To a great extent we are what we believe we are. In this sense we and those around us constantly create our self-concepts and thus ourselves.

CHANGING THE SELF-CONCEPT ◄

Having read this far, you know more clearly just what the self-concept is, how it is formed, and how it affects communication. But we still haven't focused on what may be the most important question of all: How can you change the parts of your self-concept with which you aren't happy? Sometimes the answer involves changing your *self* (for example, getting a responsible job or losing weight), and sometimes it means changing your *beliefs* (recognizing your strengths or decreasing self-criticism). Neither of these processes is simple, for there's usually no quick method for becoming the person you'd like to be: Personal growth and self-improvement are lifelong activities. But there are several suggestions that can help you move closer to your goals.

Have Realistic Expectations

It's extremely important to realize that some of your dissatisfaction might come from expecting too much of yourself. If you demand that you handle every act of communication perfectly, you're bound to be disappointed. Nobody is able to handle every conflict productively, to be totally relaxed and skillful in conversations, to ask consistently perceptive questions, or to be 100 percent helpful when others have problems. Expecting yourself to reach such unrealistic goals is to doom yourself to unhappiness at the start.

Sometimes it's easy to be hard on yourself because all those around you seem to be handling themselves so much better than you. It's important to realize that much of what seems like confidence and skill in others is a front to hide uncertainty. They may be suffering from the same self-imposed demands of perfection that you place on yourself.

Even in cases where others definitely seem more competent than you, it's important to judge yourself in terms of your own growth, not against the behavior of others. Rather than feeling miserable because you're not as talented as an expert, realize that you probably are a better, wiser, or more skillful person than you used to be and that this is a legitimate source of satisfaction. Perfection is fine as an ideal, but you're being unfair to yourself if you expect actually to reach that state.

Have a Realistic Perception of Yourself

One source of a poor self-concept is an inaccurate self-perception. As you've already read, such unrealistic pictures sometimes come from being overly harsh on yourself, believing that you're worse than the facts indicate. By sharing the self-concept list you recorded on page 23, you will be able to see whether you

have been selling yourself short. Of course, it would be foolish to deny that you could be a better person than you are, but it's also important to recognize your strengths.

An unrealistically poor self-concept can also come from the inaccurate feedback of others. Perhaps you are in an environment where you receive an excessive number of "downer" messages, many of which are undeserved, and a minimum of upper messages. We have known many women, for example, who have returned to college after many years spent in homemaking where they received virtually no recognition for their intellectual strengths. It's amazing that these women have the courage to come to college at all, so low is their self-esteem; but come they do, and most are thrilled to find that they are much brighter and more competent intellectually than they suspected. In the same way, workers with overly critical supervisors, children with cruel "friends," and students with unsupportive teachers all are prone to suffering from low self-concepts owing to excessively negative feedback.

If you fall into this category, it's important to put the unrealistic evaluations you receive into perspective and then to seek out more supportive people who will acknowledge your assets as well as point out your shortcomings. Doing so is often a quick and sure boost to self-esteem.

Have the Will to Change

Often we claim we want to change, but we aren't willing to do the necessary work. You might, for instance, decide that you'd like to become a better conversationalist. Taking the advice offered in the next section of this book, you ask your instructor or some other communication adviser how to reach this goal. Suppose you receive two suggestions: first, to spend the next three weeks observing people who handle themselves well in conversations and to record exactly what they do that makes them so skillful; second, to read several books on the subject of conversational skills. You begin these tasks with the best intentions, but after a few days the task of recording conversations becomes a burden—it would be so much easier just to listen to others talk. And your diligent reading program becomes bogged down as the press of other work fills up your time. In other words, you find you just "can't" fit the self-improvement plan into your busy schedule.

Let's be realistic. Becoming a better communicator is probably one of many goals in your life. It's possible that you'll find other needs more pressing, which is completely reasonable. However, you should realize that changing your self-concept often requires a good deal of effort, and without that effort your good intentions alone probably won't get you much closer to this goal. In communication, as in most other aspects of life, "there's no such thing as a free lunch."

Have the Skill Needed to Change

Often trying isn't enough. There are some cases where you would change if you knew of a way to do so. To see if this is the case for you, check the list of *can'ts* and *won'ts* from the exercise on page 46, and see if any items there are more appropriately "don't know how." If so, then the way to change is to learn how. You can do so in two ways.

First, you can seek advice—from books such as this one, from the references listed at the end of each chapter, and from other printed sources. You can also get suggestions from instructors, counselors, and other experts, as well as from friends. Of course, not all the advice you receive will be useful, but if you read widely and talk to enough people, you have a good chance of learning the things you want to know.

A second method of learning how to change is to observe models—people who handle themselves in the ways you would like to master. It's often been said that people learn more from models than in any other way, and by taking advantage of this principle you will find that the world is full of teachers who can show you how to communicate more successfully. Become a careful observer. Watch what people you admire do and say, not so that you can copy them, but so that you can adapt their behavior to fit your own personal style.

At this point you might be overwhelmed at the difficulty of changing the way you think about yourself and the way you act. Remember, we never said that this would be easy (although it sometimes is). But even when change is difficult, you know that it's possible if you are serious. You don't need to be perfect, but you can improve your self-concept if you choose to.

▶ SUMMARY

The chapter began by introducing the role of the self in communication. It defined the self-concept and showed the forces contributing to its development.

The chapter next examined the nature of perception, both of oneself and others. It began by introducing the steps in the perception process: selection, organization, and interpretation. It next listed several common errors in person perception and suggested empathy building and the skill of perception checking as ways of overcoming these errors.

The final section of the chapter showed how the self-concept influences perception. It discussed the desire for consistency and explained how this leads people to interpret events in ways that fit with their existing beliefs and attitudes. It showed how self-fulfilling prophecies can influence both one's own communication and the behavior of others. Finally, the chapter suggested ways of changing the self-concept.

▶ ACTIVITIES

1. This exercise will help you identify the importance of significant others in shaping a self-concept.
   a. Either by yourself or with a partner, recall someone you know or once

knew who was an "upper"—who helped enhance your self-esteem by act-ing in a way that made you feel accepted, competent, worthwhile, impor-tant, appreciated, or loved.

This person needn't have played a crucial role in your life as long as the role was positive. Often your self-concept is shaped by many tiny nudges as well as by a few giant events. A family member with whom you've spent most of your life can be an upper, but so can the stranger on the street who spontaneously smiles and strikes up a friendly conversation.

b. Now recall a "downer" from your life—someone who acted in a large or small way to reduce your self-esteem. As with uppers, downer messages aren't always intentional. The acquaintance who forgets your name after you've been introduced or the friend who yawns while you're describing an important problem can diminish your feelings of self-worth.

c. Now that you've thought about how others shape your self-concept, recall a time when you were an upper to someone else—when you delib-erately or unintentionally boosted another's self-esteem. Don't merely settle for an instance in which you were nice: Look for a time when your actions left another person feeling valued, loved, needed, and so on. You may have to ask the help of others to answer this question.

d. Finally, recall a recent instance in which you were a downer for someone else. What did you do to diminish another's self-esteem? Were you aware of the effect of your behavior at the time?

Your answer might show that some events we intend as uppers have the effect of downers. For example, you might joke with a friend in what you meant as a friendly gesture, only to discover that your remarks are received as criticism.

2. Choose a disagreement you presently have with another person or group. The disagreement might be a personal one—such as an argument about how to settle a financial problem or who is to blame for a present state of affairs—or it might be a dispute over a contemporary public issue, such as the right of women to obtain abortions on demand or the value of capital punishment.

a. In 300 words or so, describe your side of the issue. State why you believe as you do, just as if you were presenting your position to an important jury.

b. Now take 300 words or so to describe in the first-person singular how the other person sees the same issue. For instance, if you are a religious person, write this section as if you were an atheist: For a short while get in touch with how the other person feels and thinks.

c. Now show the description you wrote in step b to your "opponent," the person whose beliefs are different from yours. Have that person read your account and correct any statements that don't reflect his or her position accurately. Remember, you're doing this so that you can more clearly understand how the issue looks to the other person.

d. Make any necessary corrections in the account you wrote in step c, and again show it to your partner. When your partner agrees that you under-stand his or her position, have your partner sign your paper to indicate this.

e. Now record your conclusions to this experiment. Has this perceptual shift made any difference in how you view the issue or how you feel about your partner?

3. Identify two cases in which you committed the perceptual errors listed on pages 30–34.

4. Practice your perception checking ability by developing three-part verifications for the following situations:

   a. You made what you thought was an excellent suggestion to an instructor. The professor looked uninterested but said she would check on the matter right away. Three weeks have passed and nothing has changed.

   b. A neighbor and good friend has not responded to your "Good morning" for three days in a row. This person is usually friendly.

   c. You haven't noticed the usual weekly phone call from the folks back home in over a month. The last time you spoke, you had an argument about where to spend the holidays.

   d. An old friend with whom you have shared the problems of your love life for years has recently changed when around you: The formerly casual hugs and kisses have become longer and stronger; and the occasions where you "accidentally" brush up against one another, more frequent.

5. What communication-related self-fulfilling prophecies do you impose on yourself? What prophecies have others imposed on you? What prophecies have you imposed on others?

6. How committed are you to changing your self-concept? You can find out by responding to the steps that follow.

   a. Choose a partner and for five minutes or so take turns making and listing statements that begin with "I can't..." Try to focus your statements on your relationships with family, friends, co-workers and students, and even strangers: whomever you have a hard time communicating with.
      Sample statements:

      "I can't be myself with strangers I'd like to get to know at parties."

      "I can't tell a friend how much I care about her."

      "I can't bring myself to ask my supervisor for the raise I think I deserve."

      "I can't ask questions in class."

   b. Notice the feelings you experience as you make each statement: self-pity, regret, concern, frustration, and so on; and share these with your partner.

   c. Now go back and repeat aloud each statement you've just made, but this time change each *can't* to a *won't*. After each sentence, share with your partner whatever thoughts you have about what you've just said.

   d. After you've finished, decide whether "can't" or "won't" is more appropriate for each item, and explain your choice to your partner.

   e. Are there any instances of the self-fulfilling prophecy in your list—times when your decision that you "couldn't" do something was the only force keeping you from doing it?

1. Anthony G. Athos and John J. Gabarro, *Interpersonal Behavior: Communication and Understanding in Relationships* (Englewood Cliffs, N.J.: Prentice-Hall, 1978), p. 140.

2. Kathleen S. Berger, *The Developing Person* (New York: Worth, 1980), pp. 243–244.

3. Michael Lewis and Jeanne Brooks, "Self-knowledge and Emotional Development," in Michael Lewis and Leonard A. Rosenblum (eds.), *The Development of Affect* (New York: Plenum, 1978), pp. 205–226.

4. Arthur W. Combs and Donald Snygg, *Individual Behavior,* rev. ed. (New York: Harper & Row, 1959), p. 134.

5. Harry S. Sullivan, *The Interpersonal Theory of Psychiatry* (New York: Norton, 1953).

6. Charles H. Cooley, *Human Nature and the Social Order* (New York: Scribner's, 1902).

7. Monte D. Smith, S. A. Zingalc, and J. M. Coleman, "The Influence of Adult Expectations/Child Performance Discrepancies upon Children's Self-Concepts," *American Educational Research Journal* 15 (1978): 259–265.

8. S. Frank Miyamoto and Sanford M. Dornbusch, "A Text of Interactionist Hypotheses of Self-Conception," *American Journal of Sociology* 61 (1956): 399–403.

9. Dennis Coon, *Introduction to Psychology,* 2d ed. (St. Paul: West Publishing, 1981).

10. L. Carmichael, H. P. Hogan, and A. A. Walter, "An Experimental Study of the Effect of Language on the Reproduction of Visually Perceived Form," *Journal of Experimental Psychology* 15 (1932): 73–86.

11. Summarized in Don E. Hamachek, *Encounters with Others* (New York: Holt, Rinehart and Winston, 1982), pp. 23–30.

12. See, for example, Penny Baron, "Self-esteem, Ingratiation, and Evaluation of Unknown Others," *Journal of Personality and Social Psychology* 30 (1974): 104–109; and Elaine Walster, "The Effect of Self-esteem on Romantic Liking," *Journal of Experimental and Social Psychology* 1 (1965): 184–197.

13. See, for example, D. E. Kanouse and L. R. Hanson, "Negativity in Evaluations," in E. E. Jones, D. E. Kanouse, H. H. Kelley, R. E. Nisbett, S. Valins, and B. Weiner (eds.), *Attribution: Perceiving the Causes of Behavior* (Morristown, N.J.: General Learning Press, 1972).

14. R. G. King, *Fundamentals of Human Communication* (New York: Macmillan, 1979), p. 152.

15. D. T. Regan and J. Totten, "Empathy and Attribution: Turning Observers into Actors," *Journal of Personality and Social Psychology* 35 (1975): 850–856.

16. Hamachek, op. cit., pp. 23–24.

17. G. Cronkhite, *Communication and Awareness* (Menlo Park, Calif.: Cummings, 1976), p. 82.

18. See F. Heider, *The Psychology of Interpersonal Relations* (New York: Wiley, 1968); C. Osgood and P. Tannenbaum, "The Principle of Congruity in the Prediction of Attitude Change," *Psychological Review* 62 (1955): 42–55; and L. Festinger, *A Theory of Cognitive Dissonance* (Stanford, Calif.: Stanford University Press, 1957).

19. B. Sypher and H. E. Sypher, "Seeing Ourselves as Others See Us," *Communication Research* 11 (January 1984): 97–115.

20. Reported by D. Myers, "The Inflated Self," *Psychology Today* 14 (May 1980): 16.

21. See, for example, P. Baron, "Self-Esteem, Ingratiation, and Evaluation of Unknown Others," *Journal of Personality and Social Psychology* 30 (1974): 104–109.

22. Hamachek, op. cit., p. 3.

23. Robert Rosenthal and Lenore Jacobson, *Pygmalion in the Classroom* (New York: Holt, Rinehart and Winston, 1968).

▶ CHAPTER 3

KEY TERMS

abstraction ladder
abstract language
behavioral description
connotation
denotation
emotive language
equivocal words
euphemism
factual statement
inferential statement
language
relative words
semantic rules
syntactic rules
Whorf-Sapir hypothesis

LANGUAGE

After reading this chapter, you should understand the following:

1. The symbolic, person-centered nature of language.
2. The syntactic and semantic characteristics of language.
3. The ways in which language shapes the perceptions of users.
4. How language reflects the attitudes of users.
5. The types of linguistic misunderstandings listed in this chapter.

You should be able to do the following:

1. Identify at least two ways in which language has shaped your perceptions of a person, object, or event.
2. Identify at least two ways in which your language reflects your attitudes about a person, object, or event.
3. Identify and correct the linguistic misunderstandings listed in this chapter in a conversation or written text.
4. Translate overly abstract problems, goals, appreciations, complaints, and requests into more specific, behavioral terms.

▶ And the whole earth was of one language, and of one speech.

₂ And it came to pass, as they journeyed from the east, that they found a plain in the land of Shinar; and they dwelt there.

₃ And they said to one another, Go to, let us make brick, and burn them thoroughly. And they had brick for stone, and slime had they for mortar.

₄ And they said, Go to, let us build us a city and a tower, whose top may reach unto heaven; and let us make us a name, lest we be scattered abroad upon the face of the whole earth.

₅ And the Lord came down to see the city and the tower, which the children of men builded.

₆ And the Lord said, Behold, the people is one, and they have all one language; and this they begin to do: and now nothing will be restrained from them, which they have imagined to do.

₇ Go to, let us go down, and there confound their language, that they may not understand one another's speech.

₈ So the Lord scattered them abroad from thence upon the face of all the earth: and they left off to build the city.

₉ Therefore is the name of it called Babel; because the Lord did there confound the language of all the earth: and from thence did the Lord scatter them abroad upon the face of all the earth.

Genesis 11:1–9

It is no accident that the story of the Tower of Babel is the opening passage for this chapter. Sometimes it seems as if none of us speaks the same language. Others hear but don't understand, and we often fail to grasp the full meaning of what others say or write.

In this chapter we will explore the nature of linguistic communication. After reading the following pages, you should have a better understanding of both how we use—and misuse—language to express our thoughts and how the language we use shapes our perception of people and events.

▶ THE NATURE OF LANGUAGE

Because we use language almost constantly, we often assume that carefully chosen words can paint an accurate picture of any idea. Actually, the matter isn't this simple.

Language Is Symbolic

As you read in Chapter 1, words are symbols that represent things—ideas, events, objects, and so on. Words are not the things themselves. For instance, it's obvious that the word *coat* is not the same as the piece of clothing it describes. You would be a fool to expect the letters c-o-a-t to keep you warm in a snowstorm. This point seems so obvious as to be hardly worth mentioning, yet people often forget the nature of language and confuse symbols with their referents. For example, some students will cram facts into their heads just long enough to regurgitate them into a blue book in order to earn a high grade, forgetting that letters like *A* or *B* are only symbols and that a few lines of ink on paper don't necessarily represent true learning. In the same way, simply saying the words "I care about you" isn't necessarily a reflection of the truth although many disappointed lovers have learned this lesson the hard way.

So far we have been using the terms *language* and *symbol* interchangeably, which isn't quite correct. **Languages** consist of collections of symbols, which possess certain properties.[1] First, a language must contain certain *elements*. In English these elements consist of the letters of our alphabet along with punctuation marks such as commas, periods, and so on. In the language of mathematics the elements are the integers zero through nine plus other symbols such as plus and minus signs. The Morse code has only two elements—dots and dashes.

The elements of any language have no meaning by themselves. And in many combinations they are also meaningless. For example, the letters "flme oo usi oysk" are pure gibberish. But when rearranged into a more recognizable pattern, they become more understandable: "Kiss me, you fool!" This example illustrates the second characteristic of language, which is the existence of a body of *rules* that dictate the way in which symbols can be used.

Languages contain two types of rules. **Syntactic rules** govern the ways in which symbols can be arranged. For example, correct English syntax requires that every word contain at least one vowel and prohibits sentences such as "Have you the cookies brought?" which is a perfectly acceptable word order in a language such as German. Although most of us aren't able to describe the rules that govern our language, it's easy to recognize the existence of such rules by noting how odd a statement that violates them appears.

Semantic rules also govern our use of the language. But where syntax deals with structure, semantics governs meaning. Semantic rules reflect the ways in which speakers of a language respond to a particular symbol. Semantic rules are what make it possible for us to agree that "bikes" are for riding and "books" are for reading; they also help us to know who we will and won't encounter when we use rooms marked "Men" or "Women." Without semantic rules, communication would be impossible, for each of us would use symbols in unique ways, unintelligible to one another.

After reading the last sentence, you might object, thinking about the many cases in which people don't follow the same semantic rules. Of course, you would be correct, for there are many times when a single word has different meanings for different people. This is possible because words, being symbols, have no meaning in themselves. Ogden and Richards have illustrated this point graphically in their well-known "triangle of meaning" (Figure 3–1).[2] This triangle shows that there is only an indirect relationship—indicated by a broken line— between a word and the thing it claims to represent.* Problems arise when people mistakenly believe that words automatically represent things or when we assume that our meaning for a word is the same as someone else's. We will spend most of this chapter discussing how to avoid such linguistic problems.

---

*Some of these "things" or referents do not exist in the physical world. For instance, some referents are mythical (such as unicorns), some are no longer tangible (such as the deceased Mr. Smith), and others are abstract ideas (such as "love").

FIGURE 3–1

Ogden and Richards' triangle
of meaning

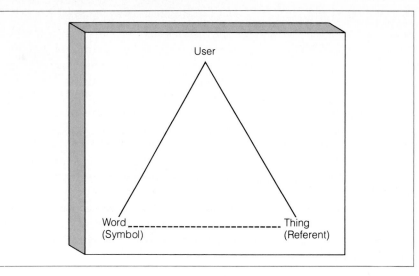

User

Word_____Thing
(Symbol)   (Referent)

Meanings Are in People, Not Words

▶ The spoken word belongs
half to the one who speaks
and half to the one who
hears.

French proverb

Show a dozen people the same symbol and ask them what it means, and you are likely to get twelve different answers. Does an American flag bring up associations of soldiers giving their lives for their country? Fourth of July parades? Mom's apple pie? How about a cross: What does it represent? The gentleness and wisdom of Jesus Christ? Fire-lit rallies of Ku Klux Klansmen? Your childhood Sunday school? The necklace your sister always wears?

Like these symbols, words can be interpreted in many different ways. And, of course, this is the basis for many misunderstandings. It's possible to have an argument about *feminism* without ever realizing that you and the other person are using the word to represent entirely different things. The same goes for *communism, Republicans, rock music,* and thousands upon thousands of other symbols. Words don't mean; people do—and often in widely different ways.

It might seem as if one remedy to misunderstandings like these would be to have more respect for the dictionary meanings of words. After all, you might think, if people would just consult a dictionary whenever they send or receive a potentially confusing message, there would be little problem.

This approach has three shortcomings. First, dictionaries show that many words have multiple definitions, and it isn't always clear which one applies in a given situation. The 500 words most commonly used in everyday communication have over 14,000 dictionary definitions, which should give you an idea of the limitations of this approach.

A second problem is that people often use words in ways you would never be able to look up. Sometimes the misuse of words is due to a lack of knowledge, as when you might ask your auto parts dealer for a new generator when you really need an alternator.

The third shortcoming of dictionaries is that they define most words in terms of *other* words, and this process often won't tell you any more about a term

> "I don't know what you mean by 'glory,' " Alice said.

Humpty Dumpty smiled contemptuously. "Of course you don't—till I tell you. I meant 'there's a nice knock-down argument for you!' "

"But 'glory' doesn't mean 'a nice knock-down argument,' " Alice objected.

"When *I* use a word," Humpty Dumpty said, in a rather scornful tone, "it means just what I choose it to mean—neither more nor less."

"The question is," said Alice, "whether you *can* make words mean so many different things."

"The question is," said Humpty Dumpty, "which is to be master—that's all."

Lewis Carroll
Through the Looking Glass

---

than you already know. In fact, it's possible to talk endlessly about a subject and sound very knowledgeable without every having the slightest idea of what your words refer to. Jessica Davidson's quiz is an example of this. Read the paragraph; then see if you can answer the questions:

> Because public opinion is sometimes marsiflate, empetricious insoculences are frequently zophilimized. Nevertheless, it cannot be overemphasized that carpoflansibles are highly traculate.

1. In the author's opinion, carpoflansibles are
    a. empetricious
    b. traculate
    c. zophilimized
2. Public opinion is sometimes
    a insoculent
    b. variable
    c. marsiflate
3. According to the text, insoculences are zophilimized
    a. often
    b. never
    c. sometimes[3]

You can see that the correct answers are 1(b), 2(c), and 3(a). But even if you scored perfectly on the quiz, do you know the meaning of the paragraph? Of course not, for the words are gibberish. But if you look closely, you'll find that many people use their own language in the same way, talking in terms they can define only by other terms.

Language Shapes Attitudes

Language does far more than describe the world. On a more fundamental level, the labels we use shape the way we look at the world and, in so doing, influence the way we behave.

CULTURE   Many social scientists believe that the structure of a culture's language shapes the worldview of its members. This idea is articulated most clearly in the **Whorf-Sapir hypothesis.**[4]

After spending several years with various North American Indian cultures, Whorf found that their patterns of thinking were shaped by the language they spoke. For example, Nootka, a language spoken on Vancouver Island, contains no distinction between nouns and verbs. The Indians who speak Nootka view the entire world as being constantly in process. Whereas English speakers see something as fixed or constant (noun), Nootka speakers view it as constantly changing. Therefore, the Nootka speaker might label a "fire" as a "burning," or a house as a "house-ing." In this sense, our language operates much like a snapshot camera whereas Nootka works more like a moving-picture camera.

What does this difference have to do with communication? Because of the static, unchanging nature of our grammar, we often regard people and things as never changing. Someone who spoke a more process-oriented language would view people quite differently, assuming their changeable nature. Some cultures, for example, allow their members to change names whenever they wish. We can speculate that this practice might make it easier to see that others change over time, and in the same way it might make it easier for individuals to escape the inhibiting effects of an obsolete self-concept.

A look at more familiar languages also shows how the linguistic world we inhabit can subtly shape our attitudes. English-speaking parents often label the mischievous pranks of their children as "bad," implying that there is something immoral about acting wild. "Be good!" they are inclined to say. On the other hand, French adults are more likely to say, *"Sois sage!"*—"Be wise." The linguistic implication is that misbehaving is an act of foolishness. Swedes would correct the same action with the words *"Var snell!"*—"Be friendly. Be kind." By contrast, German adults use the command *"Sei Artig!"*—literally "Be of your own kind"—in other words, get back in step, conform to your role as a child.[5]

Although the Whorf-Sapir hypothesis originally focused on foreign languages, Neil Postman illustrates the principle with an example closer to home. He describes a culture where physicians identify patients they treat as "doing" arthritis and other diseases instead of "having" them and where criminals are diagnosed as "having" cases of criminality instead of "being" criminals.[6]

The implications of such a linguistic difference are profound. We believe that characteristics people "have"—what they "are"—are beyond their control whereas they are responsible for what they "do." If we changed our view of

► The problems crop up when we start talking about other types of deviant behavior. We say of a person who drinks too much that he "is" an alcoholic, and we say of people who think bizarre thoughts that they "are" schizophrenic. This person is a drug addict and that person is a homosexual. Others are sadomasochists, pedophiliacs, juvenile delinquents. The English language is constructed in such a way that we speak of people *being* (certain things) when all we know is that they do certain things. . . .

That kind of identity is a myth. Admittedly, if a person believes the myth, the chances rise that he will assume the appropriate, narrowly defined role. Believing that one is an addict, an alcoholic, a schizophrenic, or a homosexual can result in relinquishing the search for change and becoming imprisoned in the role.

Edward Sagarian

---

what people "have" and what they "do," our attitudes would most likely change as well. Postman illustrates the consequences of this linguistic difference as applied to education:

In schools, for instance, we find that tests are given to determine how smart someone is or, more precisely, how much smartness someone "has." If one child scores a 138, and another a 106, the first is thought to "have" more smartness than the other. But this seems to me a strange conception—every bit as strange as "doing" arthritis or "having" criminality. I do not know anyone who *has* smartness. The people I know sometimes *do* smart things (as far as I can judge) and sometimes *do* stupid things— depending on what circumstances they are in, and how much they know about a situation, and how interested they are. "Smartness," so it seems to me, is a specific performance, done in a particular set of circumstances. It is not something you *are* or have in measurable quantities. In fact, the assumption that smartness is something you *have* has led to such nonsensical ideas as "over-" and "underachievers." As I understand it, an overachiever is someone who doesn't *have* much smartness but does a lot of smart things. An underachiever is someone who *has* a lot of smartness but does a lot of stupid things.

In any case, I am not prepared here to argue the matter through. Although I have not heard of them, there may be good reasons to imagine that smartness or honesty or sensitivity are "qualities" that people *have* in measurable proportions and that exist independently of what people actually do. What I am driving at is this: All language is metaphorical, and often in the subtlest ways. In the simplest sentence, sometimes in the simplest word, we do more than merely express ourselves. We construct reality along certain lines. We make the world according to our own imagery.[7]

The Sapir-Whorf hypothesis has never been conclusively proved or disproved. In spite of its intellectual appeal, some critics point out that it is possible to conceive of flux even in static languages like English. They suggest that Sapir and Whorf overstated the importance of their idea. Supporters of the hypothesis respond that though it is *possible* to conceptualize an idea in different languages, some languages make it much easier to recognize a term than do others.

NAMING   The power of language is so great that it even extends to personal names. Research shows that these names are more than just a simple means of identification; that, in fact, they shape the way others think of us, the way we view ourselves, and the way we act.[8]

Different names have different connotations. In one study, psychologists asked college students to rate over a thousand names according to their likability, how active or passive they seemed, and their masculinity or femininity. In spite of the large number of subjects, the responses were quite similar. Michael, John, and Wendy were likable and active and were rated as possessing the masculine or feminine traits of their sex. Percival, Isadore, and Alfreda were less likable, and their sexuality was more suspect. Other research also suggests that names have strong connotative meanings. More common names are generally viewed as being more active, stronger, and better than unusual ones.

The preconceptions we hold about people because of their names influence our behavior toward them. In another well-known study, researchers asked a number of teachers to read several essays supposedly written by fifth-grade students. The researchers found that certain names—generally the most popular ones such as Lisa, Michael, and Karen—received higher grades regardless of which essay they were attached to whereas other less popular names—Elmer, Bertha, Hubert—were consistently graded as inferior. There was one exception to the link between popular names and high grades: Unpopular Adelle received the highest evaluation of all. The researchers speculated that the teachers saw her as more "scholarly."

It's not surprising to find that the attitudes others hold toward a person because of his or her name have an effect on that person's self-concept. Over forty years ago, researchers found that students at Harvard who had unusual names were more likely to be neurotic and to flunk out of school. The negative effect of unusual names seems to be more damaging to men than women, perhaps owing to our social convention that makes such labels acceptable for females. At any rate, research such as this makes it clear that the question "What shall we name the baby?" is an important one for more than aesthetic reasons.

CREDIBILITY Scholarly speaking is a good example of how speech style influences perception. We refer to what has been called the Dr. Fox hypothesis.[9] "An apparently legitimate speaker who utters an unintelligible message will be judged competent by an audience in the speaker's area of apparent expertise." The Dr. Fox hypothesis got its name from one Dr. Myron L. Fox, who delivered a talk followed by a half-hour discussion on "Mathematical Game Theory as Applied to Physical Education." The audience included psychiatrists, psychologists, social workers, and educators. Questionnaires collected after the session revealed that these educated listeners found the lecture clear and stimulating.

Despite his warm reception by this learned audience, Fox was a complete fraud. He was a professional actor whom researchers had coached to deliver a lecture of double-talk—a patchwork of information from a *Scientific American* article mixed with jokes, non sequiturs, contradictory statements, and meaningless references to unrelated topics. When wrapped in a linguistic package of high-level professional jargon, however, the meaningless gobbledygook was judged as important information. In other words, Fox's credibility came more from his style of speaking than from the ideas he expressed.

The same principle seems to hold for academic writing.[10] A group of thirty-two management professors rated material according to its complexity rather than its content. When a message about consumer behavior was loaded with unnecessary words and long, complex sentences, the academics rated it highly. When the same message was translated into more readable English, with shorter words and clearer sentences, the professors judged the same research as less competent.

STATUS In the stage classic *My Fair Lady*, Professor Henry Higgins transformed Eliza Doolittle from a lowly flower girl into a high-society woman by replacing her Cockney accent with an upper-crust speaking style. The power of speech to influence status is a real-life fact. British researcher Howard Giles conducted experiments that conclusively demonstrated (if any proof were necessary) that, in Britain, judgments of attractiveness and status are strongly influenced by style of speech. Other research by social psychologists in North America shows that the same principle applies in the New World.[11]

SELF-ESTEEM The words we use to describe people's roles or functions in society can also shape the way they feel about themselves. Much of people's self-esteem is derived from the importance they feel their work has, a perception that often comes from the titles of their roles. For example, a theater owner had trouble keeping ushers working for more than a week or two. The ushers tired quickly of their work, which consisted mostly of taking tickets, selling popcorn, and showing people to their seats. Then, with only one change, the personnel problems ended. The manager simply "promoted" all the ushers to the "new" position of "assistant manager." Believe it or not, the new title was sufficient to make the employees happy. The new name encouraged them to think more highly of themselves and to take new pride in their work.

The significance of words in shaping our self-concept goes beyond job titles. Racist and sexist language greatly affects the self-concepts of those facing discrimination. An article in *The New York Times Magazine* by Casey Miller and Kate Swift points out some of the aspects of our language that suggest women are of lower status than men. Miller and Swift write that, except for words referring to females by definition, such as *mother* and *actress,* English defines many nonsexual concepts as male. The underlying assumption is that people in general are men. Also, words associated with males have positive connotations, such as *manly, virile, courageous, direct, strong,* and *independent* whereas words related to females are fewer and have less positive connotations, such as *feminine wiles* and *womanish tears.*[12]

Most dictionaries, in fact, define *effeminate* as the opposite of *masculine* although the opposite of *feminine* is closer to *unfeminine.* Any language expressing stereotyped sexual attitudes or assuming the superiority of one sex over

▶ **'Manholes' Called Sexist, Become 'Access Chambers'**

LONDON (UPI)—A London borough Thursday banned the use of the word *manhole* on the grounds it is sexist and ordered sewer workers to use the term *access chambers.*

"It is our policy to use nonsexist language. The word *manhole* clearly defies it," said a spokesman for the Hackney borough council in east London.

"It is an insult to women. Why not call them women-holes?" he said.

The leftist-controlled council previously banned from schools the nursery rhyme "Bah Bah, Black Sheep," saying it was racist.

▶ The most powerful stimulus for changing minds is not a chemical. Or a baseball bat. It is a word.

George A. Miller,
Past President,
American Psychological Association

another is sexist, so adding feminine endings to nonsexual words, such as *poetess* for female poet, is as sexist as *separate but equal* is racist.

Whereas sexist language usually defines the world as made up of superior men and inferior women, racist language usually defines it as composed of superior whites and other, inferior racial groups. Words and images associated with *white* are usually positive, whether it's the hero-cowboy in white or connotations of white as *pure, clean, honorable, innocent, bright,* and *shiny.* The words and images associated with black are often negative, a concept that reaches from the clothes of the villain-cowboy to connotations such as *decay, dirt, smudge, dismal, wicked, unwashed,* and *sinister.*

To the extent that our language is both sexist and racist, our view of the world is affected. For example, men are given more opportunity that women to see themselves as "good," and in the same way whites are given more opportunity than blacks. Language shapes the self-concepts of those it labels in such a way that members of the linguistically slighted group see themselves as inferior.

Many linguistic changes beginning in the late 1960s were aimed primarily at teaching speakers and writers a new vocabulary to change the destructive connotations that accompany many of our words. For example, "black is beautiful" is an effort to reduce perceived differences in status among blacks and whites.

Changes in writing style were also designed to counter the sexual prejudices inherent in language, particularly eliminating the constant use of *he* and introducing various methods either to eliminate reference to a particular sex or to refer to both sexes. Words that use *man* generically to refer to humanity at large often pose problems, but only to the unimaginative. Consider the following substitutions: *Mankind* may be replaced by *humanity, human beings, human race,* and *people; man-made* may be replaced by *artificial, manufactured,* and *synthetic; manpower* may be replaced by *human power, workers,* and *work force;* and *manhood* may be replaced by *adulthood.*

Congressmen are *members of Congress.*

Firemen are *fire fighters.*

Chairmen are *presiding officers, leaders,* and *chairs.*

Foremen are *supervisors.*

Policemen and *policewomen* are both *police officers.*

Stewardesses and *stewards* are both *flight attendants.*

Throughout this book we have used a number of techniques for avoiding sexist language: switching to the sexual neutral plural (*they*), occasionally using the passive voice to eliminate sexed pronouns, employing the *he or she* structure, carefully balancing individual masculine and feminine pronouns in illustrative material, and even totally rewriting some parts to delete conceptual sexual bias.

Language Reflects Attitudes

Besides shaping the way we view ourselves and others, language reflects our attitudes. Feelings of control, attraction, commitment, responsibility . . . all these and more are reflected in the way we use language.

► COUPLE WEDS SO THEY KNOW WHAT TO CALL EACH OTHER

This piece will use names of two people, Pietro and Tess.

For three years Pietro and Tess lived together without marrying. Such an arrangement had ceased to be scandalous when they took it up, had even become fashionable. It expressed the partners' reevaluation of the culture, or their liberation from tired old values, or something. It doesn't matter what. Pietro and Tess did it.

They were married a few weeks ago.

The canker in the love nest was the English language. Though English is the world's most commodious tongue, it provided no words to define their relationship satisfactorily to strangers. When Tess took Pietro to meet her parents the problem became troublesome. Presenting Pietro, she said, "Mommy and daddy, this is my lover, Pietro."

Pietro was not amused. "It made me sound like a sex object," he said.

A few weeks later they were invited to meet the president. Entering the reception line, Pietro was asked by the protocol officer for their names. "Pietro," he said. "And this is my mate."

As they came abreast of the president, the officer turned to Mr. Reagan and said, "Pietro and his mate."

"I felt like the supporting actress in a Tarzan movie," said Tess. It took Pietro three nights of sleeping at the YMCA to repair their relationship.

Back to the drawing board, on which they kept the dictionary.

For a while they tried "my friend." One night at a glamorous party Pietro introduced Tess to a marrying millionaire with the words, "This is my friend, Tess." To which the marrying millionaire replied, "Let's jet down to the Caribbean, Tess, and tie the knot."

"You don't understand," said Pietro. "Tess is my *friend.*"

"So don't you like seeing your friends headed for big alimony?" asked the marrying millionaire.

"She's not that kind of friend," said Pietro.

"I'm his *friend,*" said Tess.

"Ah," said the matrimonialist, upon whom the dawn was slowly breaking, "Ah—your—*friend.*"

As Tess explained at the wedding, they couldn't spend the rest of their lives rolling their eyeballs suggestively every time they said "friend." There was only one way out. "The simple thing," Pietro suggested, "would be for me to introduce you as 'my wife.' "

"And for me," said Tess, "to say, 'This is my husband, Pietro.' "

And so they were wed, victims of a failure in language.

Russell Baker
The New York Times

POWER Communication researchers have identified a number of language patterns that add to, or detract from, a speaker's ability to influence others, as well as reflecting how a speaker feels about his or her degree of control over a situation.[13] Table 3–1 summarizes some of these findings by listing several types of "powerless" language.

You can see the difference between powerful and powerless language by comparing the following statements:

"Excuse me, sir, I hate to say this, but I...uh...I guess I won't be able to turn in the assignment on time. I had a personal emergency and...well...it was just impossible to finish it by today. I'll have it in your mailbox on Monday, okay?"

"I won't be able to turn in the assignment on time. I had a personal emergency, and it was impossible to finish it by today. I'll have it in your mailbox on Monday."

LANGUAGE

TABLE 3–1 Examples of Powerless Language

Hedges	"I'm *kinda* disappointed…" "I *think* we should…" "I *guess* I'd like to…"
Hesitations	"*Uh,* can I have a minute of your time?" "*Well,* we could try this idea…" "I wish you would—*er*—try to be on time."
Intensifiers	"*So* that's how I feel…" "I'm not *very* hungry."
Polite forms	"Excuse me, *sir…*"
Tag questions	"It's about time we got started, *isn't it?*" "*Don't you think* we should give it another try?"
Disclaimers	"*I probably shouldn't say this, but* …" "*I'm not really sure but* …"

Whether or not the professor finds the excuse acceptable, it's clear that the second speaker feels confident whereas the first one is apologetic and uncertain. The first statement is a classic example of what social scientists have come to call "one-down" communication.[14]

Some relationships are characterized by what social scientists term *complementary* communication, in which one partner uses consistently powerful language while the other responds with powerless speech. A demanding boss and compliant employees or the stereotypically tyrannical husband and submissive wife are examples of complementary relationships. In other relationships, called *symmetrical,* the power is distributed more evenly between the partners: Both may use equally powerful or powerless speech. The locus of power isn't constant: As relationships pass through different stages, the distribution of power shifts, and so do the speech patterns of the partners.[15] You can test this principle for yourself. Recall situations in which you were feeling especially vulnerable, uncertain, confused, or powerless. Did your language include the characteristics listed in Table 3–1? Did these characteristics disappear when you felt more safe, confident, or powerful? What factors led to these changes? The subject being discussed? Your feelings about yourself at the moment? The way the other person was treating you?

Simply counting the number of powerful or powerless statements won't always reveal who has the most control in a relationship. Social rules often mask the real distribution of power. A boss who wants to be pleasant might say to a secretary, "Would you mind retyping this letter?" In truth, both boss and secretary know this is an order and not a request, but the questioning form makes the medicine less bitter.[16] Therefore, a knowledge of the context and the personalities of the speakers is necessary before it's safe to make any assumptions about who controls whom.

ATTRACTION AND INTEREST Social customs discourage us from expressing like or dislike in many situations. Only a clod would respond to the question "What do you think of the cake I baked for you?" by saying, "It's terrible."

Bashful or cautious suitors might not admit their attraction to a potential partner. Even when people are reluctant to speak candidly, the language they use can suggest their degree of interest and attraction toward a person, object, or idea. Morton Weiner and Albert Mehrabian outline a number of linguistic clues that reveal these attitudes.[17]

▶ *Demonstrative pronoun choice.*
  These people want our help (positive) vs. *Those* people want our help (less positive).
▶ *Negation.*
  It's *good* (positive) vs. It's *not bad* (less positive).
▶ *Sequential placement.*
  Dick and Jane (Dick is more important) vs. Jane and Dick (Jane is more important).*

RESPONSIBILITY In addition to suggesting liking and importance, language can also reveal the speaker's willingness to accept responsibility for a message.

▶ *"It" vs. "I" statements.*
▶ It's not finished (less responsible) vs. *I* didn't finish it (more responsible).
▶ *"You" vs. "I" statements.*
▶ Sometimes *you* wonder if he's honest (less responsible) vs. Sometimes *I* wonder if he's honest (more responsible).
▶ *"But" statements.*
  It's a good idea, *but* it won't work. You're really terrific, *but* I think we ought to spend less time together. (*But* cancels everything that went before the word.)
▶ *Questions vs. statements.*
  Do you think we ought to do that? (less responsible) vs. I don't think we ought to do that (more responsible).

THE LANGUAGE OF MISUNDERSTANDINGS ◀

After reading this far, you should understand that language isn't the simple tool for expressing ideas that it first seems to be. Some terms have especially high potential for being misunderstood. By becoming more aware of them, your chances for communicating accurately will grow.

Equivocal Language

Equivocal words have more than one correct dictionary definition. Some equivocal misunderstandings are simple and humorous. Not long ago we were ordering dinner in a Mexican restaurant and noticed that the menu described each item as coming with rice or beans. We asked the waitress for "a tostado with beans," but when the order arrived, we were surprised to find that instead

*Sequential placement isn't always significant. You may put "toilet bowl cleaner" at the top of your shopping list simply because it's closer to the market door than champagne.

▶ The Semantics of "I Love You"

"I love you" [is] a statement that can be expressed in so many varied ways. It may be a stage song, repeated daily without any meaning, or a barely audible murmur, full of surrender. Sometimes it means: I desire you or I want you sexually. It may mean: I hope you love me or I hope that I will be able to love you. Often it means: It may be that a love relationship can develop between us or even I hate you. Often it is a wish for emotional exchange: I want your admiration in exchange for mine or I give my love in exchange for some passion or I want to feel cozy and at home with you or I admire some of your qualities. A declaration of love is mostly a request: I desire you or I want you to gratify me, or I want your protection or I want to be intimate with you or I want to exploit your loveliness.

Sometimes it is the need for security and tenderness, for parental treatment. It may mean: My self-love goes out to you. But it may also express submissiveness: Please take me as I am, or I feel guilty about you, I want, through you, to correct the mistakes I have made in human relations. It may be self-sacrifice and a masochistic wish for dependency. However, it may also be a full affirmation of the other, taking the responsibility for mutual exchange of feelings. It may be a weak feeling of friendliness, it may be the scarcely even whispered expression of ecstasy. "I love you,"—wish, desire, submission, conquest; it is never the word itself that tells the real meaning here.

J. A. M. Meerloo
Conversation and Communication

---

of a beef tostado with beans on the side as we expected, the waitress had brought a tostado *filled* with beans. Looking back on the incident, it's obvious that the order was an equivocal one.

Other equivocal misunderstandings are more serious. A nurse once told her patient that he "wouldn't be needing" the materials he requested from home. He interpreted the statement to mean he was near death when the nurse meant he would be going home soon. A colleague of ours mistakenly sent some confidential materials to the wrong person after his boss told him to "send them to Richard," without specifying *which* Richard.

As we mentioned earlier, most of the words people use can be interpreted in a number of ways. A good rule to remember if you want to keep misunderstandings to a minimum is "If a word can be interpreted in more than one way, it probably will be." The paraphrasing and questioning skills you will learn in Chapter 4 can help overcome equivocal misunderstandings.

Relative Terms

Relative words gain their meaning by comparison. For example, is the school you attend large or small? This depends on what you compare it to: Alongside a campus like UCLA, with its almost 30,000 students, it probably looks small; but compared with a smaller institution, it might seem quite large. In the same way relative words like *fast* and *slow, smart* and *stupid, short* and *long* depend for their meaning upon what they're compared to. (The "large" size can of olives is the smallest you can buy; the larger ones are "giant," "colossal," and "super-colossal.")

▶ ...Considerably more serious is the frequent mistake committed by translators with the number word billion, which in the United States and France means a thousand millions (10^9) but in England and most continental European countries means a million millions (10^{12}): There the U.S. billion is called miliardo, Milliarde, etc. The reader will appreciate that...the difference between 10^9 and 10^{12} can mean disaster if hidden in, say, a textbook on nuclear physics.

Paul Watzlawick
How Real Is Real?

Using relative terms without explaining them can lead to communication problems. Have you ever responded to someone's question about the weather by saying it was warm, only to find out that what was warm to you was cold to the other person? Or have you followed a friend's advice and gone to a "cheap" restaurant, only to find that it was twice as expensive as you expected? Have you been disappointed to learn that classes you've heard were "easy" turned out to be hard, that journeys you were told would be "short" were long, that "unusual" ideas were really quite ordinary? The problem in each case came from failing to anchor the relative term used to a more precisely measurable term.

Emotive Language

To understand how emotive language works, we need to distinguish between **denotation** and **connotation.** A denotative definition describes an event in purely objective terms whereas connotative interpretations contain an emotional element. Consider, for example, the term *pregnant.* The denotative meaning of this word involves a condition in which a female is carrying her offspring during a gestation period. When used in this purely biological sense, most people could hear the term without a strong emotional reaction. But imagine the additional turmoil this word would create when an unmarried teenage couple find it stamped on the young woman's lab report. Certainly the meaning to these people would go far beyond the dictionary definition.

Some words have little or no connotative meaning: *the, it, as,* and so on. Others are likely to evoke both denotative and connotative reactions: *cancer, income tax,* and *final examination,* for example. There are also terms that are almost exclusively connotative, such as the *damn!* (or other oath) you would probably utter if you hammered your thumb instead of a nail.

Connotative meanings are a necessary and important part of human communication. It's a fact of life that people, as creatures with emotions, will use some words that will evoke strong reactions. Without connotative meanings, we'd be unable to describe our feelings fully.

Problems occur, however, when people claim to use words in a purely denotative way when they are really expressing their attitudes. **Emotive language,** then, contains words that sound as if they're describing something when they are really announcing the speaker's attitude toward something. Do you like that old picture frame? If so, you would probably call it "an antique," but if you think it's ugly, you would likely describe it as "a piece of junk." Now whether the picture frame belongs on the mantel or in the garbage can is a matter of opinion, not fact, but it's easy to forget this when emotive words are used. Emotive words may sound like statements of fact but are always opinions. The humorous guide "How to Tell a Businessman from a Businesswoman" illustrates how emotive language indirectly expresses the speaker's attitude.

As this list suggests, problems occur when people use emotive terms without labeling them as such. You might, for instance, have a long and bitter argument with a friend about whether a third person was "assertive" or "obnoxious," when a more accurate and peaceable way to handle the issue would be to acknowledge that one of you approves of the behavior and the other doesn't.

▶ Last night while Roy and I were preparing dinner, four-year-old Michael yelled from the family room, "Hey mom, how do you make love, again?" The expression on Roy's face clearly said, "What have you been teaching this kid?" I calmly answered Michael's question with "L-O-V-E." He had been drawing a picture for a friend and wanted to sign it, "Love, Michael," but had forgotten how to "make" love. I wonder how Roy would have answered Michael's question if I hadn't been around!

Lani Hendrick

▶ **How to Tell a Businessman from a Businesswoman**

A businessman is aggressive; a businesswoman is pushy.
He is careful about details; she's picky.
He loses his temper because he's so involved in his job; she's bitchy.
He's depressed (or hung over), so everyone tiptoes past his office; she's moody, so it must be her time of the month.
He follows through; she doesn't know when to quit.
He's firm; she's stubborn.
He makes wise judgments; she reveals her prejudices.
He is a man of the world; she's been around.
He isn't afraid to say what he thinks; she's opinionated.
He exercises authority; she's tyrannical.
He's discreet; she's secretive.
He's a stern taskmaster; she's difficult to work for.

FACT-INFERENCE CONFUSION   Some statements refer to things or acts we can observe ("She is driving a Volkswagen"), and some refer to things we can't observe directly ("She is seething with rage"). Although the two types of statements are grammatically identical, they are quite different semantically. **Factual statements** are based on direct observation and are usually easy to verify. **Inferential statements** are interpretations of sense data.

There's nothing wrong with making inferences as long as you identify them as such: "She stomped out and slammed the door. It looked to me as if she were seething with rage." The danger comes when we confuse inferences with facts and make them sound like the absolute truth.

One way to avoid fact-inference confusion is to use the perception checking skill described in Chapter 2 to test the accuracy of your inferences. Recall that a perception check has three parts: a description of the behavior being discussed, your interpretation of that behavior, and a request for verification. For instance, instead of saying, "Why are you laughing at me?" you could say, "When you laugh like that [description of behavior], I get the idea you think something I did was stupid [interpretation]. *Are* you laughing at me [question]?"

EUPHEMISMS   **Euphemisms** (from the Greek word meaning "to use words of good omen") are pleasant terms substituted for more direct but less pleasant ones. Euphemisms soften the impact of information that might be unpleasant. Unfortunately, this pulling of linguistic punches often obscures the accuracy of a message.

There are certainly cases where tactless honesty can be brutal: "What do I think of your new hairstyle? I think it's ugly!" or "How do I feel about the relationship? I can hardly wait to get away from you!" At the same time, being too indirect can leave others wondering where you stand: "What an original haircut," or "We could grow closer than we are now." When you are choosing how to broach difficult subjects, the challenge is to be as kind as possible without sacrificing either your integrity or the clarity of your message. (The guidelines for self-disclosure outlined in Chapter 6 will help you.)

Overly Abstract Language

Most objects, events, and ideas can be described with varying degrees of specificity. Consider the material you are reading. You could call it:

A book

A textbook

A communication textbook

Understanding Human Communication

Chapter 3 of *Understanding Human Communication*

Page 65 of Chapter 3 of *Understanding Human Communication*

In each case your description would be more and more specific. Semanticist S. I. Hayakawa created an **abstraction ladder** to describe this process.[18] This ladder consists of a number of descriptions of the same person, object, or event. Lower items focus specifically on the thing under discussion, and higher terms are generalizations that include the subject as a member of a larger class. These higher-level generalizations are absolutely necessary, for without them language would be too cumbersome to be useful. But though higher level abstractions allow us to focus on similarities, they also cause us to ignore differences between the objects being discussed in the category. Thus, overly abstract language can lead to several problems.

1. **Stereotyping.** Imagine someone who has had a bad experience while traveling abroad and, as a result, blames an entire country. "Yeah, those damn Hottentots are a bunch of thieves. If you're not careful, they'll steal you blind. I know because one of 'em stole my camera last year." You can see here how lumping people into highly abstract categories ignores the fact that for every thieving Hottentot there are probably 100 honest ones. It's this kind of thinking that leads to mistaken assumptions that keep people apart: "None of those kids are any damn good!" "You can't trust anybody in business." "Those cops are all a bunch of goons." Each of these statements ignores the very important fact that sometimes our descriptions are too general; that they say more than we really mean.

When you think about examples like these, you begin to see how thinking in abstract terms can lead to ignoring individual differences, which can be as important as similarities. In this sense, semantics isn't "just" a matter of words. People in the habit of using highly abstract language begin to *think* in generalities, ignoring uniqueness. And as we discussed in Chapter 2, expecting people to be a certain way can become a self-fulfilling prophecy. If I think all police officers are brutal, I'm more likely to react in a defensive, hostile way toward them, which, in turn, increases the chance that they'll react to me as a threat. If I think that no teachers care about their classes, then my defensive indifference is likely to make a potentially helpful instructor into someone who truly doesn't care.

2. **Confusing others.** Imagine the lack of understanding that results from imprecise language in situations like this:

A: "We never do anything that's fun anymore."
B: "What do you mean?"
A: "We used to do lots of unusual things, but now it's the same old stuff, over and over."
B: "But last week we went on that camping trip, and tomorrow we're going to that party where we'll meet all sorts of new people. Those are new things."
A: "That's not what I mean. I'm talking about *really* unusual stuff."
B: (*becoming confused and a little impatient*) "Like what? Taking hard drugs or going over Niagara Falls in a barrel?"
A: "Don't be stupid. All I'm saying is that we're in a rut. We should be living more exciting lives."
B: "Well, I don't know what you want."

Overly **abstract language** also leads to confusing directions:

Professor: "I hope you'll do a thorough job on this paper."
Student: "When you say thorough, how long should it be?"
P: "Long enough to cover the topic thoroughly."
S: "How many sources should I look at when I'm researching it?"

cathy

▶ Instant Blap

Anyone who is familiar with the academic, business, or government worlds knows that there often seems to be a rule which says "When choosing between a simple and a more abstract term, always pick the more confusing one."

In the past this has been a great setback for clear-headed writers and speakers. But now modern technology has found a solution: the Systematic Buzz Phrase Projector.

The projector is simple to use. Whenever you want to say nothing in an authoritative way, simply pick any three-digit number, and then find the matching word from each column. For example, 424 produces "functional monitored programming," which should impress anyone untrained in detecting high-level abstractions.

COLUMN 1	COLUMN 2	COLUMN 3
0 integrated	0 management	0 options
1 total	1 organizational	1 flexibility
2 systematized	2 monitored	2 capability
3 parallel	3 reciprocal	3 mobility
4 functional	4 digital	4 programming
5 responsive	5 logistical	5 concept
6 optional	6 transitional	6 time-phase
7 synchronized	7 incremental	7 projection
8 compatible	8 third-generation	8 hardware
9 balanced	9 policy	9 contingency

P: "You should use several—enough to show me that you've really explored the subject."
S: "And what style should I use to write it?"
P: "One that's scholarly but not too formal."
S: "Arrgh!!!"

Along with unclear complaints and vague instructions, even appreciations can suffer from being expressed in overly abstract terms. Psychologists have established that behaviors that are reinforced will recur with increased frequency. This means that your statements of appreciation will encourage others to keep acting in ways you like. But if they don't know just what it is that you appreciate, the chances of that behavior's being repeated are lessened. There's a big difference between "I appreciate your being so nice" and "I appreciate the way you spent that time talking to me when I was upset."

The best way to avoid this sort of overly abstract language is to use **behavioral descriptions** instead. Behavioral descriptions clarify the speaker's meaning whether the message describes a problem, goal, appreciation, complaint, or request. They do so by moving down the abstraction ladder to identify the specific, observable phenomenon being discussed. A thorough behavioral description should contain three elements:

1. **Who Is Involved?** Are you speaking for just yourself or for others as well? Are you talking about a group of people ("the neighbors," "women") or specific individuals ("the people next door with the barking dog," "Lola and Lizzie")?

2. **In What Circumstances Does the Behavior Occur?** Where does it occur?: Everywhere or in specific places (at parties, at work, in public)? When does it occur?: When you're tired? When a certain subject comes up?

   The behavior you are describing probably doesn't occur all the time. In order to be understood, you need to pin down what circumstances set this situation apart from other ones.

3. **What Behaviors Are Involved?** Though terms such as "more cooperative" and "helpful" might sound like concrete descriptions of behavior, they are usually too vague to do a clear job of explaining what's on your mind. Behaviors must be *observable,* ideally both to you and to others. For instance, moving down the abstraction ladder from the relatively vague term "helpful," you might come to behaviors such as "does the dishes every other day," "volunteers to help me with my studies," or "fixes dinner once or twice a week without being asked." It's easy to see that terms like these are easier for both you and others to understand than are more vague abstractions.

There is one exception to the rule that behaviors should be observable, and that involves the internal processes of thoughts and emotions. For instance, in describing what happens to you when a friend has kept you waiting for a long time, you might say, "My stomach felt as if it were in knots—I was really worried. I kept thinking that you had forgotten and that I wasn't important enough to you for you to remember our date." What you're doing when offering such a description is to make unobservable events clear.

You can get a clearer idea of the value of behavioral descriptions by looking at the examples in Table 3–2. Notice how much more clearly they explain the speaker's thought than do the vague terms.

▶ SUMMARY

To the uninitiated, using language effectively means little more than having an adequate vocabulary and following grammatical rules. This chapter shows that the business of understanding one another through the spoken and written word is much more complex.

The chapter discussed the symbolic nature of language, showing that words are arbitrary symbols that represent reality. But as meanings are in words and not in people, the mistake of assuming that others use language as we do is a dangerous one. The chapter showed that language not only describes events but also shapes our perception of them. This point is true for individual labels, which create favorable or unfavorable images for the receiver and, perhaps more significantly, for entire languages, the structure of which shapes the very way its users perceive reality.

Within the English language we saw that there are many types of words that have great potential to create misunderstandings or to distort meanings. Equivocal language, relative words, emotive descriptions, and fiction terms all need to be recognized and then either qualified or avoided.

Finally, the chapter examined the abstract nature of language, showing the problems that can arise from being overly abstract and then providing suggestions about how to begin expressing ideas in more specific, understandable ways.

TABLE 3–2 Abstract and Behavioral Descriptions

	ABSTRACT DESCRIPTION		BEHAVIORAL DESCRIPTION		REMARKS
		Who is involved	In what circumstances	Specific behaviors	
Problem	I'm no good at meeting strangers.	People I'd like to date	When I meet them at parties or at school	Think to myself, "They'd never want to date me." Also, I don't originate conversations.	Behavioral description more clearly identifies thoughts and behaviors to change.
Goal	I'd like to be more assertive.	Telephone and door-to-door solicitors	When I don't want the product or can't afford it	Instead of apologizing or explaining, say, "I'm not interested" and keep repeating this until they go away.	Behavioral description clearly outlines how to act, abstract description doesn't.
Appreciation	"You've been a great boss."	(no clarification necessary)	When I've needed to change my schedule because of school exams or assignments	"You've rearranged my hours cheerfully."	Give both abstract and behavioral descriptions for best results.
Complaint	"I don't like some of the instructors around here."	Professors A and B	In class when students ask questions the professors think are stupid.	Either answer in a sarcastic voice (you might demonstrate) or accuse us of not studying hard enough.	If talking to A or B, use only behavioral description. With others, use both abstract and behavioral descriptions.
Request	"Quit bothering me!"	You and your friends X and Y	When I'm studying for exams	Instead of asking me over and over to party with you, I wish you'd accept my comment that I need to study and leave me to do it.	Behavioral description will reduce defensiveness and make it clear that you don't *always* want to be left alone.

1. Recall an instance when you or another person mistakenly assumed that a set of symbols was an accurate reflection of reality.

   Next, describe a time when two people interpreted the same symbol in different ways.

2. Check your skill at using labels to shape perceptions by describing the following incident twice: First use language that makes the parent's behavior sound justified. Then rewrite the account to favor the child's position.

   The time is 3:30 A.M. A teenager who was due home from a party at 1:00 enters the house quietly, hoping to avoid waking his parents. This attempt fails, however, because they have been awake worrying for two hours.

   The parents ask their child why he wasn't home on time, and he explains that the family car struck a police cruiser after he failed to stop at a traffic signal.

   Both parents and teenager are upset. The parents believe that the teenager behaved irresponsibly, and the teenager claims that the accident, though unfortunate, could have happened to anyone.

3. Here's a way to see how emotive words work. According to S. I. Hayakawa, the idea of "conjugating irregular verbs" this way originated with Bertrand Russell.

   a. The technique is simple: Just take an action or personality trait and show how it can be viewed either favorably or unfavorably, according to the label we give it. For example:

      I'm casual.

      You're a little careless.

      He's a slob.

   Or try this one:

      I read love stories.

      You read erotic literature.

      She reads pornography.

   Or:

      I'm thrifty.

      You're money-conscious.

      He's a tightwad.

   b. Now try a few conjugations yourself using the following statements:
      (1) I'm tactful.
      (2) I'm conservative.
      (3) I'm quiet.
      (4) I'm relaxed.
      (5) My child is high-spirited.
      (6) I have a lot of self-pride.

   c. Now recall at least two situations in which you used an emotive word as if it were a description of fact and not an opinion. A good way to remember these situations is to think of a recent argument you had and imagine how the other people involved might have described it. How would their words differ from yours?

4. Explore your everyday use of abstract language by following these steps:
   a. Complete each of these sentences:
      (1) Women are...   (4) Blacks in America...
      (2) Men are...   (5) This college is...
      (3) In my opinion, conservatives...
   b. Share your results with another person who has also completed each of these sentences. Notice any differences in the way each of you used the same terms.
   c. Now go back over your list, reducing the subject of each sentence to whatever lower level abstractions better describe the original idea.
   d. Reflect on the unnecessarily abstract terms you use in your everyday communication. In what ways are those terms inaccurate? What misunderstandings do they cause?

NOTES ◄

1. Erwin P. Bettinghaus and Mark Milkovich, "Codes and Code Systems," in Cassandra Book (ed.), *Human Communication: Principles, Contexts, and Skills* (New York: St. Martin's, 1980), pp. 42–45.
2. C. K. Ogden and I. A. Richards, *The Meaning of Meaning* (New York: Harcourt, Brace, 1923), p. 11.
3. Jessica Davidson, "How to Translate English," in Joseph Fletcher Littell (ed.), *The Language of Man,* vol. 4 (Evanston, Ill.: McDougal Littel, 1971).
4. Benjamin Lee Shorf, in John B. Carroll (ed.), *Language, Thought, and Reality: Selected Writings of Benjamin Lee Whorf* (Cambridge, Mass.: MIT Press, 1966).
5. L. Sinclair, ed., "A Word in Your Ear," in *Ways of Mankind* (Boston: Beacon Press, 1954), pp. 28–29.
6. Neil Postman, *Crazy Talk, Stupid Talk* (New York: Delta, 1976), p. 122.
7. Ibid., pp. 123–124.
8. Research on the following pages is cited in Mary G. Marcus, "The Power of a Name," *Psychology Today* 9 (October 1976): 75–77, 108.
9. Donald H. Naftulin, John E. Ware, Jr., and Frank A. Donnelly, "The Doctor Fox Lecture: A Paradigm of Educational Seduction," *Journal of Medical Education* 48 (July 1973): 630–635. See also C. T. Cory (ed.), "Bafflegab Pays," *Psychology Today* 13 (May 1980): 12.
10. J. Scott Armstrong, "Unintelligible Management Research and Academic Prestige," *Interfaces* 10 (1980): 80–86.
11. H. Giles and P. F. Poseland, *Speech Style and Social Evaluation* (New York: Academic Press, 1975).
12. C. Miller and K. Swift, "One Small Step for Genkind," *The New York Times Magazine,* April 16, 1972. Reprinted in J. DeVito (ed.), *Language: Concepts and Processes,* (Englewood Cliffs, N.J.: Prentice-Hall, 1973), pp. 171–182.
13. See, for example, B. Erickson, E. A. Lind, B. C. Johnson, and W. M. O'Barr, "Speech Style and Impression Formation in a Court Setting: The Effects of Powerful and Powerless Speech," *Journal of Experimental Social Psychology* 14 (1978): 266–279.
14. P. Watzlawick, J. H. Beavin, and D. D. Jackson, *Pragmatics of Human Communication* (New York: Norton, 1967).
15. B. A. Fisher and G. R. Drecksel, "A Cyclical Model of Developing Relationships: A Study of Relational Control Interaction," *Communication Monographs* 50 (1983): 66–78.
16. J. Bradac and A. Mulac, "Attributional Consequences of Powerful and Powerless Speech Styles in a Crisis-Intervention Context," *Journal of Language and Social Psychology* 3 (1984): 1–19.
17. Morton Wiener and Albert Mehrabian, *A Language Within Language* (New York: Appleton-Century-Crofts, 1968).
18. S. I. Hayakawa, *Language in Thought and Action* (New York: Harcourt, Brace, 1964).

► CHAPTER 4

KEY TERMS

advising
ambushing
analyzing response
attending
defensive listening
empathic listening
evaluative listening
hearing
informational listening
insensitive listening

insulated listening
judging response
listening
paraphrasing
pseudolistening
questioning
residual message
selective listening
stage hogging
supporting response

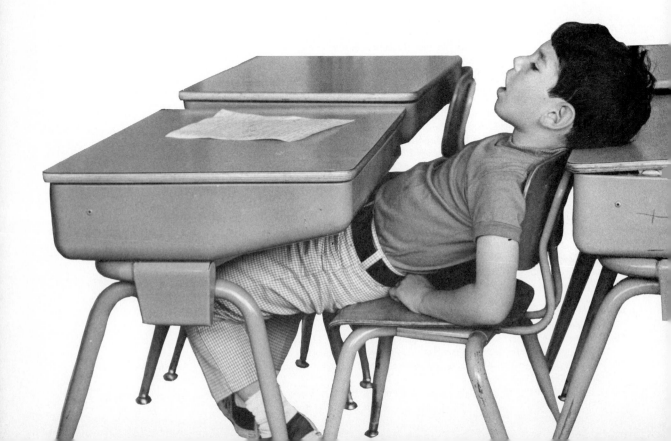

LISTENING

After reading this chapter, you should understand the following:

1. The common misconceptions about listening.

2. The four components of the listening process.

3. The nine common types of listening failure.

4. The reasons why people fail to listen effectively.

5. The characteristics of informational, evaluative, and empathic listening.

You should be able to do the following:

1. Appreciate the effort required to listen effectively.

2. Identify the situations in which you listen poorly and explain the reasons for your lack of effectiveness.

3. Demonstrate your ability to follow the guidelines for effective informational, evaluative, and critical listening given in this chapter.

In a world where almost everyone acknowledges the importance of better communication, the experience of not being listened to is all too common. The problem is especially bad when you realize that listening is the most frequent type of communication behavior. This fact was established as early as 1926, when Paul Rankin surveyed a group of businesspeople, asking them to record the percentage of time they spent speaking, reading, writing, and listening.[1] Rankin found that his subjects spent more time listening than in any other communication activity, devoting 42 percent of their time to it. Research over the past sixty years continues to show the importance of listening. A recent study (summarized in Figure 4–1) revealed that college students spent an average of 14 percent of their communicating time writing; 16 percent, speaking; 17 percent, reading; and a whopping 53 percent, listening. Listening was broken down further into listening to mass media messages, such as radio and television, and listening to face-to-face messages. Listening to media accounted for 32 percent of the students' communication time whereas listening in person accounted for 21 percent—still more than any other type of face-to-face communication.[2]

Listening, then, is one of the most frequent activities in which we engage. Despite this fact, experience shows that much of the listening we and others do is not at all effective. We misunderstand others and are misunderstood in return. We become bored and feign attention while our minds wander. We engage in a battle of interruptions where each person fights to speak without hearing the other's ideas.

As you'll soon read, some of this poor listening is inevitable. But in other cases we can be better receivers by learning a few basic listening skills. The purpose of this chapter is to help you become a better listener by giving you some important information about the subject. We'll talk about some common misconceptions concerning listening and show you what really happens when listen-

FIGURE 4–1
Types of Communication
Activities

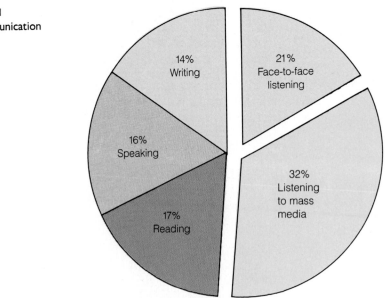

ing takes place. We'll discuss some poor listening habits, explain why they occur, and suggest better alternatives.

In spite of its importance, listening is misunderstood by most people. Because these misunderstandings so greatly affect our communication, we need to take a look at four common misconceptions that many communicators hold.

Listening and Hearing Are Not the Same Thing

Hearing is the process wherein sound waves strike the eardrum and cause vibrations that are transmitted to the brain. **Listening** occurs when the brain reconstructs these electrochemical impulses into a representation of the original sound and then gives them meaning. Barring illness, injury, or earplugs, hearing cannot be stopped. Your ears will pick up sound waves and transmit them to your brain whether you want them to or not.

Listening, however, is not so automatic. Many times we hear but do not listen. Sometimes we deliberately do not listen. Instead of paying attention to words or other sounds, we avoid them. This most often occurs when we block irritating sounds, such as a neighbor's power lawn mower or the roar of nearby traffic. We also stop listening when we find a subject unimportant or uninteresting. Boring stories, TV commercials, and nagging complaints are common examples of messages we avoid.

There are also cases when we honestly believe we're listening even though we're merely hearing. For example, recall times when you think you've "heard

it all before." It's likely that in these situations you might claim you were listening when, in fact, you had closed your mental doors to new information.

People who confuse listening with hearing often fool themselves into thinking that they're really understanding others when, in fact, they're simply receiving sounds. As you'll see by reading this chapter, true listening involves much more than the passive act of hearing.

Listening Is Not a Natural Process

Another common myth is that listening is like breathing: a natural activity that people do well. "After all," this common belief goes, "I've been listening since I was a child. Why should I have to study the subject in school?"

This attitude is understandable considering the lack of attention most schools devote to listening in comparison with other communication skills. From kindergarten to college, most students receive almost constant training in reading and writing. Every year the exposure to literature continues, from Dick and Jane through Dostoevski. Likewise, the emphasis on writing continues without break. You could probably retire if you had a dollar for every composition, essay, research paper, and bluebook you have written since the first grade. Even spoken communication gets some attention in the curriculum. It's likely that you had a chance to take a public speaking class in high school and another one in college.

Compare all this training in reading, writing, and speaking with the almost total lack of instruction in listening. Even in college there are few courses devoted exclusively to the subject. This state of affairs is especially ironic when you consider the fact that, as mentioned, over half of our communication involves listening.

The truth is that listening is a skill much like speaking: Virtually everyone listens, although few people do it well. Your own experience should prove that communication often suffers owing to poor listening. How many times have others misunderstood directions or explanations because they didn't seem to be receiving your ideas clearly? And how often have you failed to understand others accurately because you weren't receiving their thoughts accurately? The answers to these questions demonstrate the need for effective training in listening.

Listening Is Not a Passive Activity

Most people assume that listening is fundamentally a passive activity in which the receiver absorbs a speaker's ideas rather the way a sponge absorbs water. In truth, even the kind of one-way listening in the linear communication model described in Chapter 1 requires mental effort by the receiver. Probably the most familiar examples include students listening to a professor lecture or viewers paying careful attention to a television program. One-way communication also takes place in interpersonal settings as when one person dominates a conversation while the others fall into the role of audience members or when some parents lecture their children without allowing them to respond.

"I have a pet at home"

"Oh, what kind of a pet?"

"It is a dog."

"What kind of a dog?"

"It is a St. Bernard."

"Grown up or a puppy?"

"It is full grown."

"What color is it?"

"It is brown and white."

"Why didn't you say you had a full-grown, brown and white St. Bernard as a pet in the first place?"

The most important feature of one-way communication is that it contains little or no feedback. The receiver may deliberately or unintentionally send nonverbal messages that show how the speaker's ideas are being received—nods
and smiles, stifled yawns, more or less eye contact—but there's no verbal
response to indicate how—or even whether—the message has been received.

Because the speaker isn't interrupted in this type of lecture-conversation,
one-way communication has the advantage of being relatively quick. We've all
felt like telling someone, "I'm in a hurry. Just listen carefully and don't interrupt." What we're asking for here is one-way communication.

Sometimes one-way communication is an appropriate way of listening. As
you'll soon read, sometimes the best way to help people with problems is to
hear them out. In many cases, they're not looking for, nor do they need, a verbal
response. At times like these, when there's no input by the receiver, *anybody*
who will serve as a sounding board will do as a "listener." This explains why
some people find relief talking to a pet or a photograph.

One-way communication also works well when the listener wants to ease
back mentally and be entertained. It would be a mistake to interrupt a good
joke or story or to stand up in the middle of a play and shout out a question to
the performers.

But outside of these cases, one-way listening isn't very effective for the simple reason that it almost guarantees that the listener will misunderstand at least
some of the speaker's ideas. There are at least three types of misunderstandings.
As you read about each of them, think about how often they occur for you.

The first kind of misunderstanding happens when a speaker sends a clear,
accurate message that the receiver simply gets wrong. Somehow a quarter cup
of sugar is transformed into four cups, or "I'll see you at twelve" is translated
into "I'll see you at two."

In other cases, the receiver is listening carefully enough, but the speaker
sends an incorrect message. These instances are the reverse of the ones just
mentioned, and their results can be just as disastrous.

The third mix-up that comes from one-way communication is probably the
most common. The speaker sends a message that may not be incorrect but is
overly vague, and the receiver interprets the words in a manner that doesn't
match the speaker's ideas. In Chapters 2 and 3 we talked about the problems
that come from failing to check out interpretations. In this statement, "I'm a little confused," does "little" mean "slightly," or is it an understatement that could
be translated into "very"? When a lover says, "You're my best friend," is this
synonymous with the message, "Besides being such a romantic devil, I also feel
comfortable with you," or does it mean, "I want to become less of a lover and
more of a pal"? You could make your own personal list of confusing messages
and in doing so prove the point: Your assumption that you understand another's
words isn't always a sure thing. Fortunately, there's another, usually better way
of listening.

All Listeners Do Not Receive the Same Message

When two or more people are listening to a speaker, we tend to assume that
they are each hearing and understanding the same message. In fact, such uniform

comprehension isn't the case. Communication is *proactive:* Each person involved in a transaction of ideas or feelings responds uniquely. Recall our discussion of perception in Chapter 2, where we pointed out the many factors that cause each of us to perceive an event differently. Physiological factors, social roles, cultural background, personal interests, and needs all shape and distort the raw data we hear into uniquely different messages.

COMPONENTS OF LISTENING ◄

In his book *Listening Behavior,* Larry Barker describes the process of listening as having four components: hearing, attending, understanding, and remembering.[3]

Hearing

As we have already discussed, *hearing* is the physiological aspect of listening. It is the nonselective process of sound waves impinging on the ear and the ear responding to those waves that fall within a certain frequency range and are sufficiently loud. Hearing is also influenced by background noise. If such noise is the same frequency as the speech sound, then the speech sound is said to be masked; however, if the background noise is of a different frequency from speech, it is called "white noise" and may or may not detract greatly from our ability to hear. Hearing is also affected by auditory fatigue, a temporary loss of hearing caused by continuous exposure to the same tone or loudness. People who spend an evening dancing to a loud band may experience auditory fatigue, and if they are exposed often enough, permanent hearing loss may result.[4]

Attending

After the sounds are converted into electrochemical impulses and transmitted to the brain, a decision—often unconscious—is made whether to focus on what was heard. Though the listening process started as a physiological one, it quickly became a psychological one of **attending.** An individual's needs, wants, desires,

and interests determine what is attended to, or selected, to use the term introduced in Chapter 2. If you're hungry, you are more likely to attend to the message about restaurants in the neighborhood from the person next to you than the competing message on the importance of communication from the speaker in front of the room.

Understanding

The component of understanding involves interpreting a message and is composed of several elements. First, understanding a message involves some recognition of the grammatical rules used to create that message. We find the children's books by Dr. Seuss amusing because he breaks the rules of grammar and spelling in interesting ways, and we are familiar enough with the rules to recognize this. Second, understanding depends on our knowledge about the source of the message—whether the person is sincere, prone to lie, friendly, an adversary, and so on. Third, there is the *social context*. The time and place, for example, help us decide whether to take a friend's insults seriously or as a joke. Understanding depends, generally, on sharing common assumptions about the world. Consider the following two sentences.[5]

1. I bought alligator shoes.
2. I bought horseshoes.

Both sentences can be interpreted the same way because they have the same grammatical structure and may be uttered by the same person (the first two components of understanding). Both could indicate that a person bought two pairs of shoes, one made from alligator, the other from horse, or that two pairs of shoes were purchased, one for an alligator, the other for a horse. However, because of the common semantic assumptions we share about the world, we understand that the first sentence refers to shoes made *from* alligator hides and that the second refers either to shoes *for* horses (or for playing a game).

Finally, understanding often depends on the ability to organize the information we hear into recognizable form. As early as 1948, Ralph Nichols related successful understanding to a large number of factors, most prominent among which were verbal ability, intelligence, and motivation.[6]

Remembering

The complaint "You didn't listen to me" often means "You didn't remember what I said."[7] The ability to recall information is a function of several factors: the number of times the information is heard or repeated, how much information there is to store in the brain, and whether the information may be "rehearsed" or not.

Research has revealed that people remember only about half of what they hear *immediately after* hearing it.[8] This is true even if people work hard at listening. This situation would probably not be too bad if the half remembered right after were retained, but it isn't. Within two months half of the half is forgotten, bringing what we remember down to about 25 percent of the original message.

This loss, however, doesn't take two months: People start forgetting immediately (within eight hours the 50 percent remembered drops to about 35 percent). Given the amount of information we process every day—from instructors, friends, the radio, TV, and other sources—the **residual message** (what we remember) is a small fraction of what we hear.

Although it may not be necessary or desirable to listen effectively all the time, most people possess one or more bad habits that keep them from understanding truly important messages.

Pseudolistening

Pseudolistening is an imitation of the real thing. "Good" pseudolisteners give the appearance of being attentive: They look you in the eye, nod and smile at the right times, and even may answer you occasionally. Behind that appearance of interest, however, something entirely different is going on, for pseudolisteners use a polite facade to mask thoughts that have nothing to do with what the speaker is saying. Often pseudolisteners ignore you because of something on their mind that's more important to them than your remarks. Other times they may simply be bored or think that they've heard what you have to say before, and so they tune out your remarks. Whatever the reasons, the significant fact is that pseudolistening is really counterfeit communication.

Stage Hogging

Stage hogs are interested only in expressing their ideas and don't care about what anyone else has to say. These people will allow you to speak from time to time, but only so they can catch their breath, use your remarks as a basis for their own babbling, or keep you from running away. Stage hogs really aren't conversing when they dominate others—they are making a speech . . . and at the same time probably making an enemy.

Selective Listening

Selective listeners respond only to the parts of a speaker's remarks that interest them, rejecting everything else. All of us are selective listeners from time to time as, for instance, when we screen out media commercials and music while keeping an ear cocked for a weather report or an announcement of time. In other cases, selective listening occurs in conversations with people who expect a thorough hearing but get their partner's attention only when the subject turns to the partner's favorite topic—perhaps money, sex, a hobby, or some particular person. Unless and until you bring up one of these pet subjects, you might as well talk to a tree.

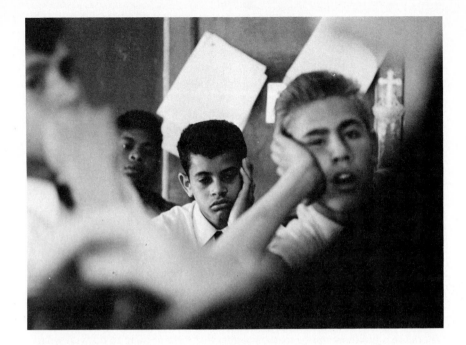

Filling in Gaps

People who fill in the gaps like to think that what they remember makes a whole story. Because we remember half or less of what we hear, these people manufacture information so that when they retell what they listened to, they can give the impression they "got it all." Of course, filling in the gaps is as dangerous as selective listening: The message that's left is only a distorted (not merely incomplete) version of the message that could have been received.

Assimilation to Prior Messages

We all have a tendency to interpret current messages in terms of similar messages remembered from the past. This phenomenon is called *assimilation to prior input.* A problem arises for those who go overboard with this and push, pull, chop, squeeze, and in other ways mutilate messages they receive to *make sure* they are consistent with what they heard in the past. This unfortunate situation occurs when the current message is in some way uniquely different from past messages.

Insulated Listening

Insulated listeners are almost the opposite of their selective-listening cousins. Instead of looking for something, these people avoid it. Whenever a topic arises they'd rather not deal with, insulated listeners simply fail to hear it or, rather, to acknowledge it. If you remind them about a problem—perhaps an unfinished job, poor grades, or the like—they'll nod or answer you and then promptly forget what you've just said.

Defensive Listening

Defensive listeners take innocent comments as personal attacks. Teenagers who perceive parental questions about friends and activities as distrustful snooping are defensive listeners as are insecure breadwinners who explode anytime their mates mention money or touchy parents who view any questioning by their children as a threat to their authority and parental wisdom. It's fair to assume that many defensive listeners are suffering from shaky public images and avoid admitting this by projecting their own insecurities onto others.

Ambushing

Ambushers listen carefully, but only because they are collecting information to attack what you have to say. The cross-examining prosecution attorney is a good example of an ambusher. Needless to say, using this kind of strategy will justifiably initiate defensiveness on the other's behalf.

Insensitive Listening

Insensitive listeners offer the final example of people who don't receive another person's messages clearly. People often don't express their thoughts or feelings openly but instead communicate them through subtle and unconscious choice of words or nonverbal clues or both. Insensitive listeners aren't able to look beyond the words and behavior to understand their hidden meanings. Instead, they take a speaker's remarks at face value.

It's important not to go overboard in labeling listeners as insensitive. Often a seemingly mechanical comment is perfectly appropriate. This most often occurs in situations involving *phatic* communication, in which a remark derives its meaning totally from context. For instance, the question "How are you?" doesn't call for an answer when you pass an acquaintance on the street. In this context, the statement means no more than "I acknowledge your existence, and I want to let you know that I feel friendly toward you." It is not an inquiry about the state of your health. Although insensitive listening is depressing, you would be equally discouraged to hear a litany of aches and pains everytime you asked, "How's it going?"

▶ i have just
wandered back
into our conversation
and find
that you
are still
rattling on
about something
or other
i think i must
have been gone
at least
twenty minutes
and you
never missed me

now this might say
something
about my
acting ability
or it might say
something about
your sensitivity

one thing
troubles me tho
when it
is my turn
to rattle on
for twenty minutes
which i
have been known to do
have you
been missing too

Ric Masten

Listening well is obviously important, yet often we do just the opposite. Why? Sad as it may be, it's impossible to listen *all* the time, for several reasons.

Effort

Listening effectively is hard work. The physical changes that occur during careful listening show the effort it takes: Heart rate quickens, respiration increases, and body temperature rises.[9] Notice that these changes are similar to the body's reaction to physical effort. This is no coincidence, for listening carefully to a speaker can be just as taxing as more obvious efforts.

Message Overload

The amount of speech most of us encounter everyday makes careful listening to everything we hear impossible. As we've already seen, many of us spend as much as one-third of the time we're awake listening to verbal messages—from teachers, co-workers, friends, family, salespeople, and total strangers. This means we often spend five hours or more a day listening to people talk. If you add this to the amount of time we tune in radio and television, you can see that it's impossible for us to keep our attention totally focused for this amount of time. Therefore, we have to let our attention wander at times.

Rapid Thought

Listening carefully is also difficult for a physiological reason. Although we are capable of understanding speech at rates up to 300 words per minute,[10] the average person speaks between 100 and 140 words per minute.[11] Thus, we have a great deal of mental "spare time" to spend while someone is talking. And the temptation is to use this time in ways that don't relate to the speaker's ideas, such as thinking about personal interests, daydreaming, planning a rebuttal, and so on. The trick is to use this spare time to understand the speaker's ideas better rather than letting your attention wander.

Psychological Noise

Another reason we don't always listen carefully is that we're often wrapped up in personal concerns that are of more immediate importance to us than the messages others are sending. It's hard to pay attention to someone else when you're anticipating an upcoming test or thinking about the wonderful time you had last night with good friends. Yet we still feel we have to "listen" politely to others, and so we continue with our charade.

Physical Noise

The world in which we live often presents distractions that make it hard to pay attention to others. The sound of traffic, music, others' speech, and the like interfere with our ability to hear well. Also, fatigue or other forms of discomfort can distract us from paying attention to a speaker's remarks. Consider, for example, how the efficiency of your listening decreases when you are seated in a crowded, hot, stuffy room that is surrounded by traffic and other noises. In such circumstances even the best intentions aren't enough to ensure clear understanding.

Hearing Problems

Sometimes a person's listening ability suffers from a physiological hearing problem. Once a hearing problem has been diagnosed, it's often possible to treat it. The real tragedy occurs when a hearing loss goes undetected. In such cases, both the person with the defect and others can become frustrated and annoyed

▶ **Duet**

When we speak we do not
listen, my son and I.
I complain of slights, hurts
inflicted on me.
He sings a counterpoint, but
not in harmony.
Asking a question, he doesn't
wait to hear.
Trying to answer, I interrupt
his refrain.
This comic opera excels in
disharmony only.

Lenni Shender Goldstein

at the ineffective communication that results. If you suspect that you or some-one you know suffers from a hearing loss, it's wise to have a physician or audiologist perform an examination.

Faulty Assumptions

We often make incorrect assumptions that lead us to believe that we're listening attentively when quite the opposite is true. If the subject is a familiar one, it's easy to think that you've "heard it all before" when, in fact, the speaker is offering new information. A related problem arises if you assume that a speaker's thoughts are too simple or obvious to deserve careful attention when the truth is that you ought to be listening carefully. At other times, just the opposite occurs: You think that another's comments are too complex to possi-bly understand (as in some lectures) and so give up trying to make sense of them. A final mistake people often make is to assume that a subject is unimpor-tant and to stop paying attention when they ought to be listening carefully.

Talking Has More Apparent Advantages

It often appears that we have more to gain by speaking than by listening. One big advantage of speaking is that it gives you a chance to control others' thoughts and actions. Whatever your goal—to have a prospective boss hire you,

▶ **Bore,** *n.* A person who talks when you wish him to listen.

Conversation, *n.* A fair for the display of the minor mental commodities, each exhibitor being too intent upon arrangement of his own wares to observe those of his neighbor.

Egotist, *n.* A person of low taste more interested in himself than me.

Heaven, *n.* A place where the wicked cease from troubling you with talk of their personal affairs, and the good listen with attention while you expound your own.

Ambrose Bierce
The Devil's Dictionary

"What? I'm sorry. I wasn't listening."

LISTENING

to convince others to vote for the candidate of your choice, or to describe the way you want your hair cut—the key to success seems to be the ability to speak well.

Another apparent advantage of speaking is the chance it provides to gain the admiration, respect, or liking of others. Tell jokes, and everyone will think you're a real wit. Offer advice, and they'll be grateful for your help. Tell them all you know, and they'll be impressed by your wisdom. But keep quiet . . . and it seems as if you'll look like a worthless nobody.

Finally, talking gives you the chance to release energy in a way that listening can't. When you're frustrated, the chance to talk about your problems can often help you feel better. In the same way, you can often lessen your anger by letting it out verbally. It is also helpful to share your excitement with others by talking about it, for keeping it inside often leaves you feeling as if you might burst.

Although it's true that talking does have many advantages, it's important to realize that listening can pay dividends, too. As you'll soon read, being a good listener is one way to help others with their problems; and what better way is there to have others appreciate you? As for controlling others, it may be true that it's hard to be persuasive while you're listening, but your willingness to hear others out will often leave them open to thinking about your ideas in return. Like defensiveness, listening is often reciprocal: You get what you give.

Lack of Training

Even if we want to listen well, we're often hampered by a lack of skill. As we've already said, listening is a skill much like speaking: Virtually everybody does it, although few people do it well. As you read through this chapter, you'll see that one reason so much poor listening exists is because most people fail to follow the important steps that lead to real understanding.

▶ TYPES OF LISTENING

Although good listening isn't easy, it is possible. An important fact to realize is that there are several different types of listening, and that each one requires a different approach.

Informational Listening

WHAT IS INFORMATIONAL LISTENING? **Informational listening** is the approach to take when you want to understand another person. As an informational listener, your goal is to make sure you are receiving the same thoughts the other person is trying to convey—not always an easy feat when you consider the forces listed on pages 83–86 that interfere with understanding.

The situations that call for informational listening are endless and varied: following an instructor's comments in class, listening to a friend's account of a night on the town, hearing a description of a new piece of equipment you're thinking about buying, learning about your family history from a relative's tales, swapping

▶ WHAT GOOD IS FREE SPEECH IF NO ONE LISTENS?

It is the law in this country, as in no other, that the individual has an extraordinary right to personal expression. The First Amendment to the Constitution protects the right to speak and to publish; these rights and the degree to which they are safeguarded are the distinguishing characteristics of American society.

For that we have only the courts to thank. Americans seem to be almost completely uninterested in any point of view other than their individual own. We are absolutely up to our necks in groups and blocs and religious and economic interests certain beyond all reason that they are correct and actively interested in imposing their rules and values and self-selected morals on the rest of us. They prattle about democracy, and use it when it suits them without the slightest regard or respect for what it means and costs and requires. These people are—please believe me—dangerous.

The right to speak is meaningless if no one will listen, and the right to publish is not worth having if no one will read. It is simply not enough that we reject censorship and will not countenance suppression; we have an affirmative responsibility to hear the argument before we disagree with it.

I think that you think that you agree with me, that you are fair and open-minded and good citizens. But if we put it to the test—if I make up some speeches about gun control, abortion, gay

rights, racial and ethnic characteristics, political terrorism and genocide—I believe that I can make you boo and jeer or at least walk out in protest.

We cannot operate that way. It's not difficult to listen to the philosophy you agree with or don't care about. It's the one that galls that must be heard. No idea is so repugnant that it must not be advocated. If we are not free to speak heresy and utter awful thoughts, we are not free at all. And if we are unwilling to hear that with which we most violently disagree, we are no longer citizens but have become part of the mob.

Nowhere is the willingness to listen more important than at a university, and nowhere is our failure more apparent than at the university whose faculty members or students think that it's legitimate to parade their own moral or political purity by shouting down the unpopular view of the day.

It will not be a week, and certainly not a month, before you will become aware that someone in your own circle of influence is saying something or thinking something very wrong. I think you have to do something about that. I think you have to help them be heard. I think you are required to listen.

Kurt Luedtke

---

ideas in a discussion about religion or politics . . . the list goes on and on. You can become more effective as an informational listener by following several guidelines.

DON'T JUDGE PREMATURELY Most people would agree with the principle that it's essential to understand a speaker's ideas before judging them. Despite this commonsense fact, all of us are guilty of forming snap judgments, evaluating others before hearing them out. This tendency is greatest when the speaker's ideas conflict with our own. Conversations that ought to be exchanges of ideas turn into verbal battles, with the "opponents" trying to ambush one another in order to win a victory. Disagreements aren't the only kind of conversation in which the tendency to judge others is strong: It's also tempting to counterattack when others criticize you, even when those criticisms might contain valuable truths and when understanding them might lead to a change for the better. Even if there is no criticism or disagreement, we tend to evaluate others based on sketchy first impressions, forming snap judgments that aren't at all valid. Not all premature judgments are negative. It's also possible to jump to overly favorable conclusions about the quality of a speaker's remarks when we like that person or agree with the ideas being expressed. The lesson contained in these negative examples is clear: Listen first. Make sure you understand. *Then* evaluate.

BE OPPORTUNISTIC   Sooner or later you will find yourself listening to information that is either so unimportant or so badly delivered that you're tempted to tune out. Although making a quick escape from such tedious situations is often the best thing to do, there are times when you can profit from paying close attention to apparently worthless communication. This is especially true when you're trapped in a situation where the only alternatives to attentiveness are pseudolistening or downright rudeness.

As an opportunistic listener you can find *some* value in even the worst situations, if you are willing to invest the effort. Consider how you might listen opportunistically when you find yourself locked in a boring conversation with someone whose ideas are worthless. Rather than torture yourself until escape is possible, you could keep yourself amused—and perhaps learn something useful—by listening carefully until you can answer the following (unspoken) questions: "Is there anything useful in what this person is saying?" "What led the speaker to come up with ideas like these?" "What lessons can I learn from this person that will keep me from sounding the same way in other situations?"

LOOK FOR KEY IDEAS   It's easy to lose patience with long-winded speakers who never seem to get to the point—or *have* a point, for that matter. Nonetheless, most people do have a central idea, or what we will call a thesis in Chapter 12. By using your ability to think more quickly than the speaker can talk, you may be able to extract the thesis from the surrounding mass of words you're hearing. If you can't figure out what the speaker is driving at, you can always ask in a tactful way by using the skills of questioning and paraphrasing, which we'll examine now.

ASK QUESTIONS AND PARAPHRASE   Questioning and paraphrasing are forms of verbal feedback, and both are quite different from the one-way passive listening style described earlier in this chapter.

Questioning involves asking for additional information to clarify your idea of the sender's message. If you ask directions to a friend's house, typical questions might be "Is your place an apartment?" or "How long does it take to get there from here?" In more serious situations, questions could include "What's bothering you?" or "Why are you so angry?" or "Why is that so important?" Notice that one key element of these questions is that they request the speaker to elaborate on information already given.

Questioning is often a valuable tool for increasing understanding. Sometimes, however, it won't help you receive a speaker's ideas any more clearly, and it can even lead to further communication breakdown. To see how this can be so, consider our example of asking directions to a friend's home. Suppose the instructions you've received are to "drive about a mile and then turn left at the traffic signal." Now imagine that a few common problems exist in this simple message. First, suppose that your friend's idea of a mile is different from yours: Your mental picture of the distance is actually closer to two miles whereas hers is closer to 300 yards. Next, consider the very likely occurrence that though your friend said "traffic signal," she meant "stop sign"; after all, it's common for us to think one thing and say another. Keeping these problems in mind, suppose you tried to verify your understanding of the directions by asking, "After I turn at the light, how far should I go?" to which your friend replied that her house is the third from the corner. Clearly, if you parted after this exchange, you would encounter a lot of frustrations before finding the elusive residence.

What was the problem here? It's easy to see that questioning didn't help, for your original ideas of how far to drive and where to turn were mistaken. And contained in such mistakes is the biggest problem with questioning, for such inquiries don't tell you whether you have accurately received the information that has *already* been sent.

Now consider another kind of feedback—one that would tell you whether you understood what had already been said before you asked additional questions. This sort of feedback, termed **paraphrasing,** involves restating in your own words the message you thought the speaker had just sent, without adding anything new. In the example of seeking directions that we've been using, such rephrasing might sound like this: "So you're telling me to drive down to the traffic light by the high school and turn toward the mountains, is that it?" Immediately sensing the problem, your friend could then reply, "Oh no, that's way

▶ Give everyman thine ear, but few thy voice.

William Shakespeare
Hamlet

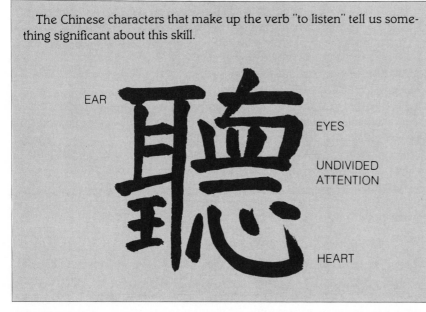

The Chinese characters that make up the verb "to listen" tell us something significant about this skill.

EAR

EYES

UNDIVIDED
ATTENTION

HEART

Calligraphy by Angie Au.

too far. I meant that you should drive to the four-way stop by the park and turn there. Did I say stop light? I always do that when I mean stop sign!"

Successful paraphrasing depends on the speaker's *restating* the sender's ideas, not parroting them. If you simply repeat the speaker's comments verbatim, you'll sound foolish or hard of hearing, and, just as important, you still might be misunderstanding what's been said.

At first, paraphrasing might seem to have little to recommend it. After all, it's an unfamiliar tool, which means that you'll have to go through a period of awkwardness while learning it. And until you become skillful at responding in this new way, you run the risk of getting odd reactions from the people to whom you're responding. In spite of these very real problems, learning to paraphrase is worth the effort, for it offers some very real advantages.

First, it boosts the odds that you'll accurately and fully understand what others are saying. We've already seen that one-way listening or even asking questions may lead you to think that you've understood a speaker when, in fact, you haven't. Paraphrasing, on the other hand, serves as a way of double-checking your interpretation for accuracy. A second advantage of paraphrasing is that it guides you toward sincerely trying to understand another person instead of using nonlistening styles such as stage hogging, selective listening, and so on. If you force yourself to reflect the other person's ideas in your own words, you'll spend your mental energy trying to understand that speaker instead of using less constructive listening styles: defensive listening, ambushing, or pseudolistening.

Evaluative Listening

Whereas the goal of informational listening is to understand a speaker, the object of **evaluative listening** is to judge—either to accept or reject an idea. Evaluative listening is appropriate when someone is trying to persuade you: as, for example, to buy a product, act in a certain way, or accept a belief. You will be most effective as an evaluative listener if you follow several guidelines.

LISTEN FOR INFORMATION BEFORE EVALUATING   The principle of listening for information before evaluating seems almost too obvious to mention, yet all of us are guilty of judging a speaker's ideas before we completely understand them. The tendency to make premature judgments is especially strong when the idea you are hearing conflicts with your own beliefs.

You can avoid the tendency to judge before understanding by following the simple rule of paraphrasing a speaker's ideas before responding to them. The effort required to translate the other person's ideas into your own words will keep you from arguing, and if your interpretation is mistaken, you'll know immediately.

EVALUATE THE SPEAKER'S CREDIBILITY   The acceptability of an idea often depends on its source. If your longtime family friend, the self-made millionaire, invited you to invest your life savings in jojoba bean futures, you might be grateful for the tip. If your deadbeat brother-in-law made the same offer, you would probably laugh off the suggestion.

Chapter 15 discusses credibility in detail, but two questions provide a quick guideline for deciding whether or not to accept a speaker as an authority:

▶ *Is the speaker competent?* Does the person have the experience or the expertise to qualify as an authority on this subject? Note that someone who is knowledgeable in one area may not be as well qualified to comment on another topic. For instance, your friend who can answer any question about computer programming might be a terrible adviser when the subject turns to romance.

▶ *Is the speaker impartial?* Knowledge alone isn't enough to certify a speaker's ideas as acceptable. People who have a personal stake in the outcome of a topic are more likely to be biased. The unqualified praise a commission-earning salesperson gives a product may be more suspect than the mixed review you get from a user. This doesn't mean you should disregard any comments you hear from an involved party—only that you should consider the possibility of deliberate or unintentional bias.

EXAMINE THE SPEAKER'S EVIDENCE   Speakers usually offer some kind of support to back up their statements. A car dealer who argues that domestic cars are just as reliable as imports might cite frequency-of-repair statistics from *Consumer Reports* or refer you to satisfied customers, for example; and a professor arguing that students don't work as hard as they used to might tell stories about then and now to back up the thesis.

Chapter 12 describes several types of supporting material that can be used to prove a point: definitions, descriptions, analogies, statistics, and so on. Whatever form the support takes, you can ask two fundamental questions to judge its quality. First, ask whether the evidence is true. Most people won't tell deliberate lies, but they may misquote the facts or even distort them out of enthusiasm—rather like an angler who exaggerates the size of a fish in a desire to make the story more impressive. In addition to making sure the speaker's statements are true, be sure to ask whether enough evidence is given. A small number of examples may not prove a point. For example, one or two bad experiences don't necessarily make it true that "all men (or women) are jerks."

EXAMINE EMOTIONAL APPEALS   Sometimes emotion alone may be enough reason to persuade you. You might lend your friend $20 just for old time's sake even though you don't expect to see the money again soon. In other cases, it's a mistake to let yourself be swayed by emotion when the logic of a point isn't sound. The excitement of fun in an ad or the lure of low monthly payments probably aren't good enough reasons to buy a product you can't afford.

Empathic Listening

We listen both informationally and evaluatively out of self-interest. In **empathic listening,** however, the goal is to help the speaker solve a problem. Sometimes others seek help for personal dilemmas: "I don't know whether to split up or to stay with him." The problem needn't be so profound, however. A friend might be trying to decide what birthday gift to buy or whether to switch jobs.

Whatever the issue, there are several ways you can respond to another person's request for help. Perhaps the most common response style is **advising:** recommending a solution to the problem. Although advice can be useful in some instances, it won't always help.

Often your suggestion may not offer the best course to follow, in which case it can even be harmful. There's often a temptation to tell others how you would behave in their place, but it's important to realize that what's right for one person may not be right for another. A related consequence of advising is that it often allows others to avoid responsibility for their decisions. A partner who follows a suggestion of yours that doesn't work out can always pin the blame on you. Finally, often people simply don't want advice: They may not be ready to accept it, needing instead simply to talk out their thoughts and feelings.

Before offering advice, then, you need to be sure that three conditions are present. First, you should be confident that your advice is correct. It's essential to resist the temptation to act like an authority on matters about which you know little. It's equally important to remember that just because a course of action worked for you doesn't guarantee that it will be correct for everybody. Second, you need to be sure that the person seeking your advice is truly ready to accept it. In this way, you can avoid the frustration of making good suggestions, only to find that the person with the problem had another solution in mind all the time. Finally, when offering advice, you should be certain that the receiver won't blame you if the advice doesn't work. You may be offering the suggestions, but the choice and responsibility of following them are up to the other person.

A **judging response** evaluates the sender's thoughts or behaviors in some way. The judgment may be favorable—"That's a good idea" or "You're on the right track now"—or unfavorable—"An attitude like that won't get you anywhere." But, in either case, it implies that the person doing the judging is in some way qualified to pass judgment on the speaker's thoughts or actions.

Sometimes negative judgments are purely critical. How many times have you heard such responses as "Well, you asked for it!" or "I *told* you so!" or "You're just feeling sorry for yourself"? Although comments like these can sometimes serve as a verbal slap that brings problem-holders to their senses, they usually make matters worse.

In other cases, negative judgments are less critical. These involve what we usually call *constructive criticism,* which is intended to help the problem-holder improve in the future. This is the sort of response given by friends about everything from the choice of clothing to jobs to friends. Another common setting for constructive criticism occurs in school, where instructors evaluate students' work to help them master concepts and skills. But whether it's justified or not, even constructive criticism runs the risk of arousing defensiveness because it may threaten the self-concept of the person at whom it is directed.

Judgments have the best chance of being received when two conditions exist. First, the person with the problem should have requested an evaluation from you. In addition, your judgments should be genuinely constructive and not designed to be disparaging. If you can remember to follow these two guidelines, your judgments will probably be less frequent and better received.

In an **analyzing response,** the listener offers an interpretation to a speaker's message. Analyses like these are probably familiar to you:

"I think what's really bothering you is...."

"She's doing it because...."

"I don't think you really meant that."

"Maybe the problem started when she...."

Interpretations are often effective ways to help people with problems to consider alternative meanings—ways they would have never thought of without your help. Sometimes a clear analysis will make a confusing problem suddenly clear either suggesting a solution or at least providing an understanding of what is occurring.

In other cases, an analysis can create more problems than it solves. There are two problems with analyzing. First, your interpretation may not be correct, in which case the speaker may become even more confused by accepting it. Second, even if your analysis is accurate, telling it to the problem-holder might not

© 1978 United Media, Inc.

be useful. There's a chance that it will arouse defensiveness (for analysis implies superiority and evaluativeness), and even if it doesn't, the person may not be able to understand your view of the problem without working it out personally.

How can you know when it's helpful to offer an analysis? There are several guidelines to follow. First, it's important to offer your interpretation in a tentative way rather than as absolute fact. There's a big difference between saying, "Maybe the reason is . . ." and insisting, "This is the truth." Second, your analysis ought to have a reasonable chance of being correct. We've already said that a wild, unlikely interpretation can leave a person more confused than before. Third, you ought to be sure that the other person will be receptive to your analysis. Even if you're completely accurate, your thoughts won't help if the problem-holder isn't ready to consider what you say. Finally, you should be sure that your motive is truly to help the other person. It's sometimes tempting to offer an analysis to show how brilliant you are or even to make the other person feel bad for not having thought of the right answer in the first place. Needless to say, an analysis offered under these conditions isn't very helpful.

A few pages ago we talked about questioning as one way for you to understand others better. A **questioning response** can also be a way to help others think about their problem and understand it more clearly. For example, questioning can help a problem-holder define vague ideas more precisely. You might respond to a friend with a line of questioning: "You said Greg has been acting 'differently' toward you lately. What has he been doing?" Another example of a question that helps clarify is as follows: "You told your roommates that you wanted them to be more helpful in keeping the place clean. What would you like them to do?"

Questions can also encourage a problem-holder to examine a situation in more detail by talking either about what happened or about personal feelings, for example, "How did you feel when they turned you down? What did you do then?" This type of questioning is particularly helpful when you are dealing with someone who is quiet or is unwilling under the circumstances to talk about the problem very much.

Although asking questions can definitely be helpful, two dangers can arise from using this style too much or at the wrong times. The first is that your questions may lead the problem-holder on a wild goose chase, away from a solution to the problem. For instance, asking, "When did the problem begin?" might provide some clue about how to solve it—but it could also lead to a long digression that would only confuse matters. As with advice, it's important to be sure you're on the right track before asking questions.

A second danger is that questioning can also be a way of disguising advice or criticism. We've all been questioned by parents, teachers, or other figures who seemed to be trying to trap or indirectly to guide us. In this way, questioning becomes a strategy and often implies that the person doing the asking already has some idea of what direction the discussion should take.

A **supporting response** can take several forms. Sometimes it involves reassuring: "You've got nothing to worry about—I know you'll do a good job." In other cases, support comes through comforting: "Don't worry. We all love you." We can also support people in need by distracting them with humor, kidding, and joking.

Sometimes a person needs encouragement, and in these cases a supporting response can be the best thing. But in many instances this kind of comment isn't helpful at all; in fact, it can even make things worse. Telling a person who is obviously upset that everything is all right or joking about what seems like a serious problem can communicate the idea that you don't think the problem is really worth all the fuss. People might see your comments as a put-down, leaving them feeling worse than before. As with the other styles we've discussed, supporting *can* be helpful . . . but only in certain circumstances.

A final type of helping response involves paraphrasing. This sort of response has several advantages. First, it provides a check on your understanding, allowing you to be sure you are responding to what the speaker is actually thinking and not to some misinterpretation. In addition, paraphrasing can be an effective way to show empathy. In order to be truly empathic, however, your response has to include the nonverbal behaviors that show you are really interested. A mechanical rephrasing won't be much help at all. Beyond assuring your understanding and demonstrating empathy, paraphrasing responses can help others sort out and solve problems for themselves.

When you use paraphrasing as a helping tool, your reflection should contain two elements. The first is a restatement of the speaker's *thoughts*. Though it might seem unnecessary to restate an idea the other person has just uttered, your paraphrasing statement can help the speaker take a more objective look at what's been said, and possibly to clarify the idea. Besides a replaying of the speaker's thoughts, it is also important to reflect the often unspoken *emotions* that accompany the verbal message.

The following suggestions will help you become a more effective empathic listener:

USE A VARIETY OF RESPONSE STYLES Most people rely too heavily on one or two styles of responding. Some are instinctive advisers whereas others reflexively try to offer help by supporting, judging, or analyzing. Although each of these responses has its place, overusing any of them is less effective than choosing the kind of feedback that seems most helpful in a given situation. When you are faced with the chance to help another person, consider which type of communication will do the best job.

LISTEN FOR FEELINGS AS WELL AS THOUGHTS In most cases, the speaker's feelings are at least as important as the thoughts being expressed. Despite this fact, people often fail to mention their feelings at all. Consider the emotions that accompany each of these statements:

"My boss has been terrible lately, but I'm afraid I'll lose my job if I speak up, and I can't afford that."

"Who does she think she is, talking to me like that? I know that's just her style, but I don't think I can take it any more."

"I really need the vacation, but I can't decide whether to spend my savings or save them for all the expenses I know will come up next year."

By paraphrasing the emotions you recognize in statements like these, you invite the speaker to explore those important feelings in depth. Focusing on just the rational parts of a message often ignores the most fundamental parts of a problem.

AVOID BEING TOO JUDGMENTAL   Although judging responses ("It's your own fault, you know.") may be correct, they rarely help. Most of us receive more judgments than we need, and often having a listener who doesn't evaluate is far more helpful than a lecture.

▶ SUMMARY

Even the best message is useless if it goes unreceived or if it is misunderstood. For this reason, listening—the process of giving meaning to an oral message—is a vitally important part of the communication process. We began our look at the subject by identifying and refuting several myths about listening. Our conclusion here was that effective listening is a skill that needs to be developed in order for us to be truly effective in understanding others.

We next took a close look at four steps in the process of listening: hearing, attending, understanding, and remembering. We examined nine types of faulty listening behavior that block understanding, showing the many ways in which we screen out or distort the messages of others. Next we identified several reasons that prevent us from listening effectively even when we want to do so.

The chapter concluded by examining three types of listening. Informational listening is the proper approach to take when the goal is to understand another person's ideas. Information can be best gained with an active approach to listening. This active approach can involve either questioning or paraphrasing—restating the speaker's message in your own words.

Evaluative listening is appropriate when the goal is to judge the quality of an idea. Evaluation will be most successful when the listener ensures correct understanding of a message before passing judgment, when the speaker's credibility is taken into account, when the quality of supporting evidence is examined, and when emotional appeals are separated from logical ones.

The aim of empathic listening is to help the speaker, not the receiver. Various helping responses include advising, judging, analyzing, supporting, and paraphrasing the speaker's thoughts and feelings. Listeners can be most helpful when they use a variety of styles, focus on the emotional dimensions of a message, and avoid being too judgmental.

▶ ACTIVITIES

1. Although failing to listen is a crime we both commit and suffer from, it often goes unnoticed. Trying this activity with a partner will demonstrate its seriousness.
   a. Each person, in turn, should take two minutes to discuss with the other his or her ideas about a current issue (abortion, capital punishment, or

some other idea that is personally important). But, as the talker shares his or her ideas, the other person should think about the unfinished business in his or her life—incomplete assignments, on-the-job work, things to discuss with the family. The partner shouldn't be rude but should respond politely every so often to the speaker, putting on a good appearance of paying close attention. Nonetheless, the idea is to think about personal concerns, not the speaker's remarks.

   b. After each partner completes the preceding step, spend some time sharing the feelings you experienced when you were talking and being listened to by the other. Also discuss how you felt as you thought about your problems instead of listening to the speaker.

   c. Next conduct a five-minute discussion with a partner in which each of you shares one personal communication problem you hope to solve. Try to be as sincere and open with your feelings as you can. But as both partners talk, each should try to keep the discussion focused on his or her own problem. Every time the other shares an idea or experience, try to turn it around to relate to your situation. Don't get sidetracked by his or her comments. Your task is to tell the other about your communication problem.

   d. After your discussion, take a few minutes to talk about how you felt during the conversation—when the other person ignored your message and when you ignored his or hers.

2. Use the categories on pages 81–83 to describe the faulty listening behaviors you use in your everyday interactions. In what circumstances do you use these behaviors: Around whom? With what subjects? In what settings? At what times? What are the main reasons for your failure to listen in these circumstances? How satisfied are you with your findings? How could you change your behavior in the unsatisfying areas?

3. You can see for yourself what a difference paraphrasing can make by trying this exercise either in class or with a companion on your own.

   a. Find a partner; then move to a place where you can talk comfortably. Designate one person as A and the other as B.

   b. Find a subject on which you and your partner apparently disagree—a personal dispute, a philosophical or moral issue, or perhaps a matter of personal taste.

   c. A begins by making a statement on the subject. B's job is then to paraphrase the idea back, beginning by saying something like "What I hear you saying is . . ." It is very important that in this step B feeds back only what he or she heard A say without adding any judgment or interpretation. B's job is simply to *understand* here, and doing so in no way should signify agreement or disagreement with A's remarks.

   d. A then responds by telling B whether or not the response was accurate. If there were some misunderstanding, A should make the correction, and B should feed back a new understanding of the statement. Continue this process until you're both sure that B understands A's statement.

   e. Now it's B's turn to respond to A's statement and for A to help the process of understanding by correcting B.

    f. Continue this process until both partners are satisfied that they have explained themselves fully and that they have been understood by the other person.

    g. Now discuss the following questions:

       (1) As a listener, how accurate was your first understanding of the speaker's statements?

       (2) How did your understanding of the speaker's position change after you used paraphrasing?

       (3) Did you find that the gap between your position and that of your partner narrowed as a result of your both using paraphrasing?

       (4) How did you feel at the end of your conversation? How does this feeling compare to your usual emotional state after discussing controversial issues with others?

       (5) How might your life change if you used paraphrasing at home? At work? With friends?

4. Recall three recent instances in which you listened evaluatively. Answer the following questions for each situation:

    a. Was this an appropriate time for evaluating, or should you have been listening for information?

    b. How did the speaker's competence and impartiality affect the merits of the topic being discussed?

    c. What kinds of evidence did the speaker offer? Was the evidence valid?

    d. Did the speaker use any emotional appeals? How did you react to them?

5. Ask a friend, a family member, or other close acquaintance to describe the response types you typically use when listening to help. Ask your informant to rate the helpfulness of these styles and to suggest better alternatives listed in this chapter.

▶ NOTES

1. Paul T. Rankin, "The Measurement of the Ability to Understand Spoken Language," *Dissertation Abstracts* 12 (1926): 847.

2. L. Barker, R. Edwards, C. Gaines, K. Gladney, and F. Holley, "An Investigation of Proportional Time Spent in Various Communication Activities by College Students," *Journal of Applied Communication Research* 8 (1981): 101–109.

3. See, for example, J. D. Weinrauch and J. R. Swanda, Jr., "Examining the Significance of Listening: An Exploratory Study of Contemporary Management," *The Journal of Business Communication* 13 (February 1975): 25–32; and Larry L. Barker, *Listening Behavior* (Englewood Cliffs, N.J.: Prentice-Hall, 1971), p. 17.

4. For a complete discussion of the physiology of hearing, see Hayes A. Newby, *Audiology* (New York: Appleton-Century-Crofts, 1972).

5. Jerrold J. Katz and Jerry A. Foder, "The Structure of a Semantic Theory," in Jay F. Rosenberg and Charles Travis (eds.), *Readings in the Philosophy of Language* (Englewood Cliffs, N.J.: Prentice-Hall, 1971).

6. Ralph G. Nichols, "Factors in Listening Comprehension," *Speech Monographs* 15 (1948): 154–163.

7. For a more complete discussion of memory and listening, see Robert N. Bostrom and Carol L. Bryant, "Factors in the Retention of Information Presented Orally: The Role of Short-Term Listening," *Western Journal of Speech Communication* 44 (Spring 1980): 137–145.

8. Nichols, op. cit.
9. Ralph G. Nichols, "Listening Is a Ten-Part Skill," in R. C. Huseman et al. (eds.), *Readings in Interpersonal and Organizational Communication* (Boston: Holbrook Press, 1969), p. 476.
10. David B. Orr, "Time Compressed Speech—A Perspective," *Journal of Communication* 17 (1967): 223.
11. Bert E. Bradley, *Fundamentals of Speech Communication,* 3d ed. (Dubuque, Iowa: W. C. Brown, 1981), pp. 205–206.

▶ CHAPTER 5

KEY TERMS

disfluency
emblems
illustrators
intimate distance
kinesics
manipulators
mixed message
nonverbal communication
paralanguage
personal distance
proxemics
public distance
social distance
territory

NONVERBAL COMMUNICATION

After reading this chapter, you should understand the following:

1. Four characteristics of nonverbal communication.

2. Four differences between verbal and nonverbal communication.

3. The six functions nonverbal communication can serve.

4. How the types of nonverbal communication described in this chapter function.

You should be able to do the following:

1. Identify and describe the nonverbal behaviors of yourself or another person in a given situation.

2. Identify nonverbal behaviors that repeat, substitute for, complement, accent, regulate, and contradict verbal messages.

3. Recognize the emotional and relational dimensions of your own nonverbal behavior.

4. Share your interpretation of another person's nonverbal behavior in a tentative manner when such sharing is appropriate.

There is often a big gap between what people say and what they feel. An acquaintance says, "I'd like to get together again" in a way that leaves you suspecting the opposite. (But how do you know?) A speaker tries to appear confident but acts in a way that almost screams out, "I'm nervous!" (What tells you this?) You ask a friend what's wrong, and the "nothing" you get in response rings hollow. (Why does it sound untrue?)

Then, of course, there are times when another's message comes through even though there are no words at all. A look of irritation, a smile, a sigh... signs like these can say more than a torrent of words.

Sometimes unspoken messages are so obvious that anyone could read them. In other cases, they are subtle, leaving you with a hunch about what's going on but unable to figure out the source of your feeling. And then there are times when you miss an unstated message so completely that the truth comes later as a complete surprise.

All situations like these have one point in common—that the message was sent nonverbally. The goal of this chapter is to introduce you to this world of nonverbal communication. Although you have certainly recognized nonverbal messages before, the following pages should introduce you to a richness of information you have never noticed. And though your experience won't transform you into a mind reader, it will make you a far more accurate observer of others ...and yourself.

We need to begin our study of nonverbal communication by defining this term. At first this might seem like a simple task. If *non* means "not" and *verbal* means "words," then *nonverbal communication* appears to mean "communication without words." This is a good starting point once we distinguish between *vocal* communication (by mouth) and *verbal* communication (with words). Once this distinction is made, it becomes clear that some nonverbal messages are vocal, and some are not. Likewise, although many verbal messages are vocal, some aren't. Table 5–1 illustrates these differences.

What about languages that don't involve words? Does American Sign Language, for example, qualify as nonverbal communication? Most scholars would

TABLE 5–1 Types of Communication

	VOCAL COMMUNICATION	**NONVOCAL COMMUNICATION**
VERBAL COMMUNICATION	Spoken words	Written words
NONVERBAL COMMUNICATION	Tone of voice, sighs, screams, vocal qualities (loudness, pitch, and so on)	Gestures, movement, appearance, facial expression, and so on.

Adapted from John Stewart and Gary D'Angelo, *Together: Communicating Interpersonally*, 2d ed. (Reading, Mass.: Addison-Wesley, 1980), p. 22.

say not.[1] Keeping this fact in mind, we arrive at a working definition of **nonverbal communication:** "oral and nonoral messages expressed by other than linguistic means." This rules out not only sign languages but written words as well, but it includes messages transmitted by vocal means that don't involve language—sighs, laughs, and other utterances we will discuss soon.

CHARACTERISTICS OF NONVERBAL COMMUNICATION ◄

Our brief definition only hints at the richness of nonverbal messages. You can begin to understand their prevalence by trying a simple experiment. Spend an hour or so around a group of people who are speaking a language you don't understand. (You might find such a group in the foreign students' lounge on campus, in an advanced language class, or in an ethnic neighborhood.) Your goal is to see how much information you can learn about the people you're observing from means other than the verbal messages they transmit. This experiment will reveal several characteristics of nonverbal communication.

Nonverbal Communication Exists

Your observations in the experiment show clearly that even without understanding speech it is possible to get an idea about how others are feeling. You probably noticed that some people were in a hurry whereas others seemed happy, confused, withdrawn, or deep in thought. The point is that without any formal experience you were able to recognize and to some degree interpret messages that other people sent nonverbally. In this chapter, we want to sharpen the skills you already have and to give you a better grasp of the vocabulary of nonverbal language.

One Can't Not Communicate

The pervasiveness of nonverbal communication brings us to its second characteristic. Suppose you were instructed to avoid communicating any messages at all. What would you do? Close your eyes? Withdraw into a ball? Leave the room? You can probably see that even these behaviors communicate messages, suggesting that you are avoiding contact. A moment's thought will show that there is no way to avoid communicating nonverbally.

This impossibility of not communicating is extremely important to understand, for it means that each of us is a kind of transmitter that cannot be shut off. No matter what we do, we give off information about ourselves.

Stop for a moment and examine yourself as you read this. If someone were observing you now, what nonverbal clues would they get about how you are feeling? Are you sitting forward or reclining back? Is your posture tense or relaxed? Are your eyes wide open, or do they keep closing? What does your facial expression communicate? Can you make your face expressionless? Don't people with expressionless faces communicate something?

► Writer (to movie producer Sam Goldwyn): Mr. Goldwyn, I'm telling you a sensational story. I'm only asking for your opinion, and you fall asleep.

Goldwyn: Isn't sleeping an opinion?

"I tell you, Mr. Arthur, this survey has no way of registering a nonverbal response!"

Reproduced by special permission of *Playboy* Magazine;
Copyright © 1977 by *Playboy*.

Of course, we don't always intend to send nonverbal messages. Consider, for instance, behaviors like blushing, frowning, sweating, or stammering. We rarely try to act in these ways, and often we are unaware of doing so. Nonetheless, others recognize signs like these and make interpretations about us based on their observations.

The fact that you and everyone around you is constantly sending nonverbal clues is important because it means that you have a constant source of information available about yourself and others. If you can tune into these signals, you will be more aware of how those around you are feeling and thinking, and you will be better able to respond to their behavior.

Nonverbal Communication Transmits Feelings

Although feelings are communicated quite well nonverbally, thoughts don't lend themselves to nonverbal channels.

You can test this principle for yourself. Following is a list that contains both thoughts and feelings. Try to express each item nonverbally, and see which ones come most easily:

You're tired. (feeling)

You're in favor of (or opposed to) capital punishment. (thought)

You're attracted to another person in the group. (feeling)

You support (or oppose) capital punishment. (thought)

You're angry at someone in the group. (feeling)

Nonverbal Communication Is Ambiguous

Before you get the idea that this chapter will turn you into a mind reader, we want to caution you and in so doing introduce a fifth feature of nonverbal communication: A great deal of ambiguity surrounds nonverbal behavior. To understand what we mean, examine the photo on page 106. What emotions do you imagine the couple are feeling: grief? anguish? agony? In fact, none of these is even close. The couple have just learned that they won $1 million in the New Jersey state lottery.

Nonverbal behavior is just as ambiguous in everyday life. For example, think of at least two meanings of a partner's silence at the end of an evening together. (Table 5–2 lists some possibilities.) Or suppose a much admired person you have worked with suddenly begins paying more attention to you than ever before. What might this mean?

Although nonverbal behavior can be quite revealing, it can have so many possible meanings that it is a serious mistake to assume your interpretations will always be accurate.

Some people are more skillful than others at accurately decoding nonverbal behavior.[2] Those who are better senders of nonverbal messages also are better

TABLE 5–2 Some Meanings of Silence

Agreement	Disagreement ("Silent Treatment")
Thoughtfulness	Ignorance
Revelation (We often say much about the people we are describing by what we choose to omit.)	Secrecy ("If he didn't have something to hide, he'd speak up.")
Warmth (Bind the participants.)	Coldness (Separate the participants.)
Submission	Attack (Not answering a letter—or worse, not answering a comment directed at you.)
Gaining attention	Boredom
Consideration	Inconsideration

Reprinted with permission from Mark L. Knapp, *Interpersonal Communication and Human Relationships* (Boston: Allyn & Bacon, 1984).

How does this couple feel? See the preceding text for the answer. (Photo courtesy of *The Record,* Hackensack, N.J.)

receivers. Decoding ability also increases with age and training, although there are still differences in ability owing to personality and occupation. For instance, extroverts are relatively accurate judges of nonverbal behavior whereas dogmatists are not. Interestingly, women seem to be better than men at decoding nonverbal messages. Over 95 percent of the studies examined in one analysis showed that women are more accurate at interpreting nonverbal signals.[3] Despite these differences, even the best nonverbal decoders do not approach 100 percent accuracy.

When you do try to make sense out of ambiguous nonverbal behavior, you need to consider several factors: The *context* in which they occur (e.g., smiling at a joke suggests a different feeling from what is suggested by smiling at another's misfortune); the *history of your relationship* with the sender (friendly, hostile, etc.); *the other's mood* at the time; and *your feelings* (when you're feeling insecure, almost anything can seem like a threat). The important idea is that when you become aware of nonverbal messages, you should think of them not as facts, but as *clues* that need to be checked out.

Much Nonverbal Communication Is Culture-Bound

Besides nonverbal communication being ambiguous, it also varies from one culture to another. Depending on your background, you may interpret a particular nonverbal behavior differently from someone who was raised in other circumstances. Also, the meaning you attribute to a particular nonverbal behavior may be the same meaning attributed to some *other* nonverbal behavior by a member of a culture different from yours. Finally, although a particular nonverbal behavior may have meaning for you, in another culture it may be perceived as little more than idiosyncratic or random behavior.

A quick look at many cultures shows the diversity of nonverbal behaviors.[4] Consider the expression of affection, for example. As members of contemporary Western civilization, we are used to embracing and kissing as signs of deepest caring. But to Mongols, the same feelings would be expressed by smelling heads; to Burmese, by pressing mouths and noses upon the other's cheek and inhaling strongly; and to Samoans, by juxtaposing noses and smelling heartily. Salutation behavior is just as varied: Polynesians stroke their own faces with the other person's hands, Lapps and Malays smell each others' cheeks, and the Dahomeans snap fingers.

Before you jump to the conclusion that examples like these are only important to anthropologists, consider the importance of understanding cross-cultural communication in this time of frequent international communication. Take, for instance, the differences between the cultural conventions of North Americans and Arabs.[5] To the former, one unstated rule about nonverbal communication is that a speaker maintains occasional eye contact with a listener, looking away from time to time during a conversation. To most Arabs, however, a greater degree of eye contact is considered normal and acceptable. Another difference between the two cultures involves body orientation. Whereas Americans are comfortable speaking to others without facing them directly, Arabs consider anything less than total confrontation impolite. Given these differences, it's easy to see how uncomfortable an American and an Arab might be, each being unaware of the other's cultural norms, and how suspiciously they could regard one another. Whereas the American might view the Arab as pushy and aggressive, the Arab would think his North American counterpart aloof and unfriendly. Imagine these feelings present during an important political or economic meeting, and you will realize the importance of learning the nonverbal as well as the verbal languages of others with whom we deal.

Even within a culture, various groups can have different nonverbal rules. For example, research in the 1970s revealed that many blacks avoid looking others directly in the eyes.[6] The findings also showed that whites in the study interpreted this lack of eye contact as a signal of disinterest and withholding. Another difference involved turn-taking in conversations: White listeners (following their own cultural rules) began to speak when black speakers paused with a sustained gaze although the blacks had not finished their statements. As long as cultural differences exist, this sort of awkwardness can be decreased when communicators are aware of the different nonverbal rules they bring to a conversation.

DIFFERENCES BETWEEN VERBAL ◄ AND NONVERBAL COMMUNICATION

The features described in the preceding section suggest some ways in which nonverbal communication differs from the spoken and written word. By examining the key differences between these two forms of communication, you will get a clearer idea of what each type can and can't accomplish.

Single vs. Multiple Channels

Most verbal messages—words, sentences, and paragraphs—reach us one at a time, rather like pearls on a string. In fact, it's physically impossible for a person to speak more than one word at a time. Unlike the spoken word, however, nonverbal messages don't arrive in such an orderly, sequential manner. Instead, they bombard us simultaneously from a multitude of channels. Consider the everyday act of meeting a stranger for the first time. On a verbal level there's relatively little information exchanged in the clichés that occupy the first few minutes of most conversations ("How's it going..." "Great weather we've been having..." "What's your major?"). But at the same moment the number of nonverbal messages available to you is overwhelming: the other person's facial expressions, postures, gestures, the clothing he or she wears, the distance he or she stands from you, and so on. In one way, this multichannel onslaught of nonverbal messages is a boon because it provides so many ways of learning about others. In another sense, however, the number of simultaneous messages is a problem, for it's difficult to recognize the overwhelming amount of nonverbal information we receive from others every moment.

Discrete vs. Continuous

Verbal messages—words, sentences, and paragraphs—form messages with clear beginnings and endings. In this sense, it's possible to say that someone either is or isn't communicating verbally by seeing whether or not he or she is speaking or writing. Unlike the written and spoken word, however, nonverbal communication is continuous and never ending. As we've already said, it's impossible not to communicate nonverbally: The postures, gestures, and other types of messages described in the following pages provide a constant flow of messages. Even the absence of a message (an unanswered letter or an unreturned phone call) is a message. As one communication expert said when referring to nonverbal communication, "Nothing never happens."

Conscious vs. Unconscious

Whereas we usually think about what we want to say before speaking or writing, most nonverbal messages aren't deliberate. Of course, we do pay attention to some of our nonverbal behavior: smiling when we want to convince others we're happy or making sure our handshakes are firm to show that we're straightforward, decisive people. But there are so many nonverbal channels that it's impossible to think about and control all of them. Thus, our slumping shoulders might contradict our smiles, and our sweating palms might cancel out all the self-confidence of our firm handshakes. The unconscious nature of most nonverbal behavior explains why it offers so many useful cues about how others are feeling.

Clear vs. Ambiguous

Although verbal communication can be confusing, we have already seen that most nonverbal cues are even more vague. Nonverbal messages aren't com-

pletely ambiguous, of course: It's probably accurate to guess that a frown signifies some sort of negative feeling and that a smile indicates a positive emotion. But we often need language to tell us *why* others feel as they do. Is the boss smiling because she likes your idea or because she finds it amusing but completely impractical? Does your instructor's frown indicate confusion with your remarks or disagreement? The best way to find out is to ask for a verbal clarification, not to depend on your reading of the nonverbal cues.

FUNCTIONS OF NONVERBAL COMMUNICATION ◄

Although verbal and nonverbal messages differ in many ways, the two forms of communication operate together on most occasions. The following discussion explains the many functions nonverbal communication can serve and shows how nonverbal messages relate to verbal ones.

Repeating

If someone asked you for directions to the nearest drugstore, you could say, "North of here about two blocks" and then repeat your instructions by pointing north. Pointing is an example of what social scientists call **emblems**—deliberate nonverbal behaviors that have precise meanings known to everyone within a cultural group. For example, we all know that a head nod means "yes," a head-shake indicates "no," a wave means "hello" or "good-bye," and a hand to the ear means "I can't hear you."

Substituting

Emblems can also replace a verbal message. When a friend asks you what's new, you might shrug your shoulders instead of answering in words. Not all substituting consists of emblems, however. Sometimes substituting responses are more ambiguous and less intentional. A sigh, smile, or frown may substitute for a verbal answer to your question, "How's it going?" As this example suggests, nonverbal substituting is especially important when people are reluctant to express their feelings in words.

Complementing

Sometimes nonverbal behaviors match the content of a verbal message. Consider, for example, a friend apologizing for forgetting an appointment with you. Your friend's sincerity would be reinforced if the verbal apology were accompanied by the appropriate nonverbal behaviors: the right tone of voice, facial expression, and so on. We often recognize the significance of complementary non-verbal behavior when it is missing. If your friend's apology were delivered with a

shrug, a smirk, and a light tone of voice, you probably would doubt its sincerity, no matter how profuse the verbal explanation was.

Much complementing behavior consists of **illustrators**—nonverbal behaviors that accompany and support spoken words. Scratching the head when searching for an idea and snapping your fingers when it occurs are examples of illustrators that complement verbal messages. Research shows that North Americans use illustrators more often when they are emotionally aroused—trying to explain ideas that are difficult to put into words—when they are furious, horrified, very agitated, distressed, or excited.[7]

Accenting

Just as we use italics to highlight an idea in print, we use nonverbal devices to emphasize oral messages. Pointing an accusing finger adds emphasis to criticism (as well as probably creating defensiveness in the receiver). Stressing certain words with the voice ("It was *your* idea!") is another way to add nonverbal accents.

Regulating

Nonverbal behaviors can control the flow of verbal communication. For example, parties in a conversation often unconsciously send and receive turn-taking cues.[8] When you are ready to yield the floor, the unstated rule is: Create a rising vocal intonation pattern, then use a falling intonation pattern, or draw out the final syllable of the clause at the end of your statement. Finally, stop speaking. If you want to maintain your turn when another speaker seems ready to cut you off, you can suppress the attempt by taking an audible breath, using a sustained intonation pattern (because rising and falling patterns suggest the end of a statement), and avoiding any pauses in your speech. Other nonverbal clues exist for gaining the floor and for signaling that you do not want to speak.

Contradicting

People often simultaneously express different and even contradictory messages in their verbal and nonverbal behaviors. A common example of this sort of **mixed message** is the experience we've all had of hearing someone with a red face and bulging veins yelling, "Angry? No, *I'm not angry!*"

Usually, however, the contradiction between words and nonverbal clues isn't this obvious. At times we all try to seem different from what we are. There are many reasons for this contradictory behavior: to cover nervousness when giving a speech or in a job interview, to keep someone from worrying about us, or to appear more attractive then we believe we really are.

Even though some of the ways in which people contradict themselves are subtle, mixed messages have a strong impact. Research suggests that when a receiver perceives an inconsistency between verbal and nonverbal messages, the unspoken one carries more weight.[9] Table 5–3 lists situations in which mixed messages are most likely to be obvious.

▶ The reality of the other person is not in what he reveals to you, but in what he cannot reveal to you.

Therefore, if you would understand him, listen not to what he says but rather to what he does not say.

Kahlil Gibran

TABLE 5–3 Leakage of Nonverbal Cues to Deception

DECEPTION CUES ARE MOST LIKELY WHEN THE DECEIVER	DECEPTION CUES ARE LEAST LIKELY WHEN THE DECEIVER
Wants to hide emotions being experienced at the moment.	Wants to hide information unrelated to his or her emotions.
Feels strongly about the information being hidden.	Has no strong feelings about the information being hidden.
Feels apprehensive about the deception.	Feels confident about the deception.
Feels guilty about being deceptive.	Experiences little guilt about the deception.
Gets little enjoyment from being deceptive.	Enjoys the deception.
Needs to construct the message carefully while delivering it.	Knows the deceptive message well and has rehearsed it.

Based on material from "Mistakes When Deceiving" by Paul Ekman, in Thomas A. Sebeok and Robert Rosenthal (eds.), *The Clever Hans Phenomenon: Communication with Horses, Whales, Apes, and People* (New York: New York Academy of Sciences, 1981), pp. 269–278.

▶ TYPES OF NONVERBAL COMMUNICATION

Now that we have examined how nonverbal messages operate as a form of communication, we can look at the various ways in which nonverbal messages are expressed. The first area we will survey is the broad field of **kinesics,** or body motion. In this section, we will explore the role that posture, gestures, body orientation, facial expressions, and eye behaviors play in our relationships with each other.

Posture

▶ Fie, fie upon her!
There's language in her
   eyes, her cheek, her lip.
Nay, her foot speaks; her
   wanton spirits look out at
   every joint and motive in
   her body.

William Shakespeare
Troilus and Cressida

Posture is one type of kinesic communication. See for yourself: Stop reading for a moment, and notice how you are sitting. What does your position say non-verbally about how you feel? Are there any other people near you now? What messages do you get from their present posture?

The main reason we miss most posture messages is that they aren't very obvious. It's seldom that people who feel weighted down by a problem hunch over so much that they stand out in a crowd, and when we're bored, we usually don't lean back and slump enough to embarrass another person. In reading posture, then, look for small changes that might be shadows of the way people feel inside.

For example, a teacher who has a reputation for interesting classes told us how he uses his understanding of posture to do a better job. "Because of my large classes, I have to lecture a lot," he said, "and that's an easy way to turn students off. I work hard to make my talks entertaining, but you know that nobody's perfect, and I do have my off days. I can tell when I'm not doing a good job of communicating by picking out three or four students before I start my talk and watching how they sit throughout the class period. As long as they're leaning forward in their seats, I know I'm doing OK, but if I look up and see them starting to slump back, I know I'd better change my approach."

▶ Who's there?...
Stand, and
   unfold yourself.

William Shakespeare
Hamlet

Psychologist Albert Mehrabian has found that other postural keys to feelings are tension and relaxation.[10] He says that we take relaxed postures in non-threatening situations and tighten up when threatened. Based on this observation, he says we can tell a good deal about how others feel simply by watching how tense or loose they seem to be. For example, he suggests that watching tenseness is a way of detecting status differences: The lower-status person is generally the more rigid, tense-appearing one whereas the one with higher status is more relaxed. This is the kind of situation that often happens when we picture a "chat" with the boss (or other authority figures), when we sit ramrod straight while the authority figure leans back, relaxed. The same principle applies to social situations, where it is often possible to tell who is uncomfortable by looking at postures. You may see people laughing and talking as if they were perfectly at home, but whose posture almost shouts nervousness. Some people never relax, and their posture shows it.

Sometimes posture communicates vulnerability in situations far more serious than mere social or business settings. One study revealed that rapists sometimes use postural clues to select victims they believe are easy to intimidate.[11] Easy targets are more likely to walk slowly and tentatively, stare at the ground, and move their arms and legs in short, jerky motions.

Gestures

Sometimes gestures are intentional—emblems like a cheery wave or thumbs up. In other cases, however, gestures are unconscious. Occasionally, an unconscious gesture will consist of an unambiguous emblem, such as a shrug that clearly means "I don't know." Another revealing set of gestures is what the psychiatrist Albert Scheflen calls "preening behaviors"—stroking or combing the hair, glancing in a mirror, and rearranging the clothing. Scheflen suggests that these behaviors signal some sort of interest in the other party: perhaps an unconscious sexual come-on or perhaps a sign of less intimate interest.[12] More often, however, gestures are ambiguous. In addition to illustrators, another group of ambiguous gestures consists of what we usually call fidgeting—movements in which one part of the body grooms, massages, rubs, holds, fidgets, pinches, picks, or otherwise manipulates another body part. Social scientists call these behaviors **manipulators.**[13] Social rules may discourage us from performing most manipulators in public, but people still do so without noticing.

Research confirms what common sense suggests—that increased use of manipulators is often a sign of discomfort.[14] But not *all* fidgeting signals uneasiness. People also are likely to use manipulators when relaxed. When they let their guard down (either alone or with friends), they will be more likely to fiddle with an earlobe, twirl a strand of hair, or clean their fingernails. Whether

113

or not the fidgeter is hiding something, observers are likely to interpret manipulators as a signal of dishonesty. Because not all fidgeters are liars, it's important not to jump to conclusions about the meaning of manipulations.

Actually, *too few* gestures may be as significant an indicator of mixed messages as *too many*.[15] Lack of gesturing may signal a lack of interest, sadness, boredom, or low enthusiasm. Illustrators also decrease whenever there is caution about speech. For these reasons, a careful nonverbal observer will look for either an increase or a decrease in the usual level of gestures.

Face and Eyes

The face and eyes are probably the most noticed parts of the body, but this doesn't mean that their nonverbal messages are the easiest to read. The face is a tremendously complicated channel of expression for several reasons.

First, it is hard even to describe the number and kinds of expressions we commonly produce with our face and eyes. For example, researchers have found that there are at least eight distinguishable positions of the eyebrows and forehead, eight more of the eyes and lids, and ten for the lower face. When you multiply this complexity by the number of emotions we experience, you can see why it would be almost impossible to compile a dictionary of facial expressions and their corresponding emotions.

Another reason for the difficulty in understanding facial expressions is the speed with which they can change. For example, slow-motion films have been taken that show expressions fleeting across a subject's face in as short a time as a fifth of a second. Also, it seems that different emotions show most clearly in different parts of the face: happiness and surprise in the eyes and lower face, anger in the lower face and brows and forehead, fear and sadness in the eyes, and disgust in the lower face.

▶ Pleads he in earnest?—
Look upon his face,
His eyes do drop no tears; his
  prayers are jest;
His words come from his
  mouth; ours, from our
  breast;
He prays but faintly, and
  would be denied;
We pray with heart and soul.

William Shakespeare
Richard II

► "It was terribly dangerous to let your thoughts wander when you were in any public place or within range of a telescreen. The smallest thing could give you away. A nervous tic, an unconscious look of anxiety, a habit of muttering to yourself—anything that carried with it the suggestion of abnormality, of having something to hide. In any case, to wear an improper expression on your face (to look incredulous when a victory was announced, for example) was itself a punishable offense. There was even a word for it in Newspeak: *facecrime,* it was called."

George Orwell
1984

Ekman and Friesen have identified six basic emotions that facial expressions reflect—surprise, fear, anger, disgust, happiness, and sadness.[16] Expressions reflecting these feelings seem to be recognizable in and between members of all cultures. Of course, **affect blends**—the combination of two or more expressions showing different emotions—are possible. For instance, it's easy to imagine how someone would look who is fearful and surprised or disgusted and angry.

Research also indicates that people are quite accurate at judging facial expressions of these emotions.[17] Accuracy increases when judges know the "target" or have knowledge of the context in which the expression occurs or when they have seen several samples of the target's expressions.

In spite of the complex way in which the face shows emotions, you can still pick up messages by watching it. One of the easiest ways is to look for expressions that seem to be overdone. Often when people are trying to fool themselves or someone else they will emphasize this mask to a point where it seems too exaggerated to be true. Another way to detect people's feelings is by watching their expression at moments when they aren't likely to be thinking about appearances. Everyone has had the experience of glancing into another car while stopped in a traffic jam or looking around at a sporting event and seeing expressions that the wearer would probably never show in more guarded moments. At other times, it's possible to watch a microexpression as it flashes across a person's face. For just a moment you see a flash of emotion quite different from the one a speaker is trying to convey. Finally, you may be able to spot contradictory expressions on different parts of someone's face: The eyes say one thing, but the expression of the mouth or eyebrows might be sending quite a different message.

The eyes themselves can send several kinds of messages. In our culture, meeting someone's glance with your eyes is usually a sign of involvement whereas looking away signals a desire to avoid contact. This is why solicitors on the street—panhandlers, salespeople, petitioners—try to catch our eye. Once they've managed to establish contact with a glance, it becomes harder for the approached person to draw away. A friend explained how to apply this principle to hitchhiking. "When I'm hitching a ride, I'm always careful to look each driver in the eye as he or she comes toward me. Most of them will try to look somewhere else as they pass, but if I can catch somebody's eye, that person will almost always stop." Most of us remember trying to avoid a question we didn't understand by glancing away from the teacher. At times like these we usually became very interested in our textbooks, fingernails, the clock—anything but the teacher's stare. Of course, the teacher always seemed to know the meaning of this nonverbal behavior and ended up picking on those of us who signaled uncertainty.

Voice

The voice itself is another form of nonverbal communication. Social scientists use the term **paralanguage** to describe nonverbal, vocal messages. You can begin to understand the power of vocal cues by considering how the meaning of a simple sentence can change just by shifting the emphasis from word to word:

This is a fantastic communication book.
(Not just any book, but *this* one in particular.)

This is a *fantastic* communication book.
(This book is superior, exciting.)

This is a fantastic *communication* book.
(The book is good as far as communication goes; it may not be so great as literature or drama.)

This is a fantastic communication *book.*
(It's not a play or record, it's a book.)

There are many other ways our voice communicates—through its tone, speed, pitch, volume, number and length of pauses, and **disfluencies** (such as stammering, use of "uh," "um," "er," and so on). All these factors can do a great deal to reinforce or contradict the message our words convey.

Sarcasm is one instance in which both emphasis and tone of voice help change a statement's meaning to the opposite of its verbal message. Experience this yourself with the following three statements. The first time through, say them literally, and then say them sarcastically.

Darling, what a beautiful little gown!

I really had a wonderful time on my blind date.

There's nothing I like better than calves' brains on toast.

Researchers have identified the communicative value of paralanguage through the use of content-free speech—ordinary speech that has been electronically manipulated so that the words are unintelligible, but the paralanguage remains unaffected. (Hearing a foreign language that you do not understand has the same effect.) Subjects who hear content-free speech can consistently recognize the emotion being expressed, as well as identifying its strength.[18]

The impact of paralinguistic cues is strong. In fact, research shows that listeners pay more attention to the vocal messages than to the words that are spoken when asked to determine a speaker's attitudes.[19] Furthermore, when vocal factors contradict a verbal message, listeners judge the speaker's intention from the paralanguage, not from the words themselves.[20]

Vocal changes that contradict spoken words are not easy to conceal. If the speaker is trying to conceal fear or anger, the voice will probably sound higher and louder, and the rate of talk may be faster than normal. Sadness produces the opposite vocal pattern: quieter, lower-pitched speech delivered at a slower rate.[21]

Touch

Besides being the earliest means we have of making contact with others, touching is essential to our healthy development. During the nineteenth and early twentieth centuries many babies died from a disease then called *marasmus,* which, translated from Greek, means "wasting away." In some orphanages the mortality rate was quite high, but even children in "progressive" homes, hospitals, and other institutions died regularly from the ailment. When researchers finally tracked down the causes of this disease, they found that many infants suffered from lack of physical contact with parents or nurses rather than poor nutrition, medical care, or other factors. They hadn't been touched enough, and as a result they died. From this knowledge came the practice of "mothering" children in institutions—picking the baby up, carrying it around, and handling it sev-

▶ The unconscious parental feelings communicated through touch or lack of touch can lead to feelings of confusion and conflict in a child. Sometimes a "modern" parent will say all the right things but not want to touch his child very much. The child's confusion comes from the inconsistency of levels: if they really approve of me so much like they say they do, why won't they touch me?

William Schutz
Here Comes Everybody

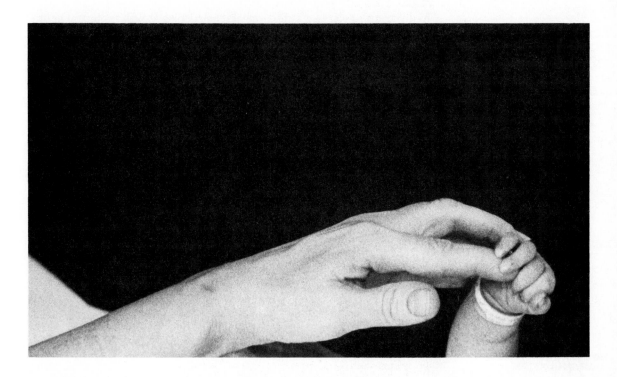

> In our now more than slightly cockeyed world, there seems to be little provision for someone to get touched without having to go to bed with whomever does the touching. And that's something to think about. We have mixed up simple, healing, warm touching with sexual advances. So much so, that it often seems as if there is no middle way between "Don't you dare touch me!" and "Okay, you touched me, so now we should make love!"

A nation which is able to distinguish the fine points between offensive and defensive pass interference, bogies, birdies, and par, a schuss and a slalom, a technical, a personal, and a player-control foul should certainly be able to make some far more obvious distinctions between various sorts of body contact.

Sidney Simon
Caring, Feeling, Touching

---

eral times each day. At one hospital that began this practice, the death rate for infants fell from between 30 and 35 percent to below 10 percent.[22]

As a child develops, the need for being touched continues. In his book *Touching: The Human Significance of the Skin,* Ashley Montagu describes research that suggests that allergies, eczema, and other health problems are, in part, caused by a person's lack of contact as an infant with her or her mother.[23] Although Montagu says that these problems develop early in life, he also cites cases where adults suffering from conditions as diverse as asthma and schizophrenia have been successfully treated by psychiatric therapy that uses extensive physical contact.

Touch seems to increase a child's mental functioning as well as physical health. L. J. Yarrow has conducted surveys that show that babies who have been given plenty of physical stimulation by their mothers have significantly higher IQs than those receiving less contact.[24]

Touch can communicate many messages. In addition to the nurturing/caring function we just discussed, it can signify many relationships:[25]

functional/professional (dental examination, haircut)

social/polite (handshake)

friendship/warmth (clap on back, Spanish *abrazo*)

love/intimacy (some caresses, hugs)

sexual arousal (some kisses, strokes)*

You might object to the examples following each of these categories, saying that some nonverbal behaviors occur in several types of relationship. A kiss, for example, can mean anything from a polite but superficial greeting to the most intense arousal. What makes a given touch more or less intense? Researchers have suggested a number of factors:

what part of the body does the touching

what part of the body is touched

---

* Other types of touch can indicate varying degrees of aggression.

how long the touch lasts

how much pressure is used

whether there is movement after contact is made

whether anyone else is present

the situation in which the touch occurs

the relationship between the persons involved

From this list you can see that there is, indeed, a complex language of touch. As nonverbal messages are inherently ambiguous, it's no surprise that this language can often be misunderstood. Is a hug playful or suggestive of stronger feelings? Is a touch on the shoulder a friendly gesture or an attempt at domination? Research suggests the interpretation can depend on a variety of factors, including the sex of the people involved, ethnic background, and marital status, among others.

Clothing

Besides protecting us from the elements, clothing is a means of nonverbal communication. One writer has suggested that clothing conveys at least ten types of messages to others.[26]

1. economic level
2. educational level
3. trustworthiness
4. social position
5. level of sophistication

6. economic background
7. social background
8. educational background
9. level of success
10. moral character

Research shows that we do make assumptions about people based on their style of clothing. In one study, a male and female were stationed in a hallway so that anyone who wished to go by had to avoid them or pass between them. In one condition, the conversationalists wore "formal daytime dress"; in the other, they wore "casual attire." Passersby behaved differently toward the couple, depending on the style of clothing: They responded positively with the well-dressed couple and negatively when the same people were casually dressed.[27] Similar results in other situations show the influence of clothing. We are more likely to obey people dressed in a high-status manner. Pedestrians were more likely to return lost coins to well-dressed people than to those dressed in low-status clothing.[28] We are also more likely to follow the lead of high-status dressers even when it comes to violating social rules. Eighty-three percent of the pedestrians in one study followed a well-dressed jaywalker who violated a "wait" crossing signal whereas only 48 percent followed a confederate dressed in lower-status clothing.[29]

"A general! Goodness gracious, you don't look like a general!"
Drawing by Richter; © 1968 The New Yorker Magazine, Inc.

Despite the frequency with which we make them, our clothing-based assumptions aren't always accurate. The stranger wearing wrinkled, ill-fitting old clothes might be a worker on vacation, a normally stylish person on the way to clean a fireplace, or even an eccentric millionaire. As we get to know others better, the importance of clothing shrinks.[30] This fact suggests that clothing is especially important in the early stages of a relationship, when making a positive first impression is necessary in order to encourage others to get to know us better. This advice is equally important in personal situations and in employment interviews. In both cases, your style of dress (and personal grooming) can make all the difference between the chance to progress further and outright rejection.

Proxemics

Proxemics is the study of the way people and animals use space.

Anthropologist Edward T. Hall has defined four distances that we use in our everyday lives.[31] He says that we choose a particular distance depending on how we feel toward the other person at a given time, the context of the conversation, and our personal goals. (These distance zones describe the behavior of North Americans and don't necessarily apply to members of other cultures.)

INTIMATE DISTANCE   The first of Hall's zones is **intimate distance.** It begins with skin contact and ranges out to about eighteen inches. The most obvious context for intimate distance involves interaction with people to whom we're emotionally close—and then mostly in private situations—making love, rough-housing playfully, comforting, and protecting. Intimate distance between individuals also occurs in less intimate circumstances: visiting the doctor or dentist, at the hairdresser's, and during some athletic contests. Allowing someone to move into the intimate zone usually is a sign of trust, an indication that we've willingly lowered our defenses. On the other hand, when someone invades this most personal area without our consent, we usually feel threatened. This explains the discomfort that sometimes comes with being forced into crowded places such as buses or elevators with strangers. At times like these the standard behavior in our society is to draw away or tense the muscles and avoid contact. This is a nonverbal way of signaling "I don't like this invasion of personal territory, but the situation has forced it."

▶ Once I heard a hospital nurse describing doctors. She said there were beside-the-bed doctors, who were interested in the patient, and foot-of-the-bed doctors, who were interested in the patient's condition. They unconsciously expressed their emotional involvement—or lack of it—by where they stood.

Edward Hall

In courtship situations, a critical moment usually occurs when one member of a couple first moves into the other's intimate zone. If the partner being approached does not retreat, this usually signals that the relationship is moving into a new stage. On the other hand, if the reaction to the advance is withdrawal to a greater distance, the initiator should get the message that it isn't yet time to get more intimate. We remember from our dating experiences the significance of where on the car seat our companions chose to sit. If they moved close to us, it meant one thing; if they stayed jammed against the opposite door, quite a different message was communicated.

PERSONAL DISTANCE　The second spatial zone, **personal distance,** ranges from eighteen inches at its closest point to four feet at its farthest. Its closer phase is the distance at which most couples stand in public. But if someone of the opposite sex stands this near one partner at a party, the other partner is likely to feel uncomfortable. This "moving in" often is taken to mean that something more than casual conversation is taking place. The far range of personal distance runs from about two and a half to four feet. It's the zone just beyond the other person's reach. As Hall puts it, at this distance we can keep someone "at arm's length." This choice of words suggests the type of communication that goes on at this range: The contacts are still reasonably close, but they're much less personal than the ones that occur a foot or so closer.

Test this for yourself. Start a conversation with someone at a distance of about three feet; then slowly move a foot or so closer. Do you notice a difference? Does the distance affect your conversation?

SOCIAL DISTANCE　The third zone is **social distance.** It ranges from four to about twelve feet. Within it are the kinds of communication that usually occur in business situations. Its closer phase, from four to seven feet, is the distance at

"Huddleston, I admire your hands-on approach to everything, but get the hell out of my office!"

Drawing by Dana Fradon; © 1986 The New Yorker Magazine, Inc.

which conversations usually occur between salespeople and customers and between people who work together. Most people feel uncomfortable when a salesclerk comes as close as three feet whereas four or five feet nonverbally signals, "I'm here to help you, but I don't mean to be too personal or pushy."

We use the far range of social distance—seven to twelve feet—for more formal and impersonal situations. This is the range at which we generally sit from our boss. Sitting at this distance signals a far different and less relaxed type of conversation than if we were to pull a chair around to the boss's side of the desk and sit only three or so feet away.

PUBLIC DISTANCE   **Public distance** is Hall's term for the farthest zone, running outward from twelve feet. The closer range of public distance is the one most teachers use in the classroom. In the farther reaches of public space—twenty-five feet and beyond—two-way communication becomes difficult. In some cases it's necessary for speakers to use public distance owing to the size of their audience, but we can assume that anyone who voluntarily chooses to use it when he or she could be closer is not interested in having a dialogue.

Physical invasion isn't the only way people penetrate our spatial bubble; we're just as uncomfortable when someone intrudes on our visual territory. If you've had the unpleasant experience of being stared at, you know this can be just as threatening as having someone get too close. In most situations, however, people respect each other's visual privacy. You can test this the next time you're walking in public. As you approach other people, notice how they shift their glance away from you at a distance of a few paces, almost like a visual dimming of headlights. Generally, strangers maintain eye contact at a close distance only when they want something—information, assistance, signatures on a petition, recognition, a handout.

Territoriality

Whereas personal space is the invisible bubble we carry around as an extension of our physical being, **territory** is fixed space. Any geographical area such as a room, house, neighborhood, or country to which we assume some kind of

A good house is planned from the inside out. First, you decide what it has to do for its occupants. Then, you let the functions determine the form. The more numerous and various those functions, the more responsive and interesting the house should be. And it may not look at all like you expect.

Dan MacMasters
Los Angeles Times

"rights" is our territory. What's interesting about territoriality is that there is no real basis for the assumption of proprietary rights of "owning" some area, but the feeling of "owning" exists nonetheless. Your room in the house is *your room* whether you're there or not (unlike personal space, which is carried around with you), and it's your room because you say it is. Although you could probably make a case for your room's *really being* your room (and not the family's or the mortgage holder's), what about the desk you sit at in each class? You feel the same way about the desk, that it's yours, even though it's certain that the desk is owned by the school and is in no way really yours.

The way people use space can communicate a good deal about power and status relationships. Generally, we grant people with higher status more personal territory and greater privacy.[32] We knock before entering our boss's office whereas a supervisor can usually walk into our work area without hesitating. In traditional schools, professors have offices, dining rooms, and even toilets that are private whereas the students, who are presumably less important, have no such sanctuaries. In the military, greater space and privacy usually come with rank: Privates sleep forty to a barracks, sergeants have their own private rooms, and generals have government-provided houses.

Copr. © 1943 James Thurber. Copr. © 1971 Helen Thurber and Rosemary A. Thurber. From *Men, Women and Dogs*, published by Harcourt Brace Jovanovich.

▶ Campuses are full of conscious and unconscious architectural symbolism. While the colleges at Santa Cruz evoke images of Italian hill towns as they might have been if the peasants had concrete, the administration building is another story. It appears to anticipate the confrontations between students and administration that marked the sixties. At Santa Cruz, administrative offices are located in a two-story building whose rough sloped concrete base with narrow slit windows gives it the look of a feudal shogun's palace. The effect is heightened by the bridge and landscaped moat that one crosses to enter the building. "Four administrators in there could hold off the entire campus," joked one student.

Sym Van Der Ryn

Environment

A large amount of research shows how the design of an environment can shape the kind of communication that takes place in it. In one experiment, researchers found that the attractiveness of a room influenced the happiness and energy of people working in it.[33] The experimenters set up three rooms: an "ugly" one, which resembled a janitor's closet in the basement of a campus building; an "average" room, which was a professor's office; and a "beautiful" room, which was furnished with carpeting, drapes, and comfortable furniture. The subjects in the experiment were asked to rate a series of pictures as a way of measuring their energy and feelings of well-being while at work. Results of the experiment showed that while in the ugly room the subjects became tired and bored more quickly and took longer to complete their task. When they moved to the beautiful room, however, they rated the faces they were judging higher; showed a greater desire to work; and expressed feelings of importance, comfort, and enjoyment. The results teach a lesson that isn't surprising: Workers generally feel better and do a better job when they're in an attractive environment.

Many businesspeople show an understanding of how environment can influence communication. Robert Sommer, a leading environmental psychologist, described several such cases in his book *Personal Space: The Behavioral Basis for Design*. He pointed out that dim lighting, subdued noise levels, and comfortable seats encourage people to spend more time in a restaurant or bar.[34] Knowing this, the management can control the amount of customer turnover. If the goal is to run a high-volume business that tries to move people in and out quickly, it's necessary to keep the lights shining brightly and not worry too much about soundproofing. On the other hand, if the goal is to keep customers in the bar or restaurant for a long time, the proper technique is to lower the lighting and use absorbent building materials that will keep down the noise level.

Furniture design can control the amount of time a person spends in an environment too. From this knowledge came the Larsen chair, which was designed for Copenhagen restaurant owners who felt their customers were occupying their seats too long without spending enough money. The chair is constructed to put an uncomfortable pressure on the sitter's back if occupied for more than a few minutes. (We suspect that many people who are careless in buying furniture for their homes get much the same result without trying. One environmental psychologist we know refuses to buy a chair or couch without sitting in it for at least half an hour to test its comfort.)

In a more therapeutic and less commercial way, physicians have also shaped environments to improve communication. Sommer found that redesigning the convalescent ward of a hospital greatly increased the interaction among patients. In the old design, seats were placed shoulder to shoulder around the edges of the ward. When the chairs were grouped around small tables so that patients faced each other at a comfortable distance, the number of conversations doubled.[35]

The design of an entire building can shape communication among its users. Architects have learned that the way housing projects are designed controls to a great extent the contact neighbors have with each other. People who live in apartments near stairways and mailboxes have many more neighbor contacts than do those living in less heavily traveled parts of the building, and tenants generally have more contacts with immediate neighbors than with people even a few doors away.[36] Architects now use this information to design buildings that either encourage communication or increase privacy, and house hunters can use the same knowledge to choose a home that gives them the neighborhood relationships they want.

So far we have talked about how designing an environment can shape communication, but there is another side to consider. Watching how people use an already existing environment can be a way of telling what kind of relationships they want. For example, Sommer watched students in a college library and found that there's a definite pattern for people who want to study alone. While the library was uncrowded, students almost always chose corner seats at one of the empty rectangular tables.[37] Finally, each table was occupied by one reader. New readers would then choose a seat on the opposite side and far end of an occupied table, thus keeping the maximum distance between themselves and the other readers. One of Sommer's associates tried violating these "rules" by sitting next to, and across from, other female readers when more distant seats were available. She found that the approached women reacted defensively, either by signaling their discomfort through shifts in posture or gesturing or by eventually moving away.

▶ SUMMARY

Nonverbal communication consists of messages expressed by nonlinguistic means. Thus, it is inaccurate to say that all wordless expressions are nonverbal or that all spoken statements are totally verbal.

There are several important characteristics of nonverbal communication. First is the simple fact that it exists—that communication occurs even in the absence of language. This leads to the second principle, namely, that it is impossible not to communicate nonverbally; humans constantly send messages about themselves that are available for others to receive. The third principle is that nonverbal communication is ambiguous; that there are many possible interpretations for any behavior. This ambiguity makes it important for the receiver to verify any interpretation before jumping to conclusions about the meaning of a nonverbal message. The fourth principle states that much nonverbal communication is culture-bound. In other words, behaviors that have special meanings in one culture may express different messages in another. Finally, we stated that nonverbal communication serves many functions: repeating, substituting, complementing, accenting, regulating, and contradicting verbal behavior.

We also examined the differences between verbal and nonverbal communication. Whereas verbal messages occupy a single channel and must be received one at a time, many nonverbal messages occur simultaneously in everyday situations. Nonverbal messages are also continuous whereas verbal ones are discrete, having beginnings and endings. Verbal messages are usually intentional whereas nonverbal ones are often expressed unintentionally. Finally, verbal messages are less ambiguous than nonverbal ones, which are almost always open to more than one interpretation.

The remainder of this chapter introduced the many ways humans communicate nonverbally: through posture, gesture, use of the face and eyes, voice, touch, clothing, distance, territoriality, and physical environment.

ACTIVITIES ◄

1. This exercise will both increase your skill in observing nonverbal behavior and show you the dangers of being too sure that you're a perfect reader of body language. You can try the exercise either in or out of class, and the period of time over which you do it is flexible, from a single-class period to several days. In any case, begin by choosing a partner, and then follow these directions:

   a. For the first period of time (however long you decide to make it), observe the way your partner behaves. Notice how he or she moves; his or her mannerisms, postures, way of speaking; how he or she dresses; and so on. To remember your observations, jot them down. If you're doing this exercise out of class over an extended period of time, there's no need to let your observations interfere with whatever you'd normally be doing: Your only job here is to compile a list of your partner's behaviors. In this step, you should be careful *not* to interpret your partner's actions; just record what you *see*.

   b. At the end of the time period, share what you've seen with your partner. He or she will do the same with you.

   c. For the next period of time, your job is not only to observe your partner's behavior but also to *interpret* it. This time in your conference you should tell your partner what you thought his or her actions revealed. For example, if your partner dressed carelessly, did you think this meant he or she overslept, that he or she is losing interest in his or her appearance, or that he or she was trying to be more comfortable? If you noticed him or her yawning frequently, did you think this meant he or she was bored, tired from a late night, or sleepy after a big meal? Don't feel bad if your guesses weren't all correct. Remember that nonverbal clues tend to be ambiguous. You may be surprised how checking out the nonverbal clues you observe can help build a relationship with another person.

2. Use your own nonverbal behavior and that of others to provide examples of each function:
   a. Repeating
   b. Substituting
   c. Complementing
   d. Accenting
   e. Regulating
   f. Contradicting

3. Explore the significance of nonverbal behavior by violating some cultural rules that govern appropriate communication. *Note:* Be sure your violations aren't so extreme that they generate a harmful reaction. Commit one violation in each of the following areas:
   a. Eye contact
   b. Vocal cues
   c. Touch
   d. Clothing
   e. Distance
   f. Territoriality

Report the results of your experiments in class.

▶ **NOTES**

1. For a survey of the issues surrounding the definition of nonverbal communication, see Mark Knapp, *Nonverbal Communication in Human Interaction,* 2d ed. (Englewood Cliffs, N.J.: Prentice-Hall, 1978), pp. 2–12.
2. See, for example, R. Rosenthal, J. A. Hall, M. R. D. Matteg, P. L. Rogers, and D. Archer, *Sensitivity to Nonverbal Communication: The PONS Test* (Baltimore: Johns Hopkins University Press, 1979).
3. J. A. Hall, "Gender, Gender Roles, and Nonverbal Communication Skills," in R. Rosenthal (ed.), *Skill in Nonverbal Communication: Individual Differences* (Cambridge, Mass.: Oelgeschlager, Gunn, and Hain, 1979), pp. 32–67.
4. Maurice M. Krout, "Symbolism," in Haig A. Bosmajian (ed.), *The Rhetoric of Nonverbal Communication* (Glenview, Ill.: Scott, Foresman, 1971), pp. 19–22.
5. Edward T. Hall, *The Hidden Dimension* (Garden City, N.Y.: Anchor, 1969), pp. 160–161.
6. M. LaFrance and C. Mayo, "Racial Differences in Gaze Behavior During Conversations: Two Systematic Observational Studies," *Journal of Personality and Social Psychology* 33 (1976): 547–552.
7. Hall, op. cit.
8. C. R. Kleinke, "Compliance to Requests Made by Gazing and Touching Experimenters in Field Settings," *Journal of Experimental Social Psychology* 13 (1977): 218–233.
9. Knapp, op. cit., p. 22.
10. Albert Mehrabian, *Silent Messages,* 2d ed. (Belmont, Calif.: Wadsworth, 1981), pp. 47–48.
11. M. B. Myers, D. Templer, and R. Brown, "Coping Ability of Women Who Become Victims of Rape," *Journal of Consulting and Clinical Psychology* 52 (1984): 73–78. See also C. Rubenstein, "Body Language That Speaks to Muggers," *Psychology Today* 20 (August 1980): 20; and J. Meer, "Profile of a Victim," *Psychology Today* 24 (May 1984): 76.
12. A. E. Scheflen, "Quasi-Courting Behavior in Psychotherapy," *Psychiatry* 228 (1965): 245–257.

13. Ekman, *Telling Lies: Clues to Deceit in the Marketplace, Politics, and Marriage* (New York: Norton, 1985), pp. 109–110.
14. P. Ekman and W. V. Friesen, "Nonverbal Behavior and Psychopathology," in R. J. Friedman and M. N. Katz (eds.), *The Psychology of Depression: Contemporary Theory and Research* (Washington, D.C.: J. Winston, 1974).
15. Ekman, *Telling Lies,* p. 107.
16. Paul Ekman and Wallace V. Friesen, *Unmasking the Face* (Englewood Cliffs, N.J.: Prentice-Hall, 1975).
17. Paul Ekman, Wallace V. Friesen, and P. Ellsworth, *Emotion in the Human Face: Guidelines for Research and an Integration of Findings* (Elmsford, N.Y.: Pergamon, 1972).
18. J. A. Starkweather, "Vocal Communication of Personality and Human Feeling," *Journal of Communication* 11 (1961): 69; and K. R. Scherer, J. Koiwunaki, and R. Rosenthal, "Minimal Cues in the Vocal Communication of Affect: Judging Emotions from Content-Masked Speech," *Journal of Psycholinguistic Speech* 1 (1972): 269–285.
19. K. L. Burns and E. G. Beier, "Significance of Vocal and Visual Channels for the Decoding of Emotional Meaning," *The Journal of Communication* 23 (1973): 118–130. See also Timothy G. Hegstrom, "Message Impact: What Percentage Is Nonverbal?" *Western Journal of Speech Communication* 43 (19779): 134–143; and E. M. McMahan, "Nonverbal Communication as a Function of Attribution in Impression Formation," *Communication Monographs* 43 (1976): 287–294.
20. A. Mehrabian and M. Weiner, "Decoding of Inconsistent Communications," *Journal of Personality and Social Psychology* 6 (1967): 109–114.
21. Ekman, *Telling Lies,* p. 93.
22. Ashley Montagu, *Touching: The Human Significance of the Skin* (New York: Harper & Row, 1972), p. 93.
23. Ibid., pp. 244–249.
24. L. J. Yarrow, "Research in Dimension of Early Maternal Care," *Merrill-Palmer Quarterly* 9 (1963): 101–122.
25. Richard Heslin and Tari Alper, "Touch: A Bonding Gesture," in John M. Wiemann and Randall Harrison (eds.), *Nonverbal Interaction* (Beverly Hills, Calif.: Sage, 1983).
26. W. Thourlby, *You Are What You Wear* (New York: New American Library, 1978), p. 1.
27. J. H. Fortenberry, J. Maclean, P. Morris, and M. O'Connell, "Mode of Dress as a Perceptual Cue to Deference," *The Journal of Social Psychology* 104 (1978).
28. L. Bickman, "Social Roles and Uniforms: Clothes Make the Person," *Psychology Today* 7 (April 1974): 48–51.
29. M. Lefkowitz, R. R. Blake, and J. S. Mouton, "Status of Actors in Pedestrian Violation of Traffic Signals," *Journal of Abnormal and Social Psychology* 51 (1955): 704–706.
30. T. F. Hoult, "Experimental Measurement of Clothing as a Factor in Some Social Ratings of Selected American Men," *American Sociological Review* 19 (1954): 326–327.
31. E. T. Hall, op. cit., pp. 113–130.
32. Mehrabian, op. cit., p. 69.
33. A. H. Maslow and N. L. Mintz, "Effects of Esthetic Surroundings," *Journal of Psychology* 41 (1956): 247–254.
34. Robert Sommer, *Personal Space: The Behavioral Basis of Design* (Englewood Cliffs, N.J.: Spectrum), pp. 122–123.
35. Leon Festinger, S. Schachter, and K. Back, *Social Pressures in Informal Groups: A Study of Human Factors in Housing* (New York: Harper & Row, 1950).
36. Sommer, op. cit., p. 78.
37. Ibid., p. 35.

▶CHAPTER 6

KEY TERMS

content message
impersonal communication
interpersonal communication
interpersonal relationship
Johari Window

metacommunication
relational message
self-disclosure
social penetration

UNDERSTANDING INTERPERSONAL RELATIONSHIPS

After reading this chapter, you should understand the following:

1. The characteristics that distinguish interpersonal relationships from impersonal ones.

2. The content and relational dimensions of every message.

3. The role of metacommunication in conveying relational messages.

4. The seven reasons for forming relationships discussed in this chapter.

5. The characteristics of disclosing and nondisclosing communication.

6. The guidelines for appropriate self-disclosure.

You should be able to do the following:

1. Identify the extent to which each of your relationships is interpersonal or impersonal, describe your level of satisfaction with these relationships, and suggest ways to make them more satisfactory.

2. Identify the content and relational dimensions of a message.

3. Describe the factors that have contributed to the formation of your important relationships.

4. Identify the degree of self-disclosure in your relationships and the functions this disclosing communication serves.

5. Compose disclosing messages that follow the guidelines listed in this chapter.

"Relationship" is one of those words people use a great deal yet have a hard time defining. See if you can explain the term before reading on: It isn't as easy as it might seem.

The dictionary defines a relationship as "the mode in which two or more things stand to one another." This is true enough: You are tall in relation to some people and short in relation to others, and we are more or less wealthy only in comparison to others. But physical and economic relationships don't tell us much that is useful about interpersonal communication.

Interpersonal relationships involve the way people deal with one another *socially*. But what is it about their social interaction that defines a relationship? What makes some relationships "good" and others "bad"? We can answer this question by recalling the three kinds of social needs introduced in Chapter 1: inclusion, control, and affection. When we judge the quality of personal relationships, we are usually describing how well those social needs are being met. Having come this far, we can define the term **interpersonal relationship** as an association in which the parties meet each other's social needs to a greater or lesser degree.

▶ CHARACTERISTICS OF INTERPERSONAL RELATIONSHIPS

What is interpersonal communication? How does it differ from other types of interaction? When and how are interpersonal messages communicated? Read on and see.

Interpersonal vs. Impersonal Communication

One way to define interpersonal communication is by looking at how many people are involved and how much access they have to one another. In this sense, a salesclerk and a customer or a police officer ticketing a speeding driver would be examples of interpersonal acts (two-person, face-to-face meetings) whereas a teacher and class or authors such as us and readers like you would not be.

You can probably sense that there's something wrong with this definition. The kind of exchanges that often go on between salespeople and their customers or bureaucrats and the public hardly seem interpersonal . . . or personal in any sense of the word. In fact, after transactions like this, we commonly remark, "I might as well have been talking to a machine." And conversely, some "public" kinds of communication seem quite personal. Teachers, religious ministers, and entertainers often establish a personal relationship with their audiences, and we certainly hope this book has at least some personal flavor.

If context doesn't make communication interpersonal, what does? When we talk about interpersonal communication in this book, we're referring to the *quality* of interaction between individuals.[1] In **interpersonal communication** we treat others as individuals whereas in **impersonal communication** we treat them as objects.[2] This definition doesn't mean that all impersonal communication is cruel or that you need to establish a warm relationship with every person you meet. The fact to remember here is that not all two-person interaction is interpersonal.

Several characteristics distinguish interpersonal relationships from impersonal ones. First, in less personal relationships we tend to classify the other person by using *labels*. We fit others into neat pigeonholes: "Anglo," "woman," "professor," "yuppie," and so on. Such labels may be accurate as far as they go, but they hardly describe everything that is important about the other person. On the other hand, it's almost impossible to use one or two labels to describe someone you know well. "She's not *just* a police officer," you want to say. Or, "Sure, he's against abortions, but there's more. ..."

A second element in interpersonal relationships is the degree to which communicators rely on *standardized rules* to guide their interactions. When we meet someone for the first time, we know how to behave because of the established social rules we have been taught. We shake hands, speak politely, and rely on socially accepted subjects: "How are you?" "What do you do?" "Lousy weather we've been having." The rules governing our interaction have little to do with us or the people with whom we interact; we are not responding to each other as individuals.

As we continue to interact, however, we sometimes gain more information about each other, and we use that information as the basis for our communicating. As we share experiences, the rules that govern our behavior will be less determined by cultural rules and more determined by the unique features of our own relationship. This doesn't mean that we abandon rules altogether but rather that we often create our *own* conventions, ones that are appropriate for

us. For example, one pair of friends might develop a procedure for dealing with conflicts by expressing their disagreements as soon as they arise whereas another could tacitly agree to withhold a series of gripes, then clear the air periodically. Although we could digress here and speculate about which procedure is more productive, the important point to recognize is that in both cases the individuals created their own rules.

A third characteristic that distinguishes interpersonal relationships from impersonal ones involve the *amount of information* the communicators have about each other. When we meet people for the first time, we have little information about them, usually no more than what we are told by others and the assumptions we make from observing what they wear and how they handle their bodies. As we talk, we gain more information in a variety of areas. The first topics we talk about are usually nonthreatening, nonintimate ones. If we continue talking, however, we may decide to discuss relatively few impersonal things. We may decide to increase the number of topics we talk about and choose to be more revealing of ourselves in doing so.

As we learn more about each other and as our information becomes more intimate, the degree to which we share an interpersonal relationship increases. This new degree of intimacy and sharing can occur almost immediately or else may grow slowly over a long period of time. In either case, we can say that the relationship becomes more interpersonal as the amount of self-disclosure increases. We'll have a great deal to say about this subject in the following pages.

If we accept the characteristics of individual regard, creation of unique rules, and sharing of personal information as criteria for a developmentally interpersonal relationship, several implications follow. First, many one-to-one relationships never reach an interpersonal state. This is not surprising in itself because establishing a close relationship takes time and effort. In fact, such relationships

are not always desirable or appropriate. Some people, however, fool themselves into thinking that they have close interpersonal friendships when, in fact, their associations are interpersonal only in a situational context.

Another implication that follows from looking at interpersonal communication in developmental terms is that the ability to communicate interpersonally is a skill people possess in varying degrees. For example, some comm;unicators are adept at recognizing nonverbal messages, listening effectively, acting supportively, and resolving conflicts in satisfying ways whereas others have no ability or no idea how to do so. The skills you will learn by studying the material in this book can help you become a more skillful communicator.

Content and Relational Messages

Virtually every verbal statement has a content dimension, containing the subject being discussed. The content of such statements as "It's your turn to do the dishes" or "I'm busy Saturday night" is obvious.

Content messages aren't the only thing being exchanged when two people communicate. In addition, almost every message—both verbal and nonverbal—also has a second, **relational** dimension, which makes statements about how the parties feel toward one another.[3] These relational messages deal with one or more social needs, most commonly inclusion, control, affection, or respect. Consider the two examples we just mentioned:

—Imagine two ways of saying "It's your turn to do the dishes": one that is demanding and another that is matter-of-fact. Notice how the different nonverbal messages make statements about how the sender views control in this part of the relationship. The demanding tone says, in effect, "I have a right to tell you what to do around the house," whereas the matter-of-fact one suggests, "I'm just reminding you of something you might have overlooked."

—You can easily visualize two ways to deliver the statement "I'm busy Saturday night": one with little affection and the other with much liking.

Notice that in each of these examples the relational dimension of the message was never discussed. In fact, most of the time we aren't conscious of the many relational messages that bombard us every day. Sometimes we are unaware of relational messages because they match our belief about the amount of respect, inclusion, control, and affection that is appropriate. For example, you probably won't be offended if your boss tells you to do a certain job because you agree that supervisors have the right to direct employees. In other cases, however, conflicts arise over relational messages even though content is not disputed. If your boss delivers the order in a condescending, sarcastic, or abusive tone of voice, you probably will be offended. Your complaint wouldn't be with the order itself but with the way it was delivered. "I may work for this company," you might think, "but I'm not a slave or an idiot. I deserve to be treated like a human being."

How are relational messages communicated? As the boss-employee example suggests, they are usually expressed nonverbally. To test this fact for yourself, imagine how you could act while saying, "Can you help me for a minute?" in a way that communicates each of the following relationships:

superiority	aloofness
helplessness	sexual desire
friendliness	irritation

Although nonverbal behaviors are a good source of relational messages, remember that they are ambiguous. The sharp tone you take as a personal insult might be due to fatigue, and the interruption you take as an attempt to ignore your ideas might be a sign of pressure that has nothing to do with you. Before you jump to conclusions about relational clues, it's a good idea to practice the skill of perception checking that you learned in Chapter 2: "When you use that tone of voice to tell me it's my turn to do the dishes, I get the idea you're mad at me. Is that right?" If your interpretation was indeed correct, you can talk about the problem. On the other hand, if you were overreacting, the perception check can prevent a needless fight.

Metacommunication

As the preceding example of perception checking shows, not all relational messages are nonverbal. Social scientists use the term **metacommunication** to describe messages that refer to other messages.[4] In other words, metacommunication is communication about communication. Whenever we discuss a rela-

"It would work with us, Francine. We share the same narrow personal interests and concerns."

Drawing by Dana Fradon; © 1979 The New Yorker Magazine, Inc.

tionship with others, we are metacommunicating: "I wish we could stop arguing so much" or "I appreciate how honest you've been with me." Verbal metacommunication is an essential ingredient in successful relationships. Sooner or later there are times when it becomes necessary to talk about what is going on between you and the other person. The ability to focus on the kinds of issues described in this chapter can be the tool for keeping the relationship on track.

Metacommunication is an important method for solving conflicts in a constructive manner. It provides a way to shift discussion from the content level to relational questions, where the problem often lies. For example, consider the case of a couple bickering because one partner wants to watch television while the other wants to talk. Imagine how much better the chances of a positive outcome would be if they used metacommunication to examine the relational problems that were behind their quarrel: "Look, it's not the TV watching itself that bothers me. It's that I imagine you watch so much because you're mad at me or bored. Are you feeling bad about us?"

Metacommunication isn't just a tool for handling problems. It is also a way to reinforce the good aspects of a relationship: "I really appreciate it when you compliment me about my work in front of the boss." Comments like this serve two functions: First, they let others know that you value their behavior. Second, they boost the odds that the other person will continue the behavior in the future.

REASONS FOR FORMING RELATIONSHIPS ◄

Why do we start to develop relationships with some people and prefer not to develop relationships with others? Social scientists have explored several possible reasons, each of which represents a theory of relationship formation and maintenance.[5]

We Like People Who Are Similar to Us—Usually

That we like people who are like us should come as no surprise. One of the first steps in getting acquainted with a stranger is the search for common ground—interests, experiences, or other factors you share. When you find similarities, you usually feel some kind of attraction toward the person who is like you.

This doesn't mean that the key to popularity is to agree with everyone about everything. Research shows that attraction is greatest when we are similar to others in a high percentage of important areas. For example, a couple who support each other's career goals, like the same friends, and have similar beliefs about human rights can tolerate trivial disagreements about the merits of sushi or Miles Davis. With enough similarity in key areas, they can even survive disputes about more important subjects, such as how much time to spend with their families or whether separate vacations are acceptable. But if the number and content of disagreements becomes too great, the relationship may be threatened.

**UNDERSTANDING
INTERPERSONAL
RELATIONSHIPS**

Similarity turns from attraction to repulsion when we encounter people who are like us in many ways but who behave in a strange or socially offensive manner. For instance, you have probably disliked people others have said were "just like you" but who talked too much, were complainers, or had some other unappealing characteristic. In fact, there is a tendency to have stronger dislike for similar but offensive people than for those who are offensive but different. One likely reason is that such people threaten our self-esteem, causing us to fear that we may be as unappealing as they are. In such circumstances, the reaction is often to put as much distance as possible between ourselves and this threat to our ideal self-image.

We Like People Who Are Different from Us—in Certain Ways

The fact that "opposites attract" seems to contradict the principle of similarity we just described. In truth, though, both are valid. Differences strengthen a relationship when they are *complementary*—when each partner's characteristics satisfy the other's needs. Couples, for instance, are more likely to be attracted to each other when one partner is dominant and the other passive. Relationships also work well when the partners agree that one will exercise control in certain areas ("You make the final decisions about money") and the other will take the lead in different ones ("I'll decide how we ought to decorate the place"). Strains occur when control issues are disputed.

Studies that have examined successful and unsuccessful couples over a twenty-year period show the interaction between similarities and differences. The research demonstrates that partners in successful marriages were similar enough to satisfy each other physically and mentally but were different enough to meet each other's needs and keep the relationship interesting. The successful couples found ways to keep a balance between their similarities and differences, adjusting to the changes that occurred over the years.

We Like People Who Like Us—Usually

Being liked by others is a strong source of attraction, especially in the early stages of a relationship. At that time, we are attracted to people who we believe are attracted to us. Conversely, we will probably not feel good about people who either attack or seem indifferent to us. After we get to know others, their liking becomes less of a factor. By then we form our preferences more from the other reasons listed in this section.

It's no mystery why reciprocal liking builds attractiveness. People who approve of us bolster our feelings of self-esteem. This approval is rewarding in its own right, and it can also confirm a self-concept that says, "I'm a likable person."

You can probably think of cases where you haven't liked people who seemed to like you. These experiences usually fall into two categories. Sometimes we think the other person's supposed liking is counterfeit—an insincere device to get something from us. The acquaintance who becomes friendly whenever he or she needs to borrow your car or the employee whose flattery of the boss seems to be a device to get a raise are examples. This sort of behavior really isn't "liking" at all. The second category of unappealing liking occurs when the other person's approval doesn't fit with our own self-concept. We cling to an existing self-concept even when it is unrealistically unfavorable. When someone tells you that you're good-looking, intelligent, and kind, but you believe you are ugly, stupid, and mean, you may choose to disregard the flattering information and remain in your familiar state of unhappiness. Groucho Marx summarized this attitude when he said he would never join any club that would have a person like him as a member.

We Are Attracted to People Who Can Help Us

Some relationships are based on a semieconomic model called *exchange theory.* It suggests that we often seek out people who can give us rewards—either physical or emotional—that are greater than, or equal to, the costs we encounter in dealing with them. When we operate on the basis of exchange, we decide (often unconsciously) whether dealing with another person is "a good deal" or "not worth the effort."

At its most blatant level, an exchange approach seems cold and calculating, but in some dimensions of a relationship it can be reasonable. A healthy business relationship is based on how well the parties help one another out, and some friendships are based on an informal kind of barter: "I don't mind listening to the ups and downs of your love life because you rescue me when the house needs repairs." Even close relationships have an element of exchange. Husbands and wives tolerate each other's quirks because the comfort and enjoyment they get make the unhappy times worth accepting. Most deeply satisfying relationships, however, are built on more than just the benefits that make them a good deal.

We Like Competent People—
Particularly When They Are "Human"

We like to be around talented people, probably because we hope their skills and abilities will rub off on us. On the other hand, we are uncomfortable around those who are *too* competent—probably because we look bad by comparison.

Given these contrasting attitudes, it's no surprise that people are generally attracted to others who are talented but who have visible flaws that show they are human, just like us. There are some qualifications to this principle. People with especially high or low self-esteem find "perfect" people more attractive than those who are competent but flawed, and some studies suggest that women tend to be more impressed by uniformly superior people of both sexes whereas men find desirable but "human" subjects especially attractive. On the whole, though, the principle stands: The best way to gain the liking of others is to be good at what you do but to admit your mistakes.

We Are Attracted to People Who Disclose Themselves to Us—
Appropriately

Telling others important information about yourself can help build liking. Sometimes the basis of this attraction comes from learning about ways we are similar, either in experiences ("I broke off an engagement myself") or in attitudes ("I feel nervous with strangers too"). Another reason why self-disclosure increases liking is because it is a sign of regard. When people share private information with you, it suggests they respect and trust you—a kind of liking that we've already seen increases attractiveness.

Not all disclosure leads to liking. People whose sharing is poorly timed often meet with bad results. It's probably unwise, for example, to talk about your sexual insecurities with a new acquaintance or to express your pet peeves to a friend at her birthday party. In addition to bad timing, opening up too much can also be a mistake. Research shows that people are judged as attractive when their disclosure matches that of the other person in a relationship. See pages 155–157 for more guidelines about when and how to self-disclose.

We Feel Strongly About People We Encounter Often

As common sense suggests, we are likely to develop relationships with people we interact with frequently. In many cases, proximity leads to liking. We're more likely to develop friendships with close neighbors than with distant ones, for instance; and several studies show that the chances are good that we'll choose a mate whom we cross paths with often. Facts like these are understandable when we consider that proximity allows us to get more information about the other people and benefit from a relationship with them.

Familiarity, on the other hand, can also breed contempt. Evidence to support this fact comes from police blotters as well as university laboratories. Thieves frequently prey on nearby victims even though the risk of being recognized is greater. Most aggravated assaults occur within the family or among close neighbors. Within the law, the same principle holds: You are likely to develop strong personal feelings of either liking or disliking regarding others you encounter frequently.

STAGES OF RELATIONAL DEVELOPMENT ◀

Although relationships come in many types and "sizes," social scientists have found that they all grow and dissolve by passing through similar phases. These phases can be broken into as few as three parts (initiation, maintenance, and dissolution) or as many as ten, which we'll now examine. These ten stages are outlined by Mark Knapp.[6] (See Table 6–1.)

Initiation

The stage of initiation involves the initial making of contact with another person. Knapp restricts this stage to conversation openers, both in initial contacts and with previous acquaintances: "Nice to meet you," "How's it going?" and so on.

Although an initial encounter *is* necessary to the succeeding interaction, its importance is overemphasized in books advising how to pick up men and women. These books suggest fail-proof openers ranging from "Excuse me, I'm from out of town, and I was wondering what people do around here at night?" to "How long do you cook a leg of lamb?" Whatever your preference for opening remarks, this stage is important because you are formulating your first impressions and presenting yourself as interested in the other person.

Experimenting

In the stage of experimenting, the conversation develops as the people get acquainted by making "small talk." We ask: "Where are you from?" or "What do you do?" or "Do you know Josephine Mandoza? She lives in San Francisco, too."

Though small talk might seem meaningless, Knapp points out that it serves four purposes:

1. It is a useful process for uncovering integrating topics and openings for more penetrating conversation.
2. It can be an audition for a future friendship or a way of increasing the scope of a current relationship.
3. It provides a safe procedure for indicating who we are and how another can come to know us better (reduction of uncertainty).
4. It allows us to maintain a sense of community with our fellow human beings.

The relationship during this stage is generally pleasant and uncritical, and the commitments are minimal. Experimenting may last ten minutes or ten years.

Knapp argues that most relationships never go beyond the experimentation stage.

Intensifying

When a relationship does go beyond experimenting, the intensification phase is one in which it develops a character of its own indicated by a common identity: "We like to dance." You come to know the other person and develop accuracy in predicting the other's wants and whims. You are more accessible to that person and may use less formal terms, including nicknames and special terms of endearment. A truly *interpersonal relationship* begins on this level.

Integrating

At the point of integrating, the sense of union of the two people is heightened further—the interpersonal synchrony is high. You become identified by others as "a pair," "an item." This oneness may be accented by similar clothing styles, increased similarities in what you talk about, phrasing of terms, and the designation of common property—for example, *our* song, *our* meeting time, or *our* project.

Bonding

When the relationship reaches the bonding stage, it achieves some formal social recognition. This can take the form of a contract to be business partners or a license to be married. During this stage, more regulations for the interaction are established. Expectations might include spending all free time together, consulting one another about spending money, or dressing only in ways that the other approves.

Differentiating

Once the two people have formed this commonality, they begin to reestablish individual identities. How are we different? How am I unique? Former identifications as "we" now emphasize "I." Differentiation often first occurs when a relationship experiences its first, inevitable conflicts. Whereas a happy employee might refer to "our company," the description might change to "their company" when a raise or some other request isn't forthcoming. We see this kind of differentiation when parents argue over the misbehavior of a child: "Did you see what *your* son just did?"

Differentiation can be positive, too, for people need to be individuals as well as parts of a relationship. The key to successful differentiation is the need to maintain commitment to a relationship while creating the space for members to be individuals as well.

Circumscribing

So far we have been looking at the growth of relationships. Although some reach a plateau of development, going on successfully for as long as a lifetime, others pass through several stages of decline and dissolution. In the circumscribing stage, communication between members decreases in quantity and quality. Restrictions and restraints characterize this stage, and dynamic communication becomes static. Rather than discuss a disagreement (which requires some degree of energy on both parts), members opt for withdrawal: either mental (silence or daydreaming and fantasizing) or physical (where people spend less time together). Circumscribing doesn't involve total avoidance, which comes later. Rather, it entails a certain shrinking of interest and commitment.

Stagnation

If circumscribing continues, the relationship begins to stagnate. Members behave toward each other in old, familiar ways without much feeling. No growth occurs. The relationship is a shadow of its former self. We see stagnation in many workers who have lost enthusiasm for their job yet continue to go through the motions for years. The same sad event occurs for some couples who unenthusiastically have the same conversations, see the same people, and follow the same routines without any sense of joy or novelty.

TABLE 6–1 An Overview of Interaction Stages

PROCESS	STAGE	REPRESENTATIVE DIALOGUE
Coming together	Initiating	"Hi, how ya doin'?" "Fine. You?"
	Experimenting	"Oh, so you like to ski...so do I." "You do?! Great. Where do you go?"
	Intensifying	"I...I think I love you." "I love you too."
	Integrating	"I feel so much a part of you." "Yeah, we are like one person. What happens to you happens to me."
	Bonding	"I want to be with you always." "Let's get married."
Coming apart	Differentiating	"I just don't like big social gatherings." "Sometimes I don't understand you. This is one area where I'm certainly not like you at all."
	Circumscribing	"Did you have a good time on your trip?" "What time will dinner be ready?"
	Stagnating	"What's there to talk about?" "Right. I know what you're going to say, and you know what I'm going to say."
	Avoiding	"I'm so busy, I just don't know when I'll be able to see you." "If I'm not around when you try, you'll understand."
	Terminating	"I'm leaving you...and don't bother trying to contact me." "Don't worry."

Reprinted with permission from Mark L. Knapp, *Interpersonal Communication and Human Relationships* (Boston: Allyn & Bacon, 1984).

Avoiding

When stagnation becomes too unpleasant, parties in a relationship begin to create distance between each other. Sometimes this is done under the guise of excuses ("I've been sick lately and can't see you") and sometimes it is done directly ("Please don't call me; I don't want to see you now"). In either case, by this point the handwriting about the relationship's future is clearly on the wall.

Termination

Characteristics of this final stage include summary dialogues about where the relationship has gone and the desire to dissociate. The relationship may end with a cordial dinner, a note left on the kitchen table, a phone call, or a legal document stating the dissolution. Depending on each person's feelings, this stage can be quite short, or it may be drawn out over time, with bitter jabs at one another. In either case, termination doesn't have to be totally negative. Understanding one another's investments in the relationship and needs for personal growth may dilute the hard feelings.

After outlining these ten steps, Knapp discusses several assumptions about his model. First, movement through the stages is generally sequential and systematic. We proceed at a steady pace and usually don't skip steps. It's unlikely, for example, to jump immediately from the initiating stage of a friendship to a bonding stage of being closest friends without moving through a time of experimenting, intensifying, and integrating.

Movement along the relational continuum isn't always straightforward. Sometimes relationships move forward, regress to previous stages, and then move forward again. Many marriages, for example, fluctuate between periods of bonding and differentiating in a cyclical manner. Partners often go through a time of intense closeness and then spend time pursuing their own interests before rebonding. In this sense, interpersonal relationships are cyclical systems.

Not every relationship moves through all the stages listed in Table 6–1. Certain relationships stabilize at a particular stage, and others follow the pattern described in the last paragraph, oscillating between two or more stages. Many superficial or limited friendships and working relationships stabilize at the experimenting stage without ever involving the kind of self-disclosure and commitment that comes with a more interpersonal bond.

SELF-DISCLOSURE IN RELATIONSHIPS ◀

We have already seen that one way to judge the strength of a relationship is by the breadth and depth of information about themselves that the parties share with one another. Furthermore, we've cited research on attraction showing that appropriate self-disclosure can increase a person's attractiveness. Given these facts, we need to take a closer look at the subject of self-disclosure. Just what is it? When is it desirable? How is it best done?

The best place to begin is with a definition. **Self-disclosure** is the process of deliberately revealing information about oneself that is significant and that would not normally be known by others. Let's take a closer look at some parts of this definition. Self-disclosure must be *deliberate*. If you accidentally mentioned to a friend that you were thinking about quitting a job or proposing marriage, that information would not fit into the category we are examining here. On the other hand, if you intentionally shared information that wasn't *significant*—the fact that you like fudge, for example—it's obvious that no important disclosure occurred. Our third requirement is that the information being disclosed would *not be known by others*. There's nothing noteworthy about telling others that you are depressed or elated if they already know how you're feeling.

Levels of Disclosing and Nondisclosing Communication

Although our definition of self-disclosure is helpful, it doesn't reveal the important fact that not all self-disclosure is equally revealing—that some disclosing messages tell more about us than others.

Social psychologists Irwin Altman and Dalmas Taylor describe two ways in which communication can be more or less disclosing.[7] Their **social penetration** model is pictured in Figure 6–1. The first dimension of self-disclosure in this model involves the *breadth* of information volunteered—the range of subjects being discussed. For example, the breadth of disclosure in your relationship with a fellow worker will expand as you begin revealing information about your life away from the job, as well as on-the-job details. The second dimension of disclosure is the *depth* of the information being volunteered, the shift from relatively nonrevealing messages to more personal ones.

Depending on the breadth and depth of information shared, a relationship can be defined as casual or intimate. In a casual relationship, the breadth may be great, but not the depth. A more intimate relationship is likely to have high depth in at least one area. The most intimate relationships are those in which disclosure is great in both breadth and depth. Altman and Taylor see the development of a relationship as a progression from the periphery of their model to its center, a process that typically occurs over time. Each of your personal relationships probably has a different combination of breadth of subjects and depth of disclosure. Figure 6–2 pictures a student's self-disclosure in one relationship.

What makes some messages deeper than others? One way to understand the various levels of self-disclosure is to picture a series of four concentric circles. (See Figure 6–3.) Each circle represents a different type of communication. As a rule, the inner levels are more revealing than the outer ones. An examination of each level will explain their differences.

FIGURE 6–1
Social Penetration Model

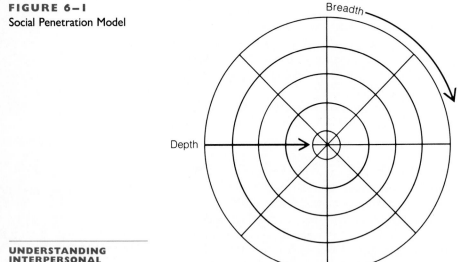

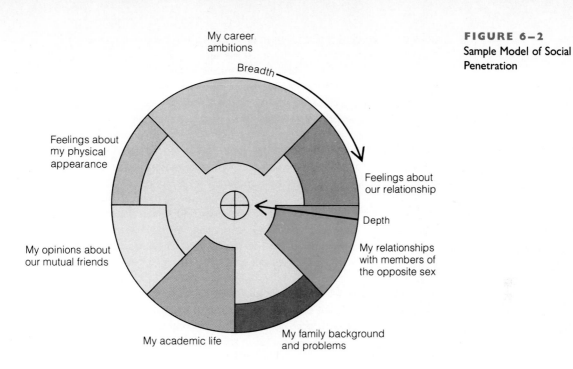

FIGURE 6-2
Sample Model of Social
Penetration

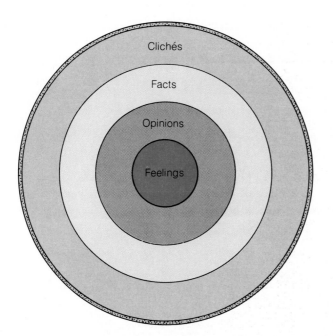

FIGURE 6-3
Levels of Self-Disclosure

UNDERSTANDING
INTERPERSONAL
RELATIONSHIPS

CLICHES The outermost layer consists of clichés: "How are you doing?" "Fine!" "We'll have to get together some time."

Remarks such as these usually aren't meant to be taken literally; in fact, the other person would be surprised if you responded to a casual "How are you?" with a lengthy speech on your health, state of mind, love life, or finances. Yet it's a mistake to consider clichés meaningless, for they serve several useful functions. For instance, they can give two speakers time to size each other up and decide whether it's desirable to carry their conversation any further. Our first impressions are generally based more on the nonverbal characteristics of the other person than on the words we hear spoken. Things like eye contact, vocal tone, facial expression, posture, and so on can often tell us more about another person than can the initial sentences in a conversation. Given the value of these nonverbal cues and the awkwardness of actually saying, "I want to take a few minutes to look you over before I commit myself to getting acquainted," the exchange of a few stock phrases can be just the thing to get you through this initial period comfortably.

Clichés can also serve as codes for other messages we don't usually express directly, such as "I want to acknowledge your presence" (for instance, when two acquaintances walk past each other). Additional unstated messages often contained in clichés are "I'm interested in talking if you feel like it" or "Let's keep the conversation light and impersonal; I don't feel like disclosing much about myself right now." Accompoanied by a different set of nonverbal cues, a cliché can say, "I don't want to be impolite, but you'd better stay away from me for now." In all these cases, clichés serve as a valuable kind of shorthand that makes it easy to keep the social wheels greased and indicates the potential for further, possibly more profound conversation.

FACTS Moving inward from clichés on our model brings us to the level of volunteering *facts*. Not all factual statements qualify as self-disclosure: They must fit the criteria of being intentional, significant, and not otherwise known:

> "This isn't my first try at college, I dropped out a year ago with terrible grades."

> "I'm practically engaged." (On meeting a stranger while away from home.)

> "That idea that everyone thought was so clever wasn't really mine. I read it in a book last year."

Facts like these can be meaningful in themselves, but they also have a greater significance in a relationship. Disclosing important information suggests a level of trust and commitment to the other person that signals a desire to move the relationship to a new level.

OPINIONS Still more revealing is the level of opinions:

> "I used to think abortion was no big deal, but lately I've changed my mind"

> "I really like Karen."

> "I don't think you're telling me what's on your mind."

Opinions like these usually reveal more about a person than facts alone. If you know where the speaker stands on a subject, you can get a clearer picture of how your relationship might develop. Likewise, every time you offer a personal opinion, you are giving others valuable information about yourself.

FEELINGS The fourth level of self-disclosure—and usually most revealing one—is the realm of feelings. At first glance, feelings might appear to be the same as opinions, but there is a big difference. As we saw, "I don't think you're telling me what's on your mind" is an opinion. Now notice how much more we learn about the speaker by looking at three different feelings that might accompany this statement:

"I don't think you're telling me what's on your mind, *and I'm suspicious.*"

"I don't think you're telling me what's on your mind, *and I'm angry.*"

"I don't think you're telling me what's on your mind, *and I'm hurt.*"

The difference between these four levels of communication suggests why relationships can be frustrating. One reason has to do with the depth of disclosure, which may not lead to the kind of relationship one or both parties are seeking. Sometimes the communicators might remain exclusively on the level of facts. This might be suitable for a business relationship but wouldn't be very likely in most other circumstances. Even worse, other communicators never get off the level of clichés. And just as a diet of rich foods can become unappealing if carried to excess, the overuse of feelings and opinions can also become disagreeable. In most cases the successful conversation is one in which the participants move from one level to another, depending on the circumstances.

The Johari Window Model of Self-Disclosure

One way to look at the important part self-disclosure plays in interpersonal communication is by means of a device called the **Johari Window**.[8] (The window takes its name from the first names of its creators, Joseph Luft and Harry Ingham.) Imagine a frame inside which is everything there is to know about you: your likes and dislikes, your goals, your secrets, your needs—everything. (See Figure 6–4.)

FIGURE 6–4

Of course, you aren't aware of everything about yourself. Like most people, you're probably discovering new things about yourself all the time. To represent this, we can divide the frame containing everything about you into two parts: the part you know about and the part you're not aware of, as in Figure 6–5.

We can also divide this frame containing everything about you in another way. In this division one part represents the things about you that others know, and the second part contains the things about you that you keep to yourself. Figure 6–6 represents this view.

FIGURE 6–5

When we impose these two divided frames one atop the other, we have a Johari Window. By looking at Figure 6–7 you can see the *everything about you* divided into four parts.

Part I represents the information of which both you and the other person are

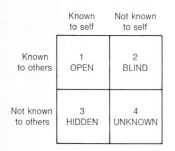

FIGURE 6–6

	Known to self	Not known to self
Known to others	1 OPEN	2 BLIND
Not known to others	3 HIDDEN	4 UNKNOWN

FIGURE 6–7

aware. This part is your *open area.* Part 2 represents the *blind area:* information of which you are unaware but the other person knows. You learn about information in the blind area primarily through feedback. Part 3 represents your *hidden area:* information that you know but aren't willing to reveal to others. Items in this hidden area become public primarily through self-disclosure, which is the focus of this chapter. Part 4 represents information that is *unknown* to both you and others. At first, the unknown area seems impossible to verify. After all, if neither you nor others know what it contains, how can you be sure it exists? We can deduce its existence because we are constantly discovering new things about ourselves. It is not unusual to discover, for example, that you have an unrecognized talent, strength, or weakness. Items move from the unknown area either directly into the open area when you disclose your insight or through one of the other areas first.

The relative size of each area in our personal Johari Windows changes from time to time, according to our moods, the subject we are discussing, and our relationship with the other person. Despite these changes, most people's overall style of disclosure could be represented by a single Johari Window. Figure 6–8 pictures windows representing four extreme interaction styles.

Style I depicts a person who is neither receptive to feedback nor willing to disclose. This person takes few risks and may appear aloof and uncommunicative. The largest quadrant is the unknown area: Such people have a lot to learn about themselves, as do others. Style II depicts a person who is open to feedback from others but does not voluntarily self-disclose. This person may fear exposure, possibly because of not trusting others. People who fit this pattern may appear highly supportive at first. They want to hear *your* story and appear willing to deny themselves by remaining quiet. Then this first impression fades, and eventually you see them as distrustful and detached. A Johari Window describing such people has a large hidden area.

Style III in Figure 6–8 describes people who discourage feedback from others but disclose freely. Like the people pictured in diagram II, they may distrust others' opinions. They certainly seem self-centered. Their largest quadrant is the blind area: They do not encourage feedback and so fail to learn much about how others view them.

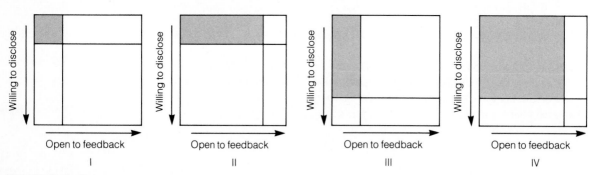

FIGURE 6–8
Four Styles of Disclosure

FIGURE 6-9

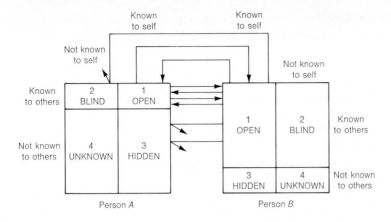

Diagram IV depicts people who are both willing to disclose information about themselves and open to others' ideas. They are trusting enough to seek the opinions of others and disclose their own. In extreme, this communication style can be intimidating and overwhelming because it violates the usual expectations of how nonintimates ought to behave. In moderation, however, this open style provides the best chance for developing highly interpersonal relationships.

Interpersonal communication of any depth is virtually impossible if the individuals involved have little open area. Going a step further, you can see that a relationship is limited by the individual who is less open, that is, who possesses the smaller open area. Figure 6–9 illustrates this situation with Johari Windows. A's window is set up in reverse so that A's and B's open areas are adjacent. Notice that the amount of communication (represented by the arrows connecting the two open areas) is dictated by the size of the smaller open area of A. The arrows originating from B's open area and being turned aside by A's hidden and blind areas represent unsuccessful attempts to communicate.

You have probably found yourself in situations that resemble Figure 6–9. Perhaps you have felt the frustration of not being able to get to know someone who was too reserved. Perhaps you have blocked another person's attempts to build a relationship with you in the same way. Whether you picture yourself more like Person A or Person B, the fact is that self-disclosure on both sides is necessary for the development of any interpersonal relationship. This chapter will describe just how much self-disclosure is optimal and of what type.

Characteristics of Self-Disclosure

The Johari Window suggests several characteristics of self-disclosure.

SELF-DISCLOSURE USUALLY OCCURS IN DYADS Although it is possible for people to disclose a great deal about themselves in groups, such communication usually occurs in one-to-one settings. Because revealing significant information about yourself involves a certain amount of risk, limiting the disclosure to one person at a time minimizes the chance that your revelations will lead to unhappy consequences.

SELF-DISCLOSURE IS USUALLY SYMMETRICAL   Note in Figure 6–9 that the amount of successful, two-way communication (represented by the arrows connecting the two open areas) is dictated by the size of the smaller open area of A. The arrows that are originating from B's open area and being turned aside by A's hidden and blind areas represent unsuccessful attempts to communicate. In situations such as this, it's easy to imagine how B would soon limit the amount of disclosure to match that of A. On the other hand, if A were willing to match the degree of disclosure given by B, the relationship would move to a new level of intimacy. In either case, we can expect that most often the degree of disclosure between partners will soon stabilize at a symmetrical level.

SELF-DISCLOSURE OCCURS INCREMENTALLY   Although occasions do occur in which partners start their relationship by telling everything about themselves to each other, such instances are rare. In most cases, the amount of disclosure increases over time. We begin relationships by revealing relatively little about ourselves; then if our first bits of self-disclosure are well received and bring on similar responses from the other person, we're willing to reveal more. This principle is important to remember. It would usually be a mistake to assume that the way to build a strong relationship would be to reveal the most private details about yourself when first making contact with another person. Unless the circumstances are unique, such baring of your soul would be likely to scare potential partners away rather than bring them closer.

RELATIVELY FEW TRANSACTIONS INVOLVE HIGH LEVELS OF SELF-DISCLOSURE   Just as it's unwise to seek great self-disclosure too soon, it's also unproductive to reveal yourself too much. Except for unique settings—such as in therapy—there's usually no need to disclose frequently or steadily.

SELF-DISCLOSURE USUALLY OCCURS IN THE CONTEXT OF POSITIVE RELATIONSHIPS   This principle makes sense. We're generally more willing to reveal information about ourselves when we feel accepted by the other person. This doesn't mean that you should avoid making disclosing statements that contain

▶ The personality of man is not an apple that has to be polished, but a banana that has to be peeled. And the reason we remain so far from one another, the reason we neither communicate nor interact in any real way, is that most of us spend our lives in polishing rather than peeling.

Man's lifelong task is simply one, but it is not simple: To remove the discrepancy between his outer self and his inner self, to get rid of the "persona" that divides his authentic self from the world.

This persona is like the peeling on a banana: It is something built up to protect from bruises and injury. It is not the real person, but sometimes (if the fear of injury remains too great) it becomes a lifelong substitute for the person.

The "authentic personality" knows that he is like a banana, and knows that only as he peels himself down to his individuated self can he reach out and make contact with his fellows by what Father Goldbrunner calls "the sheer maturity of his humanity." Only when he himself is detached from his defensive armorings can he then awaken a true response in his dialogue with others.

Most of us, however, think in terms of the apple, not the banana. We spend our lives in shining the surface, in making it rosy and gleaming, in perfecting the "image." But the image is not the apple, which may be wormy and rotten to the taste.

Almost everything in modern life is devoted to the polishing process, and little to the peeling process. It is the surface personality that we work on—the appearance, the clothes, the manners, the geniality. In short, the salesmanship: We are selling the package, not the product.

Sydney J. Harris

---

negative messages (for example, "I feel uncomfortable about what happened last night"). Such explanations are likely to be successful if they're designed to be constructive, to help your relationship grow. On the other hand, disclosure that has the effect of attacking the other person ("You sure aren't very bright") is almost guaranteed to be destructive.

Guidelines for Appropriate Self-Disclosure

One fear we've had while writing this chapter is that a few overenthusiastic readers may throw down their books and begin to share every personal detail of their lives with whomever they can find. As you can imagine, this kind of behavior isn't an example of effective interpersonal communication.

No single style of self-disclosure is appropriate for every situation. Let's take a look at some guidelines that can help you recognize how to express yourself in a way that's rewarding for you and the others involved.

IS THE OTHER PERSON IMPORTANT TO YOU? There are several ways in which someone might be important. Perhaps you have an ongoing relationship deep enough so that sharing significant parts of yourself justifies keeping your present level of togetherness intact. Or perhaps the person to whom you're considering disclosing is someone with whom you've previously related on a less personal level. But now you see a chance to grow closer, and disclosure may be the path toward developing that personal relationship.

IS THE RISK OF DISCLOSING REASONABLE?   Take a realistic look at the potential risks of self-disclosure. Even if the probable benefits are great, opening yourself up to almost certain rejection may be asking for trouble. For instance, it might be foolhardy to share your important feelings with someone you know is likely to betray your confidences or ridicule them. On the other hand, knowing that your partner is trustworthy and supportive makes the prospect of speaking out more reasonable. In anticipating risks, be sure that you are realistic. It's sometimes easy to indulge in catastrophic expectations in which you begin to imagine all sorts of disastrous consequences of your opening up when in fact such horrors are quite unlikely to occur.

ARE THE AMOUNT AND TYPE OF DISCLOSURE APPROPRIATE?   A third point to realize is that there are degrees of self-disclosure, so that telling others about yourself isn't an all-or-nothing decision you must make. It's possible to share some facts, opinions, or feelings with one person while reserving riskier ones for others. In the same vein, before sharing very important information with someone who does matter to you, you might consider testing reactions by disclosing less personal data.

IS THE DISCLOSURE RELEVANT TO THE SITUATION AT HAND?   Self-disclosure doesn't require long confessions about your past life or current thoughts unrelated to the present. On the contrary, it ought to be directly pertinent to your present situation. It's ludicrous to picture the self-disclosing person as someone who blurts out intimate details of every past experience. Instead, our model is someone who, when the time is appropriate, trusts us enough to share the hidden parts of self that affect our relationship.

Usually, then, the subject of appropriate self-disclosure involves the present, the "here and now" as opposed to "there and then." "How am I feeling now?" "How are we doing now?" These are appropriate topics for sharing personal thoughts and feelings. There are certainly times when it's relevant to bring up the past but only as it relates to what's going on in the present.

IS THE DISCLOSURE RECIPROCATED?   There's nothing quite as disconcerting as talking your heart out to someone only to discover that the other person has yet to say anything to you that is half as revealing as what you've been saying. And you think to yourself, "What am I doing?" Unequal self-disclosure creates an imbalanced relationship, one doomed to fall apart.

There are few times when one-way disclosure is acceptable. Most of them involve formal, therapeutic relationships in which a client approaches a trained professional with the goal of resolving a problem. For instance, you wouldn't necessarily expect to hear about a physician's personal ailments during a visit to a medical office. Nonetheless, it's interesting to note that one frequently noted characteristic of effective psychotherapists, counselors, and teachers is a willingness to share their feelings about a relationship with their clients.

WILL THE EFFECT BE CONSTRUCTIVE?   Self-disclosure can be a vicious tool if it's not used carefully. Psychologist George Bach suggests that every person has a psychological "belt line." Below that belt line are areas about which the person is extremely sensitive. Bach says that jabbing at a "below-the-belt" area is a surefire way to disable another person, although usually at great cost to the relationship. It's important to consider the effects of your candor before opening up to others. Comments such as "I've always thought you were pretty unintelligent" or "Last year I made love to your best friend" *may* sometimes resolve old business and thus be constructive, but they also can be devastating—to the listener, to the relationship, and to your self-esteem.

IS THE SELF-DISCLOSURE CLEAR AND UNDERSTANDABLE?   When you express yourself to others, it's important that you share yourself in a way that's intelligible. This means describing the *sources* of your message clearly. For instance, it's far better to describe another's behavior by saying, "When you don't answer my phone calls or drop by to visit anymore . . ." than to complain vaguely, "When you avoid me . . ."

It's also vital to express your *thoughts* and *feelings* explicitly. "I feel worried because I'm afraid you don't care about me" is more understandable than "I don't like the way things have been going."

SUMMARY ◄

An interpersonal relationship is an association in which two or more people meet one another's social needs to a greater or lesser degree. Communication in relationships consists of both content and relational messages. Explicit relational messages are termed metacommunication.

People are attracted to one another for a number of reasons: similarity, complementary traits, mutual liking, net gain, competency, self-disclosure, and frequency of interaction. Each of these factors has its limits, however. Whatever their basis, relationships can be divided into stages of development. These stages are sequential, although not all relationships reach the final stages.

Self-disclosure is the process of deliberately revealing significant information about oneself that would not normally be known. The breadth and depth of self-disclosure can be described by the social penetration model. The Johari Window model reveals an individual's open, blind, hidden, and unknown areas. Self-disclosure can exist on several levels of depth. The most superficial level is that of clichés, followed by facts, opinions, and feelings. Self-disclosure is not always desirable: The chapter listed several guidelines to help determine when it is and is not appropriate.

ACTIVITIES ◄

1. Make a list of several people who are "close" to you: family members, a person with whom you live, friends, co-workers, and so on. Where would you place each of these relationships on a spectrum with "interpersonal" at one end and "impersonal" at the other? Realize that "interpersonalness" isn't an

either-or matter; many relationships are partially personal and partly impersonal.

Use the information you just read to develop your answers:

Do you treat the people on your list as individuals, or do you pigeonhole and stereotype them?

Have you developed your own rules and customs, or do you rely on standardized customs?

Have you shared important personal information, or have you kept it to yourself?

Now ask yourself the most important question: How satisfied are you with the answers from your list?

2. List the names of five people with whom you have strong positive personal relationships. Use the list that follows to identify the basis of your attraction.
   a. Are their interests, attitudes, values, beliefs, or backgrounds similar to yours?
   b. Do they fill a complementary need for you?
   c. Are they attracted to you?
   d. Is your relationship a fair exchange of rewards?
   e. Are they competent but human?
   f. Have they shared personal information with you?
   g. Do you encounter them frequently?
   Now consider the five people with whom you would like to build a stronger relationship. Use the same list to decide whether you are the kind of person they would be attracted to.

3. You can use the Johari Window model to examine the level of self-disclosure in your own relationships.
   a. Use the format described in Figure 6–9 to draw two Johari Windows, representing the relationship between you and one other person. Remember to reverse one of the windows so that your open areas and those of the other person face each other.
   b. Describe which parts of yourself you keep in the hidden area. Explain your reasons for doing so. Describe the costs or benefits or both of not disclosing these parts of yourself.
   c. Look at the blind area of your model. Is this area large or small because of the amount of feedback (much or little) that you get from your partner or because of your willingness to receive the feedback that is offered?
   d. Explain whether or not you are satisfied with the results illustrated by your answers. If you are not satisfied, explain what you can do to remedy the problem.

4. Think of a person you would like to know better. Using the levels of self-disclosure in this section, identify the kind of sharing that goes on between you now. Think of two factual statements, two opinions, and two expressions of feeling that you could share as a way of increasing the level of disclosure. Before actually delivering these messages, be sure to read the guidelines on pages 155–157.

1. J. Stewart and G. D'Angelo, *Together: Communicating Interpersonally,* 2d ed. (Reading, Mass.: Addison-Wesley, 1980), pp. 75–78. See also J. Stewart, "Foundations of Dialogic Communication," *Quarterly Journal of Speech* 45 (April 1978): 183–201.

2. For a useful discussion of other dimensions of interpersonal relationships, see Mark L. Knapp, *Interpersonal Communication and Human Relationships* (Boston: Allyn and Bacon, 1984), pp. 13–20.

3. See P. Watzlawick, J. H. Beavin, D. D. Jackson, *Pragmatics of Human Communication* (New York: Norton, 1967); and W. J. Lederer and D. D. Jackson, *The Mirages of Marriage* (New York: Norton, 1968).

4. See C. M. Rossiter, Jr, "Instruction in Metacommunication," *Central States Speech Journal* 25 (1974): 36–42; and W. W. Wilmot, "Metacommunication: A Re-examination and Extension," in *Communication Yearbook 4* (New Brunswick, N.J.: Transaction Books, 1980).

5. These theories are summarized in D. E. Hamachek, *Encounters with Others: Interpersonal Relationships and You* (New York: Holt, Rinehart and Winston, 1982), pp. 52–69; and E. Berscheid and E. H. Walster, *Interpersonal Attraction,* 2d ed. (Reading, Mass.: Addison-Wesley, 1978).

6. Knapp, op. cit., pp. 32–54.

7. I. Altman and D. A. Taylor, *Social Penetration: The Development of Interpersonal Relationships* (New York: Holt, Rinehart and Winston, 1973).

8. J. Luft, *Of Human Interaction* (Palo Alto, Calif.: National Press, 1969).

► CHAPTER 7

KEY TERMS

ambiguous response
assertion
certainty
communication climate
confirming response
conflict
controlling message
crazymaking
descriptive communication
direct aggression
disconfirming response
empathy
equality
evaluative communication
Gibb categories
"I" language
impersonal response
impervious response
incongruous response
interrupting response
indirect aggression
irrelevant response
lose-lose problem solving
neutrality
nonassertion
problem orientation
provisionalism
spontaneity
strategy
superiority
tangential response
win-lose problem solving
win-win problem solving
"you" language

IMPROVING INTERPERSONAL RELATIONSHIPS

After reading this chapter, you should understand the following:

1. The role of communication climate in interpersonal relationships.
2. The types of messages that create confirming and disconfirming communication climates.
3. That conflict is unavoidable in interpersonal relationships.
4. The characteristics of nonassertive, directly aggressive, indirectly aggressive, and assertive communication.
5. The differences between win-lose, lose-lose, and win-win styles of conflict resolution.

You should be able to do the following:

1. Identify disconfirming messages and replace them with confirming ones, using the Gibb categories of supportive communication.
2. Describe the degree to which you use nonassertive, directly aggressive, indirectly aggressive, and assertive messages and choose more satisfying responses as necessary.
3. Apply the win-win approach to conflict resolution to an interpersonal conflict.

No matter how satisfying your relationships, there are almost certainly ways they could be better. At times even the best of friends, the closest of families, and the most productive co-workers become dissatisfied. Sometimes the people involved are unhappy with each other. In other cases, one person's problem is unrelated to the relationship. In either case, there's a desire to communicate in a way that makes matters better.

The ideas in this chapter can help you improve the important relationships in your life. We'll begin by talking about the factors that make communication "climates" either positive or negative. Next we'll focus on methods for understanding and resolving interpersonal conflicts.

▶ COMMUNICATION CLIMATES IN INTERPERSONAL RELATIONSHIPS

Self-disclosure may be an important ingredient in interpersonal communication, but it isn't the only characteristic that distinguishes satisfying relationships from disappointing ones. To understand the fundamental basis of rewarding relationships, we need to explore the concept of communication climate.

The term **communication climate** refers to the emotional tone of a relationship as it is expressed in the messages that the partners send and receive. Just as physical locations have characteristic weather patterns, interpersonal relationships have unique climates, too. You can't measure the interpersonal climate by looking at a thermometer or glancing at the sky, but it's there nonetheless. Every relationship has a feeling, a pervasive mood that colors the interactions of the participants.

A climate doesn't involve specific activities as much as the way people feel about each other as they carry out those activities. Consider two communication classes, for example. Both meet for the same length of time and follow the same syllabus. It's easy to imagine how one of these classes might be a friendly, comfortable place to learn whereas the other could be cold and tense—even hostile. The same principle holds for families, co-workers, and other relationships: Communication climates are a function of the way people feel about one another, not so much the tasks they perform.

Confirming and Disconfirming Climates

What makes some climates positive and others negative? A short but accurate answer is that the *communication climate is determined by the degree to which people see themselves as valued.* When we believe others view us as important, we are likely to feel good about our relationship. On the other hand, the relational climate suffers when we think others don't appreciate or care about us.

Messages that show you are valued have been called **confirming responses.**[1] Some kinds of communication are obviously confirming. Sincere *praise* or *compliments* show that you value the recipient. So does *agreeing* with others' opinions. But it isn't necessary to express praise or agreement to send confirming messages. In many cases, simply *acknowledging* the other person can be a confirmation. Stopping to exchange small talk with an acquaintance says, "You're important." So does smiling or waving when you see the other person from a distance. (If you don't believe this, recall how you felt when you were ignored.)

On a more personal level, *listening* attentively to the other person sends a confirming message. Listening is even confirming when you disagree with the speaker. For example, asking sincere questions and using the paraphrasing skills described in Chapter 4 show that you care enough about the other person to listen. When compared to the responses that characterize nonlistening (stage hogging, ambushing, pseudolistening, and so on), it's clear that sincerely trying to understand a conversational partner is a sign of respect.

In contrast to confirming communication, messages that deny the value of others have been labeled **disconfirming responses.**[2] These show a lack of regard for the other person either by disputing or ignoring some important part of that person's message. Disagreement can certainly be disconfirming, especially if it goes beyond disputing the other person's ideas and attacks the speaker personally. It may be tough to hear someone say, "I don't think that's a good idea," but a personal attack like "You're crazy" is even more insulting. However, disagreement is not the most damaging kind of disconfirmation. Far worse are responses that ignore others' ideas—or even their existence. The list of disconfirming responses in Table 7–1 shows several kinds of messages that convey a lack of appreciation. It's easy to see how these sorts of messages can create negative relational climates.

▶ The worst sin towards our fellow creatures is not to hate them, but to be indifferent to them; that's the essence of inhumanity.

George Bernard Shaw

YOU'VE OBVIOUSLY MISTAKEN ME FOR SOMEONE WHO GIVES A DAMN

TABLE 7–1 Disconfirming Messages

Disconfirming responses communicate a lack of respect or appreciation. Like their confirming counterparts, these messages can shape the climate of an entire relationship.

Impervious responses ignore the other person's attempt to communicate. Refusing to answer another person in a face-to-face conversation is the most obvious kind of impervious response although not the most common. Failing to return a phone call or write back in answer to a letter are more common impervious responses. So is not responding to a smile or a wave.

Interrupting responses occur when one person begins to speak before the other has finished. They show a lack of concern about what the other person has to say.

A: I'm looking for an outfit I can wear to work and when I travel to...
B: I've got just the thing. It's part wool and part polyester, so it won't wrinkle at all.
A: Actually wrinkling isn't that important. I want something that will work as a business outfit and...
B: We have a terrific blazer that you can dress up or down depending on the accessories you choose.
A: That's not what I was going to say. I want something that will work both here and down south. I have to go to a...
B: Say no more. I know just what you want.
A: Never mind. I think I'll look in some other stores.

Irrelevant responses are unrelated to what the other person has just said.

A: What a day! I thought it would never end. First the car overheated, and I had to call a tow truck, and then the computer broke down at work.
B: Listen, we have to talk about a present for Ann's birthday. The party is on Saturday, and I only have tomorrow to shop for it.
A: I'm really beat. Could we talk about it in a few minutes? I've never seen a day like this one.
B: I just can't figure what would suit Ann. She's got everything...

Tangential responses are conversational "take aways." Instead of ignoring the speaker's remarks completely, they use them as a starting point for a shift to a different topic.

A: I'd like to know for sure whether you want to go skiing during vacation. If we don't decide whether to go soon, it'll be impossible to get reservations anywhere.
B: Yeah. And if I don't pass my botany class, I won't be in the mood to go anywhere. Could you give me some help with this homework?...

Impersonal responses are loaded with clichés and other statements that never truly respond to the speaker.

A: I've been having some personal problems lately, and I'd like to take off work early a couple of afternoons to clear them up.
B: Ah, yes. We all have personal problems. It seems to be a sign of the times.

Ambiguous responses contain messages with more than one meaning, leaving the other party unsure of the responder's position.

A: I'd like to get together with you soon. How about Tuesday?
B: Uh, maybe so.
A: Well, how about it. Can we talk Tuesday?
B: Oh, probably. See you later.

Incongruous responses contain two messages that seem to deny or contradict each other. Often at least one of these messages is nonverbal.

A: Darling, I love you.
B: I love you, too. (giggles)

How Communication Climates Develop

As soon as two people start to communicate, a relational climate begins to develop. If the messages are confirming, the climate is likely to be a positive one. If they disconfirm one another, the relationship is likely to be hostile, cold, or defensive.

Verbal messages certainly contribute to the tone of a relationship, but many climate-shaping messages are nonverbal. The very act of approaching others is confirming whereas avoiding them can be disconfirming. Smiles or frowns, the presence or absence of eye contact, tone of voice, the use of personal space... all these and other cues send messages about how the parties feel toward one another.

Once a climate is formed, it can take on a life of its own and grow in a self-perpetuating spiral. This sort of cycle is most obvious in regressive spirals, when a dispute gets out of hand:

A: (*mildly irritated*) Where were you? I thought we agreed to meet here a half hour ago.

B. (*defensively*) I'm sorry, I got hung up at the library. I don't have as much free time as you do, you know.

A: I wasn't *blaming* you, so don't get so touchy. I do resent what you just said, though. I'm plenty busy. And I've got lots of better things to do than wait around for you!

B: Who's getting touchy? I just made a simple comment. You've sure been defensive lately. What's the matter with you?

Fortunately, spirals can work in a progressive direction, too. One confirming behavior leads to a similar response from the other person, which, in turn, leads to further confirmation by the first party.

IMPROVING
INTERPERSONAL
RELATIONSHIPS

Spirals—whether positive or negative—rarely go on indefinitely. When a negative spiral gets out of hand, the parties might agree to back off from their disconfirming behavior. "Hold on," one might say. "This is getting us nowhere." At this point, there may be a cooling-off period, or the parties might work together more constructively to solve their problem. If the partners pass the "point of no return," the relationship may end. It is impossible to take back a message once it has been sent, and some exchanges are so lethal that the relationship can't survive them. Positive spirals also have their limit: Even the best relationships go through rocky periods, in which the climate suffers. The accumulated goodwill and communication skill of the partners, however, can make these times less frequent and intense. Therefore, most relationships pass through cycles of progression and regression.

Creating Positive Communication Climates

It's easy to see how disconfirming messages can pollute a communication climate. But what are some alternative ways of communicating that encourage positive relationships? The work of Jack Gibb gives a picture of what kinds of messages lead to both positive and negative spirals.[3]

After observing groups for several years, Gibb was able to isolate six types of defense-arousing communication and six contrasting behaviors that seemed to reduce the level of threat and defensiveness. The **Gibb categories** are listed in Table 7–2. Using the supportive types of communication and avoiding the defensive ones will increase the odds of creating and maintaining positive communication climates in your relationships.

EVALUATION VS. DESCRIPTION The first type of defense-provoking behavior Gibb noted was **evaluative communication.** Most people become irritated at judgmental statements, which they are likely to interpret as indicating a lack of regard. Evaluative language has often been described as **"you" language** because most such statements contain an accusatory use of that word. For example,

You don't know what you're talking about.

You're not doing your best.

You smoke too much.

TABLE 7–2 The Gibb Categories of Defensive and Supportive Behaviors

DEFENSIVE BEHAVIORS	SUPPORTIVE BEHAVIORS
1. Evaluation	1. Description
2. Control	2. Problem orientation
3. Strategy	3. Spontaneity
4. Neutrality	4. Empathy
5. Superiority	5. Equality
6. Certainty	6. Provisionalism

▶ In interpersonal relationships, I believe first person singular is most appropriate because it places responsibility clearly.

If I say to another person, "I do not like what you did," then no contradiction is possible. No one can correct me because my perception and what I have decided to think about is mine alone. The other person may, however, suggest that I received only a portion of the information, or that I received it unclearly for one reason or another. In such a case, the meaning of the message may be tentative until it can be negotiated. It also is legitimate for me to perceive the message quite differently from the way the other person perceives it.

On the other hand, if I say "You have made me angry," then you may very well contradict me by responding with something such as "No I didn't." In fact, I am eliciting a defensiveness and also inviting "you" to attempt a control of me by your helplessness, suffering, or anger.

Only I am responsible for my behavior. Only I can change what I do. However, when I change my behavior, I may give the other person in the relationship the opportunity to evaluate his behavior and perhaps modify it.

John Narcisco and David Burkett,
Declare Yourself

Gibb contrasts evaluative "you" language with **descriptive communication** or **"I" language.** Instead of putting the emphasis on judging another's behavior, the descriptive speaker simply explains the personal effect of the other's action. For instance, instead of saying, "You talk too much," a descriptive communicator would say, "When you don't give me a chance to say what's on my mind, I get frustrated." Notice that statements such as this include an account of the other person's behavior plus an explanation of its effect on the speaker and a description of the speaker's feelings.

CONTROL VS. PROBLEM ORIENTATION A second defense-provoking message involves some attempt to control another. A **controlling message** occurs when a sender seems to be imposing a solution on the receiver with little regard for the receiver's needs or interests. The object of controls can range from where to eat dinner or what TV show to watch to whether to remain in a relationship or how to spend a large sum of money. Whatever the situation, people who act in controlling ways create a defensive climate. None of us likes to feel that our ideas are worthless and that nothing we say will change other people's determination to have their way—yet this is precisely the attitude a controller communicates. Whether done with words, gestures, tone of voice, or through some other channel; whether control is accomplished through status, insistence on obscure or irrelevant rules, or physical power, the controller generates hostility wherever he or she goes. The unspoken message such behavior communicates is "I know what's best for you, and if you do as I say, we'll get along."

In contrast, in **problem orientation** communicators focus on finding a solution that satisfies both their needs and those of the others involved. The goal here isn't to "win" at the expense of your partner but to work out some arrangement in which everybody feels like a winner. (The last section of this chapter has a great deal to say about "win-win" problem solving as a way to find problem-oriented solutions.)

STRATEGY VS. SPONTANEITY   The third communication behavior that Gibb identified as creating a poor communication climate involves the use of **strategy** or manipulation. One of the surest ways to make people defensive is to get caught trying to manipulate them into doing something for you. The fact that you tried to trick them instead of just asking for what you wanted is enough to build mistrust. Nobody likes to be a guinea pig or a sucker, and even well-meant manipulation can cause bad feelings.

Spontaneity is the behavior that contrasts with strategy. Spontaneity simply means expressing yourself honestly. Despite the misleading label Gibb chose for this kind of behavior, spontaneous communication needn't be blurted out as soon as an idea comes to you. You might want to plan the wording of your message carefully so that you can express yourself clearly. The important thing is to be honest. Often spontaneity won't get what you want, but in the long run it's usually better to be candid and perhaps miss out on some small goal than to say all the right things and be a fraud. More than once we've heard people say, "I didn't like what he said, but at least I know he was being honest."

Although it sounds paradoxical at first, spontaneity can be a strategy, too. Sometimes you'll see people using honesty in a calculating way, being just frank enough to win someone's trust or sympathy. This "leveling" is probably the most defense-arousing strategy of all because once we've learned someone is using frankness as a manipulation, there's almost no chance we'll ever trust that person again.

You may be getting the idea that using supportive behaviors such as description, problem orientation, empathy, and so on, is a good way to manipulate others. Before going any further, we want to say loudly and clearly that if you ever act supportively without being sincere in what you're saying, you've misunderstood the idea behind this chapter, and you're running a risk of causing even more defensiveness than before. None of the ideas we present in this book can go into a "bag of tricks" that can be used to control others: If you ever find yourself using them in this way, beware!

NEUTRALITY VS. EMPATHY   Gibb used the term **neutrality** to describe a fourth behavior that arouses defensiveness. Probably a better descriptive word would be *indifference*. A neutral attitude is disconfirming because it communicates a lack of concern for the welfare of another and implies that the other person isn't very important to you. This perceived indifference is likely to promote defensiveness because people do not like to think of themselves as worthless, and they'll protect a self-concept that pictures themselves as worthwhile.

The small child who has urgent things to tell a parent but is met with indifference may be expected to become upset. The physician who seems clinical and detached to his patients may wonder why they look for another doctor.

The poor effects of neutrality become apparent when you consider the hostility that most people have for the large, impersonal organizations with which they have to deal: "They think of me as a number instead of a person"; "I felt as if I were being handled by computers and not human beings." These two common statements reflect reactions to being handled in an indifferent way.

Gibb has found that **empathy** helps rid communication of the quality of indifference. When people show that they care for the feelings of another, there's little chance that the person's self-concept will be threatened. Empathy means accepting another's feelings, putting yourself in another's place. This doesn't mean you need to agree with that person. By simply letting someone know about your care and respect, you'll be acting in a supportive way. Gibb noted the importance of nonverbal messages in communicating empathy. He found that facial and bodily expressions of concern are often more important to the receiver than the words used.

SUPERIORITY VS. EQUALITY A fifth behavior creating a defensive climate involves **superiority.** How many interpersonal relationships have you dropped because you couldn't stand the superiority that the other person projected? An individual who communicates superiority arouses feelings of inadequacy in the recipients. We're not particular about the type of superiority presented to us; we just become defensive. Money, power, intellectual ability, physical appearance, and athletic prowess are all areas our culture stresses. Consequently, we often feel a need to express our superiority along these lines.

Individuals who act superior communicate that they don't want to relate on equal terms with others in the relationship. Furthermore, people like this seem to imply that they don't want feedback or need help because it would be coming from someone "inferior." The listener is put on guard because the senders are likely to attempt to reduce the receiver's worth, power, or status to maintain or advance their own superiority.

Perhaps you've had professors who continually reminded their class of their superior intellectual ability and position. Remember how delighted you were when you or a classmate caught one of these superior types in a mistake? Why do you suppose that was so satisfying? Some might argue that this is a good strategy to keep students awake, but in reality much of the students' effort is then directed to defending self-worth rather than pursuing the objectives of the course.

When we detect people communicating superiority, we usually react defensively. We "turn them off," justify ourselves, or argue with them in our minds. Sometimes we choose to change the subject verbally or even walk away. Of course, there is always the counterattack, which includes an attempt to belittle the senders of the superiority message. We'll go to great lengths "to cut them down to size." All these defensive reactions to projected superiority are destructive to an interpersonal climate.

Many times in our lives we are in a relationship with individuals who possess talents greater than ours. But is it necessary for these people to project superiority? Your own experiences will tell you that it isn't. Gibb has found ample evidence that many who have superior skills and talents are capable of projecting feelings of **equality** rather than superiority. Such people communicate that although they may have greater talent in certain areas, they see others as having just as much worth as human beings.

IMPROVING
INTERPERSONAL
RELATIONSHIPS

CERTAINTY VS. PROVISIONALISM Have you ever run into people who are positive they're right, who know that theirs is the only or proper way of doing something, who insist that they have all the facts and need no additional information? If you have, you've met individuals who project the defense-arousing behavior Gibb calls **certainty.**

How do you react when you're the target of such certainty? Do you suddenly find your energy directed to proving the dogmatic individual wrong? If you do, you're reacting normally, if not very constructively.

Communicators who regard their own opinions with certainty while disregarding the ideas of others demonstrate a rather clear lack of regard for the thoughts others hold to be important. It's likely the receiver will take the certainty as a personal affront, and react defensively.

In contrast to dogmatic communication is **provisionalism,** in which people may have strong opinions but are willing to acknowledge that they don't have a corner on the truth and will change their stand if another position seems more reasonable.

▶ RESOLVING INTERPERSONAL CONFLICT

Even the most supportive communication climate won't guarantee complete harmony. Regardless of what we may wish for or dream about, a conflict-free world just doesn't exist. Even the best communicators, the luckiest people, are bound to wind up in situations when their needs don't match the needs of others. Money, time, power, sex, humor, aesthetic taste, as well as a thousand other issues, arise and keep us from living in a state of perpetual agreement.

For many people the inevitability of conflict is a depressing fact. They think that the existence of ongoing conflict means that there's little chance for happy relationships with others. Effective communicators know differently, however. They realize that although it's impossible to *eliminate* conflict, there are ways to *manage* it effectively. And those effective communicators know the subject of this chapter—that managing conflict skillfully can open the door to healthier, stronger, and more satisfying relationships.

▶ The history of man is replete with mechanisms and attempts to control aggression. People have tried to pray it away, wish it away, or play it away. More recently they have tried to psychoanalyze it away. But it does not seem to go away.

George Bach and Herb Goldberg
Creative Aggression

The Nature of Conflict

Whatever forms they may take, all interpersonal **conflicts** share certain similarities. Joyce Frost and William Wilmot provide a thorough definition of conflict. They state that conflict is an *expressed struggle between at least two interdependent parties who perceive incompatible goals, scarce rewards, and interference from the other parties in achieving their goals.*[4] Let's look at the various parts of this definition so as to develop a clearer idea of conflicts in people's lives.

EXPRESSED STRUGGLE Another way to describe this idea is to say that both parties in a conflict know that some disagreement exists. For instance, you may be upset for months because a neighbor's loud stereo keeps you from getting to sleep at night, but no conflict exists between the two of you until the neighbor learns about your problem. Of course, the expressed struggle doesn't have to be verbal. You can show your displeasure with somebody without saying a word. A dirty look, the silent treatment, or avoiding the other person are all ways of expressing yourself. But one way or another both parties must know that a problem exists before they're in conflict.

PERCEIVED INCOMPATIBLE GOALS All conflicts look as if one party's gain will be another's loss. For instance, consider the neighbor whose stereo keeps you awake at night. Does somebody have to lose? A neighbor who turns down the noise loses the enjoyment of hearing the music at full volume; but if the neighbor keeps the volume up, then you're still awake and unhappy.

But the goals in this situation really aren't completely incompatible—solutions do exist that allow both parties to get what they want. For instance, you could achieve peace and quiet by closing your windows and getting the neighbor to do the same. You might use a pair of earplugs. Or perhaps the neighbor could get a set of earphones and listen to the music at full volume without bothering anyone. If any of these solutions prove workable, then the conflict disappears.

Unfortunately, people often fail to see mutually satisfying answers to their problems. And as long as they *perceive* their goals to be mutually exclusive, then, although the conflict is unnecessary, it is still very real.

PERCEIVED SCARCE REWARDS Conflicts also exist when people believe there isn't enough of something to go around. The most obvious example of a scarce resource is money—a cause of many conflicts. If a person asks for a raise in pay and the boss would rather keep the money or use it to expand the business, then the two parties are in conflict.

Time is another scarce commodity. As authors and family men, both of us are constantly in the middle of struggles about how to use the limited time we have to spend. Should we work on this book? Visit with our wives? Play with our kids? Enjoy the luxury of being alone? With only twenty-four hours in a day we're bound to wind up in conflicts with our families, editors, students, and friends—all of whom want more of our time than we have available to give.

INTERDEPENDENCE However antagonistic they might feel toward each other, the parties in a conflict are usually dependent on each other. The welfare and satisfaction of one depends on the actions of another. If this weren't true, then even in the face of scarce resources and incompatible goals there would be no need for conflict. Interdependence exists between conflicting nations, social groups, organizations, friends, and lovers. In each case, if the two parties didn't need each other to solve the problem, each would go separate ways. In fact, many conflicts go unresolved because the parties fail to understand their interdependence. One of the first steps toward resolving a conflict is to take the attitude that "we're all in this together."

Styles of Conflict

Table 7–3 describes four ways people can act when their needs are not met. Each one has very different characteristics.

▶ **Conflict Basic as Hunger?**

Psychologists often find themselves in the position of proving scientifically what people have always known implicitly.

So it is with new data on the value of conflict.

Conflict, a Canadian psychologist reported in Scientific American, 215:82, 1966, may be the same sort of driving force as hunger, thirst, sexual appetite and pain. If so, it can be placed among the ranks of those conditions which are most efficient in producing learning, with important implications for education.

All of the basic drives have in common the fact that they arouse the individual physically, sharpen his faculties, motivate him to act and enhance his learning capacity.

Science News

NONASSERTIVE BEHAVIOR   Nonassertive communicators handle conflict in one of two ways. Sometimes they ignore their needs, keeping quiet when things don't go their way. A second nonassertive course of action is to acknowledge that a problem exists and then simply to accept the situation, hoping that it will clear up by itself.

Unfortunately, most problems don't solve themselves. In addition, a nonassertive person often grows more and more angry at the other party, poisoning the relationship. Furthermore, failing to act often leads to a loss of self-respect. Clearly, **nonassertion** is usually not a very satisfying course of action.

DIRECT AGGRESSION   Whereas nonassertion is characterized by underreaction, **direct aggression** is typified by overreaction. The usual consequences of aggressive behaviors are anger and defensiveness or hurt and humiliation on the part of the receiver. In either case, aggressive communicators build themselves up at the expense of others.

INDIRECT AGGRESSION   In several of his works, psychologist George Bach describes behavior that he terms "**crazymaking**,"[5] another term for **indirect aggression.** Crazymaking occurs when people have feelings of resentment, anger, or rage that they are unable or unwilling to express directly. Instead of keeping these feelings to themselves, the crazymakers send these aggressive messages in subtle, indirect ways, thus maintaining the front of kindness: hinting, joking, gossiping, and so on. This amiable facade eventually crumbles, however, leaving the crazymaker's victim confused and angry at having been fooled. The

TABLE 7–3   Styles of Conflict

	NONASSERTIVE	DIRECTLY AGGRESSIVE	INDIRECTLY AGGRESSIVE	ASSERTIVE
Approach to others	I'm not OK, you're OK.	I'm OK, you're not OK.	I'm OK, you're not OK. (But I'll let you think you are.)	I'm OK. You're OK
Decision making	Let others choose	Chooses for others. They know it.	Chooses for others. They don't know it.	Chooses for self
Self-sufficiency	Low	High or low	Looks high but usually low	Usually high
Behavior in problem situations	Flees; gives in	Outright attack	Concealed attack	Direct confrontation
Response of others	Disrespect, guilt, anger, frustration	Hurt, defensiveness, humiliation	Confusion, frustration, feelings of manipulation	Mutual respect
Success pattern	Succeeds by luck or charity of others	Beats out others	Wins by manipulation	Attempts "win-win" solutions

Adapted with permission from Stanlee Phelps and Nancy Austin, *The Assertive Woman* (San Luis Obispo, Calif.: Impact, 1975), p. 11; and Gerald Piaget, American Orthopsychiatric Association, 1975. Further reproduction prohibited.

targets of the crazymaker can either react with aggressive behavior of their own or retreat to nurse their hurt feelings. In either case, indirect aggression seldom has anything but harmful effects on a relationship.

ASSERTION **Assertive** people handle conflicts skillfully by expressing their needs, thoughts, and feelings clearly and directly but without judging others or dictating to them. They have the attitude that most of the time it is possible to resolve problems to everyone's satisfaction. Possessing this attitude and the skills to bring it about doesn't guarantee that assertive communicators will always get what they want, but it does give them the best chance of doing so. An additional benefit of such an approach is that whether or not it satisfies a particular need, it maintains the self-respect of both the assertors and those with whom they interact. As a result, people who manage their conflicts assertively may experience feelings of discomfort while they are working through the problem. They usually feel better about themselves and each other afterward—quite a change from the outcomes of no assertiveness or aggression.

Approaches to Conflict Resolution

So far, we've looked at individual styles of communication. Whereas assertive problem solving may be the most satisfying and productive of these, it's obvious

▶ Not everything that is faced can be changed, But nothing can be changed until it is faced.

James Baldwin

that not everyone uses it. Even when one person behaves assertively, there's no guarantee that others will do so. There are three quite different outcomes of the various interactions among nonassertive, indirectly aggressive, directly aggressive, and assertive communicators. By looking at each of them, you can decide which ones you'll seek when you find yourself facing an interpersonal conflict.

WIN-LOSE **Win-lose** conflicts are ones in which one party achieves its goal at the expense of the other. People resort to this method of resolving disputes when they perceive a situation as being an "either-or" one: Either I get what I want or you get your way. The most clear-cut examples of win-lose situations are certain games such as baseball or poker in which the rules require a winner and a loser. Some interpersonal issues seem to fit into this win-lose framework: two co-workers seeking a promotion to the same job, for instance, or a couple who disagree on how to spend their limited money.

Power is the distinguishing characteristic in win-lose problem solving, for it is necessary to defeat an opponent to get what you want. The most obvious kind of power is physical. Some parents threaten their children with warnings such as "Stop misbehaving, or I'll send you to your room." Adults who use physical power to deal with each other usually aren't so blunt, but the legal system is the implied threat: "Follow the rules, or we'll lock you up."

Real or implied force isn't the only kind of power used in conflicts. People who rely on authority of many types engage in win-lose methods without ever

threatening physical coercion. In most jobs, supervisors have the potential to use authority in the assignment of working hours, job promotions, and desirable or undesirable tasks and, of course, in the power to fire an unsatisfactory employee. Teachers can use the power of grades to coerce students to act in desired ways.

Even the usually admired democratic principle of majority rule is a win-lose method of resolving conflicts. However fair it may be, this system results in one group's getting its way and another group's being unsatisfied.

There are some circumstances when the win-lose method may be necessary as when there are truly scarce resources and where only one party can achieve satisfaction. For instance, if two suitors want to marry the same person, only one can succeed. And to return to an earlier example, it's often true that only one applicant can be hired for a job. But don't be too willing to assume that your conflicts are necessarily win-lose: As you'll soon read, many situations that seem to require a loser can be resolved to everyone's satisfaction.

There is a second kind of situation when win-lose is the best method. Even when cooperation is possible, if the other person insists on trying to defeat you, then the most logical response might be to defend yourself by fighting back. "It takes two to tango," the old cliché goes, and it also often takes two to cooperate.

A final and much less frequent justification for trying to defeat another person occurs when the other party is clearly behaving in a wrong manner and where defeating that person is the only way to stop the wrongful behavior. Few people would deny the importance of restraining a person who is deliberately harming others even if the aggressor's freedom is sacrificed in the process. The danger of forcing wrongdoers to behave themselves is the wide difference in opinion between people about who is wrong and who is right. Given this difference, it would only seem justifiable to coerce others into behaving as we think they should in the most extreme circumstances.

LOSE-LOSE In **lose-lose problem solving** neither side is satisfied with the outcome. Although the name of this approach is so discouraging that it's hard to imagine how anyone could willingly use the method, in truth lose-lose is a fairly common approach to handling conflicts.

Compromise is the most respectable form of lose-lose conflict resolution. In it all the parties are willing to settle for less than they want because they believe that partial satisfaction is the best result they can hope for.

In his valuable book on conflict resolution, Albert Filley offers an interesting observation about our attitudes toward this method.[6] Why is it, he asks, that if someone says, "I will compromise my values," we view the action unfavorably, yet we talk admiringly about parties in a conflict who compromise to reach a solution? Though compromises may be the best obtainable result in some conflicts, it's important to realize that both people in a dispute can often work together to find much better solutions. In such cases, *compromise* is a negative word.

Most of us are surrounded by the results of bad compromises. Consider a common example: the conflict between one person's desire to smoke cigarettes

and another's need for clean air. The win-lose outcomes on this issue are obvious: Either the smoker abstains or the nonsmoker gets polluted lungs—neither very satisfying. But a compromise in which the smoker only gets to enjoy a rare cigarette or must retreat outdoors and in which the nonsmoker still must inhale some fumes or feel like an ogre is hardly better. Both sides have lost a considerable amount of both comfort and goodwill. Of course, the costs involved in other compromises are even greater. For example, if divorced parents compromise on child care by haggling over custody and then finally grudgingly agree to split the time with their youngsters, it's hard to say that anybody has won.

Compromises aren't the only lose-lose solutions or even the worst ones. There are many instances in which the parties will both strive to be winners, but, as a result of the struggle, both wind up losers. On the international scene, many wars illustrate this sad point. A nation that gains military victory at the cost of thousands of lives, large amounts of resources, and a damaged national consciousness hasn't truly won much. On an interpersonal level the same principle holds true. Most of us have seen battles of pride in which both parties strike out and both suffer. It seems as if there should be a better alternative, and fortunately there often is.

WIN-WIN In **win-win problem solving,** the goal is to find a solution that satisfies the needs of everyone involved. Not only do the partners avoid trying to win at the other's expense, but there's also a belief that by working together it is possible to find a solution in which all parties reach their goals without needing to compromise.

One way to understand how win-win problem solving works is to look at a few examples.

A boss and a group of employees get into a conflict over scheduling. The employees often want to shift the hours they're scheduled to work in order to accommodate personal needs whereas the boss needs to be sure that the operation is fully staffed at all times. After some discussion they arrive at a solution that satisfies everyone: The boss works up a monthly master schedule indicating the hours during which each employee is responsible for being on the job. Employees are free to trade hours among themselves as long as the operation is fully staffed at all times.

A conflict about testing arises in a college class. Owing to sickness or other reasons, certain students need to take exams on a makeup basis. The instructor doesn't want to give these students any advantage over their peers and doesn't want to go through the task of making up a brand-new test for just a few people. After working on the problem together, instructor and students arrive at a win-win solution. The instructor will hand out a list of twenty possible exam questions in advance of the test day. At examination time five of these questions are randomly drawn for the class to answer. Students who take makeups will draw from the same pool of questions at the time of their test. In this way, makeup students are taking a fresh test without the instructor's having to create a new exam.

A newly married husband and wife found themselves arguing frequently over their budget. The wife enjoyed buying impractical but enjoyable items for herself and the house whereas the husband feared that such purchases would ruin their carefully constructed budget. Their solution was to set aside a small amount of money each month for such purchases. The amount was small enough to be affordable yet gave the wife a chance to escape from their Spartan life-style. Additionally, the husband was satisfied with the arrangement because the luxury money was now a budget category by itself, which got rid of the "out-of-control" feeling that came when his wife made unexpected purchases. The plan worked so well that the couple continued to use it, even after their income rose, by increasing the amount devoted to luxuries.

The point here isn't that these solutions are the correct ones for everybody with similar problems: The win-win approach doesn't work that way. Different people might have found other solutions that suited them better. What the win-win method does is give you an approach—a way of creatively finding just the right answer for your unique problem. By using it, you can tailor-make a way of resolving your conflicts that everyone can live with comfortably.

You should understand that the win-win approach doesn't call for compromises in which the participants give up something they really want or need. Sometimes a compromise is the only alternative, but in the method we're talking about you find a solution that satisfies everybody—one in which nobody has to lose.

Win-Win Problem Solving

Of these three styles the win-win approach is clearly the most desirable one in most cases. It is also the hardest one to achieve—for two reasons. First, it requires a noncompetitive attitude and a number of skills that we'll soon discuss. Second, it requires a certain amount of cooperation from the other person, for it's difficult to arrive at a win-win solution with somebody who insists on trying to defeat you.

In spite of these challenges, it is definitely possible to become better at resolving conflicts. In the following pages, we will outline a method to increase your chances of being able to handle your conflicts in a win-win manner, so that both you and others have your needs met. As you learn to use this approach, you should find that more and more of your conflicts wind up with win-win solutions. And even when total satisfaction isn't possible, this method can help by showing you how to solve problems in the most satisfying way possible and also by preventing individual conflict from spoiling your future interactions with the person involved.

The method is patterned after techniques developed by George Bach[7] and Thomas Gordon,[8] and it has proved successful with many people, both young and old, in a variety of settings.

Before we introduce you to this method, there are a few ideas you should keep in mind. This technique is a highly structured activity. While you're learning how to use it, it's important that you follow all the stages carefully. Each step is essential to the success of your encounter, and skipping one or more can lead to misunderstandings that might threaten your meeting and even cause a "dirty fight." After you've practiced the method a number of times and are familiar with it, this style of conflict will become almost second nature to you. You'll then be able to approach your conflicts without the need to follow the step-by-step approach. But for the time being, try to be patient, and trust the value of the following pattern.

As you read the following steps, try to imagine yourself applying them to a problem that's bothering you now.

IDENTIFY YOUR PROBLEM AND UNMET NEEDS Before you speak out, it's important to realize that the problem that is causing conflict is yours. Whether you want to return an unsatisfactory piece of merchandise, complain to a noisy neighbor because your sleep is being disturbed, or request a change in working conditions from your employer, the problem is yours. Why? Because in each case *you* are the person who is dissatisfied. You are the one who has paid for the defective article; the merchant who sold it to you has the use of your good money. You are the one who is losing sleep as a result of your neighbors' activities; they are content to go on as before. You are the one who is unhappy with your working conditions, not your boss.

▶ Let us begin anew, remembering on both sides that civility is not a sign of weakness.

John F. Kennedy

Realizing that the problem is yours will make a big difference when the time comes to approach your partner. Instead of feeling and acting in an evaluative way, you'll be more likely to share your problem in a descriptive way, which will not only be more accurate but will also reduce the chance of a defensive reaction.

Once you realize that the problem is yours, the next step is to identify the unmet needs that leave you feeling dissatisfied. For instance, in the barking dog incident, your need may be to get some sleep or to study without interruptions. In the case of a friend who teases you in public, your need would probably be to avoid embarrassment.

Sometimes the task of identifying your needs isn't as simple as it first seems. Consider these cases:

A friend hasn't returned some money you loaned long ago. Your apparent need in this situation might be to get the cash back. But a little thought will probably show that this isn't the only, or even the main, thing you want. Even if you were rolling in money, you'd probably want the loan repaid because of your most important need: *to avoid feeling victimized by your friend's taking advantage of you.*

Someone you care about who lives in a distant city has failed to respond to several letters. Your apparent need may be to get answers to the questions you've written about, but it's likely that there's another, more fundamental need: *the reassurance that you're still important enough to deserve a response.*

As you'll soon see, the ability to identify your real needs plays a key role in solving interpersonal problems. For now, the point to remember is that before you voice your problem to your partner, you ought to be clear about which of your needs aren't being met.

MAKE A DATE Unconstructive fights often start because the initiator confronts a partner who isn't ready. There are many times when a person isn't in the right frame of mind to face a conflict: perhaps owing to fatigue, being in too much of a hurry to take the necessary time, upset over another problem, or not feeling well. At times like these, it's unfair to "jump" a person without notice and expect to get full attention for your problem. If you do persist, you'll probably have an ugly fight on your hands.

After you have a clear idea of the problem, approach your partner with a request to try to solve it. For example: "Something's been bothering me. Can we talk about it?" If the answer is yes, then you're ready to go further. If it isn't the right time to confront your partner, find a time that's agreeable to both of you.

DESCRIBE YOUR PROBLEM AND NEEDS Your partner can't possibly meet your needs without kowing why you're upset and what you want. Therefore, it's up to you to describe your problem as specifically as possible. When you do so, it's important to use terms that aren't overly vague or abstract. Recall our discussion of behavioral descriptions in Chapter 3 when clarifying your problem and needs.

PARTNER CHECKS BACK   After you've shared your problem and described what you need, it's important to make sure that your partner has understood what you've said. As you can remember from our discussion of listening in Chapter 4, there's a good chance—especially in a stressful conflict situation—of your words being misinterpreted.

It's usually unrealistic to insist that your partner paraphrase your problem statement, and fortunately there are more tactful and subtle ways to make sure you've been understood. For instance, you might try saying, "I'm not sure I expressed myself very well just now—maybe you should tell me what you heard me say so I can be sure I got it right." In any case, be absolutely sure that your partner understands your whole message before going any further. Legitimate agreements are tough enough, but there's no point in getting upset about a conflict that doesn't even exist.

George Bach suggests a very good idea at this point. Because being really understood is so rare and gratifying, once you're sure your partner understands you, why not express your appreciation with a "thank-you"? Besides reinforcing the importance of good listening, such a gesture can show caring at what is probably a tense time.

SOLICIT PARTNER'S NEEDS   Now that you've made your position clear, it's time to find out what your partner needs in order to feel satisfied about this issue. There are two reasons why it's important to discover your partner's needs. First, it's fair. After all, the other person has just as much right as you to feel satisfied, and if you expect help in meeting your needs, then it's reasonable that you behave in the same way. But in addition to decency, there's another, practical reason for concerning yourself with what the other person wants. Just as an unhappy partner will make it hard for you to become satisfied, a happy one will be more likely to cooperate in letting you reach your goals. Thus, it is in your own self-interest to discover and meet your partner's needs.

You can learn about your partner's needs, simply by asking about them: "Now I've told you what I want and why. Tell me what you need to feel OK about this." Once your partner begins to talk, your job is to use the listening skills discussed earlier in this book to make sure you understand.

Not having studied interpersonal communication, your partner might state intentions in terms of means rather than ends, for instance, saying things like "I want you to be around when I call" instead of "I need to know where you are when I need you." In such cases, it's a good idea to rephrase the statements in terms of ends, thus making it clear to you both what your partner really needs to feel satisfied.

CHECK YOUR UNDERSTANDING OF PARTNER'S NEEDS   Reverse the procedure in Step 4 by paraphrasing your partner's needs until you're certain you understand them. The surest way to accomplish this is to use the paraphrasing skills you learned in Chapter 4.

NEGOTIATE A SOLUTION   Now that you and your partner understand each other's needs, the goal becomes finding a way to meet them. This is done by

▶ We struggled together, knowing. We prattled, pretended, fought bitterly, laughed, wept over sad books or old movies, nagged, supported, gave, took, demanded, forgave, resented—hating the ugliness in each other, yet cherishing that which we were.... Will I ever find someone to battle with as we battled, love as we loved, share with as we shared, challenge as we challenged, forgive as we forgave? You used to say that I saved up all of my feelings so that I could spew forth when I got home. The anger I experienced in school I could not vent there. How many times have I heard you chuckle as you remembered the day I would come home from school and share with you all of the feelings I had kept in. "If anyone had been listening they would have thought you were punishing me, striking out at me. I always survived and you always knew that I would still be with you when you were through." There was an honesty about our relationship that may never exist again.

Vian Catrell

---

trying to develop as many potential solutions as possible and then evaluating them to decide which one best meets everyone's needs.

Probably the best description of the win-win approach has been written by Thomas Gordon in his book *Parent Effectiveness Training*. The following steps are a modification of his approach.

1. **Identify and Define the Conflict.** We've discussed this process in the preceding pages. It consists of discovering each person's problem and needs, setting the stage for meeting all of them.
2. **Generate a Number of Possible Solutions.** In this step the partners work together to think of as many means as possible to reach their stated ends. The key word here is *quantity:* It's important to generate as many ideas as you can think of without worrying about which ones are good or bad. Write down every thought that comes up, no matter how unworkable; sometimes a farfetched idea will lead to a more workable one.
3. **Evaluate the Alternative Solutions.** This is the time to talk about which solutions will work and which ones won't. It's important for all concerned to be honest about their willingness to accept an idea. If a solution is going to work, everyone involved has to support it.
4. **Decide on the Best Solution.** Now that you've looked at all the alternatives, pick the one that looks best to everyone. It's important to be sure everybody understands the solution and is willing to try it out. Remember, your decision doesn't have to be final, but it should look potentially successful.

FOLLOW UP THE SOLUTION   You can't be sure the solution will work until you try it out. After you've tested it for a while, it's a good idea to set aside some time to talk over how things are going. You may find that you need to make some changes or even rethink the whole problem. The idea is to keep on top of the problem, to keep using creativity to solve it.

Win-win solutions aren't always possible. There will be times when even the best-intentioned people simply won't be able to find a way of meeting all their needs. In cases like this, the process of negotiation has to include some compromising. But even then the preceding steps haven't been wasted. The genuine desire to learn what the other person wants and to try to satisfy those desires will build a climate of goodwill that can help you find the best solution to the present problem and also improve your relationship in the future.

Letting Go

One typical comment people have after trying the preceding method of handling conflicts is "This is a helpful thing sometimes, but it's so rational! Sometimes I'm so uptight I don't care about defensiveness or listening or anything . . . I just want to yell and get it off my chest!"

When you feel like this, it's almost impossible to be rational. At times like these, probably the most therapeutic thing to do is to get your feelings off your chest in what Bach calls a "Vesuvius"—an uncontrolled, spontaneous explosion. A Vesuvius can be a terrific way of blowing off steam, and after you do so, it's often much easier to figure out a rational solution to your problem.

So we encourage you to have a Vesuvius with the following qualifications: Be sure your partner understands what you're doing and realizes that whatever you say doesn't call for a response. He or she should let you rant and rave for as long as you want without getting defensive or "tying in." Then, when your eruption subsides, you can take steps to work through whatever still troubles you.

▶ SUMMARY

This chapter explored several factors that help make interpersonal relationships satisfying or unsatisfying. We began by defining communication climate as the emotional tone of a relationship as it is expressed in the messages sent and received. We examined factors that contribute to positive and negative climates, learning that the underlying determining factor is the degree to which a person feels valued by others. We looked at research on the causes and reduction of defensiveness, a major problem in interpersonal relationships.

The final section of the chapter dealt with the matter of interpersonal conflict. We began by asserting that conflict is natural and inevitable, pointing out that when it is handled skillfully, it can be a means of improving relationships. We looked at several styles of conflict that individuals take, then examined three interpersonal approaches to resolving a conflict. We examined one of these approaches, the win-win orientation, in some detail, showing that it is often a possible and realistic method of resolving disputes.

▶ ACTIVITIES

1. You can probably recognize the communication climate in each of your relationships without much analysis. But answering the following questions will

help explain *why* these climates exist. Following these steps may also suggest how to improve negative climates.

▶ Identify the communication climate of an important interpersonal relationship. Using weather metaphors (sunny, gloomy, calm) may help.

▶ List the confirming or disconfirming communication that created and now maintains this climate. Be sure to identify both verbal and nonverbal messages.

▶ Describe what you can do either to maintain the existing climate (if positive) or to change it (if negative). Again, list both verbal and nonverbal behaviors.

2. Approach an important person in your life, and request some help in learning more about yourself. Inform the other person that your discussion will probably take at least an hour, so make sure both of you are prepared to invest this amount of time.

▶ Begin by explaining all twelve of the Gibb behaviors to your partner. Be sure to give enough examples so that each category is clearly understood.

▶ When your explanation is complete and you've answered all your partner's questions, ask him to tell you which of the Gibb categories *you use*. Seek specific examples so that you are certain to understand the feedback fully. (As you are requesting an evaluation, be prepared for a little defensiveness on your own part at this point.) Inform your partner that you are interested in discovering both the defense-arousing and the supportive behaviors you use and that you are sincerely interested in receiving a candid answer. (*Note:* if you don't want to hear the truth from your partner, don't try this exercise.)

▶ As your partner speaks, record the categories he lists in sufficient detail for both of you to be sure that you have understood his comments.

▶ When you have finished your list, show it to your partner. Listen to his or her reactions, and make any corrections that are necessary to reflect an accurate understanding of his or her comments. When your list is accurate, have your partner sign it to indicate that you have understood him or her clearly.

▶ In a concluding statement, note
   a. How you felt as your partner was describing you.
   b. Whether you agree with the evaluation.
   c. What effect your use of the various Gibbs categories has on your relationship with your partner.

3. How does your conflict-related communication affect your relationships? You can find out by answering the following questions:
   a. Recall five conflicts you've been involved in. The more recent they are, the better, and they should be involvements with people who are relatively important to you.
   b. Turn an 8½-by-11-inch sheet of paper horizontally, and divide it into three columns. In the first one describe the nature of each conflict: who it involved and what it was about. In the second column describe how you handled the conflict: what you said and how you acted. Use the third col-

umn to describe the results of each conflict: how you felt, how the others involved felt, and your satisfaction with the outcome.

   c. Based on your findings here, answer the following questions:

     (1) Are you happy with the way you've handled your conflicts? Do you come away from them feeling better or worse than before?

     (2) Have your conflicts left your relationships stronger or weaker?

     (3) Do you recognize any patterns in your conflict style? For example, do you hold your angry feelings inside? Are you sarcastic? Do you lose your temper easily?

     (4) If you could, would you like to change the way you deal with your conflicts?

4. Identify your conflict style by describing five recent interpersonal conflicts. (You can use the ones from the preceding activity if you completed it.) For each situation, describe

   a. Your communication style: nonassertive, directly aggressive, indirectly aggressive, or assertive.

   b. Your level of satisfaction with the style you used.

   c. Responses that would fit the three other styles you did not use (that is, if you behaved nonassertively, describe directly and indirectly aggressive and assertive responses.)

Based on the responses you identified here, how effective is your present conflict style? How could you improve it?

5. This exercise will help you develop a win-win solution for a problem in your own life.

   a. Make a list of the situations in your life where there's a conflict of needs that's creating tension between you and someone else.

   b. Analyze what you're doing at present to resolve such conflicts, and describe whether your behavior is meeting with any success.

   c. Pick at least one of the problems you just listed, and, together with the other people involved, try to develop a win-win solution by following the steps listed earlier.

   d. After following the process described on pages 178–182, share the results of your conference with the class. After you've had time to test your solution, report the progress you've made, and discuss the follow-up conference described on pages 181–182.

▶ NOTES

1. E. Sieburg, "Confirming and Disconfirming Communication in an Organizational Setting," in J. Owen, P. Page, and G. Zimmerman (eds.), *Communication in Organizations* (St. Paul, Minn.: West, 1976), pp. 129–149.

2. Ibid.

3. J. Gibb, "Defensive Communication," *Journal of Communication* 11 (September 1961): 141–148. See also W. F. Eadie, "Defensive Communication Revisited: A Critical Examination of Gibb's Theory," *Southern Speech Communication Journal* 47 (1982): 163–177.

4. J. L. Hocker and W. W. Wilmot, *Interpersonal Conflict*, 2d ed. (Dubuque, Iowa: W. C. Brown, 1985), pp. 22–29.

5. George R. Bach and Herb Goldberg, *Creative Aggression* (Garden City, N.Y.: Doubleday, 1974).
6. Albert C. Filley, *Interpersonal Conflict Resolution* (Glenview, Ill.: Scott, Foresman, 1975), p. 23.
7. George Bach and Yetta Bernhard, *Aggression Lab: The Fair Fight Training Manual* (Dubuque, Iowa: Kendall-Hunt, 1971).
8. Thomas Gordon, *Parent Effectiveness Training* (New York: New American Library, 1975), pp. 263–264.

▶CHAPTER 8

KEY TERMS

closed question
direct question
factual question
indirect question
interview
interviewing

open question
opinion question
primary question
probe
prod
secondary question

INTERVIEWING

After reading this chapter, you should understand the following:

1. The most common types of interviews.

2. The characteristics that define interviewing and distinguish it from other types of communication.

3. The types and uses of interview questions.

4. The roles of interviewer and interviewee, both before and during an interview.

5. The functions of each stage in an interview.

You should be able to do the following:

1. Identify the types of interviews you will most commonly encounter.

2. Define the purpose of an interview in which you might participate.

3. Develop a list of questions to accomplish the goal of an interview.

4. Participate effectively in an interview both as interviewer and interviewee.

A potential employer greets a job applicant: "Let's begin by talking about exactly why you're interested in this opening."

A professor calls a student aside after class: "Neither of us was very happy with your grade on the last exam. I'd like to see where the problem is so you'll do better on the final."

A customer replies to the salesperson's offer of help: "I've been thinking about buying a tape deck, and I'd like to see what you have."

One guest approaches another at a party: "I want to do some backpacking next summer, and I've heard that you've spent a lot of time in the mountains. I was hoping you could suggest some trails and tell me what to expect."

Mention the word **interview,** and most people will think of a news correspondent questioning some public figure or a job applicant facing a potential employer. Though these images are accurate, they tell only part of the story. We all take part in interviews. Some are work-related, determining whether you will get the job you want and how you will do once you have landed the position. Others center on important personal relationships, focusing on everything from finding the perfect birthday gift to solving personal problems. Interviewing also comes into play when you want to learn important information from people with whom you aren't personally involved, perhaps about school, vacationing, how to fix a car, where to find a good restaurant, or what it was like to meet a famous person. Some interviews are formal, and others are casual. Sometimes you are the one who asks the questions; sometimes you are the person who responds. But in all these cases, the ability to get and give information is an important one.

▶ THE NATURE OF INTERVIEWING

What is interviewing, and how does it differ from other kinds of communication? These are the questions the next few pages will answer.

Interviewing Defined

Most communication experts would agree with a definition of **interviewing** as a form of oral communication involving two parties, at least one of whom has a preconceived and serious purpose, and both of whom speak and listen from time to time.[1] This description tells us several important characteristics of interviewing.

The phrase *oral communication* emphasizes the critical role of the spoken word. A verbal interview is far superior to a written one in several ways. First, a spoken exchange gives the interviewer a chance to follow up on ideas that emerge as important. Another advantage of face-to-face interviewing comes from the nonverbal messages that accompany a spoken exchange. Tone of voice, emphasis on certain words, disfluencies such as stammers and stutters, and the other paralinguistic clues we discussed in Chapter 5 add a new dimension to any interaction. For the same reason, in-person interviewing with its accompanying postures, gestures, facial expressions, and so on offers more information than does a written exchange or even one over the telephone.

The phrase *two parties* needs some explanation. There are certainly cases when one person is questioned by a panel of interviewers and other times when two or more respondents face a single interviewer. But no matter how many participants are involved, in every case interviews are *bipolar:* One person or group is exploring issues with another person or group.

When we say that at least one party *has a preconceived and serious purpose,* we distinguish interviews from casual interactions in which the only goal is to pass the time. The fact that an interview has a serious purpose doesn't mean that enjoyment is against the rules—simply that the goal goes beyond sociability.

The words *both of whom speak and listen from time to time* make it clear that interviews are exchanges of messages. In most cases, this exchange involves questions and answers. If either the speaker or the listener dominates the situation, then the interaction becomes a public-speaking situation even though there may be only one person in the audience.

How Interviewing Differs from Conversation

One way to understand the nature of interviewing is to see what it is not. There are several ways in which interviews differ from conversations.

PURPOSE We have already seen that conversations can occur without the participants having any serious preconceived purpose: Two people chat between

floors in an elevator; friends swap jokes at a party; a boss and employees take a break around the coffee machine. An interview, on the other hand, always has a goal.

STRUCTURE   Conversations can be aimless affairs in which neither person knows (or cares) when the exchange will end or exactly what topics will be covered. Any good interview, in contrast, has several distinct parts, which we'll discuss in a few pages.

CONTROL   Whereas conversations don't require any guidance from one of the parties, an interviewer should always be acting in ways that keep the exchange moving toward the preset purpose.

BALANCE   Though most conversations involve roughly the same amount of input from each person, authorities on interviewing suggest that participation ought to be in the 70 to 30 percent ratio, with the interviewee doing most of the talking.[2]

▶ PLANNING THE INTERVIEW

A good interview begins long before you sit down to face the other person. There are several planning steps you can take to boost your chances for success.

The Interviewer's Role

Using Tables 8–1 and 8–2 as guides, choose the most important situation in which you will be an interviewer. Think about yourself in this situation as you read the following section.

TABLE 8–1   Types of Interviews

Information-gathering	Problem and Evaluation
Investigating products and services	Appraisal/performance (employment and
Research	academic)
Career exploration	Counseling (personal and professional)
On-the-job (caseworker, medical, and	Complaint/grievance
so on)	**Persuasive**
Personal interest	Selling products
Survey (market, political, and so on)	Selling services
Journalistic	Quasi-commercial selling (charitable,
Selection	political, religious, and so on)
Hiring	
Promotion	
Placement	

TABLE 8—2 Subjects of Interviews

Job-related	**Financial**
Investigating career	Advice
Employment selection	Assistance (loans, and so on)
Job performance	Investigation (tax audit, and so on)
Employee grievance	Other_____
Counseling	**Other**
Sales	Personal problems
Other_____	Information
School	Family
Investigating courses, major,	Recreation
and so on	Other_____
Understanding coursework	Other_____
Expressing dissatisfaction with course,	
program, and so on	
Other_____	
Consumer	
Investigating products	
Investigating services	
Complaining about products or services	
Other_____	

CLARIFY THE PURPOSE   What do you want to accomplish in the interview? The answer to this question will often seem obvious. For example, in an information-gathering interview, you might want to find the best places to go on an upcoming vacation or to find out more about "the old days" from an older relative. But often a purpose that seems clear will prove too vague to get you what you want. For example, your questions about a vacation could result in a list of places too expensive for you or unrelated to your interests. In the same way, your request for information about the old days could bring on a string of stories about long-dead (and uninteresting) relatives when you are really interested in events rather than personalities.

The more clearly you can define the goal of your interview, the greater your chances for success will be. One way to set clear goals is to think about specific content areas you'll need to explore to achieve your general purpose. See how this process of focusing on a goal works in the following situations:

GENERAL GOAL	SPECIFIC CONTENT OBJECTIVES
Learn best place to go.	Discover affordable, beautiful place that is different from home.
Learn about old days.	Learn how daily routines differed from now, how area looked before it was built up, what social relationships were like, what people did for recreation.

GENERAL GOAL	SPECIFIC CONTENT OBJECTIVES
Choose best roommate to fit with present occupants of apartment.	Find person with similar or compatible study habits, dating life, ideas about neatness; also, person must be financially responsible.
Get mechanic's opinion about whether I should fix up present car or get a newer one.	Explore cost of repairing old one vs. expense of fixing up newer one; determine life expectancy, performance, mileage of old vs. new.

DEVELOP TENTATIVE QUESTIONS More than any other factor the quality of the interviewer's questions and the way they are asked will determine the success or failure of an interview. Truly good questions rarely come spontaneously, even to the best of interviewers. After you define your goals and content objectives, the next step is to develop a list of questions. You need to think about several factors in planning questions:

1. **Relationship to Purpose.** Your questions should cover all the content objectives you developed in the previous step. Furthermore, it's important to cover each area in the amount of depth that suits your needs. For example, in interviewing an instructor about how best to prepare for an exam, you should briefly cover the areas you feel confident about while spending enough time on tougher subjects to be sure you're prepared. This suggestion may seem obvious, but many inexperienced interviewers find to their dismay that they have wasted most of their time discussing trivial areas and have failed to get their most important questions answered.

2. **Factual vs. Opinion Questions.** Some questions involve matters of fact: "What's the difference between an integrated amplifier and a preamplifier?" or "How many points will I need to earn an *A* for the course?" These can be called **factual questions.** In other cases, you'll want to ask **opinion questions:** "What occupations do you think will offer the best chance for advancement in the next few years?" or "How do you think I should go about apologizing?" When planning an interview, you should ask yourself whether you're more interested in facts or opinions and plan your questions accordingly.

   In some cases, you can approach a question either factually or subjectively, often with quite different results. For example, imagine that you're interviewing two close friends, trying to resolve a conflict between them. Notice the difference between asking, "Where do you think the problem lies?" (a broad, subjective question that invites disagreement between the disputants) and "What are some of the things bothering each of you?" (a factual question that doesn't call for the parties to read each other's minds). Again, you need to think clearly about whether you're seeking facts or opinions.

3. **Open vs. Closed Questions.** You have almost certainly had the frustrating experience of trying to draw out an uncommunicative partner:

   You "How've you been?"
   Other "Fine."

▶ You start a question, and it's like starting a stone. You sit quietly on the top of a hill; and away the stone goes, starting others.

Robert Louis Stevenson

You "Up to anything new lately?"

Other "Nope. Same old stuff."

You "You look good. Have you been getting a lot of exercise?"

Other "Not really."

▶ Judge a man, not by his answers, but by his questions.

Voltaire

Although the respondent here could have certainly done better at holding up the other end of the conversation, much of the problem grew out of the type of questions being asked. All of them were *closed*: questions that could be answered in a word or two. Though some talkative subjects will freely amplify on a closed question, less outgoing ones will give you the briefest response possible. The best way to encourage interviewees to talk up is by asking **open questions,** which require the subject to answer in detail:

"If you had the chance to start your career over again, what things would you do differently?"

"What were some of the things you liked best about New York?"

"Start at the beginning and tell me just what happened."

It will take time and thought to develop a list of open questions to cover all your content areas, but your effort will be rewarded in several ways. First, you will almost certainly have enough lengthy responses to fill the allotted time, soothing a common fear of inexperienced interviewers. Your open questions, inviting comment as they do, will also make your subject feel more comfortable. Furthermore, the way in which your subject chooses to answer your open questions will tell you more about him or her than you could probably learn by only asking more restrictive **closed questions,** which can be answered in a few words.

Closed questions aren't all bad: For one thing they're easy for many subjects to answer, and you can ask many of them in a short period of time. Also, closed questions are appropriate for some subjects. For example, you wouldn't want long-winded replies to questions such as "What's the cost of part #1234?" or "What is your social security number?" As an interviewer, you should decide what type of information you need and then choose the combination of open and closed questions that will get it for you.

4. **Direct vs. Indirect Questions.** Most of the time the best way to get information is to ask a **direct question:**

"Have you had any experience in this kind of work?"

"How much were you planning to spend for a new coat?"

"What kinds of things are you looking for in an apartment and new room-mates?"

There are times, however, when a subject won't be able to answer a direct question. At one time or another, most of us have been so confused that we've answered the question "What don't you understand?" by replying in exasperation, "Everything!" In other cases, you've heard yourself or someone else sincerely answer the question "Do you understand?" in the affirmative, only to find out later that this wasn't true.

There are also times when a subject might be *able* to answer a question sincerely but isn't *willing* to do so. This sort of situation usually occurs when a candid answer would be embarrassing or risky. For instance, when interviewing a prospective roommate, you'd be naive to ask, "Do you always pay your share of the rent on time?" because a truly shifty person would probably answer yes.

At times like these it's wise to seek information by using **indirect questions,** which do not directly request the information you are seeking. You could ask potential roommates whether their share of the rent money would be coming from current work (then check to see if they're employed) or from savings. In the same way, instead of asking, "Are you creative?" a prospective employer might present a job applicant with a typical or hypothetical situation, looking for an innovative solution.

5. **Primary vs. Secondary Questions.** Sometimes you will need to ask only an initial, **primary question** to get the fact or opinion you need in a given content area. But more often you will need to follow up your first question with others to give you all the information you need. These follow-up **probes** are called **secondary questions.**

> **Primary Question:** "In your opinion who are the best people for me to ask about careers in the computer field?"

> **Secondary Questions:** "How could I meet them?" "Do you think they'd be willing to help?" "How could each one help me?"

It's a good idea to develop a list of secondary questions in each content area so you can be sure to get all the information you need. Why fumble on the spot for a way to follow up an incomplete answer when you can plan in advance?

ARRANGE THE SETTING Even the best questions won't help an interview that takes place in a bad setting. To avoid such problems, keep these two considerations in mind as you arrange a meeting with your subject.

The first is *time.* Just as you should pick a time that is convenient for you, it's equally important for you to do the same for the interviewee. When arranging an appointment with your subject, be sure you've avoided predictably busy days or hours when the press of unfinished business may distract your interviewee. If you can, tactfully discover whether the subject is a morning or evening person—some people function especially well or poorly at certain times of the day. You should also make sure that the interviewee doesn't have appointments or other obligations that will overlap with your scheduled time.

The right *place* for an interview is also important. The most important consideration is to have a spot that is free of distractions. A constantly ringing telephone or other people dropping by to ask questions or chat can throw you and your subject off the track. If any of your questions call for confidential answers, the setting should be private. It's also important for the location to be convenient for both parties. Neither you nor the interviewee will do best if you've had to struggle for a parking place or gotten lost trying to find the right spot. Finally, your setting should be comfortable and attractive enough to put your

subject at ease. Don't go overboard and choose too relaxed a setting: Too many beers or the pleasures of a beach might lead you or your interviewee to forget your main reason for meeting.

The Interviewee's Role

Because most of the responsibility for planning an interview rests with the interviewer, the subject has an easier time during the planning phase. There are, however, some things a respondent can do in advance to make the interview a good one.

CLARIFY THE INTERVIEWER'S GOALS   It's important to know just what the interviewer is seeking from you. Sometimes the interviewer's goals are obvious. The insurance sales representative who wants "to see if you're paying too much for your present coverage" is trying to sell you a new policy, and a friend who wants to know how you've repaired an object or fixed a recipe is probably looking for your expertise.

TABLE 8–3 Checklist for Interview Planning

INTERVIEWER	INTERVIEWEE
Goals	**Goals**
☐ General purpose defined	☐ Interviewer's goals clearly understood
☐ Specific content areas listed	☐ Interviewee's goals clearly defined
Tentative Questions	**Preparation**
☐ Cover all content areas in specific depth	☐ Necessary information, materials collected
☐ Each question properly phrased as factual or opinion	☐ Thought given to interviewer's probable questions
☐ Each question properly worded as open or closed	
☐ Each question properly worded directly or indirectly	
Setting	
☐ Best time chosen for both interviewer and subject	
☐ Private, comfortable, distraction-free setting chosen	

In other cases, the interviewer's goal isn't quite so clear. Sometimes you know the general goal of the interview but need to understand the specific content areas more clearly. For example, suppose you are preparing for an employment interview. You know that the company is looking for the best applicant to fill the job. But just what kinds of qualities are they seeking? Are education and training most important? Experience? Initiative? Knowing these criteria in advance will boost your chances of doing well in the interview.

There will be times when an interviewer has hidden goals, which you should do your best to discover. For instance, your boss's questions about your daily job routine might really be part of the managerial process of deciding whether to promote (or fire) you. An acquaintance's ostensible questions about factual information might really be aimed at building a friendship. This last example shows that not all hidden goals are malicious, but in any case you'll feel more comfortable and behave more effectively when you know what the interviewer wants from you.

CLARIFY YOUR OWN GOALS Sometimes the subject's only role in an interview is to help the questioner. But there are other times when you, as an interviewee, will have your own agenda. Although a sales representative might be trying to sell you an insurance policy, you could be interested in getting an education on the subject. When your boss conducts an interview assessing your performance, you might want to learn by observation how to do the same thing later in your career when you're a manager. Keep your own goals in mind when thinking about the upcoming session.

DO YOUR HOMEWORK There are many cases in which a subject can make an interview run quickly and well by preparing materials or answers in advance. If you know that the interviewer will be seeking certain information, get it together before your meeting. Sometimes you'll need to bring facts and figures as when you need to justify your claims during an income tax audit. At other times an interviewee should collect materials. For instance, an interviewer describing what college is like to a graduating high school senior might bring along class schedules, catalogs, textbooks, and exams.

Preparation is an important step in interviewing. But once the interviewer and subject get together, there's more to do than simply ask and answer the prepared questions.

Stages of an Interview

An interview, like the speeches you'll read about in later chapters, has three distinct parts.

OPENING   This beginning stage serves two important functions. Most important, it establishes the tone of the relationship between interviewer and subject: formal or informal, relaxed or tense, serious or humorous. Just as the first stages of a date or party will generally shape what comes later, the success or failure of an interview is often determined before the first question is asked. Besides setting the tone, a good introduction will also give the interviewee a preview (or reminder) of the interviewer's goals and what subjects will be covered.

The usual format for an opening begins with some sort of greeting, which includes any introductions that are necessary. A period of informal conversation sometimes follows, in which the interviewer and subject talk about subjects of mutual interest not necessarily related to the interview topic. This period gives both people a chance to get settled and acquainted before getting down to business. This greeting stage may sound artificial—which it often is. But there's no need to discuss obviously trivial subjects or act phony here: the idea is to establish some common ground sincerely between interviewer and subject.

In the final stage of the opening, the interviewer should preview topics of discussion and brief the subject on plans for proceeding: "I appreciate your giving me the time. I expect my questions will take about forty-five minutes. I'd like to start by learning how you got started, then go on to talk about what you've learned during your career, and finish by asking for any suggestions you have that might help me in my career."

BODY   This middle stage of the interview is the longest. It's here that the interviewer asks the questions that were planned before the meeting.

Although the list of questions is important, it's sometimes a mistake to follow them precisely. Some areas will need more exploration whereas others won't seem worth pursuing. The trick in the body of the interview is to focus on all the important content areas in a way that seems most comfortable to both interviewer and subject. (We'll have more to say about the roles of each party shortly.)

CLOSING   In many ways, the closing is similar to the opening. Instead of previewing, however, the conclusion is a time for reviewing what's occurred during the interview. This helps ensure that the interviewer has correctly understood any points that might be unclear and has gotten the general tone of the subject matter correctly.

The closing is also a time to establish the future of the relationship between interviewer and subject: to decide if any future meetings are necessary, possibly to set a date for them. Finally, it's usually good to conclude the interview with an exchange of sincere pleasantries. Table 8–4 summarizes the points to remember when planning, conducting, and evaluating an interview.

The Interviewer's Role

During the session the interviewer has several responsibilities:

CONTROL AND FOCUS THE CONVERSATION   The interviewer's job is to ensure that each stage of the conversation—opening, body, and closing—takes the right amount of time and that all important content areas are covered. It's easy to get off on a tangent and discover too late that the available time is up.

HELP THE SUBJECT FEEL COMFORTABLE   In simplest terms, this includes making sure that the setting is physically comfortable. But it's just as important that the interviewer use the listening, relational, and nonverbal skills we discussed earlier in this book to help the subject feel at ease. For example, suppose the interviewee seems reluctant to share personal information in an important

TABLE 8–4   Checklist for Evaluating Interviews

Opening
- ☐ Sincere, appropriate pleasantries exchanged to help both parties feel comfortable
- ☐ Proper tone established (formal vs. informal, serious vs. casual)
- ☐ Interviewer previews subject and approach

Body
- ☐ Interviewer's nonverbal behavior reflects interest and lack of threat to subject
- ☐ Interviewer asks enough questions to cover all content areas established in advance
- ☐ Interviewer uses probes to explore client's responses (repetition, amplification, paraphrasing, silence)
- ☐ Interviewee gives clear, detailed answers
- ☐ Interviewee keeps on subject
- ☐ Interviewee corrects any misunderstandings of interviewer
- ☐ Interviewee achieves own goals

Closing
- ☐ Interviewer reviews results of interview
- ☐ Future relationship between interviewer and interviewee established
- ☐ Sincere pleasantries exchanged

content area. The interviewer might then remember that self-disclosure is reciprocal and volunteer some information such as the reasons for asking all the questions.

PROBE FOR IMPORTANT INFORMATION Sometimes your first question in a certain area won't give you all the information you need. At times like this it's important to probe for the facts or beliefs you're seeking by asking secondary or follow-up questions. There are several types of probes you can use as an interviewer:

1. **Repeat.** Either because of evasiveness or fuzzy thinking, subjects sometimes need to hear a question several times before giving a full answer.

   Adult   (*breaking up fight between two children*) "Hey, what's this all about?"
   Child A   "He's a punk!"
   Adult   "But what were you fighting about?"
   Child B   "It's not my fault! She started it!"
   Adult   "But what were you fighting about?"
   Child A   "I did *not* start it. *You* started it!"
   Adult   "I don't care who started it. I just want to find out what you're fighting about."

2. **Amplify.** When an answer is incomplete, you need to get more information.

   Customer   "I want to buy some running shoes."
   Salesperson   "What kind of running do you do?"
   Customer   "Oh, mostly just for fun."
   Salesperson   "I mean how far do you run and on what kind of surfaces?"
   Customer   "I mostly run on the track at the high school . . . a few miles."
   Salesperson   "When you say a few miles, do you mean three or four each time you run, or more?"

3. **Paraphrase.** Paraphrasing, as discussed in Chapter 4, serves two purposes. First, it helps to clarify a vague answer. In addition it encourages the speaker to give more information about the topic.

   A   "I'm so fed up with that class that I'm ready to drop it. I just wanted to talk it over with you before I did."
   B   "So you're pretty sure that the right thing to do would be to quit because the class is giving you so much trouble."
   A   "Well, I'm just not sure. The semester is almost over, and if I did drop it now, I'd just have to repeat the class later."
   B   "So you're really not sure what to do, is that it?"
   A   "Oh, I guess I ought to stick it out. It's just that I'm really tired. I'll sure be glad when the semester is over."

4. **Silence and Prods.** A bit of experimenting will show you the value of pauses and **prods**—brief but encouraging phrases such as "Really?" "Uh-huh," "I see," and "Tell me more about it." Often a subject will be anxious to talk about a topic if simply given a sympathetic and interested ear.

▶ He was so preoccupied with the mechanics of taking notes that he never listened. I wanted to scream at him, "put away your pencil and *listen* to me!" But I knew he'd never hear me. He'd just write it down.

Interview subject quoted by Ken Metzler
Creative Interviewing

The Interviewee's Role

There are several things you can do as a subject to make the interview a success.

GIVE CLEAR, DETAILED ANSWERS Put yourself in the interviewer's shoes, and be as specific and helpful as you hope others would be for you. Although the interviewer ought to draw you out skillfully, make that job easier by being helpful yourself.

KEEP ON THE SUBJECT It is sometimes tempting to go overboard with your answers, sidetracking the discussion into areas that won't help the interviewer. It's often a good idea to ask the questioner whether your answers are being helpful and then to adjust them accordingly.

CORRECT ANY MISUNDERSTANDINGS Sometimes an interviewer will misinterpret your ideas. When this happens, be sure to correct the mistaken impression. Of course, one way to be certain that the message was received correctly is to invite the interviewer to paraphrase what he or she thinks you said. When an important issue is in question, any conscientious interviewer will be willing to do so.

COVER YOUR OWN AGENDA As we pointed out earlier in this chapter, interviewees often have their own goals, which are sometimes different from those of the interviewer. It's important to keep these in mind during the session so that you can satisfy your own needs in a way that is compatible with the questioner's purpose.

▶ THE SELECTION INTERVIEW

For many people, the short time spent facing a potential employer is the most important interview of a lifetime. After all, a great deal is at stake. Most of us spend the greatest part of our adult lives on the job: roughly 2,000 hours per year for a full-time employee. In addition, the financial difference between an unrewarding position and a well-paying one can be staggering. Even without considering the effects of inflation, a gap of only $200 per month can amount to almost $100,000 over the course of a career. Finally, the emotional stakes of having the right position are high. A frustrating job not only can block the chances for advancement and lead to unhappiness at work; these dissatisfactions have a way of leaking into nonworking hours as well.

How important is an interview in getting the right job? The Bureau of National Affairs, a private research firm that serves both the government and industry, conducted a survey to answer this question.[3] They polled 196 personnel executives to find out what factors are most important in hiring applicants. The results of their survey showed that the employment interview is the single most important factor in landing a job.

Employment Strategies

Most people naively believe that the best candidate gets the job. Although this principle might be fair and logical, the employment process usually doesn't work this way. In reality, *the person who knows the most about getting hired* usually gets the desired position. Though job-getting skills are no substitute for qualifications once the actual work begins, they are necessary if you are going to be hired in the first place.

What is the best strategy for getting the job offer you want? The advice job seekers often get is certainly important: Scan sources of job announcements for positions, and prepare a thorough, professional resumé. But beyond these steps are other strategies that can often give you a critical boost over other applicants.[4]

BACKGROUND RESEARCH　Your first step should be to explore the types of work and specific organizations for which you'd like to work. This phase in-

volves looking into all those areas that have interested you in the past. Through library research, reading magazine and newspaper articles, taking classes, and simply fantasizing, find out as much as possible about jobs that might be interesting to you. The result of your research should be a list of organizations and of people who can tell you more about your chosen field and help you make contacts.

BACKGROUND INTERVIEWS At this point arrange to meet the people on the list you have just developed. These meetings are *not* employment interviews in which you're specifically asking for the job. Rather, they serve three purposes:

1. To help you learn more about the fields and companies that interest you.
2. To help you make contacts that might later lead to a job offer from your interview subject.
3. To develop leads about other people you might contact for help in your job search.

These background interviews are information-gathering in nature, so it's wise to read the section of this chapter that deals with this subject before beginning this step.

TABLE 8–5 Common Job Interview Questions

Questions from the Employer

What makes you think you're qualified to work for this company? (How can you help us?)
What have you been doing since your last job?
Why are you interested in this company? This job?
What do you want in your career?
What would you do if…(hypothetical situation)
Where do you see yourself in five years?
Tell me about your experience.
What did you like (not like) about your last job?
What's your greatest strength (limitation) for this job?

Questions for the Employer

Will you describe the duties of the job for me, please?
Will you tell me where this job fits within the organization?
What characteristics do you most hope to find in people for this kind of assignment?
Can you tell me about the prospects for advancement beyond this level?
What is the biggest problem facing your staff now? How have past and current employees had trouble solving this problem?
What have been the best results produced by people in this job?
What are the primary results you would like to see me produce?
Can you describe the ideal candidate for this job? Then we can see how closely I fit your requirements?

TABLE 8–6 Common Interviewer Complaints About Job Applicants

1. Is caught lying.
2. Shows lack of interest in the interview, merely shopping around.
3. Has a belligerent attitude, is rude or impolite.
4. Lacks sincerity.
5. Is evasive concerning information about himself or herself.
6. Is concerned only about salary.
7. Is unable to concentrate.
8. Displays a lack of initiative.
9. Is indecisive.
10. Has an arrogant attitude.
11. Has a persecuted attitude.
12. Tries to use pull to get a job.
13. Has dirty hands or face.
14. Is cynical.
15. Is intolerant and has strong prejudices.
16. Is late for the interview.
17. Has a limp-fish handshake.
18. Is unable to express himself or herself clearly.
19. Shows lack of planning for career.
20. Has not done research into the history and products of the company.
21. Wants to start in an executive position.
22. Lacks maturity.
23. Has low moral standards.
24. Presents extreme appearance.
25. Oversells case.

Based on Charles S. Goetzinger, Jr., "An Analysis of Irritating Factors in Initial Employment Interviews of Male College Graduates," unpublished doctoral dissertation, Purdue University, 1954. Cited in Charles J. Stewart and William B. Cash, Jr., *Interviewing: Principles and Practices,* 2d ed. (Dubuque, Iowa: W. C. Brown, 1978).

Tips for the Interviewee

Once you are in the interview itself, there are several important points to keep in mind.

FOLLOW THE INTERVIEWER'S LEAD   Let the interviewer set the emotional tone of the session: amount of humor, level of formality, and so forth. A great deal depends on the personal chemistry between interviewer and candidate, so try to match the interviewer's style without becoming phony.

RESPOND TO THE EMPLOYER'S NEEDS   Though you may need a job to repay your student loan or finance your new Porsche, these concerns won't impress a potential employer. (See Table 8–6.) Companies hire an employee to satisfy *their* needs. Your approach in an interview, then, should be to show your potential employer how your skills match up with the company's concerns. Here's where your background research will pay off: If you've spent time learning about your potential employer, you'll be in a good position to talk about that company's concerns and how you can satisfy them.

RECOGNIZE AND RESPOND TO HIDDEN QUESTIONS   As you read earlier in this chapter, some questions are indirect. For example, the question "Where do you see yourself five years from now?" most likely means "How ambitious are you? How well do your plans fit with this company's goals? How realistic are you?" In the same way, when an interviewer asks, "Why did you leave your last job?" the real questions are probably "Are you competent? Can you get along with others?"

BE HONEST   Whatever else an employer may be seeking, honesty is a key job requirement. If an interviewer finds that you've misrepresented yourself by lying or exaggerating about even one answer, everything else you say will be suspect. Emphasize your strengths, and downplay your weak areas, of course, but always be honest.

KEEP YOUR ANSWERS BRIEF   It's easy to rattle on in an interview either out of enthusiasm, a desire to show off your knowledge, or nervousness; but in most

"*Yes, I'm sure you are, but unfortunately this place is already crawling with 'swell guys.'*"

Drawing by Woodman; © 1981 The New Yorker Magazine, Inc.

cases, long answers are not a good idea. The interviewer probably has lots of ground to cover, and long-winded answers won't help this task. A good rule of thumb is to keep your responses under two minutes.

LOOK GOOD AND BEHAVE WELL   You should obviously present a good image. Dress neatly and appropriately, be on time, and bring along any necessary materials.

HAVE YOUR OWN QUESTIONS ANSWERED   Any good employer will recognize that you have your own concerns about the job. After you've answered the interviewer's questions, you should be prepared to ask a few of your own. See Table 8–5 for some suggestions.

THE INFORMATION-GATHERING INTERVIEW ◀

Although you might not label them as such, you almost certainly take part in a great many information-gathering interviews. Whenever you investigate an offer of goods or services, seek advice about the future, explore another person's opinions or background, or seek specific facts, you are conducting an interview. The following suggestions will help you do a good job.

Collecting Background Information

Sometimes a period of research can pay dividends when the actual interview begins. Suppose, for instance, that you have decided to treat yourself to a foreign vacation. You have heard about a travel agent who arranges unusual trips— river rafting, mountain climbing, tramp steamer voyages, and so on. You've made an appointment to talk with the agent and hear some suggestions. Of course, it's the agent's job to interview *you* to find out what kind of trip suits your interests; but at the same time your advance research can help you both in answering the agent's questions and in asking some of your own. What parts of the world interest you? Read about those areas to discover any interesting features you'd like to see. What about types of transportation? Climates? Life-styles? Having thought about areas like these will boost the chances that you'll arrange the best vacation.

Choosing the Right Interviewee

Sometimes the most obvious subject for an interview isn't the best person to answer your questions. Asking an instructor about how a course is taught might not be as productive as talking to students who have taken it in the past. Seeking financial advice from a wealthy person might not be helpful if that subject made the money in times that were different from these or if the subject's interests or skills are different from yours. Sometimes knowing *whom* to ask is just as important as knowing *what* to ask.

Informational Interviewing Tips

In addition to the general suggestions on pages 191–195, follow these pointers when conducting informational interviews.

In addition to the general suggestions on pages 191–195,

▶ He who asks is a fool for five minutes. He who does not ask is a fool forever.

Chinese proverb

BE CURIOUS Whereas matters like wording questions correctly and choosing the right environment are important, another essential ingredient for success in interviewing is honest curiosity, as shown by a willingness to follow a line of questioning until you're satisfied and to ask about points that interest you. Your sincere curiosity will often warm up an interviewee, who will be flattered by your interest. And an inquiring attitude will help you think of new and important questions during your interview, transforming it from what might be a sterile recitation of the questions you prepared in advance.

CHECK YOUR UNDERSTANDING After reading Chapter 4, you know that much listening is inaccurate. Keeping this fact in mind, you will find it a good idea to check your understanding of important ideas with the interviewee. Sometimes the consequences of misunderstanding are fairly small: a botched recipe (was it a tablespoon or a cup of vinegar?) or getting lost (were you supposed to turn right or left?). In other cases, however, misunderstandings can be more serious. The fact that you thought you understood an instructor's explanation won't change your low grade on a final exam, and the Internal Revenue Service won't forgive your tax penalties because you thought the local agent said something that turned out to be something else. Whenever there's a chance of misinterpretation, it's a good idea to use the active listening skills you learned earlier in this book.

USE THE BEST INTERVIEWING STRATEGY In many cases, your best approach is to ask questions in the simplest, most straightforward manner. There are times, however, when a more strategic approach will produce better results.

You have already read about the value of asking indirect questions when direct ones will be embarrassing or difficult to answer. Instead of asking a merchant, "Will your advice about products or service be any good?" you could ask about some product that you already know about.

There are also times when the personality of your interviewing subject calls for a strategic way of presenting yourself. For instance, if you are talking to someone whose self-image is one of being an authority or a wise person, you might take a *naive* approach: "Gee, I'm new at this, and you know so much." A little flattery never hurts. At other times you might want to act more like an *interrogator,* particularly when you think a subject is trying to treat you like a fool. For instance, you could show your knowledge and seriousness to a car mechanic by saying, "Why did you suggest a valve job without running a compression check?" (Here's one case where gathering background information on automotive repair could improve your interviewing and save you a healthy chunk of money.) In still other cases, a *sympathetic* or *chummy* approach can be helpful. Investing the time and money to chat over coffee or beers can shake loose information a subject might be unwilling to share in a more formal setting.

The Persuasive Interview

The most recognizable type of persuasive interview involves the selling of some commercial product, either merchandise or service. But there are also noncommercial situations in which the interview aims at changing the attitudes or behavior of a subject. Candidates meet with prospective voters, either in person or via broadcast media; religious people try to influence the beliefs of others; and representatives of charitable organizations are constantly seeking more funds for their causes, often in interview settings.

There are several steps to follow for a successful persuasive interview:

DEFINE YOUR GOAL   In Chapter 11 we'll talk in detail about defining a public speaking goal. Some of the same principles apply here. You ought to have a clear idea of just what kind of change you're seeking in your subject. Your goal should be specifically worded, and it should be a realistically attainable one.

UNDERSTAND THE INTERVIEWEE   A persuasive approach that will convince one person will be ineffective with others. Your best chance of success will come from understanding your subjects—their interests, concerns, level of knowledge, and background.

USE PERSUASIVE STRATEGIES   Chapter 15 contains a list of persuasive strategies that are useful in both public speaking and interview settings. In addition to the items there, you should consider these guidelines:[5]

1. Welcome the subject's questions and reactions. They tell you how the interviewee is responding to your approach, giving you a chance to adapt and keep on target. It is important, however, for you to choose the time when the other person voices his or her concerns. You should keep control of the interview to avoid complicating the discussion.
2. Show that you understand the interviewee's position. The fact that you understand will leave the other person feeling more positive about you, diminishing the "hard-sell" image.
3. Keep your approach clear and simply stated. Only bring up one subject at a time, and organize your presentation logically. See Chapters 12 and 13 for more suggestions in this area.

The Appraisal Interview

Appraisal interviews are most common in school and job settings, where a student's or employee's performance is judged. At its best, the appraisal process is a tool for recognizing accomplishments and finding ways to improve performance in problem areas. But, in practice, things sometimes work out differently. It's not hard to see why: Appraisal is a form of evaluation and, as such, has a high potential for arousing defensiveness. Here are a few suggestions for making appraisal interviews truly productive.

As an interviewee:

1. Remember that criticism of your work in one area doesn't mean you're no good as a person or even in other areas in which you interact with the interviewer.
2. Approach the interview with a sincere desire to do better. View the interview as a chance to start improving your performance. This attitude will impress the interviewer and will help you grow.
3. When faced with vague descriptions of your behavior ("You're doing well" or "You're not keeping up"), ask the interviewer for specific examples. Your goal here isn't to be argumentative but to understand exactly what the interviewer is talking about.
4. Do your best to avoid behaving defensively by counterattacking or withdrawing. Though reactions like these are understandable, they probably won't make you feel any better and are likely to lower your stature in the interviewer's eyes.

As an interviewer:

1. Acknowledge good work as well as pointing out problem areas.
2. Be improvement-oriented. Try to focus on making things better rather than simply criticizing. Set specific behavioral goals (see Chapter 3) for the upcoming evaluation period.
3. Be descriptive, not evaluative. Describe how the interviewee's behavior affects you and the organization.
4. Be a good listener. Try really to understand the respondent's point of view. Remember the value of paraphrasing when someone else is upset.

The Counseling Interview

Few people are professional counselors or therapists, but at one time or another we're all faced with the chance to help solve another person's problem: love, career, family, money . . . the list of troublesome areas is a long one.

There are two approaches to counseling others with problems—directive and nondirective. The directive approach includes a good deal of question asking, analysis, and advice. There are definitely situations in which this approach is the best one, most often when the counselor has greater knowledge than the interviewee. For example, a friend might approach you for advice on how to get help from some consumer-protection agency. If you know the right procedure, you surely would share this information and suggest how your friend ought to proceed.

There are many other cases when a directive approach isn't the best one. Suppose your problem-ridden friend asks for advice about whether or not to get married. Even the best advice can be ignored or rejected at times like this. There is another risk in giving advice: If your friend follows your suggestions and things don't work out, you are the one who's likely to be held responsible.

The most important decision in counseling interviews, then, is whether to use a directive or nondirective approach. Be sure to base your decision on knowledge of the person seeking help and on the nature of the problem. In any case,

it's essential to know just how much help and guidance one can give as a friend and when it's dangerous to begin playing counselor without the necessary training. It's better to say, "I don't know what to tell you" than to give bad advice to a person in need.

The Survey Interview

Surveys are a type of information gathering in which the responses of a sample of a population are collected to disclose information about a larger group. Surveys are used in government, businesses, and educational concerns. Interviews are a valuable way of surveying, for they provide greater respondent cooperation, depth of response, and flexibility than other means of gathering data, such as questionnaires.

In order to be effective, survey interviews must collect data from a representative sample of the population in question. A classic example of poor sampling occurred in the 1936 presidential election, when a popular magazine, *Literary Digest,* interpreted the results of over two million survey responses to mean that Alfred Landon would beat Franklin D. Roosevelt by a landslide. Hindsight showed that the incorrect prediction arose from the fact that the respondents were chosen from telephone directories and automobile registration lists. During the Great Depression only upper- and middle-class people fell into these categories. Thus, the survey failed to give adequate representation to the millions of less affluent Democrats who were to choose Roosevelt.

Most survey interviews are highly structured, with respondents all being asked identical questions in identical order. This sort of structure ensures that all respondents are, in fact, being approached in the same way. Survey interviewers are trained to standardize their approach, even to the extent of repeating the same nonverbal behaviors from one situation to the next. For example, a smile in one interview might encourage responses that would differ from those elicited by a more restrained approach.

▶ SUMMARY

Interviewing is a special kind of conversation, being more purposeful, structured, controlled, and one-sided than other types of two-party interaction. There are many types of interviews—information-gathering, selection, problem and evaluation, and persuasive. Each of these types contains several subcategories, which are listed in Table 8–1.

A successful interview begins with a planning phase before the parties meet. During that time, the interviewer should define the goal of the session, develop tentative questions, and arrange the setting. The questions should be closely related to the purpose of the interview. Thought should also be given as to whether questions will be factual or opinion-seeking, open or closed, and direct or indirect. When necessary, primary questions should be followed up by secondary inquiries. In the preparation stage, the interviewee should clarify the interviewer's goals as much as possible and do whatever planning will help the session run smoothly.

Interviews consist of three stages—opening, body, and closing. During the session, the interviewer should control and focus the conversation, help the subject feel comfortable, and probe for important information. The interviewer's role includes giving clear, detailed answers, keeping on the subject, and correcting any misunderstandings. In addition, interviewers should also be sure to accomplish their own goals.

Though the steps outlined early in the chapter are useful in all contexts, specific types of interviews have their own requirements. Selection and information-gathering interviews were discussed in some detail; and persuasive, appraisal, counseling, and survey interviews were briefly described.

▶ ACTIVITIES

1. Almost everybody takes part in interviews. This exercise will help you identify the subjects and types of interviews that play a role in your life.
   a. Use Table 8–2 to identify interviewing situations that you have experienced. In addition to noting situations in which you have been involved in the past, you can also list the kinds of interviews in which you will be involved in the future. (For example, you may know you'll take part in an employment interview and realize that you should also seek advice about potential employers before doing so.)
   b. For each subject, indicate the type of interview in which you'll be involved, using Table 8–2 as a guide.

c. For each situation, indicate whether you will play the role of interviewer or interviewee.

d. Finally, for each item you've checked, write the name of the person or persons with whom you'll be speaking. If you don't know any names, describe them as best you can (for example, potential boss, irate customer).

2. Choose one situation in which you'll be an interviewer. Using that situation
   a. List your objectives for the interview.
   b. Translate these goals into content areas.
   c. Write a list of tentative questions sufficient to explore each content area. Be sure your questions follow the suggestions in this chapter.

3. How well do you understand the nature of interview questions? Find out by identifying each of the following questions as either open or closed, factual or opinion-seeking, primary or secondary. For each primary question you identify, write two secondary questions. For each closed question, write an open question that would generate additional useful information.
   a. "Have you been hospitalized in the last five years?"
   b. "I don't blame you for wanting good roommates. What kinds of things do you think make a roommate good?"
   c. "You've been awfully quiet lately. Are you upset?"
   d. "Now that you've told me which parkas you have in stock, do you think the more expensive one is worth the extra money?"
   e. "Can you give me some examples of the type of questions we'll need to answer in each area?"

4. This exercise will help you build your skill at probing for more information when interviewing subjects. For each statement that follows, write an appropriate probing response. Be sure to use each of the following types of response at least once:
   a. "I'd never hire her!"
   b. "Career advice? I'd check with the placement office on campus." (You asked about advice from people already in business.)
   c. "I'm not sure how to answer that."
   d. "I'm probably wasting your time."
   e. "I guess what I'm looking for are some useful courses."
   f. "The book by Jones and Smith might help you."

NOTES ◄

1. Robert S. Goyer, W. Charles Redding, and John T. Rickey, *Interviewing Principles and Techniques: A Project Text* (Dubuque, Iowa: Kendall-Hunt, 1968), pp. 6–7.

2. Charles J. Stewart and William B. Cash, Jr., *Interviewing: Principles and Practices*, 3d ed. (Dubuque, Iowa: W. C. Brown, 1982), p. 10.

3. Cited in Richard N. Bolles, *What Color Is Your Parachute?: A Practical Manual for Job-Hunters and Career Changers*, rev. ed. (Berkeley, Calif.: Ten Speed Press, 1980), p. 140.

4. These steps are based on the suggestions of Bolles, op. cit.

5. Cal Downs, Wil Linkugel, and David M. Berg, *The Organizational Communicator* (New York: Harper & Row, 1977), pp. 120–121.

▶CHAPTER 9

KEY TERMS

consensus
dysfunctional role
explicit norms
functional role
group
group goals
growth group
hidden agenda

individual goals
implicit norms
learning group
maintenance roles
networks
procedural norms
problem-solving group
roles

social goals
social group
social norms
task norms
task roles
task-related goals

THE NATURE OF GROUPS

After reading this chapter, you should understand the following:

1. The characteristics that distinguish groups from other collections of people.

2. The types of goals that operate in groups.

3. The various types of groups.

4. The characteristics of groups described in this chapter.

5. The advantages and disadvantages of the decision-making methods introduced in this chapter.

You should be able to do the following:

1. Identify the groups you presently belong to and those you are likely to join in the future.

2. List the personal and group goals in groups you observe or belong to.

3. Identify the norms, roles, and interaction patterns in groups you observe or belong to.

4. Choose the most effective decision-making method for a group task.

How important are groups?

You can answer this question for yourself by trying a simple experiment. Start by thinking of all the groups you belong to now and have belonged to in the past: the family you grew up with, the classes you have attended, the teams you have played on, the many social groups you have been a member of. . . . The list is a long one. Now, one by one, imagine that you had never belonged to each of these groups. Start with the less important ones, and the results aren't too dramatic; but very soon you will begin to see that a great deal of the information you have learned, the benefits you have gained . . . even your very identity have all come from group membership.

This doesn't mean that every group experience is a good one. Some are vaguely unrewarding, rather like eating food that has no taste and gives no nourishment. And others are downright miserable. Sometimes it is easy to see why a group succeeds or fails, but in other cases matters aren't so clear.

This chapter will help you understand better the nature of group communication. It will start by explaining just what a group is—for not every collection of people qualifies. It will go on to examine the reasons people form groups and then look at several different types of groups. Finally, it will conclude by looking at some common characteristics all groups share.

▶ WHAT IS A GROUP?

Imagine that you are taking a test on group communication. Which of the following would you identify as groups?

a crowd of onlookers gawking at a burning building

several passengers at an airline ticket counter discussing their hopes to find space on a crowded flight

an army battalion

As all these situations seem to involve groups, your experience as a canny test taker probably tells you that a commonsense answer will get you in trouble here—and you're right. When social scientists talk about groups, they use the word in a special way that excludes each of the preceding examples.

What are we talking about when we use the term *group*? For our purposes a **group** consists of a *small collection of people who interact with each other, usually face to face, over time in order to reach goals*. A closer examination of this definition will show why none of the collections of people described in the preceding quiz qualify as groups.

Interaction

Without interaction, a collection of people isn't a group. Consider, for example, the onlookers at a fire. Though they all occupy the same area at a given time, they have virtually nothing to do with each other. Of course, if they should begin interacting—working together to give first aid or to rescue victims, for

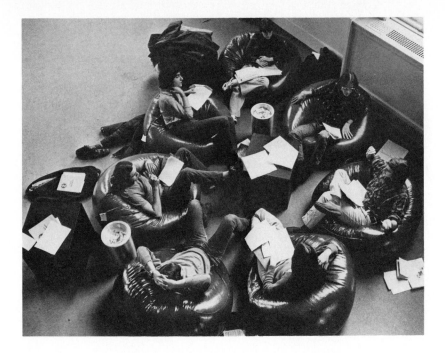

example—the situation would change. This requirement of interaction high-lights the difference between true groups and collections of individuals who merely *coact*—simultaneously engaging in a similar activity without communicat-ing with one another. For example, students who passively listen to a lecture don't technically constitute a group until they begin to exchange messages with each other and their instructor. (This explains why some students feel isolated even though they spend so much time on a crowded campus. Despite being sur-rounded by others, they really don't belong to any groups.)

As you read in Chapters 3 and 5, there are two types of interaction that go on in any communication setting. The most obvious type is verbal, in which group members exchange words either orally or in writing. But people needn't talk to each other in order to communicate as a group: Nonverbal channels can do the job, too. We can see how by thinking again about a hypothetical class-room. Imagine that the course is in its tenth week and the instructor has been lecturing nonstop for the entire time. During the first few meetings there was very little interaction of any kind: Students were too busy scribbling notes and wondering how they would survive the course with grade-point averages and sanity intact. But as they became more used to the class, the students began to share their feelings with each other. Now there's a great amount of eye rolling and groaning as the assignments are poured on, and the students exchange re-signed sighs as they hear the same tired jokes for the second and third time. Thus, even though there's no verbal exchange of sentiments, the class has become a group—interestingly, in this sense a group that doesn't include the professor.

Is this a group?

Time

A collection of people who interact for a short while don't qualify as a group. As you'll soon read, groups that work together for any length of time begin to take on characteristics that aren't present in temporary aggregations. For example, certain standards of acceptable behavior begin to evolve, and the way individuals feel about each other begins to affect their behavior toward the group's task and toward each other. According to this criterion, onlookers at a fire might have trouble qualifying as a group even if they briefly cooperated with one another to help out in the emergency. The element of time clearly excludes temporary gatherings such as the passengers gathered around the airline ticket counter. Situations like this simply don't follow many of the principles you'll be reading about in the next two chapters.

Size

Our definition of groups included the word *small*. Most experts in the field set the lower limit of group size at three members. This decision isn't arbitrary, for there are some significant differences between two- and three-person communication. For example, the only way two people can resolve a conflict is either to change one another's minds, give in, or compromise; in a larger group, however, there's a possibility of members' forming alliances either to put increased pressure on dissenting members or to outvote them.[1]

There is less agreement about when a group stops being small. Though no expert would call a 500-member army battalion a group in our sense of the word (it would be labeled an organization), most experts are reluctant to set an arbitrary upper limit. Probably the best description of smallness is the ability for each member to be able to know and react to every other member. It's sufficient to say that our focus in these pages will be on collections of people ranging in size from three to between seven and twenty.

Goals

Group membership isn't always voluntary, as draftees and prison inmates will testify. But whenever people choose to join groups, they do so because membership will help them achieve one or more goals. At first the goal-related nature of group membership seems simple and obvious. In truth, however, there are several types of goals, which we will now examine.

GOALS OF GROUPS AND THEIR MEMBERS ◄

We can talk about two types of goals when we examine groups. The first category involves **individual goals**—the motives of individual members—whereas the second involves **group goals**—the outcome the group seeks to accomplish.

Individual Goals

TASK-RELATED GOALS   The most obvious reason individuals join groups is to accomplish **task-related goals**—to get a job done. Some people join study groups, for example, in order to improve their knowledge. Others belong to religious groups as a way of improving the quality of their lives and those of others. (There may be additional reasons for going to school and church, as we will soon see.)

Sometimes a member's task-related goals will have little to do with a group's stated purpose. Many merchants, for example, join service clubs such as Kiwanis, Rotary, or Lions primarily because doing so is good for business. The fact that these groups help achieve worthy goals such as helping the blind or disabled is fine, of course, but for many people it is not the prime motive for belonging.

SOCIAL GOALS   What about groups with no specifically defined purpose? Consider, for instance, gatherings of regulars at the beach on sunny weekends or a group of friends who eat lunch together several times a week. Collections such as these meet the other criteria for being groups: They interact, meet over time, and have the right number of members. But what are the members' reasons for belonging? In our examples here, the goals can't be sunbathing or eating because these activities could be carried out alone. The answer to our question introduces **social goals,** the second type of group goals. In many cases, people join together in order to get the inclusion, control, and affection we mentioned in Chapter I.

We join many, if not most, groups in order to accomplish both task and social goals. School becomes a place both to learn important information and to meet desirable friends. Our work becomes a means of putting food on the table and getting recognition for being competent. The value of making a distinction between task and social goals comes from recognizing that the latter are usually important but often not stated or even recognized by group members. Thus, asking yourself whether social goals are being met can be one way of identifying and overcoming blocks to group effectiveness.

Group Goals

So far we have discussed the forces that motivate individual group members. In addition to these individual motives, there also exist group goals. For example, athletic teams exist to compete with each other, and academic classes strive to transmit knowledge.

Sometimes there is a close relationship between group and individual goals. In athletic teams the group goal is to win whereas individual members' goals include helping the group succeed. If you think about it for a moment, however, you'll see that the individual members have other goals as well: improving their physical ability, having a good time, overcoming the personal challenges of competition, and often gaining the social benefits that come from being an athlete. The difference between individual and group goals is even more pronounced when the two are incompatible. Consider, for instance, the case of an athletic team that has one player more interested in being a "star" (satisfying personal needs for recognition) than in helping the team win. Or recall classes you have known in which a lack of student enthusiasm made the personal goal of many students getting by with the smallest possible amount of work—hardly consistent with the stated group goal of conveying information. Sometimes the gap between individual and group goals is public whereas in other cases an individual's goal becomes a **hidden agenda.** In either case, this discrepancy can be dangerous for the well-being of the group and needs to be dealt with. We'll have more to say about this subject in Chapter 10.

▶ TYPES OF GROUPS

So far we have seen that there are a variety of goals that groups fulfill. Another way of examining groups is to look at some of the functions they serve.

Learning Groups

When the term "**learning group**" comes up, most people think first about school. Although academic settings certainly qualify as learning groups, they aren't the only ones. Members of a scuba-diving class, friends who form a Bible study group, and members of a League of Women Voters chapter all belong to learning groups. Whatever the setting or subject, the purpose of learning groups is to increase the knowledge or skill of each member.

Learning groups take a variety of formats. Most familiar is the lecture, in which one or more speakers dispense information to several listeners. Learning also takes place in two-way exchanges of information, when each member is both a contributor and receiver of knowledge. Sometimes the learning becomes more active, as when skiers or aspiring musicians develop their skill by practicing it.

Growth Groups

Unlike learning groups, in which the subject matter is external to the members, **growth groups** focus on teaching the members more about themselves. Consciousness-raising groups, Marriage Encounter workshops, counseling, and group therapy are all types of growth groups. These are unlike most other types of groups in that there is no real collective goal: The entire purpose of the group is to help the members identify and deal with their personal concerns.

Problem-solving Groups

Problem-solving groups work together to resolve a mutual concern. Sometimes the concern involves the group itself, as when a family decides how to handle household chores or when co-workers meet to coordinate vacation schedules. In other instances, the problem is external to the group. For instance, neighbors who organize themselves to prevent burglaries or club members who plan a fund-raising drive are focusing on external problems.

Problem-solving groups can take part in many activities: One type is gathering information, as when several students compile a report for a class assignment. At other times, a group makes policy—a club's deciding whether or not to admit the public to its meetings being an example. Some groups make individual decisions; an interview committee that decides which candidate to hire is fulfilling this function.

Social Groups

We have already mentioned that some groups serve strictly to satisfy the social needs of their participants. Some **social groups** are organized whereas others are informal. In either case, the inclusion, control, and affection that such groups provide are reason enough for belonging.

CHARACTERISTICS OF GROUPS ◄

Whatever their function, all groups have certain characteristics in common. Understanding these characteristics is a first step to behaving more effectively in your own groups.

Norms

Norms are agreements about how people should behave toward one another.[2] Some norms—called "laws" or "rules" by sociologists—are *explicit,* spelling out what behaviors are appropriate and prohibited. In a classroom, **explicit norms** include matters such as how many absences are permitted, whether papers must be typed or may be handwritten, and so on. Although **implicit norms** are just as powerful and important as explicit ones, they are not stated overtly. For instance, you probably won't find a description of what jokes are and aren't acceptable in the bylaws of any groups you belong to, yet you can almost certainly describe the unstated code if you think about it. Is sexual humor acceptable? How much, and what types? What about religious jokes? How much kidding of other members is proper? Matters such as these vary from one group to another, according to the norms of each one.

There are three categories of group norms: social, procedural, and task.[3] **Social norms** govern the relationship of members to each other. How honest and direct will members be with one another? What emotions will and won't be expressed, and in what ways? Matters such as these are handled by the establishment of social norms, usually implicit ones. **Procedural norms** outline how the group should operate. Will the group make decisions by accepting the vote of the majority, or will the members keep talking until consensus is reached? Will one person run meetings, or will discussion be leaderless? **Task norms** focus on how the job itself should be handled. Will the group keep working on a problem until everyone agrees that its product is the best one possible, or will members settle for an adequate, if imperfect, solution? The answer to this question results in a task-related norm. All groups have social norms whereas problem-solving, learning, and growth groups also have procedural and task norms.

Table 9–1 lists some of the norms most people bring to a task-oriented group's first meeting. It is important to realize that cultural norms such as these

▶ A fighter pilot soon found he wanted to associate only with other fighter pilots. Who else could understand the nature of the little proposition (right stuff/death) they were all dealing with? And what other subject could compare with it? It was riveting! To talk about it in so many words was forbidden, of course. The very words *death, danger, bravery, fear* were not be uttered except in the occasional specific instance or for ironic effect. Nevertheless, the subject could be adumbrated in *code* or *by example*... They diced that righteous stuff up into little bits, bowed ironically to it, stumbled blindfolded around it, groped, lurched, belched, staggered, bawled, sang, roared, and feinted at it with self-deprecating humor. Nevertheless!—they never mentioned it by name.

Tom Wolfe
The Right Stuff

---

are *idealized* and that a group's actual norms emerge as its members spend time together. Consider the matter of punctuality, for example. A cultural norm in our society is that meetings should begin at the scheduled time, yet some groups soon generate the usually unstated agreement that the real business won't commence until ten or so minutes later. On a more serious level, one cultural norm is that other people should be treated politely and with respect, but in some groups failure to listen, sarcasm, and even outright hostility make the principle of civility a sham.

TABLE 9–1 Expected Norms for a Discussion Group's First Meeting

SOCIAL	PROCEDURAL	TASK
Do	**Do**	**Do**
—serve refreshments	—introduce people	—criticize ideas, not people
—dress casually	—plan to participate	—support the best idea
—use first names	—establish goals	—commit yourself to group
—discuss uncontroversial	—build agenda	solutions
subjects	—hold routine meetings one	—share in the work load
—tell humorous jokes	hour in length	—say so if you disagree
—tell political jokes (they will be	—have someone in charge	—ask questions about group
tolerated)	—sit face-to-face	ideas
—tell trend or one-line jokes	**Don't**	**Don't**
—tell cultural truisms	—leave meetings without cause	—push your idea on the group
Don't	—monopolize conversation	—support ideas just because of
—smoke (perhaps)	—stand up and speak in small-	people who presented them
—swear	group meetings (generally)	—be verbally violent if you
—arrive late	—demand to lead	disagree with ideas
—be absent without apology	—refuse to speak when	—consider your ideas as the only
—tell sexist, racist, ethnic, agist,	addressed	ones of merit
or religious jokes		

Reprinted by permission from *Communication in Small Group Discussions* by John F. Cragan and David W. Wright, copyright © 1980, West Publishing Co. All rights reserved.

▶ "What are we? Humans? Or animals? Or savages? What's grownups going to think? Going off—hunting pigs—letting fires out—and now!"

A shadow fronted him tempestuously.

"You shut up, you fat slug!"

There was a moment's struggle and the glimmering conch jigged up and down. Ralph leapt to his feet.

"Jack! Jack! You haven't got the conch! Let him speak."

Jack's face swam near him.

"And you shut up! Who are you, anyway? Sitting there telling people what to do. You can't hunt, you can't sing—"

"I'm chief. I was chosen."

"Why should choosing make any difference? Just giving orders that don't make any sense—"

"Piggy's got the conch."

"That's right—favor Piggy as you always do—"

"Jack!"

Jack's voice sounded in bitter mimicry.

"Jack! Jack!"

"The rules!" shouted Ralph. "You're breaking the rules!"

"Who cares?"

Ralph summoned his wits.

"Because the rules are the only thing we've got!"

William Golding
Lord of the Flies

Roles

Where norms define acceptable group standards, **roles** refer to the patterns of behavior expected of individual members.[4] Just like norms, some roles are formally recognized. These explicit roles usually come with a label, such as "professor," "chairperson," or "student." Other roles are informal; they are very real although group members may not acknowledge—or even consciously realize—their existence. For instance, you can probably think of many informal groups in which some members are clearly leaders and others followers although these positions have never been discussed.

Formal titles don't describe all the roles that operate in groups. Social scientists have found that there are certain **functional roles** that also must be filled if task-related groups are to get a job done (see Table 9–2). These functional roles are not formally assigned to members. In fact, they are rarely even recognized as existing. Many of the roles may be filled by more than one member, and some of them may be filled by different people at different times. The important fact is that, at crucial times, each of the functional roles must be filled by someone.

The list of functional roles in Table 9–2 is a valuable tool because it can serve as a checklist you can use to diagnose why a group is or isn't working effectively. Notice that the roles fall into two categories, task and maintenance. **Task roles** help the group accomplish its goals, and **maintenance roles** (also called "social roles") keep the relationships among members running smoothly. Table

TABLE 9–2 Functional Roles of Group Members

TASK ROLES	TYPICAL BEHAVIORS	EXAMPLES
1. Initiator/contributor	Contributes ideas and suggestions; proposes solutions and decisions; proposes new ideas or states old ones in a novel fashion.	"How about taking a different approach to this chore. Suppose we…"
2. Information seeker	Asks for clarification of comments in terms of their factual adequacy; asks for information or facts relevant to the problem; suggests information is needed before making decisions.	"Do you think the others will go for this?" "How much would the plan cost us?" "Does anybody know if those dates are available?"
3. Information giver	Offers facts or generalizations that may relate to the group's task.	"I bet Chris would know the answer to that." "*Newsweek* ran an article on that a couple of months ago. It said…"
4. Opinion seeker	Asks for clarification of opinions made by other members of the group and asks how people in the group feel.	"Does anyone else have an idea on this?" "That's an interesting idea, Ruth. How long would it take to get started?"
5. Opinion giver	States beliefs or opinions having to do with suggestions made; indicates what the group's attitude should be.	"I think we ought to go with the second plan. It fits the conditions we face in the Concord plant best…"
6. Elaborator/clarifier	Elaborates ideas and other contributions; offers rationales for suggestions; tries to deduce how an idea or suggestion would work if adopted by the group.	"If we followed Lee's suggestion, each of us would need to make three calls." "Let's see…at 35 cents per brochure, the total cost would be $525.00."
7. Coordinator	Clarifies the relationships among information, opinions, and ideas or suggests an integration of the information, opinions, and ideas of subgroups.	"John, you seem most concerned with potential problems. Mary sounds confident that they can all be solved. Why don't you list the problems one at a time, John, and Mary can respond to each one."
8. Diagnostician	Indicates what the problems are.	"But you're missing the main thing, I think. The problem is that we can't afford…"
9. Orienter/summarizer	Summarizes what has taken place; points out departures from agreed-on goals; tries to bring the group back to the central issues; raises questions about the direction in which the group is heading.	"Let's take stock of where we are. Helen and John take the position that we should act now. Bill says, 'Wait.' Rusty isn't sure. Can we set that aside for a moment and come back to it after we…"
10. Energizer	Prods the group to action.	"Come on, guys. We've been wasting time. Let's get down to business."

(continued on next page)

TABLE 9–2 Functional Roles of Group Members (*continued*)

TASK ROLES	TYPICAL BEHAVIORS	EXAMPLES
11. Procedure developer	Handles routine tasks such as seating arrangements, obtaining equipment, and handing out pertinent papers.	"I'll volunteer to see that the forms are printed and distributed." "I'd be happy to check on which of those dates are free."
12. Secretary	Keeps notes on the group's progress.	"Just for the record, I'll put these decisions in a memo and get copies to everyone in the group."
13. Evaluator/critic	Constructively analyzes group's accomplishments according to some set of standards; checks to see that consensus has been reached.	"Look, we said we only had two weeks, and this proposal will take at least three. Does that mean that it's out of the running, or do we need to change our original guidelines?"

SOCIAL/MAINTENANCE ROLES	TYPICAL BEHAVIORS	EXAMPLES
1. Supporter/encourager	Praises, agrees with, and accepts the contributions of others; offers warmth, solidarity, and recognition.	"I really like that idea, John." "Priscilla's suggestion sounds good to me. Could we discuss it further?"
2. Harmonizer	Reconciles disagreements; mediates differences; reduces tensions by giving group members a chance to explore their differences.	"I don't think you two are as far apart as you think. Henry, are you saying ——? Benson, you seem to be saying —— is that what you mean?"
3. Tension reliever	Jokes or in some other way reduces the formality of the situation; relaxes the group members.	"Let's take a break…maybe have a drink." "You're a tough cookie, Bob. I'm glad you're on our side!"
4. Conciliator	Offers new options when his or her own ideas are involved in a conflict; disciplines himself or herself to admit his or her errors so as to maintain group cohesion.	"Looks like our solution is halfway between you and me, John. Can we look at the middle ground?"
5. Gatekeeper	Keeps communication channels open; encourages and facilitates interaction from those members who are usually silent.	"Susan, you haven't said anything about this yet. I know you've been studying the problem. What do you think about ——?"
6. Feeling expresser	Makes explicit the feelings, moods, and relationships in the group; shares own feelings with others.	"I'm really glad we cleared things up today." "I'm just about worn out. Could we call it a day and start fresh tomorrow?"
7. Follower	Goes along with the movement of the group passively, accepting the ideas of others sometimes serving as an audience.	"I agree. Yes, I see what you mean. If that's what the group wants to do, I'll go along…"

TABLE 9-2 Functional Roles of Group Members (*continued*)

DYSFUNCTIONAL ROLES	TYPICAL BEHAVIORS	EXAMPLES
1. Blocker	Interferes with progress by rejecting ideas or taking a negative stand on any and all issues; refuses to cooperate.	"Wait a minute! That's not right! That idea is absurd." "You can talk all day, but my mind is made up."
2. Aggressor	Struggles for status by deflating the status of others; boasts; criticizes.	"Wow, that's really swell! You turkeys have botched things again." "Your constant bickering is responsible for this mess. Let me tell you how you ought to do it."
3. Deserter	Withdraws in some way; remains indifferent, aloof, sometimes formal; daydreams; wanders from the subject; engages in irrelevant side conversations.	"I suppose that's all right...I really don't care."
4. Dominator	Interrupts and embarks on long monologues; is authoritative; tries to monopolize the group's time.	"Bill, you're just off base. What we should do is this. First..."
5. Recognition seeker	Attempts to gain attention in an exaggerated manner; usually boasts about past accomplishments; relates irrelevant personal experiences, usually in an attempt to gain sympathy.	"That reminds me of a guy I used to know..." "Let me tell you how I handled old Marris..."
6. Playboy	Displays a lack of involvement in the group through inappropriate humor, horseplay, or cynicism.	"Why try to convince these guys? Let's just get the mob to snuff them out." "Hey, Carla, wanna be my roommate at the sales conference?"

Adapted from Gerald L. Wilson and Michael S. Hanna, *Groups in Context: Leadership and Participation in Decision-Making Groups.* © Random House, Inc., 1986, pp. 144–146.

9–2 also lists several **dysfunctional roles** that prevent a group from working effectively.

ROLE EMERGENCE   We said earlier that most group members aren't aware of the existence of functional roles. You will rarely find members saying things like "You ask most of the questions, I'll give opinions, and she can be the summarizer." Yet it's fairly obvious that over time certain members do begin to fulfill specific functions. How does this process occur?

There are two answers to this question. One factor in role differentiation is certainly the personal characteristics of each member. Some people, for example, seem to be more critical than others and thus feel comfortable as diagnosers and evaluators. Others are particularly aware of personality dynamics and find it easy to get along with other members, which makes them good harmonizers and interpersonal problem solvers.

In addition to the personal skills and traits of individual members, the idiosyncrasies of each particular group shape the roles that each member takes. In other words, each of us plays a different role in different groups. For example, a normally nonassertive person might act as a starter or direction giver in a group where no one else was performing that necessary task. In some cases, this assumption of uncharacteristic roles isn't voluntary: Members informally assign functions to members who wouldn't otherwise have taken them. This kind of role assignment shows up in movies, where the hapless passenger or the untrained but courageous flight attendant saves the plane after an accident wipes out the pilot. In more humdrum but common situations, you've probably heard people assigning roles by saying things like "You know something about that, what do you think?"—a clear invitation to become an information or opinion giver.

ROLE-RELATED PROBLEMS   Groups can suffer from at least two role-related problems. The first occurs when one or more important functional roles go unfilled. The most common example of this happens in groups where there is no information giver to provide some vital knowledge. A more subtle (but equally dangerous) role vacuum occurs when maintenance functions aren't filled. If nobody relieves interpersonal tensions, gives praise, or solves interpersonal problems at critical times, a group will have a hard time accomplishing its task. There are other cases when the problem isn't an *absence* of candidates to fill certain roles, but an *overabundance* of them. This situation can lead to unstated competition between members, which gets in the way of group effectiveness. You have probably seen groups in which two people both want to be the tension-relieving comedian. In such cases, the problem arises when the members in question become more concerned with getting laughs than with getting the group's job done.

Patterns of Interaction

In Chapter 1 we said that communication involves the flow of information between and among people. It almost goes without saying that this exchange needs to be complete and efficient for the communicators to reach their goals. In interpersonal and public speaking settings, information exchange is relatively uncomplicated, taking basically two routes: either between the two individuals in an interpersonal dyad or between speaker and audience in a public speaking situation.* In groups, however, things aren't so simple. The mathematical formula that identifies the number of possible interactions between individuals is

$$\frac{N\,(N-1)}{2}$$

---

*Actually, this is a slight oversimplification. In public-speaking situations, members of an audience also exchange messages with one another with their laughter, restless movements, and so on. It's still fair to say, however, that the exchange of information is basically two-way.

where N equals the number of members in a group.[5] Thus, in even a relatively small five-member group, there are ten possible combinations of two-person conversations and a vastly greater number of potential multiperson interactions. Besides the sheer quantity of information exchange, the more complex structure of groups affects the flow of information in other ways, too.

PHYSICAL ARRANGEMENT   It's obviously easier to interact with someone you can see well. Lack of visibility isn't a serious problem in dyadic settings, but it can be troublesome in groups. For example, group members seated in a circle are more likely to talk with persons across from them than with those on either side.[6] Different things happen when members are seated in rectangular arrangements. Research with twelve-person juries showed that those sitting at either end of such tables participated more in discussions and were viewed by other members as having more influence on the decision-making process.[7] Rectangular seating patterns have other consequences as well. Research conducted on six-person groups seated at rectangular tables showed that as distance between two persons increased, other members perceived them as being less friendly, less talkative, and less acquainted with each other.[8]

COMMUNICATION NETWORKS   When group members meet face-to-face, information can flow freely among them. But this open structure doesn't always exist. For instance, think about working groups in which members occupy separate offices or even social groups where members talk with each other one at a time over the telephone. The patterns that individual channels of communication form between group members are called **networks.** Figure 9–1 pictures several communication networks for six-person groups. The circles represent group members, and lines represent communication among them.

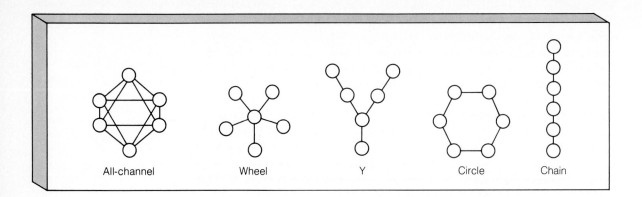

All-channel   Wheel   Y   Circle   Chain

FIGURE 9–1
Small-Group Communication Networks

Does the structure of a communication network have any effect on group interaction? Much experimentation indicates that it does. Perhaps the most significant effect involves leadership emergence. In groups with no formal leader, the person who occupies a central position in any network has the greatest chance of emerging as a leader.[9] This principle contains a practical tip for aspiring leaders: Do whatever you can to become the clearinghouse for your group's information. Offer to keep members informed of any news, collect information from them, be present whenever there's a subgroup meeting, and chat casually with other members whenever you get the chance.

Communication networks also affect group problem solving. As Figure 9–1 shows, there are two basic types of networks, centralized and each-to-all. In the centralized pattern, one person serves as the clearinghouse for all information and solves the problem, using the information provided from others. In each-to-all groups, on the other hand, every member has equal access to information and potentially has an equal chance to contribute to solving the group's problems. Extensive research has shown that centralized networks work better in some situations whereas each-to-all arrangements are more productive in others. When the group faces an ambiguous task, an each-to-all approach works most effectively—probably because the greater amount of input boosts the chances of finding a good solution.* A centralized approach works best with simple, routine tasks, because there is less time occupied by communication that interferes with getting the job done.[10]

Decision-making Methods

Another way to classify groups is according to the approach they use to make decisions. There are several methods a group can use to decide matters. We'll look at each of them now, examining their advantages and disadvantages.[11]

AUTHORITY RULE WITHOUT DISCUSSION   Authority rule without discussion is the method most often used by autocratic leaders (see Chapter 10). Though

---

*Centralized group structures such as chains and stars (see Fig. 9–1) can still manage tasks in an each-to-all manner by using memos, verbal message passing, and other methods. Although such feats are possible, they are difficult. When decentralized communication is appropriate, it's far better to structure the group accordingly.

it sounds dictatorial, there are times when such an approach has its advantages. First, the method is quick: There are some cases when there simply isn't time for a group to decide what to do. The method is also perfectly acceptable with routine matters that don't require discussion in order to gain approval. When overused, however, this approach causes problems. As Chapter 10 will show, much of the time group decisions are of higher quality and gain more support from members than those made by an individual. Thus, failure to consult with members can lead to a decrease of effectiveness even when the leader's decision is a reasonable one.

EXPERT OPINION   Sometimes one group member will be defined as an expert and, as such, will be given the power to make decisions. This method can work well when that person's judgment is truly superior. For example, if a group of friends are backpacking in the wilderness and one becomes injured, it would probably be foolish to argue with the advice of a doctor in the group. In most cases, however, matters aren't so simple. Who is the expert? There is often disagreement on this question. Sometimes a member might think he or she is the best qualified to make a decision, but others will disagree. In a case like this, the group probably won't support that person's advice, even if it is sound.

AUTHORITY RULE AFTER DISCUSSION   The method of authority rule after discussion is less autocratic than the preceding two, for it at least takes into consideration the opinions of more than one person. Thus, the unilateral decisions of an open-minded authority gain some of the increases in quality and commitment that come from group interaction while also enjoying the quickness that comes from avoiding extensive discussion. This approach has its disadvantages, however. Often other group members will be tempted to tell the leader what they think he or she wants to hear, and in other cases they will compete to impress the decision maker.

MAJORITY CONTROL   A naive belief of many people (perhaps coming from overzealous high school civics teachers) is that the democratic method of majority rule is always superior. This method does have its advantages in cases where the support of all members isn't necessary, but in more important matters it is risky. Remember that even if a 51 percent majority of the members favor a plan, 49 percent might still oppose it—hardly sweeping support for any decision that needs the support of all members in order to work.

MINORITY CONTROL   Sometimes a few members of a group will decide matters. This approach works well with noncritical questions that would waste the whole group's time. In the form of a committee, a minority of members also can study an issue in greater detail than can the entire group. When an issue is so important that it needs the support of everyone, it's best at least to have the committee report its findings for the approval of all members.

CONSENSUS   **Consensus** occurs when all members of a group support a decision. The advantages of consensus are obvious: Full participation can increase the quality of the decision as well as the commitment of members to support it.

▶ During a [second grade] science project...one of the 7 year olds wondered out loud whether the baby squirrel they had in class was a boy or a girl. After pondering the issue for a few minutes, one budding scientist offered the suggestion that they have a class discussion about it and then take a vote.

Cal Downs, Wil Linkugel, and David M. Berg
The Organizational Communicator

Consensus is especially important in decisions on critical or complex matters; in such cases, methods using less input can diminish the quality of or enthusiasm for a decision. Despite its advantages, consensus also has its drawbacks. It takes a great deal of time, which makes it unsuitable for emergencies. In addition, it is often very frustrating: Emotions can run high on important matters, and patience in the face of such pressures is difficult. Because of the need to deal with these emotional pressures, consensus calls for more communication skill than do other decision-making approaches. As with many things in life, consensus has high rewards, which come at a proportionately high cost.

Which of these methods is best? There's no single answer. The most effective method in a given situation depends on the circumstances: the amount of time available, the importance of the decision, the abilities of the group's leader, and the members' attitudes toward that person. The best approach might be to use the preceding descriptions of each method as guidelines in deciding which method to use in a particular situation.

▶ SUMMARY

Groups play an important role in many areas of our lives—families, education, on the job, and in friendships, to name a few. Groups possess several characteristics that distinguish them from other communication contexts. They involve interaction over time among a small number of participants with the purpose of achieving one or more goals. Groups have their own goals, as do individual members. Member goals fall into two categories: task-related and social. Sometimes individual and group goals are compatible, and sometimes they conflict.

Groups can be put into several classifications—learning, growth, problem-solving, and social. All these types of groups share certain characteristics: the existence of group norms, individual roles for members, patterns of interaction that are shaped by the group's structure, and the choice of one or more ways of reaching decisions.

▶ ACTIVITIES

1. Think about two groups to which you belong.
   a. What are your task-related goals in each?
   b. What are your social goals?
   c. Are your personal goals compatible or incompatible with those of other members?
   d. Are they compatible or incompatible with the group goals?
   e. What effect does the compatibility or incompatibility of goals have on the effectiveness of the group?
2. You can understand the nature of norms by thinking of one specific group to which you belong as you answer the following questions.
   a. What explicit norms govern your group's behavior? How were they announced?
   b. What implicit norms are in operation? What is the evidence of their existence?

c. Use the examples from the preceding steps plus others to identify two social norms, two procedural norms, and two task norms.
3. Think of a group to which you belong.
a. What functional roles do you fill in that group?
b. Are those roles similar or different in other groups to which you belong?
c. Are there any roles that are going unfilled in your group? How does this absence affect the group's functioning?
4. Draw a visual representation of the shape of the communication network in one group to which you belong. How does this type of network affect the decisions the group makes? Would a different type of network be better?
5. What is the physical setting in which your group meets? What effect does that setting have on the communication? Consider factors such as seating arrangement, level of light, ventilation, background noise, and degree of privacy. Are there any changes in the physical environment that could improve the group's effectiveness? How could you help make those changes?
6. Describe the methods of decision making used in family, classroom, and on-the-job groups to which you have belonged. Then answer the following questions for each group:
a. Does the group use the same decision-making method in all circumstances, or does it use different methods at different times?
b. After reading the advantages and disadvantages of each method, do you think the methods used by each group are appropriate? If not, what methods would be better? Why?

NOTES ◄

1. C. David Mortensen, *Communication: The Study of Human Interaction* (New York: McGraw-Hill, 1972), pp. 267–268.
2. Earl R. Babbie, *Society by Agreement: An Introduction to Sociology* (Belmont, Calif.: Wadsworth, 1977).
3. John F. Cragan and David W. Wright, *Communication in Small Group Discussions: A Case Study Approach* (St. Paul, Minn.: West Publishing, 1980), p. 56.
4. Albert C. Kowitz and Thomas J. Knutson, *Decision Making in Small Groups: The Search for Alternatives* (Boston: Allyn & Bacon, 1980), p. 98.
5. E. M. Rogers, *Diffusion of Innovations,* 3d ed. (New York: Free Press, 1983), p. 294.
6. B. Steinzor, "The Spatial Factor in Face-to-Face Discussion Groups," *Journal of Abnormal and Social Psychology* 45 (1950): 552–555.
7. F. L. Strodtbeck and L. H. Hook, "The Social Dimensions of a Twelve Man Jury Table," *Sociometry* 24 (1961): 397–415.
8. N. F. Russo, "Connotations of Seating Arrangements," *Cornell Journal of Social Relations* 2 (1967): 37–44.
9. Marvin E. Shaw, *Group Dynamics: The Psychology of Small Group Behavior,* 3d ed. (New York: McGraw-Hill, 1981), p. 153.
10. Ibid., p. 156.
11. Adapted from David W. Johnson and Frank P. Johnson, *Joining Together: Group Theory and Group Skills* (Englewood Cliffs, N.J.: Prentice-Hall, 1975), pp. 80–81.

►CHAPTER 10

KEY TERMS

authoritarian leadership style
brainstorming
coercive power
cohesiveness
democratic leadership style
expert power
force field analysis
forum
information power
laissez-faire leadership style
leader
leadership
legitimate power
managerial grid
nominal leader
panel discussion

parliamentary procedure
participative decision making
probative question
referent power
reward power
situational leadership
symposium
trait theories of leadership

SOLVING PROBLEMS IN GROUPS

After reading this chapter, you should understand the following:

1. The advantages of solving problems in groups.

2. The characteristics of several common discussion formats.

3. The six basic problem-solving steps.

4. The importance of effective listening and conflict resolution methods in group problem solving.

5. The factors that contribute to group cohesiveness.

6. The factors that contribute to balanced participation in groups.

7. The differences between a "leader" and "leadership."

8. The various types of power in groups.

9. The various approaches to studying leadership.

10. The dangers in group discussion outlined in this chapter.

You should be able to do the following:

1. Use the problem-solving steps outlined in this chapter in a group task.

2. Suggest ways to build the cohesiveness and participation in a group.

3. Analyze the sources of leadership and power in a group.

4. Suggest the most effective leadership approach for a specific group task.

5. Identify the obstacles to effective functioning of a specific group and suggest more effective ways of communicating.

Chapter 9 described various types of groups—learning, growth, social, and problem-solving. Of all these, problem-solving groups have been studied most intensively by social scientists. Once we understand the nature of problem solving, the reason becomes clear. *Problems,* as we define them here, don't refer only to situations where something is wrong. Perhaps *meeting challenges* and *performing tasks* are better terms. Once you recognize this, you can see that problem solving not only occupies a major part of our working life but plays an important role in other areas as well. At one time or another, all groups need to solve problems.

There are two sets of communication skills that any group must possess in order to come up with successful solutions. The first has to do with the group task itself: how to analyze the problem, choose the best solution, and make it work. A second area involves building and maintaining good relationships: making sure, first, that members feel good about each other and, second, that they enjoy the experience of working together.

This chapter will focus on both the task and relational aspects of problem-solving groups. In addition, it will explore the nature of leadership, defining that important term and suggesting how groups can be led most effectively. Finally, it will list several common problems task-oriented groups can encounter and describe how to overcome them.

▶ WHY USE GROUPS FOR PROBLEM SOLVING?

To many people, groups are to communication what Muzak is to music or Twinkies are to food—a joke. The snide remark "A camel is a horse designed by a committee" reflects this attitude as does this ditty:

> Search all your parks in all your cities ...
> You'll find no statues to committees!!![1]

This unflattering reputation is at least partly justified. Most of us would wind up with a handsome sum if we had a dollar for every hour wasted in groups. On the other hand, it's unfair to view all groups as bad, especially when this accusation implies that other types of communication are by nature superior. After all, we also have wasted time listening to boring lectures, reading worthless books, and making trivial conversation.

So what's the truth? Is group problem solving a waste of effort, or is it the best way to manage a task? As with most matters, the truth falls somewhere between these two extremes. Groups do have their shortcomings, which we will discuss in a few pages. But extensive research has shown that when these shortcomings can be avoided, groups are clearly the most effective way to handle many tasks.

Research over fifty years that has compared problem solving by groups and by individuals shows that, in most cases, groups can produce more solutions to a problem than individuals working alone ... and that the solutions will be of higher quality.[2]

Another meeting! One after another without coming up with a proposal that would fly.

This one took place in early September and (not surprisingly) only a few people showed up—12, to be precise. And so they talked for some days and finally came up with a plan for still another meeting, eight months hence. It was hoped this would offer sufficient time to generate interest in the matter.

They also moved the location. It was not that the September site had been unpleasant—on the contrary, the facilities were quite good—but variety in meeting places might induce more individuals to attend.

Of the 74 invitees, 55 showed up. But they didn't all come at once. They were supposed to convene on Monday, May 14, but it wasn't until Friday, May 25, that enough were present to conduct business. They decided to work diligently from that day on until they finished their proposal. They even agreed to put a lid on their deliberations.

They were a relatively young group; the average age was 42. The youngest was 30 and the oldest 82 and prone to nod during long meetings. Although some were lackluster in ability, most were able and would later move to high executive positions.

They were together for 116 days, taking off only Sundays and 12 other days. And you might have guessed it: During a very hot summer they were without air conditioning. In addition to the formal sessions of the entire group, much of their work was done in committee and after hours.

The formal sessions sometimes got out of hand. One faction had come with a proposal that was almost the reverse of an outline offered by another group. The advocates of each seemed unwilling to bend, and by the end of June tempers were flaring so much that the oldest participant suggested beginning each session with an invocation.

By early June, they got wind of a way out of their impasse: Adopt a portion of each plan. By compromising, they might be better able to sell their product to a broad market. Yet even this task of drawing the line between two extremes was not easy, and so some decided to go home or back to their offices. It simply was not worth the effort.

Even among those who remained there was still criticism of the final proposal. It was much too short, some argued—only 4,000 words. Four months of work and only 4,000 words! It was scarcely enough to fill a few sheets of paper. But 39 of them felt it was the best they could come up with. It was good enough to sign, which they did on the 17th day of September, 1787.

And they called their proposal the Constitution of the United States.

Thomas V. DiBacco

Groups have proved superior at a wide range of tasks—everything from assembling jigsaw puzzles to solving complex reasoning problems. There are several reasons why groups are effective.[3]

Resources

For many tasks, groups possess a greater collection of resources than do most individuals. Sometimes the resources are physical. For example, three or four people can put up a tent or dig a ditch better than a lone person. But on other problems the pooled resources lead to *qualitatively* better solutions. Think, for instance, about times when you have studied with other students for a test, and you will remember how much better the group was at preparing for all the questions that might be asked and at developing answers to them. (This, of course, assumes that the study group members cared enough about the exam to have studied for it before the group meeting.) Groups not only have more resources than individuals; through interaction among the members they also are better able to mobilize them. Talking about an upcoming test with others can jog your memory about items you might not have thought of if you had been working alone.

Accuracy

Another benefit of group work is the increased likelihood of catching errors. At one time or another, we all make stupid mistakes like the man who built a boat in his basement and then wasn't able to get it out the door. Working in a group increases the chance that foolish errors like this won't slip by. Sometimes, of course, errors aren't so obvious, which makes groups even more valuable as an error-checking mechanism. Another side to the error-detecting story is the risk that group members will support each other in a bad idea. We'll discuss this problem when we focus on comformity later in this chapter.

Commitment

Besides coming up with superior solutions, groups also generate higher commitment to carrying them out. Members are most likely to accept solutions they have helped create, and they will work harder to carry out those actions. This fact has led to the principle of **participative decision making,** in which the people who will live with a plan help make it.[4] This is an especially important principle for those in authority such as supervisors, teachers, and parents. As professors, we have seen the difference between the sullen compliance of students who have been forced to accept a policy with which they disagree and the much more willing cooperation of classes who have helped develop it. Though the benefits of participative decision making are great, we need to insert a qualification here: There are times when an autocratic approach of imposing a decision without discussion is most effective. We will discuss this question of when to be democratic and when to be directive in the section on leadership later in this chapter.

▶ TYPES OF PROBLEM-SOLVING FORMATS

Groups meet to solve problems in a variety of settings and for a wide range of reasons. The formats they use are also varied. Some groups meet before an audience to address a problem. The onlookers may be involved in, and affected by, the topic under discussion like the citizens who attend a typical city council meeting or voters who attend a candidate's debate. In other cases, the audience members are simply interested spectators, as occurs in televised discussions such as "Meet the Press" and "Face the Nation."

Most problem-solving meetings do not occur before an audience. The members meet privately because it is most efficient for a small number of decision makers to tackle the problem facing a larger group or because their discussions are confidential or because there is no interest in the problem beyond the people present.

Problem-solving meetings can follow a variety of formats. A session that uses **parliamentary procedure** observes specific rules about how topics may be discussed and decisions made. The standard reference book for parliamentary procedure is *Robert's Rules of Order.* Although the parliamentary rules may seem stilted and cumbersome, when well used, they do keep a discussion on track and protect the rights of the minority against domination by the majority.

Another common problem-solving format is the **panel discussion,** in which the participants talk over the topic informally, much as they would in an ordinary conversation. A leader (called a "moderator" in public discussions) may help the discussion along by encouraging the comments of some members, cutting off overly talkative ones, and seeking consensus when the time comes for making a decision.

In a **symposium** the participants divide the topic in a manner that allows each member to deliver in-depth information without interruption. Although

this format lends itself to good explanations of each person's decision, the one-person-at-a-time nature of a symposium won't lead to a group decision. The contributions of the members must be followed by the give-and-take of an open discussion.

A **forum** allows nonmembers to add their opinions to the group's deliberations before the group makes a decision. This approach is commonly used by public agencies to encourage the participation of citizens in the decisions that affect them.

▶ STEPS IN PROBLEM SOLVING

You read earlier in this chapter that people working in groups have the potential to be effective problem solvers. This doesn't mean that *all* problem-solving groups are successful. What makes some groups succeed and others fail? Research shows that, to a great degree, a group's effectiveness is determined by whether or not it approaches the problem rationally and systematically. Just as a poor blueprint or a shaky foundation can weaken a house, groups can fail by skipping one or more of the necessary steps in solving a problem.

As early as 1910, John Dewey introduced his famous "reflective thinking" method as a systematic method for solving problems.[5] Since then, other experts have suggested modifications of Dewey's approach. Some emphasize answering key questions whereas others seek "ideal solutions" that meet the needs of all members. Research comparing various methods has clearly shown that, although no single approach is best for all situations, *some* structured procedure produces better results than "no pattern" discussions.[6]

The following problem-solving model contains the elements common to most structured approaches developed in the last 75 years:

1. Identify the problem
   a. What are the group's goals?
   b. What are individual members' goals?
2. Analyze the problem
   a. Word the problem as a probative question
   b. Gather relevant information
   c. Identify impelling and restraining forces
3. Develop alternative solutions
   a. Avoid criticism at this stage
   b. Encourage "freewheeling" ideas
   c. Develop a large number of ideas
   d. Combine two or more individual ideas
4. Evaluate the solutions by asking which solution
   a. Will best produce the desired changes
   b. Is most achievable
   c. Contains the fewest serious disadvantages
5. Implement the plan
   a. Identify specific tasks
   b. Determine necessary resources

SOLVING PROBLEMS IN
GROUPS

   c. Define individual responsibilities
   d. Provide for emergencies
6. Follow up on the solution
   a. Meet to evaluate progress
   b. Revise approach as necessary

Identify the Problem

Sometimes a group's problem is easy to identify. The crew of a sinking ship, for example, doesn't need to conduct a discussion to understand that its goal is to avoid drowning or being eaten by some large fish.

There are many times, however, when the problems facing a group aren't so clear. As an example, think of an athletic team stuck deep in last place well into the season. At first the problem seems obvious: an inability to win any games. But a closer look at the situation might show that there are other unmet goals—and thus other problems. For instance, individual members may have goals that aren't tied directly to winning: making friends, receiving acknowledgment as good athletes . . . not to mention the simple goal of having fun—of playing in the recreational sense of the word. You can probably see that if the coach or team members took a simplistic view of the situation, looking only at the team's win-lose record, analyzing player errors, training methods, and so on, some important problems would probably go overlooked. In this situation, the team's performance could probably be best improved by working on the basic problems—the frustration of the players about having their personal needs met. What's the moral here? That *the way to start understanding a group's problem is to identify the concerns of each member.*[7]

What about groups that don't have problems? Several friends planning a surprise birthday party or a family deciding where to go for its vacation don't seem to be in the dire straits of a losing athletic team: They simply want to have fun. In cases like these, it may be helpful to substitute the word *challenge* for the more gloomy term *problem.* However we express it, the same principle applies to all task-oriented groups: The best place to start work is to identify what each member seeks as a result of belonging to the group.

B.C. by permission of Johnny Hart and Creator's Syndicate, Inc.

Analyze the Problem

Once you have identified the general nature of the challenge facing the group, you are ready to look at the problem in more detail. There are several steps you can follow to accomplish this important job.

WORD THE PROBLEM AS A PROBATIVE QUESTION[8]   If you have ever seen a formal debate, you know that the issue under discussion is worded as a proposition: "The United States should reduce its foreign aid expenditures," for example. Many problem-solving groups define their task in much the same way. "We ought to spend our vacation in the mountains," suggests one family member. The problem with phrasing problems as propositions is that such wording invites people to take sides. Though this approach is fine for formal debates (which are contests rather like football or card games), premature side-taking creates unnecessary conflict in most problem-solving groups.

A far better approach is to state the problem as a question. Note that this should be a **probative question**—an open one that encourages exploratory thinking. Asking, "Should we vacation in the mountains or at the beach?" still forces members to choose sides. A far better approach involves asking a question to help define the general goals that came out during the problem-identification stage: "What do we want our vacation to accomplish?" (that is, "relaxation," "adventure," "low cost," and so on).

Notice that this question is truly exploratory. It encourages the family members to work cooperatively, not forcing them to make a choice and then defend it. This absence of an either-or situation boosts the odds that members will listen openly to one another rather than listening selectively in defense of their own positions. There is even a chance that the cooperative, exploratory climate that comes from wording the question probatively will help the family arrive at consensus about where to vacation, eliminating the need to discuss the matter any further.

GATHER RELEVANT INFORMATION   Groups often need to know important facts before they can make decisions or even understand the problem. We remember one group of students who determined to do well on a class presentation. One of their goals, then, was "to get an *A* grade." They knew that, to do so, they would have to present a topic that interested both the instructor and the students in the audience. Their first job, then, was to do a bit of background research to find out what subjects would be well received. They interviewed the instructor, asking what topics had been successes and failures in previous semesters. They tested some possible subjects on a few classmates and noted their reactions. From this research they were able to modify their original probative question—"How can we choose and develop a topic that will earn us an *A* grade?"—into a more specific one—"How can we choose and develop a topic that contains humor, action, and lots of information (to demonstrate our research skills to the instructor) and that contains practical information that will

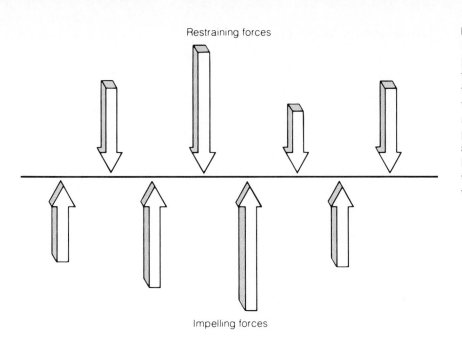

Restraining forces

Impelling forces

FIGURE 10—1
Force field. The arrows pointing downward represent forces that keep a group from reaching its goal whereas the upward arrows reflect the forces that support change. Notice that the arrows are of different lengths, representing the fact that some forces are stronger than others.

either improve the audience's social life, academic standing, or financial condition?"

IDENTIFY IMPELLING AND RESTRAINING FORCES Once members understand what they are seeking, the next step is to see what forces stand between the group and its goals. One useful tool for this kind of analysis is the **force field analysis.**[9] The easiest way to understand the force field concept is to look at Figure 10—1. By returning to our earlier example of the troubled team, we can see how the force field operates. Suppose the group defined its problem-question as "How can we (a) have more fun and (b) grow closer as friends?"

One restraining force in area (a) was clearly the team's losing record. But, more interestingly, discussion revealed that another damper on enjoyment came from the coach's obsession with winning and his infectiously gloomy behavior when the team failed. The main blocking force in area (b) proved to be the lack of socializing between team members in nongame situations. The driving forces in the first area included the sense of humor possessed by several members and the confession by most players that winning wasn't nearly as important to them as everyone had suspected. The impelling force in the area of friendship was the desire of all team members to become better friends. In addition, the fact that members shared many interests was an important plus.

It's important to realize that most problems have many impelling and constraining forces, all of which need to be identified during this stage. This may call for another round of research.

Once the force field is laid out, the group is ready to move on to the next step—namely, deciding how to strengthen the impelling forces and weaken the constraining ones.

SOLVING PROBLEMS IN GROUPS

Develop Alternative Solutions

Once the group has set up a list of criteria for success, its next job is to consider a number of ways to reach its goal. During this development phase, creativity is essential. The goal is to generate a number of approaches, not to choose just one. The biggest danger here is the tendency of members to defend their own idea and criticize others'. This kind of behavior leads to two problems. First, evaluative criticism almost guarantees a defensive reaction from members whose ideas have been attacked. A second consequence is the stifling of creativity. People who have just heard an idea rebuked—however politely—will find it hard even to think of more alternatives, let alone share them openly and risk possible criticism.

Probably the best-known method for encouraging creativity and avoiding the dangers just described is the process of **brainstorming.**[10] There are four important rules connected with this approach:

1. **Criticism Is Forbidden.** As we have already said, nothing will stop the flow of ideas more quickly than negative evaluation.
2. **"Freewheeling" Is Encouraged.** Sometimes even the most outlandish ideas prove workable, and even an impractical suggestion might trigger a workable idea.
3. **Quantity Is Sought.** The more ideas generated, the better the chance of coming up with a good one.
4. **Combination and Improvement Are Desirable.** Members are encouraged to "piggyback," by modifying ideas already suggested, and to combine previous suggestions.

Evaluate Possible Solutions

Once it has listed possible solutions, the group can evaluate the usefulness of each. One good way of identifying the most workable solutions is to ask three questions:[11]

1. **Will This Proposal Produce the Desired Changes?** One way to find out is to see whether it successfully overcomes the restraining forces in your force field analysis.
2. **Can the Proposal Be Implemented by the Group?** Can the members strengthen impelling forces and weaken constraining ones? Can they influence others to do so? If not, the plan isn't a good one.
3. **Does the Proposal Contain Any Serious Disadvantages?** Sometimes the cost of achieving a goal is too great. For example, one way to raise money for a group is to rob a bank. Although this plan might be workable, it raises more problems than it solves.

Implement the Plan

Everyone who makes New Year's resolutions knows the difference between making a decision and carrying it out. There are several important steps in developing and implementing a plan of action.[12]

► Creativity Killers in Group Discussion

Nothing squelches creativity like criticism. Although evaluating ideas is an important part of problem solving, judging suggestions too early can discourage members from sharing potentially valuable ideas. Here is a list of creativity-stopping statements that people should avoid making in the development phase of group work.

"That's ridiculous."
"It'll never work."
"You're wrong."
"What a crazy idea!"
"We tried it before and it didn't work."
"It's too expensive."
"There's no point in talking about it."
"It's never been done like that."
"We could look like fools."
"It's too big a job."
"We could never do that."
"It's too risky."
"You don't know what you're talking about."

IDENTIFY SPECIFIC TASKS TO BE ACCOMPLISHED   What needs to be done? Even a relatively simple job usually involves several steps. Now is the time to anticipate all the tasks facing the group. Remember everything now, and you will avoid a last-minute rush later.

DETERMINE NECESSARY RESOURCES   Identify the equipment, material, and other resources the group will need in order to get the job done.

DEFINE INDIVIDUAL RESPONSIBILITIES   Who will do what? Do all members know their jobs? The safest plan here is to put everyone's duties in writing, including due date. This might sound compulsive, but experience shows that it increases the chance of having jobs done on time.

PROVIDE FOR EMERGENCIES   Murphy's Law states, "Whatever can go wrong, will." Anyone experienced in group work knows the truth of this statement. People forget or welsh on their obligations, get sick, or quit. Machinery breaks down. (One corollary of Murphy's Law is "the copying machine will be out of order whenever it's most needed.") Whenever possible, you ought to develop contingency plans to cover foreseeable problems. Probably the single best suggestion we can give here is to plan on having all work done well ahead of the deadline, knowing that, even with last minute problems, your time cushion will allow you to finish on time.

Follow Up on the Solution

Even the best plans usually require some modifications once they're put into practice. You can improve the group's effectiveness and minimize disappointment by following two steps.

MEET PERIODICALLY TO EVALUATE PROGRESS Follow-up meetings should be part of virtually every good plan. The best time to schedule these meetings is as you put the group's plan to work. At that time, a good leader or member will suggest: "Let's get together in a week (or a few days or a month, depending on the nature of the task). We can see how things are going and take care of any problems."

REVISE THE GROUP'S APPROACH AS NECESSARY These follow-up meetings will often go beyond simply congratulating everyone for coming up with a good solution. Problems are bound to arise, and these periodic meetings, in which the key players are present, are the place to solve them.

Although these steps provide a useful outline for solving problems, they are most valuable as a general set of guidelines and not as a precise formula that every group should follow. As Table 10–1 suggests, certain parts of the model may need emphasis depending on the nature of the specific problem; the general approach will give virtually any group a useful way to consider and solve a problem.

▶ MAINTAINING POSITIVE RELATIONSHIPS

The task-related advice in the preceding pages will be little help if the members of a group don't get along. We therefore need to look at some ways to maintain good relationships among members. Many of the principles described in Chapters 4, 6, and 7 apply here. Because these principles are so important, we will review them here.

Basic Skills

Probably the most important ingredient in good personal relationships is mutual respect, and the best way to demonstrate respect for the other person is to *listen* carefully. A more natural tendency, of course, is to assume you understand the other members' positions and to interrupt or ignore them. Even if you are right, however, these reactions can create a residue of ill feelings. On the other hand, careful listening can at least improve the communication climate . . . and it may even teach you something.

Groups are bound to disagree sooner or later. When they do, the win-win problem-solving methods outlined in Chapter 7 boost the odds of solving the immediate issue in the most constructive way. As you read in Chapter 9, taking votes and letting the majority rule can often leave a sizable minority whose unhappiness can haunt the group's future work. Consensus is harder to reach in the short term but far more beneficial in the long run.

Building Cohesiveness

Cohesiveness can be defined as the totality of forces that cause members to feel themselves a part of a group and make them want to remain in that group.

TABLE 10–1 Adapting Problem-solving Methods to Special Circumstances

CHARACTERISTIC	EMPHASIZE
Members have strong feelings about the problem.	Consider allowing a period of emotional ventilation before systematic problem solving.
Task difficulty is high.	Follow structure of problem-solving method carefully.
Many possible solutions.	Emphasize brainstorming.
High level of member acceptance required.	Carefully define needs of all members, and seek solutions that satisfy all needs.
High level of technical quality required.	Emphasize evaluation of ideas; consider inviting outside experts.

Adapted from John Brilhart, *Effective Group Discussion,* 5th ed. (Dubuque, Iowa: W. C. Brown, 1986), p. 310.

You might think of cohesiveness as the glue that bonds individuals together, giving them a collective sense of identity. Groups become cohesive when certain conditions exist. If you understand these conditions, you can apply them to any group. You will then have a way of both measuring the group's cohesiveness and understanding how to increase it. There are eight factors that lead to increased cohesiveness.[13]

SHARED OR COMPATIBLE GOALS People draw closer when they share a similar aim or when their goals can be mutually satisfied. For example, members of a conservation group might have little in common until a part of the countryside they all value is threatened by development. Some members might value the land because of its beauty; others, because it provides a place to hunt or fish; and still others, because the nearby scenery increases the value of their property; but as long as their goals are compatible, this collection of individuals will find that a bond exists that draws them together.

PROGRESS TOWARD THESE GOALS While a group is making progress, members feel highly cohesive; when progress stops, cohesiveness decreases. All other things being equal, members of an athletic team feel closest when the team is winning. During extended losing streaks, it is likely that players will feel less positive about the team and less willing to identify themselves as members of the group.

SHARED NORMS AND VALUES Although successful groups will tolerate and even thrive on some differences in members' attitudes and behavior, wide variation in the group's definition of what actions or beliefs are proper will reduce cohesiveness. If enough members hold different ideas of what behavior is acceptable, the group is likely to break up. Disagreements over values or norms can fall into many areas, such as humor, finance, degree of candor, and proportion of time allotted to work and play.

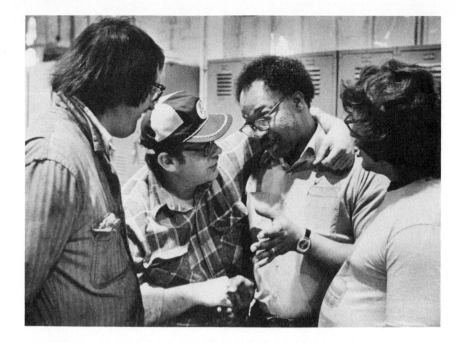

LACK OF PERCEIVED THREAT BETWEEN MEMBERS Cohesive group members see no threat to their status, dignity, and material or emotional well-being. When such interpersonal threats do occur, they can be very destructive. Often competition arises within groups, and as a result members feel threatened. Sometimes there is a struggle over who will be nominal leader. At other times, members view others as wanting to take over a functional role (problem solver, information giver, and so on), either through competition or criticism. Sometimes the threat is real, and sometimes it's only imagined, but in either case the group must neutralize it or face the consequences of reduced cohesiveness.

INTERDEPENDENCE OF MEMBERS Groups become cohesive when their needs can be satisfied only with the help of other members. When a job can be done just as well by one person alone, the need for membership decreases. This factor explains the reason for food cooperatives, neighborhood yard sales, and community political campaigns. All these activities enable the participants to reach their goal more successfully than if they acted alone.

THREAT FROM OUTSIDE THE GROUP When members perceive a threat to the group's existence or image (groups have self-concepts, just as individuals do), they grow closer together. Almost everyone knows of a family whose members seem to fight constantly among themselves—until an outsider criticizes one of them. At this point, the internal bickering stops, and for the moment the group unites against its common enemy. The same principle works on a larger scale when nations often bind up their internal differences in the face of external aggression.

MUTUAL PERCEIVED ATTRACTIVENESS AND FRIENDSHIP The factor of mutual attraction and friendship is somewhat circular because friendship and mutual attraction often are a result of the points just listed, yet groups often do become close simply because members like each other.

SHARED GROUP EXPERIENCES When members have been through some unusual or trying experience, they draw together. This explains why soldiers who have been in combat together often feel close and stay in touch for years after; it also accounts for the ordeal of fraternity pledging and other initiations. Many societies have rituals that all members share, thus increasing the group's cohesiveness.

It's important to realize that the eight factors just described interact with one another, often in contradictory ways. For instance, members of many groups are good friends who have been through thick and thin together (cohesiveness builders), but they find themselves less dependent on each other than before and now struggle over playing certain roles. In cases like this, cohesiveness can be figured as the net sum of all attracting and dividing forces.

Encouraging Participation

In most groups, there is an unequal amount of participation from member to member. Though it probably isn't desirable to have every person speak equally on every subject, neither is it good to have one or more members keep almost totally quiet. There are two reasons why: First, the group could probably benefit from hearing the additional information; second, having wallflowers in a group can become nerve-racking both for the quiet ones themselves and for the contributors. How, then, can participation be encouraged?

KEEP THE GROUP SMALL Common sense suggests that as a group grows larger, there is less time for each member to speak. But, just as important, the imbalance between talkers and nontalkers grows with membership.[14] In small groups of three or four members, participation is roughly equal; but once the size increases to between five and eight, there's a dramatic gap between the contributions of members. Therefore, one simple way to increase participation is to keep the group small whenever the task permits.

SOLICIT CONTRIBUTIONS FROM QUIET MEMBERS Sometimes contributions from quiet members can be obtained by simply asking for a member's input, ideally using open questions to guarantee a complete response: "What can you suggest to improve that idea, Gus?" In other cases, the nominal leader can assign quiet members certain tasks that will ensure their participation, such as reporting to the group on research.

REINFORCE CONTRIBUTIONS When a quiet member does make a contribution, it is especially important for others in the group to acknowledge it. Acknowledgment can be direct: "Thanks for suggesting that, Lisa." Another way to reinforce a comment is to refer to it later in the discussion: "That ties in with what Will said a while ago about ..."

Of course, there's a danger of becoming a phony, being overly complimentary. Gushing undeserved praise at shy people will probably discourage them from contributing again, so be sure to keep your reinforcements sincere and not effusive.

When we first read over these suggestions for encouraging participation, they sounded so obvious that we almost tossed them in the trash basket. But before doing so, we took a look at groups we belong to and realized that following these three simple steps really does draw out quiet speakers. So we encourage you not to discount these obvious but effective suggestions.

▶ LEADERSHIP IN GROUPS

For most of us, leadership ranks not far below motherhood in the hierarchy of values. "What are you, a leader or a follower?" we're asked, and we know which position is the good one. On the job, for instance, leadership means promotion. Even in the earliest grades of school, we knew who the leaders were, and we admired them. What is leadership all about?

Leadership and Leaders: A Matter of Power

Most people use the terms *leader* and *leadership* interchangeably when, in fact, there is a big difference between these two concepts. Some leaders don't exert leadership, and much leadership doesn't come from leaders...or at least people we identify by that term. Let us explain.

We can begin by defining **leadership** as *the ability to influence the behavior of others in a group.* And how are people influenced? By some sort of power. Power comes in several forms.[15]

LEGITIMATE POWER   The ability to influence others through **legitimate power** comes from the position one holds—supervisor, parent, professor, and so on. In many situations, this sort of power comes from the title alone: We follow the directions of police officers in traffic because we figure they know what they're doing. At other times, however, a person's title isn't the prime motivation.

COERCIVE POWER   Sometimes we do what the boss tells us, not out of any respect for the wisdom of the decision but because the consequences of not obeying would be unpleasant. Economic hardship, social disapproval, unpleasant work, even physical punishment...all are coercive forces that can shape behavior.

REWARD POWER   The ability to reward is the reverse side of coercive power. Like punishments, rewards can be social, material, or physical.

EXPERT POWER   Sometimes we are influenced by people because of what they know or can do. For example, when a medical emergency occurs, most group

"I was just going to say 'Well, I don't make the rules.' But, of course, I do make the rules."

Drawing by Leo Cullum; © 1986 The New Yorker Magazine, Inc.

members would gladly let a doctor, nurse, or paramedic call the shots (no pun intended) because of that person's obvious knowledge.

REFERENT POWER We might regard **referent power** as social power because we are talking about the influence that comes from the members' respect, attraction, or liking for someone in the group.

INFORMATION POWER Sometimes a member's knowledge of otherwise obscure facts can make a big difference in how the group operates. If you're working on a group project for one of your classes, the experiences of a fellow student who has taken another class from your instructor can give you important clues about how to approach the topic. This example shows the difference between **expert power** ("I can use an on-line computer data base to search for that information") and **information power** ("This professor is a fanatic about spelling and formatting mistakes"). Both technical expertise and insider information are important, but they can be possessed by different members.

Logic suggests that if leadership is the power to influence others, then the **leader** is someone who exerts that influence. But a look at the discussion you have **just** read shows that matters aren't this simple. For instance, there are some times when the **nominal leader**—the person who is designated by title to direct the group's functioning—really has very little influence on a group. We remember those happy days of junior high school when a certain substitute teacher took control (and we use that term loosely) of one civics class. She may have reigned, but she certainly didn't rule. Instead, a band of rowdy students, headed by two ringleaders with great referent power, ran the show: telling jokes, falling out of chairs, and finally escaping from the room through open windows. In the end, the dean's coercive power was the only way to put down the rebellion.

The lesson in this story of teenage mayhem is that some nominal leaders don't really lead and that some superficially powerless members are, in fact, the real movers and shakers of the group. One way to analyze the influence of a nominal leader is to identify that person's true power in the group by applying the six dimensions we just discussed. If the nominal leader scores high in most of these categories, we can say that he or she is a "strong leader." If the power is spread throughout the group, however, that leader's influence isn't as great.

Don't conclude from this that highly visible, powerful, centralized leadership is the best way to get a job done. There are many cases in which shared leadership is every effective. One mark of many effective leaders is their ability to enlist subtly the powerful support—by reward, coercive, expert, and referent methods—of other members to back a policy. Even leaders who want to take a highly influential and visible role can't do everything. Recall our discussion of functional roles in Chapter 9, and you'll realize that no single person can possibly perform every task necessary to have the group achieve its goal. We will

have more to say about the pros and cons of directive, centralized leadership in a few pages, when we discuss autocratic and democratic styles of designated leaders.

What Makes Leaders Effective?

Because the position of nominal leader is such an important one in our society, the next few pages will describe the factors that contribute to leader effectiveness.

TRAIT ANALYSIS Over 2,000 years ago Aristotle proclaimed, "From the hour of their birth some are marked out for subjugation, and others for command."[16] This is a radical example of the "great man" (or "great woman") view of leadership. Social scientists began their studies of leader effectiveness by conducting literally hundreds of studies that compared leaders with nonleaders. The results of all this research were mixed. Yet a number of distinguishing characteristics did emerge in several categories:[17]

Physical Appearance As a rule, leaders tend to be slightly taller, heavier, and physically more attractive than others. They also seem to possess greater athletic ability and stamina.

Sociability The category of sociability involves behaviors related to maintaining personal relationships within the group. For example, leaders talk more often and more fluently and are regarded as more popular, cooperative, and socially skillful.

Goal Facilitation Leaders have skills that help groups perform their tasks. They are somewhat more intelligent, possess more task-relevant information, and are more dependable than other members.

Desire for Leadership Leaders *want* that role and act in ways that will help them get it. They exercise initiative, are persistent, and express their beliefs assertively.

Despite these general findings, the research on **trait theories of leadership** is of only limited practical value: Later research has shown that many other factors are important in determining leader success, and not everyone who possesses these traits becomes a leader. We'll now examine this body of knowledge.

LEADERSHIP STYLE Some leaders have an **authoritarian leadership style,** using **legitimate, coercive,** and **reward power** to dictate what will happen in a group. Others use a more **democratic leadership style,** inviting other members to share in decision making. In a third style, called the **laissez-faire leadership style,** the leader gives up the power to dictate, transforming the group into a leaderless collection of equals. Early research suggested that the democratic style produced the highest-quality results,[18] but later experiments showed that matters weren't so simple. For instance, groups with autocratic leaders proved more productive under stressful conditions, but democratically led groups did better when the situation was nonstressful.[19]

CONTEMPORARY APPROACHES   After more than half a century of research, it seemed that certain types of leadership worked well in one set of circumstances but poorly in another. In an effort to pin down what approach works best in a given type of situation, psychologist Fred Fiedler attempted to find out when a task-oriented approach was most effective and when a more relationship-oriented style produced the best results.[20] From his research, Fiedler developed a **situational** theory of **leadership.** Although the complete theory is too complex to describe here, its general conclusion is that a leader's style should change with the circumstances. A task-oriented approach works best when conditions are either highly favorable (good leader-member relations, strong leader power, and clear task structure) or highly unfavorable (poor leader-member relations, weak leader power, and an ambiguous task) whereas a more relationship-oriented style is appropriate in moderately favorable or moderately unfavorable conditions.

Two researchers in the field of organizational communication, Robert R. Blake and Jane S. Mouton, have also examined the interaction of task and relationship factors in leadership, but with somewhat different conclusions.[21] They developed a **Managerial Grid**® consisting of a two-dimensional model (see Figure 10–2). The horizontal axis measures the leader's concern for production. This involves a focus on accomplishing the organizational task, with efficiency being

FIGURE 10–2
The Managerial Grid®. From Robert R. Blake and Jane S. Mouton, *The Managerial Grid III,* Houston: Gulf Publishing Co., Copyright © 1985, p. 12. Reproduced by permission.

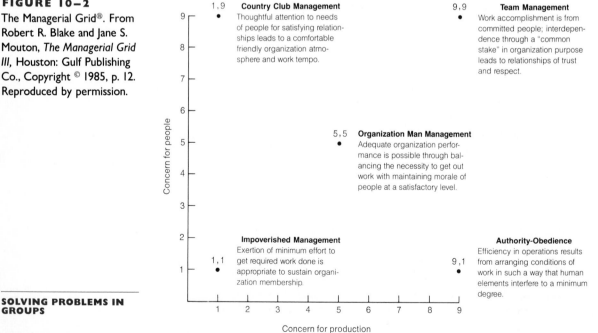

the main concern. The vertical axis measures the leader's concern for people's feelings and ideas. Blake and Mouton suggest that the most effective leader is one who adopts a 9,9 style—showing high concern for both task and relationships.

To summarize, situational theorists suggest that a good leader doesn't adopt either a 1,9 (high-relationship) or 9,1 (high-task) approach and stick with it; rather, effectiveness comes from adjusting to whatever approach the situation demands. Grid proponents urge leaders to exhibit high concern for both task and relationships at all times.[22] This book isn't the place to settle the dispute between situational and "one best style" adherents. Despite the unresolved controversy, one important and useful point emerges: Leaders need to consider the relationship needs of their subordinates as well as the demands of the task at hand.

DANGERS IN GROUP DISCUSSION ◄

Even groups with the best of intentions often find themselves unable to reach satisfying decisions. At other times, they make decisions that later prove to be wrong. Though there's no foolproof method of guaranteeing high-quality group work, there are several dangers to avoid.

Absence of Critical Information

Many groups are so anxious to make decisions that they do so without having important information. We know of one group that scheduled a fund-raising party without enough forethought and later found that their event had to compete with a championship football game. A bit of checking could have prevented much disappointment and earned the group more sorely needed funds.

Domination by a Minority

We have already said that participation in most groups is unequal. Besides leaving quieter members feeling hurt and unenthusiastic, domination by the vocal few can reduce a group's ability to solve a problem effectively. Research shows that the proposal receiving the largest number of favorable comments is usually the one chosen even if it isn't the best one.[23] Furthermore, ideas of high-status members (who aren't always talkers) are given more consideration than those of lower-status people.[24] The moral to this story? Don't assume that quantity of speech or the status of the speaker automatically defines the quality of an idea: Instead, seek out and seriously consider the ideas of quieter members.

Pressure to Conform

There's a strong tendency for group members to go along with the crowd, which often results in bad decisions. A classic study by Solomon Asch illustrated this point.[25] College students were shown three lines of different lengths and

Drawing by Levin; © 1983. The New Yorker Magazine, Inc.

asked to identify which of them matched with a fourth line. Although the correct answer was obvious, the experiment was a setup: Asch had instructed all but one member of the experimental groups to vote for the wrong line. As a result, fully one-third of the uninformed subjects ignored their own good judgment and voted with the majority. If simple tasks like this one generate such conformity, it is easy to see that following the (sometimes mistaken) crowd is even more likely in the much more complex and ambiguous tasks that most groups face. It's interesting to note that pressures toward conformity are strongest when group members have low confidence in their ability to solve a problem and are highly attracted to the group and when the conforming majority is relatively large.[26]

Premature Decision Making

Probably because uncertainty is not a happy state, many groups become emotionally attached to an alternative early in the decision-making process.[27] Such attachment leads members to ignore other ideas that might prove to be better. This tendency explains why the brainstorming process described on page 244 should be considered without criticism during early stages of discussion.

Confusing Disagreement with Dislike

Many group members see criticism of their ideas as a personal attack. This often leads them either to withdraw from the discussion or to lash back at the personality or proposal of the original critic. Hard as it sometimes is, it's important to distinguish disagreement from dislike.[28]

▶ When we look a little closer, we see an inconsistency in the way our society seems to feel about conformity (team playing) and nonconformity (deviance). For example, one of the great best-sellers of the 1950s was a book by John F. Kennedy called *Profiles in Courage*, wherein the author praised several politicians for their courage in resisting great pressure and refusing to conform. To put it another way, Kennedy was praising people who refused to be good team players, people who refused to vote or act as their parties or constituents expected them to. Although their actions earned Kennedy's praise long after the deeds were done, the immediate reactions of their colleagues were generally far from positive. The nonconformist may be praised by historians or idolized in films or literature long after the fact of his nonconformity, but he's usually not held in high esteem, at the time, by those people to whose demands he refuses to conform.

Elliot Aronson
The Social Animal

SUMMARY ◀

Despite the bad reputation of groups in some quarters, research shows that they are often the most effective setting for problem solving. They command greater resources, both quantitatively and qualitatively, then either single individuals or a collection of persons working in isolation; their work can result in greater accuracy; and the participative nature of the solutions they produce generates greater commitment from members.

Groups use a wide variety of discussion formats when solving problems. Some use parliamentary procedure to govern decision-making procedures. Others use moderated panel discussions, symposia, or forums. The best format depends on the nature of the problem and the characteristics of the group.

Groups stand the best chance of developing effective solutions to problems if they begin their work by identifying the problem, avoiding the mistake of failing to recognize hidden needs of individual members. Their next step is to analyze the problem, including identification of forces both favoring and blocking progress. Only at this point should the group begin to develop possible solutions, taking care not to stifle creativity by evaluating any of them prematurely. During the implementation phase of the solution, the group should monitor the situation carefully and make any necessary changes in its plan.

Groups that pay attention only to the task dimension of their interaction risk strains in the relationships among members. Many of these interpersonal problems can be avoided by using the skills described in Chapter 7 as well as by following the guidelines in this chapter for building group cohesiveness and encouraging participation.

Many naïve observers of groups confuse the concepts of leader and leadership. We defined leadership as the ability to influence the behavior of other members through the use of one or more types of power—legitimate, coercive, reward, expert, or referent. We saw that many nominal leaders share their power with other members. Leadership has been examined from many perspectives—trait analysis, leadership style, and situational variables.

The chapter concluded with a list of several common dangers that can hamper the effectiveness of problem-solving groups: lack of critical information, domination by vocal members, pressures to conform, premature decision making, and the confusion of disagreement and dislike among members.

▶ ACTIVITIES

1. Apply the principles summarized in Table 10–1 to a problem-solving group you belong to. (Class projects or informal study groups are good subjects to study here.) Do your best to follow each step carefully, and note any differences between the results of this approach and others you've tried in the past.
2. Observe a problem-solving group in action, and use Table 10–1 to see whether the group follows each of the steps thoroughly. What are the consequences of omitting one or more of the steps? If the group hired you as a consultant, how could you advise them to increase their problem-solving effectiveness?
3. Recall two groups to which you have belonged: one with a low level of cohesiveness and one highly cohesive one. Use the factors listed on pages 247–249 to analyze what contributed to the level of commitment of each group. How could matters be improved in the low-cohesiveness group?
4. Think of one low-level participant in a group you have observed. Using the guidelines on pages 249–250, suggest how the quiet member's contributions could be increased.
5. Think of two effective leaders you have known. How would you describe the style of each one: autocratic, democratic, or laissez-faire? Task- or relationship-oriented? Imagine that the two leaders were transferred, so that each one was directing the other's group. Would the same approach work equally well in each situation? Why or why not?

▶ NOTES

1. Cal Downs, David M. Berg, and Wil A. Linkugel, *The Organizational Communicator* (New York: Harper & Row, 1977), p. 127.
2. Marvin E. Shaw, *Group Dynamics: The Psychology of Small Group Behavior*, 3d ed. (New York: McGraw-Hill, 1981), pp. 61–64.
3. Ibid., p. 391.
4. Charles W. Redding, *Communication Within the Organization* (New York: Industrial Communication Council, 1972).
5. John Dewey, *How We Think* (New York: Heath, 1910).
6. See R. Y. Hirokawa, "Group Communication and Problem-Solving Effectiveness: An Investigation of Group Phases," *Human Communication Research* 9 (1983): 291–305, Edward R. Marby and Richard E. Barnes, *The Dynamics of Small Group Communication* (Englewood Cliffs, N.J.: Prentice-Hall, 1980), p. 78; Norman R. F. Maier and Robert A. Maier, "An Experimental Test of the Effects of 'Developmental' vs. 'Free' Discussions on the Quality of Group Decisions," *Journal of Applied Psychology* 41 (1957): 320–323; and Ovid L. Bayless, "An Alternative Model for Problem-Solving Discussion," *Journal of Communication* 17 (1967): 188–197.

7. Bobby R. Patton and Kim Giffin, *Problem-Solving Group Interaction* (New York: Harper & Row, 1973), p. 131.

8. Adapted from David Potter and Martin P. Andersen, *Discussion in Small Groups: A Guide to Effective Practice* (Belmont, Calif.: Wadsworth, 1976), pp. 20–22.

9. Kurt Lewin, *Field Theory in Social Science* (New York: Harper & Row, 1951), pp. 30–59.

10. Alex Osborn, *Applied Imagination* (New York: Scribner's, 1959).

11. Patton and Giffin, op. cit., pp. 167–168.

12. Ibid., adapted from pp. 182–185.

13. Adapted from Ernest G. Bormann, *Discussion and Group Methods: Theory and Practice,* 2d ed. (New York: Harper & Row, 1975), pp. 141–171.

14. R. F. Bales, F. L. Strodtbeck, T. M. Mills, and M. E. Roseborough, "Channels of Communication in Small Groups," *American Sociological Review* 16 (1951): 461–468.

15. John R. French and Bertram Raven, "The Basis of Social Power," in Dorwin Cartwright and Alvin Zander (eds.), *Group Dynamics* (New York: Harper & Row, 1968), p. 565.

16. Aristotle, *Politics* (New York: Oxford University Press, 1958), Book 7.

17. John F. Cragan and David W. Wright, *Communication in Small Group Discussions: A Case Study Approach* (St. Paul, Minn.: West Publishing, 1980), p. 74.

18. Kurt Lewin, R. Lippitt, and R. K. White, "Patterns of Aggressive Behavior in Experimentally Created Social Climates," *Journal of Social Psychology* 10 (1939): 271–299.

19. L. L. Rosenbaum and W. B. Rosenbaum, "Morale and Productivity Consequences of Group Leadership Style, Stress, and Type of Task," *Journal of Applied Psychology* 55 (1971): 343–358.

20. Fred E. Fiedler, *A Theory of Leadership Effectiveness* (New York: McGraw-Hill, 1967).

21. Robert R. Blake and Jane S. Mouton, *The Managerial Grid* (Houston: Gulf Publishing, 1964).

22. Robert R. Blake and Jane S. Mouton, *Toward Resolution of the Situationalism vs. "One Best Style ..." Controversy in Leadership Theory, Research, and Practice* (Austin, Tex.: Scientific Methods, 1981).

23. L. Richard Hoffman and Norman R. F. Maier, "Valence in the Adoption of Solutions by Problem-Solving Groups: Concept, Method, and Results," *Journal of Abnormal and Social Psychology* 69 (1964): 264–271.

24. E. P. Torrence, "Some Consequences of Power Differences on Decision Making in Permanent and Temporary Three-Man Groups," *Research Studies,* Washington State College, 22 (1954): 130–140.

25. Solomon E. Asch, "Effects of Group Pressure upon the Modification and Distortion of Judgments," in H. Guetzkow (ed.), *Groups, Leadership and Men* (Pittsburgh: Carnegie Press, 1951), pp. 177–190.

26. Shaw, op. cit., p. 398.

27. Hoffman and Maier, op. cit.

28. Patton and Giffin, op. cit., p. 158.

▶ PART FOUR
PUBLIC COMMUNICATION

▶ CHAPTER II

KEY TERMS

attitude
audience analysis
belief
demographics
general purpose
on-line data base
purpose statement
specific purpose
survey research
thesis statement
value

CHOOSING AND DEVELOPING A TOPIC

After reading this chapter, you should understand the following:

1. The importance of defining a clear speech purpose.

2. The difference between a general and a specific speech purpose.

3. The necessity of analyzing a speaking situation.

4. The importance of audience analysis.

You should be able to do the following:

1. Choose an effective topic.

2. Formulate a purpose statement that will help you develop that topic.

3. Analyze the three components of a speaking situation.

4. Perform an audience analysis.

5. Gather information on the topic from a variety of sources.

. . . I am, God help me, about to do it for the fifth time. My hands I know will be wet and my mouth dry. There will even be an actual bumping inside my chest as I scrape back my chair and walk unsteadily to the podium. "Thank you very much" (gulp . . . weak smile), "and good evening, ladies and gentlemen."

My horror of stages, speeches, spotlights and footlights is old stuff. I am a born spectator. My natural habitat is the audience. I know my place and it is not in the spotlight. It is back up there in the snug anonymous dark. . . .

I first emerged from the wings in a walnut shell towed by two mice. It was a fourth-grade production of *Thumbelina,* and my mortifying costume was a leaf. Merciful obscurity closed in after that until the time came to make a speech at my eighth-grade graduation. By then I was burdened with 20 pounds of overweight, a mouthful of braces and a broken leg. The event was so traumatic that for the next 20 years I stayed resolutely off the stage, refusing to take part in school plays, team athletics, dance contests or campus politics. I even got my college diploma by mail. Though my wedding took place in the relative privacy of my parents' living room, I would have preferred the even greater anonymity of city hall.

For years I refused all invitations to participate in panel discussions, disk-jockey interviews, political rallies, awards ceremonies or tree plantings. I never asked questions from the floor at lectures or volunteered to help the magician in the nightclub. At raffles, half of me hoped I didn't have the lucky number.

The carrot that finally coaxed me out of the wings was of all things a journalism award. No acceptance speech, they said, no award. O vanity, vanity! I said I'd be there.

But there was something more to it than that. I really started speaking for the same reason that I stopped smoking. I was ashamed of myself. It was time to grow up. But the older one gets, it seems, the harder that is to do.

As my D-day approached, I retreated. Friends had rallied round with all sorts of advice, mostly contradictory. Don't be afraid to write it out. Read it. Memorize it. Put it on cards. Speak it off the cuff. Start funny. Start dull—an early joke lets them off the hook of curiosity. Turn from side to side so they can all see you. Find one nice face in the audience and tell it all to him. Get a new dress. Get a little drunk.

By the afternoon of the speech, trying to follow all this advice at once, I sat stupefied with terror in my room in the hotel where the banquet was to be held. My new gown hung on the back of the door, flowers and telegrams began to arrive. Were they condolences? Had I already died? . . . I barely remember going downstairs to the hotel ballroom, or the dais, or the dinner, or anything at all until I felt my wet palms gripping the smooth sides of the lectern, and heard my own weird, oddly magnified voice rumble out over the crowd.

I was most unprepared for my own total unpreparedness: I didn't know where to look, where to put my hands, where to pitch my voice, when to pause, when to smile. To be *that* unknowing rarely happens to an adult; it gave me a giddy feeling; nothing to do but push on.

After a few moments I heard faint laughter. I was not quite conscious of it at first, but then it came again a bit stronger, until I was sure I heard it, and then as I was reading I began to wait for it, and to make spaces in sentences for it, to enjoy it, and finally to play with the words and with the audience, to swoop and glide and describe arabesques with all the nutty abandon of Donald Duck on ice skates.

Success. Triumph. Waves of applause. The night came to a kind of crescendo Andy Hardy finish that I have never been able to recapture. In the next three speeches I was nearly as scared as the first time, but not nearly as good. But I am going to try it again. I am getting to know the ropes.

Shana Alexander

Most people view the prospect of standing before an audience with the same enthusiasm they have for a trip to the dentist or the tax auditor. In fact, giving a speech seems to be one of the most anxiety-producing things we can do: *The Book of Lists* claims that Americans fear public speaking more than they do insects, heights, accidents, and even death.[1]

Despite the discomfort that speech giving causes, sooner or later most of us will need to talk to an audience of some kind: while giving a class report, as part of our jobs, or as part of a community-action group. And even in less "speech-like" situations, we often need the same skills good speakers possess: the ability to talk with confidence, to organize ideas in a clear way, and to make those ideas interesting and persuasive.

Getting to "know the ropes" in public speaking is, as Shana Alexander suggests in the reading on page 264, at least partially a matter of practice. But practice doesn't always make perfect; without a careful analysis of *what* you are practicing, practice has a tendency to make old public speaking habits permanent rather than perfect. The final section of this book will provide you with some tools to analyze your performance as a public speaker.

CHOOSING A TOPIC ◄

Often the difference between a successful and an unsuccessful speech is the choice of topic. It should be familiar enough for your audience to understand, yet be innovative enough to hold their attention. This chapter will discuss a number of approaches to choosing and developing the right topic. The following guidelines will help you pick a topic that is appropriate for you, your audience, and your assignment.

Look for a Topic Early

The best student speakers usually choose a topic as soon as possible after a speech is assigned by their instructor, and then they stick with it. One reason to look for a topic early is so that you will have plenty of time to complete the speech and practice it. Adequate practice time is essential to effective speech-making. And yet the reasons for choosing a topic early run even deeper than that. Ideas seem to come automatically to speakers who have a topic in mind; things they read or observe or talk about that might have otherwise been meaningless suddenly relate to their topic, providing material or inspiration for sources of material.[2] The earlier you decide on a topic, the more of these happy coincidences you can take advantage of.

Choose a Topic That Interests You

If you are not interested in your topic, it will be difficult for you to interest anyone else. Your interest in a topic will improve your ability to investigate it. It will also increase your confidence when it comes time to present it.

Needless to say, your topic should also have the potential of being interesting to your audience. But no matter how "good" the topic, if it isn't interesting to you, you'll have a hard time involving your audience.

Sometimes it's difficult to pinpoint *what* your interests are—especially when you're being pressed to come up with a speech topic. If that happens to you, we suggest the following steps:

1. Review a few recent issues of your favorite newspapers and magazines—which articles did you find interesting?
2. Browse through your bookshelf at home, or mentally review the books you've read—any consistent themes or topics?
3. Inspect your possessions—any equipment for sports, hobbies, or interests that would suggest a topic?
4. Think about the way you spend your free time—anything there that would suggest a major interest?

These steps are just examples, of course. Television programs, films, bookstores, walks in the neighborhood, talks with friends, and dozens of other activities can all spur your memory about the things that interest you.

Choose a Topic You Know Something About

The main problem for most people is realizing how *much* they know. It is a mistake to think that you have nothing new to say; your experiences, your thoughts, and your investigation of a topic will be, by definition, unique.

One student who felt he had no unique knowledge came up with the following list after reviewing his interests:

1. Cars: driving them, different types, safety features and problems.
2. Learning English as a second language: from his experiences as both a student and a tutor.
3. Dealing with adoption (he was adopted).
4. Different forms of discrimination: age, sex, racial and student discrimination, to be specific.
5. Religion: He was deeply involved with his own and very interested in others.

With these preliminary guidelines out of the way, we can turn to the next step in choosing and developing your topic: defining your purpose.

▶ DEFINING PURPOSE

All Communication Is Purposeful

No one gives a speech—or expresses *any* kind of message—without having a reason to do so. This is easy to see in those messages that ask for something: "Pass the salt" or "How about a movie this Friday?" or "Excuse me. That's my foot you're standing on." but even in subtler messages the speaker always has a purpose—to evoke a response from the listener.

Sometimes purposes are misunderstood or confused by the speaker. This causes wasted time both in the preparation and in the presentation of the speech. It is essential, therefore, that the speaker keep in mind a clear purpose.

The first step in understanding your purpose is to formulate a clear and precise purpose statement. This requires an understanding of both *general purpose* and *specific purpose*.

General Purpose

Most students, when asked *why* they are giving a speech in a college class, will quickly cite course requirements. But you have to analyze your motives more deeply than that to develop a complete speech purpose. Even if you are only giving your speech for the grade, you still have to affect your audience in some way to earn that grade.

If your motive for speaking is to learn effective speech techniques (as we hope it is), you still have to influence your audience to accomplish your goal because that is what effective speaking is all about.

When we say you have to influence your audience, we mean you have to *change* them in some way. If you think about all the possible ways you could change an audience, you'll realize that they all boil down to three options, which happen to be the three basic **general purposes** for speaking:

1. To Entertain: To relax your audience by providing them with a pleasant listening experience.
2. To Inform: To enlighten your audience by teaching them something.
3. To Persuade: To move your audience toward a new attitude or behavior.

A brief scrutiny of these purposes will reveal that no speech could ever have *only* one purpose. These purposes are interrelated because a speech designed for one purpose will almost always accomplish a little of the other purposes; even a speech designed purely to entertain might change audience attitudes or teach that audience something new. In fact, these purposes are *cumulative* in the sense that, to inform an audience, you have to make your remarks entertaining enough to hold their interest—at least long enough to convince them your topic is worth learning about.

Deciding your general purpose is like choosing the "right" answer on one of those multiple-choice tests in which *all* the answers are right to a certain degree, but *one* answer is more right than the others. Thus, we say that any speech is *primarily* designed for one of these purposes. A clear understanding of your general purpose gets you on the right track for choosing and developing a topic. Understanding your **specific purpose** will keep you on that track.

Specific Purpose

Whereas your general purpose is only a one-word label, your **specific** goal is expressed in the form of a **purpose statement**—a complete sentence that describes exactly what you want your speech to accomplish. The purpose statement usually isn't used word for word in the actual speech; its purpose is to keep you focused as you plan your speech.

► Let him never make a speech until he has something to say. This last is about the hardest advice to follow, perhaps.

Mark Twain

There are three criteria for a good purpose statement.[3]

1. A Purpose Statement Must Describe the Result You Are Seeking. As we mentioned earlier, all communication seeks some response from a receiver. This receiver orientation should be reflected in your purpose statement. For example, if you were giving an informative talk on gourmet cooking, this would be an inadequate purpose statement:

"My purpose is to tell my audience about gourmet cooking."

As that statement is worded, your purpose is "to tell" an audience something, which means that the speech could be successful even if no one listens. Your purpose statement should refer to the response you want from your audience: It should tell what the audience members will know or be able to do after listening to your speech. Thus, the purpose statement above could be improved this way:

"After listening to my speech, my audience will know more about gourmet cooking."

That's an improvement because you now have stated what you expect from your audience. But this purpose statement could still be improved through the judicious application of a second criterion:

2. A Purpose Statement Must Be Specific. To be effective, a purpose statement should be worded specifically, with enough details so that you would be able to measure or test your audience, after your speech, to see if you had achieved your purpose. In the example given earlier, simply "knowing about gourmet cooking" is too vague; you need something more specific, such as:

"After listening to my speech, my audience will be able to cook *coq au vin* at home."

At least now you've limited your purpose to a single dish rather than the entire world of gourmet cooking. This is an improvement, but it can still be made better by applying a third criterion:

3. **A Purpose Statement Must Be Realistic.** You must be able to accomplish your purpose as stated. Some speakers insist on formulating purpose statements such as "My purpose is to convince my audience to make federal budget deficits illegal." Unfortunately, unless your audience happens to be a joint session of Congress, it won't have the power to change United States fiscal policy. But any audience can write their congressional representative or sign a petition. Similarly, an audience will not "learn how to play championship tennis" or "understand the dangers of business regulation" in one sitting. You must aim for an audience response that is possible to accomplish. In your gourmet cooking speech, it would be impossible for you to be sure that each of your audience members will actually be able to cook a meal. You might have no idea, for example, if they all have access to a kitchen. So a better purpose statement for this speech might sound something like this:

> "After listening to my speech my audience will be able to list the five steps for preparing *coq au vin* at home."

This purpose statement is audience-oriented, precise, and attainable. It also suggests an organizational pattern for the speech ("the five steps").

Consider the following sets of purpose statements:

Less Effective	**More Effective**
To tell my audience about day-care centers. (not result-oriented)	After listening to my speech, my audience will be able to identify the three basic types of day-care centers.
After listening to my speech, my audience will understand solar power. (not realistic)	After listening to my speech, my audience will understand how solar power can be used at home, in business, and in government. (Once again, this type of purpose statement can be particularly effective because it shows you what your main points will be.)
After listening to my speech, my audience will know about drunken driving. (not specific)	After listening to my speech, my audience members will think twice before driving a car after having had more than two drinks.

THE THESIS STATEMENT ◄

So far we have discussed how to select a topic, how partially to focus that topic through its general purpose, and how to focus it further through its specific purpose. Your next step in the focusing process is to formulate your thesis statement. The **thesis statement** tells you what the central idea of your speech is. It tells you the one idea that you want your audience to remember after they have forgotten everything else you had to say. The thesis statement for your *coq au vin* speech might be worded like this:

Cooking *coq au vin* is a simple, five-step process that can start you on the road to gourmet cooking.

Unlike your purpose statement, your thesis statement is often spoken directly to your audience. The thesis statement contains more information than the purpose statement, and it is usually formulated later in the speechmaking process after you have done some research on your topic. The progression from topic to central idea is, therefore, another focusing process as you can see in the following examples:

Topic: Why must an injured horse be destroyed?

General Purpose: To inform

Specific Purpose: After listening to my speech, my audience will understand why certain types of equine injuries cannot be healed. They will not criticize people who put horses to sleep for good reasons.

Thesis Statement: If a horse cannot recover, it is more humane to destroy it than to let it suffer a slow, agonizing death.

Topic: The Bottle Bill

General Purpose: To persuade

Specific Purpose: After listening to my speech, at least half my audience members will sign my petition to the governor supporting a state bottle bill.

Thesis Statement: Returnable-container laws reduce litter, create new employment, and save resources.

Once again, this thesis statement evolved after research. This thesis statement is particularly useful because it reveals the three main points of the speech. Another example:

Topic: Saving Water

General Purpose: To persuade

Specific Purpose: After listening to my speech, audience members will use less water in their daily activities.

Thesis Statement: Conserving water is a relatively simple process that will save us from much greater inconveniences in the future.

▶ ANALYZING THE SPEAKING SITUATION

A good speech purpose should be attainable, but it's impossible to know just what you can expect to attain—or the best way to go about attaining it—without analyzing the speaking situation.

There are three components to analyze in any speaking situation: the speaker, the audience, and the occasion. To be successful, every choice you make in putting together your speech—your choice of purpose, topic, and all the material you use to develop your speech—must be appropriate to all three of these components.

You, the Speaker: Self-analysis

"Above all else," Polonius urged Hamlet, "to thine own self be true." This is good advice to follow in speech preparation. Don't become so involved in finding a "correct" topic or material that you lose yourself.

One student, after analyzing his own life experience, came up with the topic of "Mandatory Recertification of Medical Doctors." His speech began as follows:

> Last summer I entered a hospital with symptoms that required a spinal tap for further diagnosis. Some 1,500 miles away, 12-year-old Rebecca Valada entered Miami Baptist Hospital also requiring a spinal tap. Like the majority of Americans who seek medical care, I had blind trust in my physician. I was not the least bit worried about his competence. As I expected, my test went fine. Becky's blind trust, however, betrayed her and, owing to her doctor's incompetence, she went into cardiac arrest and died within an hour.[4]

Self-analysis is largely a matter of staying in touch with three factors you have already considered: your own purpose, feelings, and unique knowledge and interests.

PURPOSE   We already discussed one step in self-analysis when we considered your purpose as a speaker. The first question to ask yourself when planning a speech (or any other act of communication) is, "What do I want to accomplish?" Having answered this question, you should check every decision that follows to be sure it contributes to your goal.

YOUR FEELINGS   After your purpose has been clarified, a second kind of self-analysis involves your feelings about yourself in the specific speaking situation. As we discussed in Chapter 2, the perceptions of both the speaker and the listener can greatly alter the outcome of any act of communication. Your perception of yourself as a speaker will influence you along every step of the speech-preparation process. If you have a negative self-concept or if you feel negative about the topic, those feelings will show through in the final product. You will be just a little "off" in terms of the topic you've selected, the information you've gathered, the way you present that information, and in every other aspect of your speech. Therefore it's important to look at yourself objectively and to choose a purpose, topic, and material about which you can feel confident and enthusiastic. If you really don't care about gourmet cooking, the barter economy, consumer credit, or any other subject, then that's not an appropriate topic for you as a speaker—no matter how potentially interesting that topic is to your audience.

YOUR UNIQUE KNOWLEDGE AND INTERESTS   A third step in your self-analysis involves recognizing and building on your uniqueness as a person. Though you are obviously similar in many ways to your audience, there are also many respects in which you are different. You can capitalize on this uniqueness by offering the audience something new—your knowledge, your experiences, or perhaps your opinions. Analyze yourself from the point of view of how you are different from your audience. This will give you insight into what you have to offer them. For example, if you have been the object of discrimination or if you know someone who has, then you have an area of uniqueness to talk about.

At the same time, this third step in your self-analysis will help you keep your message close to the listeners' interests and backgrounds; if you know where you're different from them, you'll know where you have to explain things in depth and add human-interest touches to keep from losing their attention. This brings us to our second step in analyzing the situation: your analysis of the audience.

The Listeners: Audience Analysis

When you choose a gift, it's important to consider the person who will receive it; what would be an ideal present for one person could be a disaster for another. In the same way, you need to think about your audience—especially in terms of their interests—when planning a speech. Because the audience's reaction determines the success or failure of a speech we say that public speaking is "audience-oriented." In essence, this means that the more you know about your audience, the more successful your speech will be.

Audience adaptation is something that we have a tendency to do naturally. Research suggests, for example, that in everyday conversations what we say to children and the elderly is simpler, more redundant, and less complex than what we say to other adults.[5] Your speeches will tend to be successful if you extend

this principle of audience adaptation to your prepared remarks to a group of listeners.

There are several factors to consider in **audience analysis.**

AUDIENCE TYPE   There are at least three types of audience you are likely to encounter—we could call these types "passersby," "captives," and "volunteers." Each type suggests different audience interests.[6]

"Passersby," as the name implies, are people who aren't much interested—at least not in advance—in what you have to say. A crowd milling around the student union or a shopping mall would fit into this category. With this type of audience, your first concern is to make them aware of you as a speaker either by interesting them in the topic or in you as a speaker. You might have to pick a really sensational topic or begin developing your topic by using some kind of device or gimmick to get their attention, such as the loud costumes or wild theatrics street speakers often rely on.

"Captives" are audience members who have gathered for some reason besides the joy of hearing you speak. Students in a required class often begin as a type of "captive" audience. So do military formations, mandatory work meetings, and other "required" gatherings. With captives you don't have to worry about devices and gimmicks to make them aware of you as a speaker; you do, however, have to use material that will get them interested and keep them interested in what you have to say.

"Volunteers" are audience members who have gathered together because of a common interest. Students in elective courses, especially those with long waiting lists, would fit into this category. So would gatherings of most clubs, social organizations, and "action" groups. Even with an audience of volunteers, you still have to maintain the listeners' interest; you never lose that responsibility. But when the audience is informed and involved, as volunteers tend to be, you can treat your topic in greater depth without worrying about *losing* their interest.

Most college speech classes are a mixture of captives and volunteers, which means that you don't have to sensationalize your topic or use gimmicks, but you do have to maintain interest and provide depth.

AUDIENCE PURPOSE   Just as you have a purpose for speaking, the audience members have a purpose for gathering. Sometimes virtually all members of your audience will have the same, obvious goal. Expectant parents at a natural childbirth class are all seeking a healthy, relatively painless delivery, and people attending an investment seminar are looking for ways to increase their net worth.

There are other times, however, when audience purpose can't be so easily defined. In some instances, different listeners will have different goals, some of which might not be apparent to the speaker. Consider a church congregation, for example. Whereas some members might listen to a sermon with the hope of applying religious principles to their lives, others might be interested in being entertained or in appearing pious. In the same way, the listeners in your speech class probably have a variety of motives for attending; becoming aware of as many of these motives as possible will help you predict what will interest them.

▶ There is no such thing as an uninteresting subject. There are only uninterested people.

G. K. Chesterton

CHOOSING AND DEVELOPING A TOPIC

DEMOGRAPHICS **Demographics** are characteristics of your audience that can be labeled, such as number of people, age, sex, group membership, and so on. Demographic characteristics might affect your speech planning in a number of ways.[7] For example:

1. **Number of People.** Topic appropriateness varies with the size of an audience. With a small group you can be less formal and more intimate—you can, for example, talk more about your own inner feelings and personal experiences. If you gave a speech before five people as impersonally as if they were a standing-room-only crowd in a lecture hall, they would probably find you stuffy. On the other hand, if you talked to 300 people about your unhappy childhood, you'd probably make them uncomfortable. Also, the larger your audience, the broader the range of interests and knowledge; with a small audience, you can choose a more specific topic.

2. **Sex.** Traditionally, men and women have tended to be interested in different topics. These differences are becoming less pronounced as time goes on because men and women are becoming conscious of sexual stereotypes and are rebelling against them. Still, the differences in interest that prevail are of concern to a speaker in choosing and developing a topic. There are still more men than women interested in automotive engineering and more women than men interested in cooking. The guideline here might be: *Do not exclude or offend any portion of your audience on the basis of sex.* Every speech teacher has a horror story about a student getting up in front of a class composed primarily, but not entirely, of men and speaking on a subject such as "Picking up Chicks." The women, once they realize that the speech is not about methods of handling poultry, are invariably offended. And most of the men will feel the same way.

    As with any of these demographic characteristics, the point is to *analyze,* not *stereotype* your audience. This will enable you to adapt your idea (rather than throwing it away) according to who is in your audience. The speaker who wants to speak to a mixed audience on how man meets woman, or vice versa, may still do so; the topic of the speech, however, should be "meeting people." That way it can be treated in a manner that would be appropriate for both men and women. This is true of topics like "weight lifting" (which could be changed to "body conditioning") and "home economics" (which could be changed to "survival for singles").

3. **Age.** In many areas younger people and older people have different interests. Topics such as social security, child rearing, and school success are all influenced by the age of the audience. These differences run relatively deep; Aristotle observed long ago that young people "have strong passions," that "their lives are spent not in memory but in expectation," and that they have high ideals because "they have not been humbled by life or learned its necessary limitations." Older people, on the other hand, tend to have more practical interests.

4. **Group Membership.** Organizations to which the audience members belong provide more clues to audience interests. By examining the groups to which they belong, you can surmise an audience's political leanings (Young

Republicans or Young Democrats), religious beliefs (CYO or Hillel), or occupation (Bartenders Union or Speech Communication Association). Group membership is often an important consideration in college classes. Consider the difference between "typical" college day classes and "typical" college night classes. At many colleges the evening students are generally older and tend to belong to civic groups, church clubs, and the local chamber of commerce. Daytime students tend to belong to sororities and fraternities, sports clubs, and social-action groups.

These four demographic characteristics are important examples, but the list goes on and on. Other demographic characteristics include ethnic background, religion, educational level, economic status, and occupation; demographics that might be important in a college class include hometown, year in school, and major subject. A student at North Dakota State University adapted her speech on adult illiteracy to her college audience by beginning it like this:

College campuses are saturated with Greek-named sorority and fraternity houses. If you're unaccustomed to Kappa, Rho, or Delta, these letters are as meaningless as a blank piece of paper. Or picture yourself in downtown Tokyo trying to translate the written squiggles on a billboard into common words like "restaurant" or "bus stop." Fortunately, most of us don't have these problems in everyday life. But there are individuals who must interpret the written English language in much the same way.[8]

Here is how another student adapted her speech on "Learning to Communicate" to an audience of speech majors:

With backgrounds in speech, we can be the solution to this problem. It's actually very simple. Since we possess the skills that the children need to learn, we can instruct them in the basics of oral communication. This solution involves no tricky legislation or money, just a little time....[9]

As these examples show, audience consideration doesn't stop with prior analysis. You should use your understanding of your audience to include audience references within your speech. In short, any demographic characteristic of the audience that you can identify should be used as part of your audience analysis.

A final factor to consider in audience analysis concerns their attitudes, beliefs, and values.

ATTITUDES, BELIEFS, AND VALUES An audience's feelings about you, your subject, and your intentions for them are central issues in audience analysis. One way to approach these questions is through a consideration of attitudes, beliefs, and values. These characteristics are structured in human consciousness like layers of an onion. They are all closely interrelated, but attitudes lie closest to the surface whereas beliefs and values underlie them. An **attitude** is a predisposition to respond to something in a favorable or unfavorable way. A **belief** is an underlying conviction about the truth of something, which is often based on cultural training. A **value** is a deeply rooted belief about a concept's inherent worth or worthiness. An audience might hold the value that "freedom is a good thing," for example, which will be expressed in a belief such as "people should be free to choose their political leaders," which, in turn, will lead to the attitude

▶ **Length Versus Depth**

The speaker steps up on the
    podium
To give his speech of praise
    or odium,
And as he lays his papers out
And ranges them with care
    about
And thinks, "My speech is for
    the ages,"
His hearers try to count the
    pages.

Richard Armour

**CHOOSING AND
DEVELOPING A TOPIC**

275

that "voting is an important right and responsibility for all citizens." This, in short, leads to a predisposition to vote—in other words, a positive attitude toward voting.

In diagram form, attitudes, beliefs and values might appear as shown in Figure 11–1.

Experts in audience analysis often try to concentrate on values. As one team of researchers pointed out, "Values have the advantage of being comparatively small in number, and, owing to their abstract nature, are more likely to be shared by large numbers of people."[10]

Take, for example, a corporate recruiter who addresses a college class about job opportunities. By complimenting the students for choosing to delay their careers until they earn degrees, he or she might create a positive audience attitude. After all, an audience made up of college students will probably hold a basic value of respecting education. In diagram form, this speaker's situation might be represented as shown in Figure 11–2.

On the other hand, for another audience, such as a group of blue-collar workers, the speaker's strategy might not work so favorably.

You can often make an inference about audience attitudes by recognizing beliefs and values they are likely to hold. For example, a group of religious fundamentalists might hold the value of "obeying God's word." This might lead to the belief—based on their interpretation of the Bible—that women are not meant to perform the same functions in society as men. This, in turn, might lead to the attitude that women ought not to pursue careers as fire fighters, police officers, or construction workers.

FIGURE 11–1
Structure of Values, Beliefs, and Attitudes

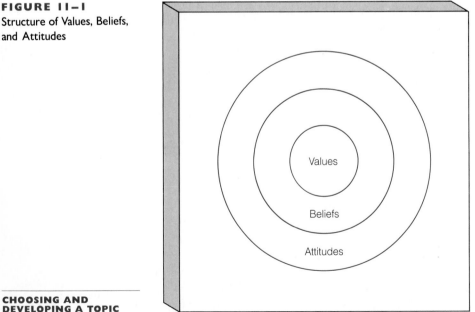

You can also make a judgment about one attitude your audience members hold based on your knowledge of other attitudes they hold. If your audience is made up of undergraduates who have a positive attitude toward liberation movements, it is a good bet they also have a positive attitude toward civil rights and ecology. If they have a negative attitude toward collegiate sports, they probably also have a negative attitude toward fraternities and sororities. This should not only suggest some appropriate topics for each audience, but it should also suggest ways that those topics could be developed.

The Occasion

The third phase in analyzing a speaking situation focuses on the occasion. The "occasion" of a speech is determined by the circumstances surrounding it. Three of these circumstances are time, place, and audience expectations.

TIME Your speech occupies a space in time that is surrounded by other events. For example, other speeches might be presented before or after yours, or comments might be made that set a certain tone or mood. There are also external events (such as elections, the start of a new semester, or even the weather) that color the occasion in one way or the other. The date on which you give your speech might have some historical significance. If that historical significance relates in some way to your topic, you can use it to help build audience interest.

The time *available* for your speech is also an essential consideration. You should choose a topic that is broad enough to say something worthwhile but

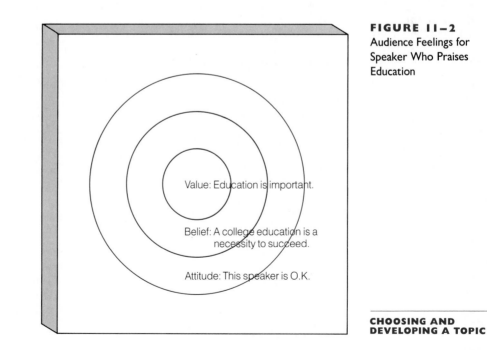

FIGURE 11–2
Audience Feelings for Speaker Who Praises Education

Value: Education is important.

Belief: A college education is a necessity to succeed.

Attitude: This speaker is O.K.

Audience: Sons of Italy Club

Situation: Acceptance speech for scholarship award.

Purposes
1. The audience will know that I'm grateful for receiving the scholarship.
2. The audience will realize that I'm not the stereotyped bookworm that scholarship recipients are usually viewed as.
3. The audience will think that they've given the scholarship to the right person.

When I began planning the speech, I couldn't decide if I wanted to do it in Italian or English. I was considering Italian because of the nature of the club and because I thought it would impress the audience if I used that language: They might think "She's a good Italian" and "She's bright." In the end I decided to speak in English. Even though most of the audience would understand my Italian, there were a few important people who didn't speak it.

My audience consisted of mostly middle-aged and older people. There were about 150 to 200 of them. Among the special guests were the mayor and some club representatives from out of town. I knew that I had to sound sincere and yet be organized enough to show that I had a "good head on my shoulders." On the other hand, I didn't want to give the audience the impression that I was superstudious and did nothing but study. For this reason, I began the speech by acknowledging the audience's feelings of boredom after sitting through forty minutes of other speeches. I thought this would show that I was one of them. I acknowledged this feeling because from past experiences with this particular audience I know that they are more interested in the festivities and dancing following dinner than with any ceremonies.

Also to get away from the bookworm stereotype, I dressed in a very sophisticated (yet not too sexy—I'm a "nice Italian girl"!) manner, in a black midcalf dress.

My entire speech supported the idea that I was honored to receive the scholarship by describing my sincere feelings of enthusiasm. I also threw in a few Italian phrases for authenticity and concluded the speech by encouraging everyone to have a great time that evening.

The speech was a big success. I was very sincere and emotional while giving it, so the audience knew it was coming from my heart. My happiness showed in my smile. I felt comfortable looking at the audience a lot because I had practiced the speech well and because I knew they were behind me. Because of my nervousness and excitement my voice was quivery, but I think even this helped my purpose although I didn't plan it that way.

The reception I received from the audience was tremendous, which made me feel good because it made me realize that I had accomplished my purposes.

---

brief enough to fit your time limits. "Wealth," for example, might be an inherently interesting topic to some college students, but it would be difficult to cover such a broad topic in a ten-minute speech and still say anything significant. But a topic like "How to Make Extra Money in Your Spare Time" could conceivably be covered in ten minutes in enough depth to make it worthwhile. All speeches have time limitations, whether they are explicitly stated or not. If you are invited to say a few words and you present a few volumes, you won't be invited back.

PLACE   Your speech also occupies a physical space. The beauty or squalor or your surroundings or the noise or stuffiness of the room should all be taken into consideration. These physical surroundings can be referred to in your speech if appropriate. If you were talking about world poverty, for example, you could compare your surroundings to those that might be found in a poorer country.

AUDIENCE EXPECTATION   Finally, your speech is surrounded by audience expectations. A speech presented in a college class, for example, is usually expected to reflect a high level of thought and intelligence. This doesn't necessarily mean that it has to be boring or humorless; wit and humor are, after all, indicative of intelligence. But it does mean that you have to put a little more effort into your presentation than if you were discussing the same subject with friends over coffee.

When you are considering the occasion of your speech, as well as when you are considering your audience and yourself as a speaker, it pays to remember that every occasion is unique. Although there are obvious differences between the occasion of a college class, a church sermon, and a bachelor party "roast," there are also many subtle differences that will apply only to the circumstances of each unique event.

GATHERING INFORMATION ◄

This discussion about planning a speech purpose and analyzing the speech situation makes it apparent that it takes time, interest, and knowledge to develop a topic well. Much of the knowledge you present in your speech will be based on your own thoughts and experience. Setting aside a block of time to reflect on your own ideas is essential. However, you will also need to gather information from outside sources.

There are three types of information you need for a speech. We've already discussed the first category, which is information dealing with the speaking situation (you, the audience, and the occasion). In addition, you also need information about the *ideas* you use and *facts* to substantiate and help develop your ideas. By this time, of course, you are familiar with library research as a form of gathering information. Sometimes, however, speakers overlook some of the less obvious resources of the library; more often they also overlook interviewing, personal observation, and survey research as equally effective methods of gathering information. We will review all these methods here and perhaps provide a new perspective on one or more of them.

► A library is a sacred place. For four thousand years, humanity has gone through dreadful horrors, dreadful turmoils, varied glories. How do we distill the past? How do we retain the memories? Libraries.

Vartan Gregorian

Library Research

Libraries, like people, tend to be unique. It's important to get to know your own library, to see what kind of special collections and services it offers, and just to find out where everything is. There are, however, a few resources that are common to most libraries, including the card catalog, reference works, periodicals, and nonprint materials.

CHOOSING AND DEVELOPING A TOPIC

THE CARD CATALOG   The card catalog is an ancient and noble information-storing device. Today many card catalogs are computerized or stored on microfilm. Whatever its form, the card catalog is your key to all the books in the library, filed according to subject, author, and title, so that you can look under general topics as well as for specific books and authors.

REFERENCE WORKS   Reference works will also be listed in the card catalog, but it would be a better idea to spend some time wandering through the reference room yourself. There are wonders there that could turn you into a trivia expert for life. There are encyclopedias galore, even specialized ones such as *The Encyclopedia of Social Sciences* and *The Encyclopedia of American History;* there are statistical compilations such as *The World Almanac, Facts on File,* and *The Guinness Book of World Records;* you can find out *Who's Who in America* or even *Who Was Who.* You can collect a lot of facts in a short time in the reference room. Reference works are good for uncovering basic information, definitions, descriptions, and sources for further investigation.

PERIODICALS   Magazines, journals, and newspapers are good resources for finding recently published material on interesting topics. Indexes such as *The Readers' Guide to Periodical Literature* will enable you to find popular magazine articles on just about any subject. Specialized indexes such as *The Education Index* and *Psychological Abstracts* can be used to find articles in specific fields, and newspaper indexes such as *The New York Times Index* can be used to find microfilmed newspaper articles. Periodicals are a good source of high-interest, up-to-date information on your topic.

NONPRINT MATERIALS   Most libraries are also treasuries of nonprint and audiovisual materials. Films, records, tapes, and videotapes can be used not only as research tools but as aids during your presentation. Your library probably has

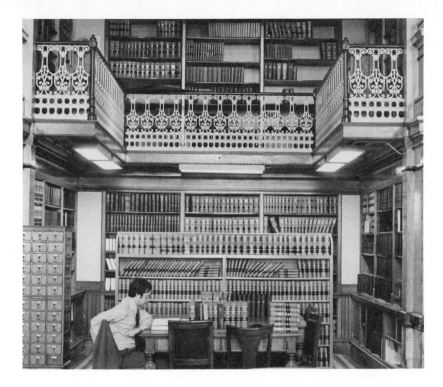

an orientation program that will acquaint you with what it has to offer in the way of nonprint materials.

ON-LINE DATA BASES A growing number of libraries have access to **on-line data bases.** These are computerized collections of information that can be searched via telephone link. One popular collection of data bases is Dialog Information Retrieval Service. Dialog contains over 80,000,000 records from news services, magazines, scholarly journals, conference papers, books, and other sources. With the right search strategy, you can locate scores of citations on your topic in just a few minutes rather than spending hours or weeks looking manually. Once you have located the items you want, it is possible to read abstracts or even entire articles on the screen of the library's computer terminal—or even have printouts mailed to you. For more information about on-line data bases, consult a librarian.

LIBRARIANS If you have explored all the sources mentioned in the preceding section and you still can't find exactly what you need, seek out a librarian. Today's librarians are trained in special search techniques, and their familiarity with the resources of their library is exhaustive. Of course, part of the effectiveness of your interaction with the librarian will depend on your communication skills: your ability to ask clear, specific questions; to be direct but polite; and

▶ The mind of the orator grows and expands with the subject. Without ample materials no splendid oration was ever yet produced.

Tacitus, A.D. 80

to listen effectively. This is also true in other forms of information-gathering interviews.

Interviewing

As we discussed in Chapter 8, the information-gathering interview is an especially valuable form of research on a college campus because so many experts of every stripe run loose there. The interview allows you to view your topic from an expert's perspective, to take advantage of that expert's years of experience, research, and thought. You can use an interview to collect facts and to stimulate your own thinking. Often the interview will save you hours of library research and allow you to present ideas that you could not have uncovered any other way. And because the interview is a face-to-face interaction with an expert, many ideas that otherwise would be unclear can become more understandable.

Personal Observation

Personal *experience* is one of the basic ingredients of any speech, but unsupported personal *opinions* can be detrimental. As a method of gathering information, personal observation gives some extra weight to your personal opinion. For example, if you were suggesting to an audience that the TV sets in your student union should be removed, you might say this:

> I think people would interact more here if the televisions were removed from the student union.

But all you have there is personal opinion, which could be based on anything, including a purely emotional hatred of television or of college students. The use of personal observation, however, might allow you to say this:

> Last Wednesday I spent 7:00 to 10:00 P.M. in the lounge of the student union. Only three times during the evening did anyone attempt to start a conversation. Two of those attempts were met with a request for silence in deference to the television.

If you wanted to prove your point further, you could go one step beyond and observe the same situation under different circumstances:

> This Wednesday I received permission to remove the television from the student union. During those same hours, 7:00 to 10:00 P.M., I observed the following behavior in that lounge, this time without television:
> 1. Thirty conversations were begun.
> 2. Twenty-four of these conversations continued, in depth, for more than ten minutes.
> 3. Seven groups of students decided on alternative entertainment for the evening, including table games, singing, dancing, and going to the library.
> 4. Four new male-female acquaintances were made, one of which resulted in a TV date for the following Wednesday night.

Personal observation is used to collect information about human beings. Because your job as a public speaker is communicating with human beings and because human beings love information about themselves, observing their behavior firsthand can be an extremely valuable form of investigation. Survey research is also valuable in this respect.

Survey Research

One advantage of handing out a survey to your audience (a week or so before your speech) is that it gives you up-to-date answers concerning "the way things are" for a specific audience. Consider the following ideas, either of which might be presented in a speech on giving children a right to divorce their parents:

A survey conducted in 1980 suggests that five out of ten college students are in favor of greater civil rights for children. (library-type data)

According to a survey I conducted last week, 90 percent of the students in this class are in favor of greater civil rights for children. And yet the same proportion—nine out of ten—are undecided about granting children the right to divorce their parents. (survey-type data)

That second statement would probably be of more immediate interest to an audience of students. That is one advantage of conducting your own survey. Another advantage is that it is one of the best ways to find out about your audience: It is in fact *the* best way to collect the demographic data mentioned earlier. The one disadvantage of conducting your own survey is that, if it is used as evidence, it might not have as much credibility as published evidence found in the library. But, all in all, the advantages seem to outweigh the disadvantages of **survey research** in public speaking.

No matter how you gather your information, remember that it is the *quality* rather than the quantity of the research that is most important. The key is to determine carefully what type of research will answer the questions you need to have answered. Sometimes only one type of research will be necessary; at other times every type mentioned here will have to be used.

SAMPLE SPEECH ◄

The sample speech for this chapter was given by Bobbye Perrin, a student at Central Michigan University. Bobbye's choice of topic demonstrates how an idea that is right in front of us—and never far from anyone's consciousness—can be the topic for an original, creative speech. Her analysis of this topic is informative as well as entertaining.

Bobbye's general purpose for this speech was "to inform." Her specific purpose could be stated as follows:

After listening to my speech, my audience members will accept the physical reality of sexual chemistry.

Her thesis statement:

"Sexual chemistry" is a biological fact; understanding it can enhance all our interactions with others.

Bobbye won first place in expository speaking in the 1984 National Forensics Association National Tournament with this speech. Notice how she maintains her focus throughout the speech.

Sexual Chemistry[11]

Bobbye Perrin, Central Michigan University

In the autumn of 1954, my mother suffered a severe physical affliction. An affliction that would change her life forever. She was in college at the time and one day her adrenal glands began secreting excessive amounts of unknown substances into her bloodstream. Her pulse rate increased incredibly, her blood pressure soared, and she began talking senselessly. What happened to my mother has the power to affect everyone in this room, and oddly enough, we'd probably welcome its unsettling effects. On that day my mother met my father, and it was "love at first sight." This phenomenon is something which scientific researchers and research psychologists have labeled "sexual chemistry." In all its strength, sexual chemistry is an internal, emotional sensation that has biological symptoms. For some of us, sexual chemistry may be one of the most pivotal experiences of our lives. For others, social psychologists believe it will enhance our interpersonal dynamics by drawing connections to their physical origins. In any case, it warrants a closer look at its biological factors, physical components, and how chemistry of the sexual kind can work for us.

Research psychologists in the United States and Germany have developed a sound biological background for the phenomenon of sexual chemistry. When we meet someone who interests us intensely, there is a moment of understanding. With that, our sympathetic nervous system begins to secrete hormones into our nerve endings and adrenal glands. In our nerve endings, there are more than thirty neurotransmitters that carry impulses to the brain. Two of these neurotransmitters, norepinephrine and dopamine, are responsible for what we feel when we experience "love at first sight": our breath quickens, pulses race, there's an overwhelming compulsion to speak... we feel happy and excited, according to Dr. Michael Liebowitz, assistant professor of psychiatry at Columbia University. All these neurotransmitters connect to the limbic system in the brain—our body's pleasure system. Dr. José Delgado, a neurophysicist at Yale University, has done much research on the limbic system by using rhesus monkeys. He concludes that a tiny electrical charge sent through the skull of a rhesus monkey is enough to make the monkey give up food and water for his continued pleasure. I say, "Why let the monkeys have all the fun, let's get in touch with our limbic systems!" Our two neurotransmitters, norepinephrine and dopamine, further act as triggering agents to a naturally occurring, amphetamine-like substance in the brain. It is this elusive substance that makes sexual chemistry so special. It is the moment of awakening within our transmitters that stimulates our nervous system even further. That intensified feeling is sexual chemistry. We are then tuned-in and turned-on in a truly chemical sense of the phrase. Sexual chemistry is not limited to possible sexual relationships only. It forms a special type of friendship. It crosses every boundary of gender, wealth, and origin. But it must be mutual. If only one person feels the attraction, there is no chemistry. However, it can lie dormant in a person, and under the right conditions, suddenly be brought to life, according to Julius Fast, coauthor of the book *Sexual Chemistry*. What sexual chemistry needs, then, is the proper setting: the correct energy, enthusiasm, and strength.

Now that we know what happens on the inside for sexual chemistry to take place, let's see what sexual chemistry is composesd of on the outside. Well, the eyes have it!, according to Meredith Bernstein, coauthor of *Sexual Chemistry*. It is the instant of recognition, a moment that tells us what we see is good, that arouses sexual chemistry. For every situation, there is a moral looking time. That is, the length of time we can hold somsone's eye contact and still be within the bounds of propriety. Violate that time for even a second and a message is sent. In a social setting, the message is usually, "I like you, I'm interested in you." Well naturally, there's more to this than just running around and looking at people. It is important that we become aware of the moral looking time for every situation; if not instinctively, then by learning. A starting point would be having an awareness of the environment in which we're involved. For example, the moral looking time involved in a board meeting of superiors will differ significantly from the moral looking time involved in addressing an audience.

The second component of sexual chemistry is an unbeatable smile! After eye contact is made, Fast and Berstein say, a smile changes the tone of any message previously sent. It's as if we smile and the whole world smiles with us . . . or at least there's a greater chance of it. A smile makes communication official when it's coupled with positive feedback from our viewers. For example, when you nod at me, I know you're listening and that you understand. When we as speakers receive this, although we may not be aware, we feel the other person is sympathetic. Thus, a special bond is established.

Lastly, and perhaps most deadly, is the tender touch. In a recent study conducted by researchers to establish just how effective touch was, librarians were asked to touch, or not to touch, the subjects. With only the slightest touch to book-borrowers, the whole functioning system of the library was viewed as a more personal place by those who acquired books. Politicians are also aware of this element during campaign time when they "press the flesh" of constituents. Touching can vary in its impact. It can act as a consoling gesture or a deliberate attempt to break down barriers we set up around us. Although it may take time, we can master the components of sexual chemistry.

Assuming we have, let's go all the way, well maybe not that far, and see how sexual chemistry can work for us. The advertising aspect of business has always been aware of sexual chemistry to sell a product. Beautiful female models and well-groomed men create just the right rapport with any audience to increase sales. It's in their eyes, their smiles, the overall feeling they generate about the product that stimulates the audience.

California salesman Barrie Stein had a record-breaking reputation in sales. When Julius Fast examined his approach, it was realized that he would always touch the arm of the patron, establishing immediate rapport. When we begin to incorporate the components of sexual chemistry into our own lives, the contacts we then experience are heightened to an even greater degree.

Sexual chemistry can reflect a positive feeling into our self-images. The theory of sexual chemistry says if the image we project can suggest to others a quality or characteristic they see in themselves, or would like to see, the chemical reaction can be readily enhanced by emotional ties: whether it's friendship, respect, or, ultimately, love. If we wish to strengthen our self-images, according to Norman Cavoir in a doctoral thesis for West Virginia University, we can imitate the body language of a more self-confident person. If we do this continually, we will begin to feel more secure and self-confident in ourselves. As this becomes habitual it also becomes easier. So whether it's for business or for pleasure, putting a little chemical fire into our and other people's lives can work to our advantage.

Sexual chemistry has the power to stimulate our bodies as well as our minds. Neurotransmitters never lie. Nor do the components of sexual chemistry. The eyes that are the windows to the soul in cooperation with a sweet, simple smile, a nod of approval, and an exciting touch can stimulate new responses. But most important is how all these elements combined can make each human experience fill with the polymers of passion. Sexual chemistry: a chemical explosion and a great feeling!

▶ SUMMARY

This chapter dealt with your first tasks in preparing a public speech: choosing and developing a topic.

Some guidelines for choosing a topic include these: Look for a topic early and stick with it, choose a topic you find interesting, and choose a topic you know something about to begin with.

One of your tasks is to understand your purpose so that you can stick to it as you prepare your speech. General purposes include entertaining, informing, and persuading. Specific purposes are expressed in the form of purpose statements, which must be audience-oriented, precise, and attainable.

Your next step is to formulate a thesis statement, which tells what the central idea of your speech is.

Another early task is to analyze the three components of the speaking situation—yourself, the audience, and the occasion. When analyzing yourself, you should consider your feelings about your topic and your unique knowledge and interests, as well as your purpose. When analyzing your audience, you should consider the audience type (passersby, captives, volunteers), purpose, demographics, attitudes, beliefs, and values. When analyzing the occasion, you should consider the time (and date) your speech will take place, the time available, the location, and audience expectations.

Although much of your speech will be based on personal reflection about your own ideas and experiences, it is usually necessary to gather some information from outside sources. Techniques for doing so include interpersonal research (such as interviewing), personal observation, and surveys, as well as library research.

Throughout all these preliminary tasks you will be organizing information. This process will be discussed in the next chapter.

1. Analyze your strengths and weaknesses as a speaker. Think back to the most recent "speech" you gave—a class presentation, for example. Answer the following questions about that speech:

    a. How interested was your audience in what you had to say?

    b. How well did they understand you?

    c. Did your speech accomplish what you wanted it to accomplish?

    d. How did *you* feel about your presentation?

2. For practice in formulating purpose statements that adhere to the criteria mentioned in this chapter, try writing one for each of the following speeches:

    a. An afterdinner speech at an awards banquet in which you will honor a team that has a winning, but not championship, record. (You pick the team.)

    b. A classroom speech in which you explain how to do something. (Once again, you choose the topic: rebuilding an engine, cooking a favorite dish, playing a guitar, or whatever.)

    c. A campaign speech in which you support the candidate of your choice.

Answer the following questions about each of your purpose statements: Is the purpose audience-oriented? Is it precise? Is it attainable?

3. For practice in formulating thesis statements, turn each of the following purpose statements into a statement that expresses a possible central idea:

    a. At the end of my speech the audience members will be willing to sign my petition requesting our congressional representative to support a balanced federal budget.

    b. After listening to my speech, the audience members will be able to list five advantages of recycling.

    c. During my speech on the trials and tribulations of sailing, the audience members will show their interest by paying attention and their amusement by occasionally laughing.

4. For practice in formulating thesis statements, try the following: Imagine that Congress has just passed a law requiring that all young people—male and female, without exception—perform two years of required national service immediately after high school (or at the age of eighteen, for those who don't finish high school). This period of national service could be spent in the military, park service, or any government agency. Pay would be at the subsistence level, below minimum wage.

The exercise proceeds as follows:

    a. Decide whether you will support or oppose this law.

    b. Write a purpose statement for a speech in support of your position.

    c. Draw up a list of points you might like to make in the speech.

    d. With the help of this list, select your thesis and main point.

5. For practice in choosing topics through self-analysis, list the following:

    a. Three topics you feel are *inappropriate* for you as a speaker, and for your class as an audience.

    b. Three topics you feel are *appropriate* for you, and for your class.

Briefly explain *why* each of these topics is appropriate or inappropriate.

**CHOOSING AND
DEVELOPING A TOPIC**

6. For practice in analyzing speech situations, carry out the following exercise with your classmates:
   a. Prepare, in advance, three index cards: one with a possible topic for a speech, one with a possible audience, and one with a possible occasion.
   b. Form groups of three members each, and place your cards face down, with one member's "audience" matched with a second member's "topic" and a third member's "occasion," and so on.
   c. Turn the cards over. For each set, decide which characteristics of the audience, topic, and occasion would most likely affect the way the speech was developed.
   d. Compare notes with the other groups to see who had the most unlikely matchup, as well as the best analysis.

A sample set of cards might look like this:

Topic: Morals on campus.
Audience: The women's auxiliary for the local ambulance squad. All women, all between the ages of thirty-five and fifty, and all married to members of the volunteer ambulance squad.
Occasion: Annual awards banquet, at which you're about to receive an award for special achievement in your topic area.

7. This exercise will give you practice in gathering information.
   a. Choose a current expression with a derivation that you are interested in but unsure about. For example, you might choose a term in general usage such as *nerd, gut course,* or *cramming;* or you might choose one that enjoys only local currency, such as *megabooking* now has on at least one large Eastern campus.
   b. Once you have decided on an expression, try to find out as much as you can about its derivation. Use the library, conduct an interview or two, do a survey, and observe the context in which your chosen expression is used around your campus and among your friends and acquaintances.

► **NOTES**

1. David Wallechinsky, Irving Wallace, and Amy Wallace, *The Book of Lists* (New York: William Morrow, 1977), p. 469.
2. One article that offers advice on choosing and developing a topic is B. F. Skinner, "How to Discover What You Have to Say: A Talk to Students," *Behavior Analyst* 4 (September 1981): 1–7.
3. Leon Fletcher, *How to Design and Deliver a Speech* (New York: Chandler, 1973).
4. Timothy Helms, "Mandatory Recertification of Medical Doctors," *Winning Orations, 1984* (Interstate Oratorical Association, 1984), p. 40.
5. Gwen Asburn and Alice Gordon, "Features of Simplified Register in Speech to Elderly Conversationalists," *International Journal of Psycholinguistics* 8:3 (1981): 7–31.
6. Different theorists mention different audience "types." See, for example, H. L. Hollingsworth, *The Psychology of the Audience* (New York: American Book, 1935), pp. 19–32.
7. An example of how demographics such as race, age, and union membership affect an audience's perception of messages can be found in Carl H. Botan and Lawrence R. Frey, "Do Workers Trust Labor Unions and Their Messages?" *Communication Monographs* 50 (September 1983): 233–244.

8. Joan Braaten, "It's English," *Winning Orations, 1984* (Interstate Oratorical Association, 1984), p. 64.

9. Marcie Groover, "Learning to Communicate: The Importance of Speech Education in Public Schools," *Winning Orations, 1984,* p. 9.

10. Randall K. Stutman and Sara E. Newell, "Beliefs Versus Values: Salient Beliefs in Designing a Persuasive Message," *Western Journal of Speech Communication,* 48:4 (Fall 1984): 364. For an example of how values are used in the analysis of political speeches, see Steve Goldzwig, "James Watt's Subversion of Values: An Analysis of Rhetorical Failure," *Southern Speech Communication Journal,* L:4 (Summer 1985): 305–326. According to Goldzwig, Watt "violated the sacred values and shibboleths of the American Dream."

11. Bobbye Perrin, "Sexual Chemistry," speech presented at the 1984 NFA national tournament; reprinted by permission of Bobbye Perrin.

▶ CHAPTER 12

KEY TERMS

analogy	diagram	number chart	topic patterns
anecdote	example	pictograms	transitions
bar charts	exhaustiveness	pie charts	visual aids
basic speech structure	focus	problem-solution patterns	word charts
cause-effect patterns	formal outline	quantification	working outlines
climax patterns	hypothetical example	space patterns	
column charts	introduction (of a speech)	statistics	
conclusion (of a speech)	line chart	testimony	
coordination	model	time patterns	

ORGANIZATION AND SUPPORT

After reading this chapter, you should understand the following:

1. The importance of clear speech organization.

2. The basic structure of a speech.

3. The steps involved in organizing the body of a speech.

4. The importance of effective introductions, conclusions, and transitions.

5. The functions and types of supporting material.

You should be able to do the following:

1. Construct an effective formal speech outline, using the organizing principles described in this chapter.

2. Develop an effective introduction, conclusion, and transitions.

3. Choose verbal supporting material for a speech to make your points clear, interesting, memorable, and convincing.

4. Choose appropriate visual aids for a presentation.

Knowing what you want to say and *communicating* that knowledge aren't the same thing. It's frustrating to know you aren't expressing your thoughts clearly, and it's equally unpleasant to know another speaker has something worth saying, yet be unable to figure out just what it is.

In the following pages, you will learn methods of organizing your thoughts in a way that others can follow. Clarity isn't the only benefit of good organization: Structuring a message effectively will help you refine and clarify your own ideas and then present them in a way that is comprehensible and persuasive

▶ STRUCTURING THE SPEECH

A good speech is like a good building: Both grow from a careful plan. In Chapter 11 you began this planning by analyzing your audience, formulating a purpose, and conducting research. Now you will learn how to apply the information you developed there.

Outlining the Speech

An outline is the framework on which your speech is built. It contains your main ideas and shows how they relate to one another and your thesis. Virtually every speech outline ought to follow the basic structure outlined in Figure 12–1.

This **basic speech structure** demonstrates the old aphorism for speakers: "Tell what you're going to say, say it, and then tell what you said." Although this structure sounds redundant, the research on listening cited in Chapter 4 demonstrates that receivers forget most of what they hear. The clear, repetitive nature of the basic speech structure reduces the potential for memory loss because audiences have a tendency to listen more carefully during the beginning and ending of a speech.[1] Outlines come in all shapes and sizes, but they can generally be classified in one of three categories.

WORKING OUTLINES   **Working,** or "scratch," **outlines** are construction tools used in building your speech. Unlike a formal outline, a working outline is a constantly changing, personal device. You begin organizing your speech material from a rough working outline; then, as your ideas solidify, your outline changes accordingly.

A working outline is for your eyes only. No one else need understand it, so you can use whatever symbols and personal shorthand you find functional. In fact, your working outline will probably become pretty messy by the time you are ready to create a formal outline for others to see.

FORMAL OUTLINES   The basic pattern given earlier is a **formal outline.** It uses a consistent format and set of symbols to identify the structure of ideas. Roman numerals are usually used to separate the main divisions of the speech: introduction, body, and conclusion. Each of those sections is then divided and subdivided with capital letters, Arabic numerals, and lowercase letters.

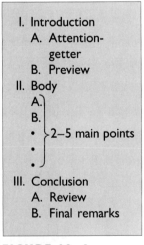

I. Introduction
  A. Attention-
      getter
  B. Preview
II. Body
  A.⎤
  B.⎥
  • ⎬2–5 main points
  • ⎥
  • ⎦
III. Conclusion
  A. Review
  B. Final remarks

FIGURE 12–1
Basic Speech Structure

A formal outline serves several purposes. It can be used as a visual aid (on a poster board, for example, or distributed as a handout). It can serve as a record of a speech that was delivered. Many organizations send outlines to members who miss meetings at which presentations were given. Finally, in speech classes, outlines are often used by the instructor to analyze student speeches.

A formal outline contains only the structural units of a speech—main points and subpoints (the division of main points, including sub-subpoints and sub-sub-subpoints). In formal outlines, main points and subpoints almost always represent a division of a whole. As it is impossible to divide something into less than two parts, you will usually have at least two main points for every topic. Then, if your main points are divided, you will always have at least two subpoints, and so on. Thus, the rule for formal outlines is, never a *I* without a *II*, never an *A* without a *B*, and so on.

Formal outlines can be written in full-sentence or key-word form. If you were speaking on the topic "The Causes of Modern Illness" you might divide the body of your topic as shown in Figure 12–2.

A key-word outline is sometimes too brief to communicate the structure of the speech to someone else (as when an outline is used to substitute for a speech that someone missed). When a more complete model of the speech is necessary, a full-sentence outline is usually more appropriate.

A full speech outline should also include the points to be made in the introduction and conclusion. Many instructors prefer that a formal speech outline include a purpose statement, a thesis statement, and also the various transitions and internal summaries. With these features added, a full-sentence outline for the "Modern Illness" speech might look like the one in Figure 12–3.

Notice that those parts of the outline not needed to be divided—supporting material, transitions, and so on—are listed on the outline without structural symbols.

Many instructors ask that a bibliography accompany a formal speech outline. Your bibliography should conform to the rules of a standard style sheet, such as Kate Turabian's *Student's Guide for Writing College Papers.*[2] A bibliography for the "Modern Illness" speech might look like the one in Figure 12–4.

A. Poor Diet [main point]
  1. Lack of Nutrition [subpoint]
  2. Chemical Toxins [subpoint]
  3. Irregular Intake [subpoint]
B. Pollution [main point]
  1. Air Pollution [subpoint]
  2. Water Pollution [subpoint]
  3. Noise Pollution [subpoint]
C. Stress [main point]
  1. Work-related Stress [subpoint]
  2. Day-to-Day Stress [subpoint]

FIGURE 12–2
Formal Outline (with Subpoints) for the Body of a Speech Entitled "Causes of Modern Illness"

FIGURE 12–3
Sentence Outline for Speech

Topic: "The Causes of Modern Illness"

Purpose: After listening to my speech, my audience members will be able to list at least three ways to avoid typical modern illness.

Thesis: The three main causes of modern illness are poor diet, pollution, and stress, all of which can be controlled to some extent by each of us.

I. Introduction
   A. Do you ever feel like this?
      Quotation: Adelle Davis on exhaustion.
   B. You *can* make yourself feel better. (Preview main points)
      Transition: The first step is to recognize what causes us to get sick.

II. The Body
   A. Modern people often suffer from poor diets.
      1. Too many convenience foods can cause malnutrition.
      2. Too many chemical preservatives can cause toxic reactions.
      3. Irregularly scheduled meals can cause gastric disorders.
         Internal summary: What to do about it.
         Transition: Diet is only one form of "pollution."
   B. Modern people are subjected to more pollution than ever before.
      1. Air pollution contributes to respiratory diseases.
      2. Water pollution contributes to digestive diseases.
      3. Noise pollution contributes to nervous disorders.
         Internal summary: What to do about it.
         Transition: Noise pollution is only one cause of stress.
   C. Modern people are subjected to more stress than ever before.
      1. Work-related stress contributes to nervous disorders.
      2. The day-to-day stress of modern living contributes to circulatory diseases.
         Internal summary: What to do about it.

III. Conclusion
   A. Review the problem.
   B. Review what we can do about it.
   C. One final thought.
      Quotation: Michael Smith on the pleasures of good health.

SPEAKING NOTES Like your working outline, your speaking notes are a personal device, so the format is up to you. Many teachers suggest that speaking notes should be in the form of a brief key-word outline, with just enough information listed to jog your memory but not enough to get lost in.

Many teachers also suggest that you fit your notes on one side of one 3-by-5-inch card. Other teachers recommend that you also have your introduction and conclusion on note cards, and still others suggest that your references and quotations be written out on them. Your speaking notes for a speech on the ASPCA (the American Society for the Prevention of Cruelty to Animals) might look like the ones in Figure 12–5.

FIGURE 12–4
Sample Bibliography

BIBLIOGRAPHY

Bergsman, Jurrit. Health Care: Its Psychosocial Dimensions. Atlantic Highlands, N.J.: Humanities Press, 1982.

Calabrese, Edward J., and Michael W. Dorsey. "How to Insure Your Health in a Dangerous World." Redbook 162 (January 1984): 94.

Kissick, William L. "Health Care in the 80's: Changes, Consequences, and Choices." Vital Speeches of the Day. 52 (January 15, 1986): 213.

Leonard, George B. "Ultimate Fitness: Esquire's 10 keys to High-Level Health and Athletic Performance." Esquire 101 (May 1984): 87.

Smith, Michael J. Personal interview on September 22, 1987. At Illinois State University.

Survey on Health Habits Conducted at Illinois State University on September 24, 1987.

Principles of Outlining

There are three principles that relate to all outlines, working or formal. A good outline will follow all three: division, coordination, and order.

DIVISION   The first principle of outlining is to divide your topic into main points that completely cover your thesis. Correct division is said to be exhaustive and focused. **Exhaustiveness** means that all the necessary information can be included under one of the divisions of that idea. If you are speaking on jury selection and are explaining that lawyers are able to recognize certain biases in prospective jurors, you might divide the idea of bias like this:

A. Racial bias
B. Sexual bias

If those are the two most important parts of the idea of bias, then it can be said that the divisions of that idea are exhaustive. If, however, you also want to discuss the fact that some jurors are biased in terms of the defendant's age, you might have to divide the idea of bias like this:

A. Racial bias
B. Sexual bias
C. Age bias

If everything you want to say could be included under one of these three subpoints, then the idea is properly divided. If not, the division of the idea would not be exhaustive.

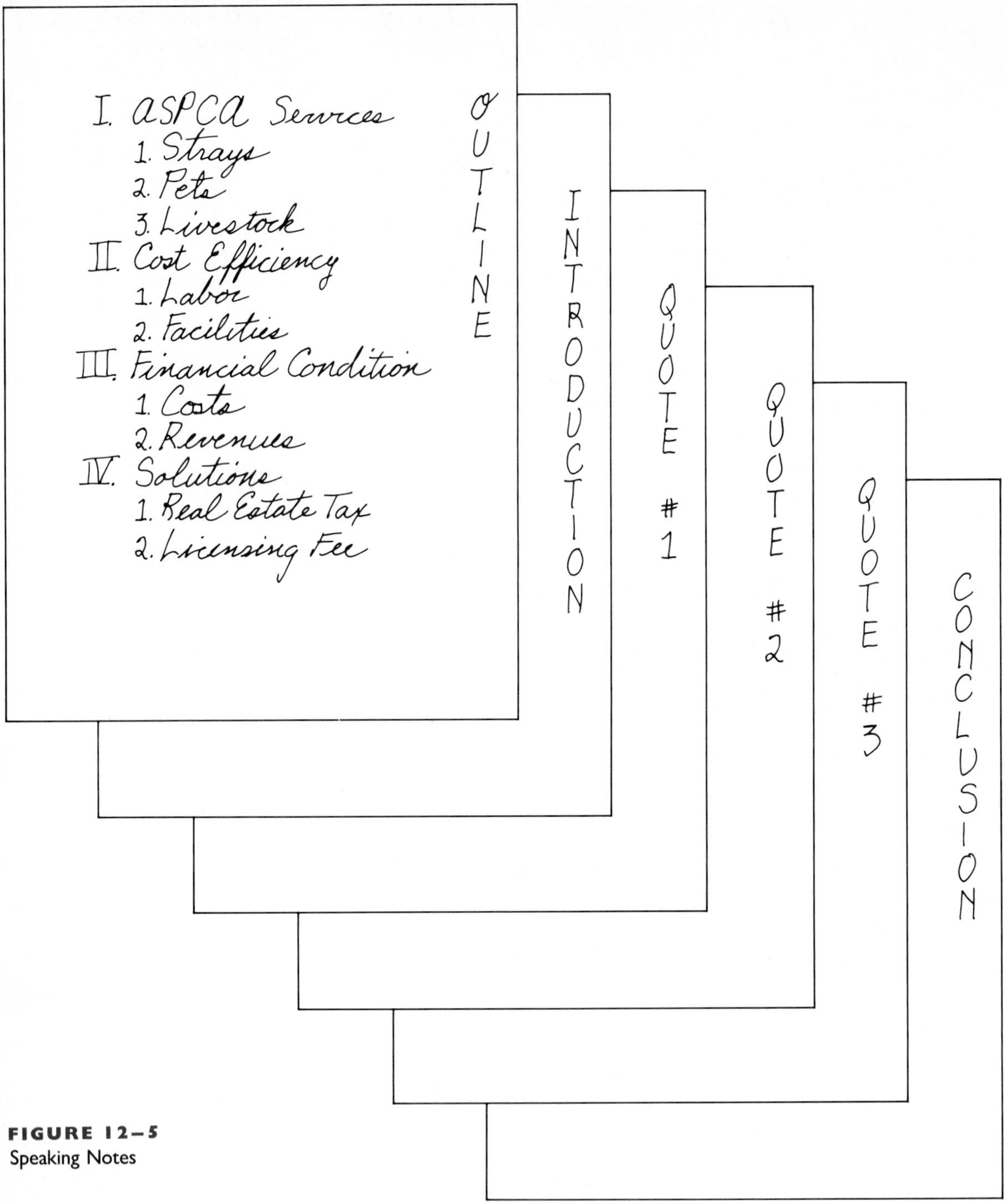

FIGURE 12–5
Speaking Notes

A speech has **focus** when each division contains one, and only one, idea. If you were discussing cures for indigestion, your topic might be divided incorrectly if your main points looked like this:

I. "Preventive cures" help you before eating.
II. "Participation cures" help you during and after eating.

You might actually have three ideas there and thus three main points:

I. Preventive cures (before eating).
II. Participation cures (during eating).
III. Postparticipation cures (after eating).

It is important for all messages to be divided in an exhaustive and focused manner. But speeches have one further requirement: They should have no more than five main points (three or four are considered ideal), and each point should be broken up into no more than five subpoints (and so on for sub-subpoints). Research shows that this will allow for maximum comprehension within the limits of human information processing.[3]

COORDINATION **Coordination** is the state of being equal in rank, quality, or significance. The principle of coordination requires that all your main points be of *similar* importance and that they be *related* to one another. The principle of coordination is reflected in the wording of your main points. Points that are equal in significance and related to one another can easily be worded in a similar manner. Because of this, the principle of coordination is sometimes referred to as the principle of "parallel wording." For example; if you are developing a speech against capital punishment, your main points might look like this:

A. Crime did not decrease during the 1950s, when capital punishment was enforced.
B. The Eighth Amendment to the U.S. Constitution protects against cruel and unusual punishment.
C. Most civilized countries have abandoned the notion of capital punishment.

The relationship of those points might seem obvious to you as a speaker, but chances are they would leave the audience confused. Parallel wording, which requires that each of these main points be written in a similar way, helps to guard against this confusion.

A. Capital punishment is not effective: It is not a deterrent to crime.
B. Capital punishment is not constitutional: It does not comply with the Eighth Amendment.
C. Capital punishment is not civilized: It does not allow for a reverence for life.

ORDER An outline should reflect a logical order for your points. You might arrange them from newest to oldest, largest to smallest (or vice versa), best to worst (or worst to best), or in a number of other ways we will soon discuss. The organizing pattern you choose ought to be the one that best develops your thesis. Organizing patterns are discussed as follows.

▶ First, you must know the truth about the subject you speak or write about; that is to say, you must be able to isolate it in definition, and having so defined it you must understand how to divide it into kinds, until you reach the limit of division.

Plato

The body makes up the bulk—usually 80 percent or more—of the speech. Because the body contains the main ideas you will express, it makes sense to begin preparing the actual speech by starting here rather than with the introduction or conclusion.

The body of any speech should contain two types of information: the points you want to make and supporting material to back up those points. The last half of this chapter will focus on supporting material. In the next pages we will examine the various ways in which you can organize the main points themselves.

TIME PATTERNS Arrangement according to periods of time, or chronology, is one of the most common patterns of organization. The period of time could be anything from centuries to seconds. The "cures for indigestion" example given earlier is an example of a **time pattern.** In a speech on the history of the ASPCA, a time pattern might look like this:

A. Early attempts by the city to control animals, 1900–1920.
B. The ASPCA takes over: 1920–present.
C. The outlook for the future.

Arranging points according to the steps that make up a process is another form of time patterning. The topic "Getting That Big Date" might use this type of patterning:

A. The first step: Choosing an appropriate person.
B. The second step: Breaking the ice.
C. The third step: Asking for the date.

SPACE PATTERNS **Space patterns** are organized according to area. The area could be stated in terms of continents or centimeters or anything in between. If you were discussing the ASPCA in New York City, for example, you could arrange your points according to borough:

A. Manhattan
B. Queens
C. Brooklyn
D. Bronx
E. Staten Island

TOPIC PATTERNS A topical arrangement or **topic pattern** is based on types or categories. These categories could be either well known or original; both have their advantages. For example, a division of college students according to well-known categories might look like this:

A. Freshmen
B. Sophomores
C. Juniors
D. Seniors

Well-known categories are advantageous because audiences are generally more receptive to ideas that they can associate with their present knowledge. But familiarity also has its drawbacks. One disadvantage is the "Oh, this again" syndrome. If members of an audience feel they have nothing new to learn about the components of your topic, they might not listen to you. To avoid this, you could invent original categories that freshen up some topics by suggesting an original analysis. For example, original categories for "college students" might look like this:

A. Grinds—the students who go to every class and read every assignment before it is due and who are usually seen in dormitories telling everyone to turn their stereos down.
B. Renaissance students—the students who find a satisfying blend of scholarly and social pursuits. They go to most of their classes and do most of their assignments, but they don't let school get in the way of their social life.
C. Burnouts—the students who have a difficult time finding the classroom, let alone doing the work.

PROBLEM-SOLUTION PATTERNS   The **problem-solution pattern,** as you might guess from its no-nonsense title, describes what's wrong and proposes a way to make things better. It is usually (but not always) divisible into these two distinct parts. One variation of the problem-solution arrangement contains five steps and has come to be known as the motivated sequence.[4]

1. **The Attention Step** draws attention to your subject. (For example, "Have you ever gotten all dressed up to go out for a meal in a nice restaurant and then been choked by smoke from the table next to you?")
2. **The Need Step** establishes the problem. ("Ambient smoke—that is, smoke from someone else's cigarette, cigar, or pipe—is a threat to your health as well as a general nuisance.")
3. **The Satisfaction Step** proposes a solution. ("The State Clean Air Act will provide for separate smoking and nonsmoking areas in restaurants.")
4. **The Visualization Step** describes the results of the solution. ("Imagine—clean air in every public place, without denying smokers their rights in any way.")
5. **The Action Step** is a direct appeal for the audience to do something. ("Sign this petition, and you will have done your part.")

CAUSE-EFFECT PATTERNS   **Cause-effect patterns** are similar to problem-solution patterns in that they are basically two-part patterns: First you discuss something that happened; then you discuss its effects. For example, many speakers feel that the topic of inflation is amenable to this pattern because the reason people tend to misunderstand inflation is that they confuse causes with effects. These speakers would organize a speech on inflation as follows:

A. Causes
   1. Government budget deficits
   2. Increase in money supply

B. Effects
   1. Rising prices
   2. Rising wages

A variation of this pattern is reversing the order and presenting the effects first and then the causes. Effect-to-cause patterns would work well with a topic such as "the terrorism crisis"; the audience would presumably already be interested in, and knowledgeable about, the effects, and discussing them first might increase interest in your analysis of the causes.

CLIMAX PATTERNS   **Climax patterns** are used to create suspense. For example, if you wanted to create suspense in a speech about military intervention, you could chronologically trace the steps that eventually led us into World War II or the wars in Korea or Vietnam in such a way that you build up your audience's curiosity. If you told of these steps through the eyes of a soldier who was drafted into military service right before one of those wars, you would be building suspense as your audience wonders what will become of him.

This pattern can also be reversed. When it is, it is called *anticlimactic* organization. If you started your military-intervention speech by telling the audience that you were going to explain why so-and-so was killed in such-and-such a war and then you went on to explain the things that caused him to become involved in that war, you would be using anticlimactic organization. This pattern is helpful when you have an essentially uninterested audience and you need to build interest early in your speech to get them to listen to the rest of it.

Once you have organized the body of your speech, you can turn to your introduction and conclusion.

▶ BEGINNING AND ENDING THE SPEECH

▶ The beginning is the most important part of the work.

Plato

The **introduction** and **conclusion** of a speech are vitally important although they usually will occupy less than 20 percent of your speaking time. Listeners form their impressions of a speaker early, and they remember what they hear last; it is, therefore, vital to make those few moments at the beginning and end of a speech work to your advantage.

The Introduction

As you have already read, the first part of your introduction should capture the attention of your listeners. There are several ways to get an audience's attention. The following discussion shows how some of these ways might be used in a speech entitled "Communication Between Plants and Humans."

REFER TO THE AUDIENCE   The technique of referring to the audience is especially effective if it is complimentary, as "It's great to have the opportunity to address this group of young scholars…" Of course, to be effective, the compliment has to be sincere.

REFER TO THE OCCASION   A reference to the occasion could be a reference to the event of your speech, as "We are gathered here today, as we are on every Tuesday and Thursday at this time, to examine the phenomenon of human communication..." This might also be a reference to the date, as "On this date, just five years ago, a little-known botanist made a breakthrough that set the scientific world on its ear..."

REFER TO THE RELATIONSHIP BETWEEN THE AUDIENCE AND THE SUBJECT   "My topic, 'Communicating with Plants,' ties right in with our study of human communication. We can gain several insights into our communication with one another by examining our interactions with our little green friends."

REFER TO SOMETHING FAMILIAR TO THE AUDIENCE   The technique of referring to something familiar to the audience is especially effective if you are discussing a topic that might seem new or strange to the audience. Audience attention will be attracted to the familiar among the new in much the same way that we are able to pick out a friend's face in a crowd of strangers. For example, "See that lilac bush outside the window? At this very moment it might be reacting to the joys and anxieties that you are experiencing in this classroom."

CITE A STARTLING FACT OR OPINION   A statement that surprises an audience is bound to make them sit up and listen. This is true even for a topic that the audience considers old hat; if the audience members think they've heard it all before about plant-human communication, you might mention, "There is now actual scientific evidence that plants appreciate human company, kind words, and classical music."

ASK A QUESTION   A rhetorical question is one that causes your audience to think rather than to answer out loud. "Have you ever wondered why some people seem to be able to grow beautiful, healthy plants effortlessly whereas others couldn't make a weed grow in the best soil you could get?" This question is designed to make the audience respond mentally, "Yeah, why is that?"

TELL AN ANECDOTE   A personal story perks up audience interest because it shows the human side of what might otherwise be dry, boring information. "The other night, while taking a walk in the country, I happened on a small garden that was rich with lush vegetation. But it wasn't the lushness of the vegetation that caught my eye at first. There, in the middle of the garden, was a man who was talking quite animatedly to a giant sunflower."

USE A QUOTATION   Quotable quotes sometimes have a precise, memorable wording that would be difficult for you to say as well. Also, they allow you to borrow from the credibility of the quoted source. For example, "Thorne Bacon, the naturalist, recently said about the possibility of plants and humans communicating, 'Personally, I cannot imagine a world so dull, so satiated, that it should reject out of hand arresting new ideas which may be as old as the first amino acid in the chain of life on earth.' "

▶ A bad beginning makes a bad ending.

Euripides

ORGANIZATION AND SUPPORT

TELL A JOKE If you happen to know or can find a joke that is appropriate to your subject and occasion, it can help you build audience interest: "We once worried about people who talked to plants, but that's no longer the case. Now we only worry if the plants talk back." Be sure, though, that the joke is appropriate to the audience, as well as to the occasion and to you as a speaker.

After you capture the attention of the audience, an effective introduction will almost always state the speaker's thesis and give the listeners an idea of the upcoming main points. Katherine Graham, the chairperson of the board of the Washington Post Company, addressed a group of businessmen and their wives in this way:

> I am delighted to be here. It is a privilege to address you. And I am especially glad the rules have been bent for tonight, allowing so many of you to bring along your husbands. I think it's nice for them to get out once in a while and see how the other half lives. Gentlemen, we welcome you.
>
> Actually, I have other reasons for appreciating this chance to talk with you tonight. It gives me an opportunity to address some current questions about the press and its responsibilities—whom we are responsible to, what we are responsible for, and generally how responsible our performance has been.[5]

Thus, Mrs. Graham previewed her main points:

1. To explain whom the press is responsible to.
2. To explain what the press is responsible for.
3. To explain how responsible the press has been.

Sometimes your preview of main points will be even more straightforward:

"I have three points to discuss: They are _____, _____, and _____."

Sometimes you will not want to refer directly to your main points in your introduction. Your reasons might be based on a plan calling for suspense, humorous effect, or stalling for time to win over a hostile audience. In that case, you might preview only your thesis:

"I am going to say a few words about _____."
"Did you ever wonder about _____?"
"_____ is one of the most important issues facing us today."

The attention-getter and preview of every speech should accomplish two functions in addition to their stated purposes:

SETTING THE MOOD AND TONE OF YOUR SPEECH   Notice, in the example just given, how Katherine Graham began her speech by joking with her audience. She was speaking before an all-male organization; the only women in the audience were the members' wives. That is why Mrs. Graham felt it necessary to put her audience members at ease by joking with them about women's traditional role in society. By beginning in this manner, she assured the men that she would not berate them for the sexist bylaws of their organization. She also showed them that she was going to approach her topic with wit and intelligence. Thus, she set the mood and tone for her entire speech. Imagine how different that mood and tone would have been if she had begun this way:

Before I start today, I would just like to say that I would never have accepted your invitation to speak here had I known that your organization does not accept women as members. Just where do you Cro-Magnons get off, excluding more than half the human race from your little club?

DEMONSTRATING THE IMPORTANCE OF YOUR TOPIC TO YOUR AUDIENCE
Your audience will listen to you more carefully if your speech relates to them as individuals. Based on your audience analysis, you should state directly *why* your topic is of importance to your audience. This importance should be related as closely as possible to their specific needs at that specific time. For example, if you were speaking to your class about why they should help support the Red Cross, you might begin like this:

Lives have been lost in the time it takes an ambulance or doctor to reach the victim of accidents. Too many people have died from accidentally severed veins or arteries, drowning, choking on food, or swallowing iodine, plant-spray, arsenic, or other poisons.

If someone on the scene had known what emergency measures to take, tragedy could have been averted.

The Red Cross, with vast experience in the latest, most successful lifesaving techniques, has put together a handy, easy-to-follow manual, *Standard First Aid and Personal Safety.* The information it contains could save your life—or that of someone dear to you. This book is available only through the Red Cross, and we'd like to send it to you free.[6]

This introduction establishes an immediate importance: The audience members don't have to wait until they need blood or until an emergency or a disaster strikes. Acquiring the free booklet is something that is important to them right now as healthy, reasonably secure members of a college class.

The Conclusion

The conclusion, like the introduction, is an especially important part of your speech. Your audience will have a tendency to listen carefully as your speech draws to a close; they will also have a tendency to consider what you say at the end of your speech as important. Because of this, the conclusion has two essential functions: to review the thesis and to leave the audience remembering your speech by using effective final remarks. You can review your thesis either through direct repetition or by paraphrasing it in different words. Either way your conclusion should include a short summary statement:

> And so, after listening to what I had to say this afternoon, I hope you agree with me that the city cannot afford to lose the services of the ASPCA.

You might also want to review your main points. This can be done directly: "I made three main points about the ASPCA today. They are..."

The review of your main points can also be done artistically. For example, first look back at that example of an introduction by Katherine Graham; then read her conclusion to that speech:

> ...So instead of seeking flat and absolute answers to the kinds of problems I have discussed tonight, what we should be trying to foster is respect for one another's conception of where duty lies, and understanding of the real worlds in which we try to do our best. And we should be hoping for the energy and sense to keep on arguing and questioning, because there is no better sign that our society is still healthy and strong.[7]

Let's take a closer look at how and why this conclusion was effective. Mrs. Graham posed three questions in her introduction. She dealt with those questions in her speech and reminded her audience, in her conclusion, that she had answered the questions.

PREVIEW	REVIEW
1. To whom is the press responsible?	1. To its own conception of where its duty lies.
2. What is the press responsible for?	2. For doing its best in the "real world."
3. How responsible has the press been?	3. It has done its best.

Your final remarks are important because they are the last words your audience will hear from you in the speech. You can make them most effective by avoiding the following mistakes:

DO NOT END ABRUPTLY   Make sure that your conclusion accomplishes everything it is supposed to accomplish. Develop it fully. You might want to use a "pointer phrase" such as "and now, in conclusion..." or "to sum up what we've been talking about here..." to let your audience know that you have reached the conclusion of the speech.

BUT DON'T RAMBLE EITHER   Prepare a definite conclusion, and never, never end by mumbling something like "Well, I guess that's about all I wanted to say..."

DON'T INTRODUCE NEW POINTS   The worst kind of rambling is "Oh, yes, and something I forgot to mention is..."

DON'T APOLOGIZE   Don't say, "I'm sorry I couldn't tell you more about this" or "I'm sorry I didn't have more time to research this subject" or any of those sad songs. They will only highlight the possible weaknesses of your speech, and there's a good chance those weaknesses were far more apparent to you than to your audience.

Instead, it is best to end strong. You can use any of the attention-getters suggested for the introduction to make the conclusion memorable. In fact, one kind of effective closing is to refer to the attention-getter you used in your introduction and remind your audience how it applies to the points you made in your speech.

You can use elements of surprise or suspense to make a point memorable; you can also use mnemonic devices, which are often formulated as collections of meaningful letters:

> Think of recycling in the same terms as you think of gas mileage: MPG. Only, in recycling, MPG stands for *metals, paper,* and *glass,* the three materials you stand to conserve.

Whatever device you use, end with a flourish, as John F. Kennedy did when he said, "Ask not what your country can do for you; ask what you can do for your country," or as General MacArthur did when he said, "Old soldiers never die; they just fade away."

Transitions

You should tie all your ideas together through the use of **transitions,** which join ideas together by showing how one is related to another. Transitions keep your message moving forward, they tell how the introduction relates to the body of the speech, they tell how one main point relates to the next main point, they tell how your subpoints relate to the points they are part of, and they tell how your supporting points relate to the points they support (see Figure 12–3 on p. 294 for an example of how transitions perform these functions). Transitions, to be effective, should refer to the previous point and to the upcoming point, showing how they relate to one another and to the thesis. They usually sound something like this:

"...Like (*previous point*), another important consideration in (*topic*) is (*upcoming point*).

"...But _____ isn't the only thing we have to worry about. _____ is even more potentially dangerous."

"...Yes, the problem is obvious. But what are the solutions? Well, one possible solution is..."

Sometimes a transition includes an internal review, a preview of upcoming points, or both:

"...So far we've discussed _____, _____, and _____. Our next points are _____, _____, and _____."

The actual process of organizing a speech usually takes place in the order outlined in Table 12–1.

▶ **SUPPORTING MATERIAL**

It is important to organize ideas clearly and logically. But clarity and logic by themselves won't guarantee that you'll interest or persuade others; these functions call for the use of supporting materials. These materials—the facts and information that back up and prove your ideas and opinions—are the flesh that fills out the skeleton of your speech.

Functions of Supporting Material

There are four purposes for supporting material:

TO CLARIFY As explained in Chapter 3, people of different backgrounds tend to attach different meanings to words. For example, if you were talking about recycling, every member of your audience could have a different idea about what you meant. To some, recycling refers just to aluminum beer cans; to others, the term means reusing everything that is normally thrown away as refuse. You could use supporting material to clarify this idea:

> The type of recycling I'm talking about here involves separating from the rest of your trash all glass, metals, newspapers, and magazines. The papers and magazines must be bundled, and containers must be uncapped and washed, and labels must be removed from the cans. The material is then placed in a separate container for removal once a week to a municipal recycling center.

TO MAKE INTERESTING A second use of support is to make an idea interesting or to catch your audience's attention. The audience might know what you mean by "recycling" but still not care. Supporting material could be used to bolster their interest in your topic:

> Outside New York City, where waste material has been dumped into the ocean for years, a large mass of thick, life-choking sludge is slowly inching its way toward the

shore. It might be too late for New York, but *we* can avoid the same problem here, if we take action now.

TO MAKE MEMORABLE   A third purpose of supporting materials, related to the preceding one, is to make a point memorable. We have already mentioned the importance of "memorable" statements in a speech conclusion; use of supporting material in the introduction and body of the speech provides another way to help your audience retain important information.

The most common way to make a point memorable is to use supporting material that is impressive because it stresses the importance of the point. For example:

The State Environmental Protection Agency recently measured the air in this area, and what they found suggests that each and every one of us, at this moment, are breathing

TABLE 12–1   Checklist for Outlining a Speech

Develop Main Points

——Division (Is the topic covered clearly and completely?)
  ——Is the coverage *exhaustive*? (Does it include all necessary information about the topic?)
  ——Is the coverage *focused*? (Does each point cover one—and only one—idea?)
——Coordination (Is the relationship between the main points clear?)
——Order (Are the main points arranged in the most logical way?)
  ——Time
  ——Space
  ——Topic
  ——Problem-solution
  ——Cause-effect
  ——Climax
  ——Other

Plan the Introduction

——Do the opening remarks gain the attention of the audience?
——Does the introduction preview the thesis and main point?
——Do introductory remarks set the proper tone for the topic and occasion?
——Does the introduction demonstrate the importance of the topic to the audience?

Plan the Conclusion

——Do you restate the thesis and review main points?
——Do you close the speech with strong, memorable remarks?

Develop Transitions

——Do transitions occur between the introduction and body, between the main points within the body, and between the body and conclusion?
——Does each transition refer to the previous and upcoming points, showing how they relate to one another and to the thesis?

ORGANIZATION AND SUPPORT

poisons into our systems. These are cumulative, carcinogenic, chemical toxins; and they are caused by our township incinerator's burning garbage that could just as easily be sold and reused.

TO PROVE   Finally, a supporting material can be used as evidence, to prove the truth of what you are saying. For example, if you said, "The way our local landfill area is filling up, it might have to be closed in a year or so," your audience would find it easy to disagree with you. But supporting material makes it less easy to disagree:

According to Tom Murray, our village chief sanitation engineer and the man in charge of landfill areas, all our landfills will be filled to capacity and closed within one year. This means, in no uncertain terms, that we are not going to have anywhere to put our garbage.

Types of Support

As you may have noted, each function of support could be fulfilled by several different types of material. An examination of these different types of supporting material follows.

DEFINITIONS   It's a good idea to give your audience definitions of your key terms, especially if those terms are unfamiliar to them or are being used in an unusual way. A good definition is simple and concise and is stated in such a way that no other terms within the definition need to be defined.

Dictionary definitions are a handy way of determining the most acceptable meaning for a word, but you should be careful about using them to define terms in your speech. Your own carefully chosen words are usually more interesting and clearer than a dictionary definition. Dictionaries are written for very general audiences. If you were speaking on the abortion issue and relying on a dictionary definition, you might be stuck with:

By abortion I mean the expulsion of a nonviable fetus...

This might be an accurate definition, but it is probably too clinical for a college audience. It might be clearer to say:

By abortion I mean the termination of pregnancy before the twelfth week of gestation...

if that's what you mean.

Another problem with dictionaries is that they sometimes give you a definition that includes the term itself and that will sometimes make it seem as if you are clarifying an idea when you actually aren't:

By abortion, I mean the abortion of a fetus...

One last problem with dictionary definitions is that they have a tendency to change more slowly than the reality they represent. You might use the term *female chauvinist sexist* in a speech about women employers who discriminate against men. However, if you looked up those terms in *The Random House College Dictionary*, 1972 edition, you would find that *female* means "woman" (as you might expect), but *chauvinist* means "patriot," and *sexist* means "someone who discriminates against women." According to this dictionary, therefore, a female chauvinist sexist is a woman patriot who discriminates against women!

There are two different types of definitions: traditional and operational. A traditional definition places something in a class and tells how it is different from other things in that class. The classic example of this is proposed by Aristotle: "Man [or "woman," we might add] is a featherless biped." Humans are, therefore, defined as belonging to a class (bipeds) but different from that class in that they do not have feathers. (For Aristotle, fur was a type of "feathers.")

Operational definitions tell what you would have to do to experience the thing being described. We could use an operational definition to define recycling: First you separate glass, metals, newspapers, and magazines from the rest of your trash, and so on. Operational definitions for the term *man* might sound something like this:

> You want to know what a man is? Go down to the graduation ceremonies for marine boot camp. Now *those* are men.

or,

> You want to know what a man is? Go to the state school for the retarded, and watch the men who work with those kids every day with compassion and unfailing patience. Those are men.

DETAILED DESCRIPTION A description is a "word picture," a direct rendering of the details that summarize an idea from your perspective. Martin Luther King, Jr., used description in his famous "I Have a Dream" speech, when he described the plight of the black American:

> There are those who are asking the devotees of civil rights, "When will you be satisfied?" We can never be satisfied as long as our bodies, heavy with the fatigue of travel, cannot gain lodging in the motels of the highways and the hotels of the cities. We cannot be satisfied as long as the Negro's basic mobility is from a smaller ghetto to a larger one. We can never be satisfied as long as our children are stripped of their selfhood and robbed of their dignity by signs stating "for whites only."[8]

Dr. King's description helps us to imagine pain and fatigue as well as the sight of a sign that says "for whites only." These things can be truly perceived only through the senses, but he manages to give us an image of them by capturing their essence in a few words. In his description, as in all good description, it is the choice of details that makes the difference.

ANALOGIES/COMPARISON-CONTRAST We use **analogies,** or comparisons, all the time, often in the firm of figures of speech such as similes and metaphors. A simile is a direct comparison that usually uses *like* or *as* whereas a metaphor is an implied comparison that does not use *like* or *as*. So if you said, "Student unrest is like psoriasis: It flares up, then subsides, but never quite goes away," you would be using a simile. If you used phrases such as "simmering student unrest" or "an avalanche of student unrest," you would be using metaphors because you have implied comparisons between student unrest and slowly boiling liquids and snowslides.

ORGANIZATION AND SUPPORT

Analogies are extended metaphors. We run across analogies all the time. Here, for example, is the way Ingmar Bergman describes old age:

> Old age is like climbing a mountain. You climb from ledge to ledge. The higher you get, the more tired and breathless you become, but your view becomes much more extensive.

Here's the way Carl Sagan explains the age of the universe through analogy:

> The most instructive way I know to express this cosmic chronology is to imagine the fifteen-billion-year lifetime of the universe (or at least its present incarnation since the Big Bang) compressed into the span of a single year.... It is disconcerting to find that in such a cosmic year the Earth does not condense out of interstellar matter until early September: Dinosaurs emerge on Christmas Eve; flowers arise on December 28th; and men and women originate at 10:30 P.M. on New Year's Eve. All of recorded history occupies the last ten seconds of December 31; and the time from the waning of the Middle Ages to the present occupies little more than one second.[9]

Here's how a newspaper reporter pointed out how relatively inexpensive bike lanes can be:

> The proposed four-mile long freeway in New York City at $1.6 billion could finance 100,000 miles of rural bikeways. Or, alternatively, ribbon bikeways could be built paralleling the whole 40,000-mile national Interstate System of highways.[10]

Analogies can be used to compare or contrast an unknown concept with a known one. For example, if you had difficulty explaining to a public speaking class composed mostly of music majors why they should practice their speeches out loud, you might use this analogy:

> We all realize that great masters often can compose music in their heads; Beethoven, for example, composed his greatest masterpieces after he had gone deaf and couldn't even hear the instruments play out his ideas. However, beginners have to sit down at a piano or some other instrument and play their pieces as they create them. It is much the same way for beginning public speakers. When composing their speeches, they need to use their instruments—their voices—to hear how their ideas sound.

For an audience of music majors, this analogy might clarify the concept of practicing a speech. For a class of electrical engineers who may not know Mozart from Madonna, this analogy might confuse rather than clarify. It is important to remember to make your analogies appropriate to your audience.

ANECDOTES An **anecdote** is a brief story with a point, often (but not always) based on personal experience. (The word *anecdote* comes from the Greek meaning "unpublished item.") Anecdotes can add a lively, personal touch to your explanation. For example, a minister used the following anecdote to demonstrate the communication problems he sometimes has with members of his congregation.

> I ought not to be surprised by anything at my time of life, but one of my flock did manage to take my breath away. I was preaching about the Father's tender wisdom in caring for us all; illustrated by saying that the Father knows which of us grows best in sunlight and which of us must have shade. "You know you plant roses in the sunshine," I said, "and heliotrope and geraniums; but if you want your fuchsias to grow they must

be kept in a shady nook." After the sermon, which I hoped would be a comforting one, a woman came up to me, her face glowing with pleasure that was evidently deep and true. "Oh, Dr. _____, I am so grateful for that sermon," she said, clasping my hand and shaking it warmly. My heart glowed for a moment while I wondered what tender place in her heart and life I had touched. Only for a moment, though. "Yes," she went on fervently, "I never knew before what was the matter with my fuchsias."[11]

The minister's anecdote contains an analogy, which makes it a good example of how two types of supporting material can be combined. And that brings us to our next type of supporting material: examples.

EXAMPLES An **example** is a specific case that is used to demonstrate a general idea. Examples can be either factual or hypothetical, personal or borrowed. They can also be combined with other types of support. Vic Vieth, a student at Winona State University in Minnesota, used graphic examples in his speech entitled "Prisoners of Conscience."

One student used examples to begin her speech on the possible dangers of Nutrasweet:

Jason Domingo was experiencing unprovoked fits of violence, very unusual for a 4-year-old boy. Fifty-year-old Dr. James Bowen's speech was slurred. Along with this, his movements were very uncoordinated. Joellen Embry, 28, was suffering from very severe headaches, a bloated feeling, and her periods were coming much later or being skipped altogether.

What is the recurring factor in each of these situations? The fact that each of these victims had consumed an artificially sweetened beverage containing aspartame, more commonly known as Nutrasweet.[12]

Hypothetical examples can be often more powerful than factual examples, because hypothetical examples ask the audience to imagine something—thus causing them to become active participants in the thought. If you were speaking on the subject of euthanasia (mercy killing), you might ask your audience to imagine that someone they loved was suffering and being kept alive by a machine. If you were dealing with street crime, you might begin by saying, "Imagine you're walking down a dark street and you hear footsteps..." One way to generate a hypothetical example is to consider the possible consequences of some current trend or occurrence. One student, in a speech on censorship in school libraries, used a hypothetical example this way:

Imagine for a moment. We are in the year 2025. The place, the typical public school library for this time period. No longer do the bookshelves carry novels by such great authors as Huxley, Orwell, Joyce, Vonnegut, and Hemingway. Books that have been read by past American generations, the classics, like *To Kill a Mockingbird, The Grapes of Wrath, Brave New World,* can no longer be found. The children are all complacent and content with the books they are reading, those of an idealistic world. They are totally oblivious to the realities of their own society. Above the librarian's desk is a large sign in huge black lettering for all to see. It states, "Any book found in this library expressing controversial views about sex, race, politics, or personal behavior will be destroyed."[13]

Examples can be effective in clarifying information and making it interesting and memorable. Strictly speaking, however, they do not prove a point because they refer only to isolated instances that might not be representative. To prove an idea with examples, you have to collect a number of them; at that point they become statistics.

QUANTIFICATION AND STATISTICS   **Quantification** is the use of numbers to clarify a concept, to make it more specific. One example of quantification comes from a lecture given by a professor at Columbia University. He wanted to develop the idea that inflation lowers the value of paper currency, so he used quantification (developed in an anecdote) in the following way:

> Some time ago, I found a postcard which I had written to my father on November 23, 1923, while I was attending a boarding school in Germany. The card asked that my father send the bursar "immediately 1.2 trillion marks. If the tuition is not paid by the end of the month, you will have to pay four gold marks."
>
> Those two figures—1.2 trillion paper and four gold marks—illustrate the catastrophic fraud of the great German inflation which resulted in a revolutionary change in the economic and above all the social order of the country.[14]

Statistics are numbers that are arranged or organized to show how a fact or principle is true for a large number of cases. Statistics are actually collections of examples, which is why they are often more effective as proof than are isolated examples. If you wanted to develop the idea that American youths are not well informed about the American economic system, the following example would be insufficient proof:

> I asked my younger brother the other day if he knew the difference between collectivism and a free-enterprise society, and he had no idea. He didn't even know that the U.S. economy is based on free enterprise.

"Can you cut it a little finer, Mergeson, than 'umpteen'?"

Drawing by Donald Reilly; © 1985 The New Yorker Magazine, Inc.

Proof based on *lots* of people's younger siblings would be more effective:

A 1987 study by the Joint Council on Economic Education showed that 50 percent of high school students could not distinguish between collectivism and a free-enterprise society, and 50 percent did not know the U.S. economy was based on free enterprise.

Because statistics are potentially powerful proof, you have the ethical responsibility to cite them exactly as they were published or tabulated. It's usually all right to "round off" a percentage or other figure, but it's considered bad form to manipulate your statistics so they sound better than they are. For example, the term *average* is often used to manipulate statistics. As there are actually three measures of central tendency, or "averages" (mean, median, and mode), it is important to be clear about which one you mean. Imagine that you had the following list of annual incomes for a group of five people:

1. $0
2. $0
3. $500
4. $750
5. $23,750

The mode (most frequent value) for that group would be $0, the mean (arithmetic average) would be $5,000, and the median (the point at which 50 percent of the values are greater and 50 percent are less) would be $500. Any of these could be cited as the "average" by an unscrupulous speaker.

Another responsibility calls for you to cite the complete source of your statistic along with any other information that would have a bearing on its validity. Established professional pollsters such as Gallup, Roper, and Harris, as well as the best magazines and newspapers, have reputations for accuracy. If you cite them, your audience can be relatively sure that your statistics are reliable. Sometimes the source of a statistic will cause it to be suspect, as when, years ago, a cigarette company mailed cartons of cigarettes to doctors and then sent those same doctors a questionnaire asking which brand of cigarettes they were then smoking. Shortly afterward, advertising for the company stated that seven out of ten doctors reported smoking that brand.[15]

A third rule about the use of statistics is based on effectiveness rather than ethics. You should reduce the statistic to a concrete image if possible. For example, $1 billion in $100 bills would be about the same height as a sixty-story building. Using concrete images such as this will make your statistics more than "just numbers" when you use them.

QUOTATION/TESTIMONY Using a familiar, artistically stated saying will enable you to take advantage of someone else's memorable wording. For example, if you were giving a speech on personal integrity, you might quote Mark Twain, who said, "Always do right. This will gratify some people, and astonish the rest." A quotation like that fits Alexander Pope's definition of "true wit": "What was often thought, but ne'er so well expressed."

You can also use quotations as **testimony,** to prove a point by using the support of someone who is more authoritative or experienced on the subject than you. Theresa Clinkenbeard, a student at Regis College in Colorado, used quotation for this purpose in her speech entitled "The Loss of Childhood":

> "As a distinctive childhood culture wastes away, we watch with fascination and dismay." This insight of Neil Postman, author of *The Disappearance of Childhood,* raised a poignant point. Childhood in America is vanishing. Gradually, subtly. and to many, almost imperceptibly.... As Postman stated it, "The language, games, tastes, sexuality and clothing of our children and adults are becoming indistinguishable." During a recent ABC News report, it was stated that "one of the major reasons children are turning to alcohol, drugs, early sexual activity and suicide is to alleviate the pressures to grow up fast."[16]

You can usually signal to your audience that you are using a quotation simply by pausing or by changing your pace or inflection slightly. If you want to be more formal, you can preface the quotation with some variation of "And I quote ..." and end it with some variation of "end of quote" although that technique becomes tiresome if used too often.

▶ VISUAL AIDS

▶ Be sure of it; give me the ocular proof.

Shakespeare
Othello

Sometimes information is clearer, more interesting, more persuasive, and more memorable when it is presented visually. Figure 12–6 provides one example. Saying that a billion is a thousand millions isn't nearly as effective as demonstrating that fact graphically. (Imagine how you might use this display in a speech on the increasing national debt.)

Visual aids serve several purposes. They can show how things look (photos of your trek to Nepal or the effects of malnutrition). They can show how things work (demonstration of a new ski binding, a diagram of how seawater is made drinkable). Visual aids can also show how things relate to one another (the million-billion example in Figure 12–6; a graph showing the relationship between gender, education, and income). Finally, visual aids can show important information clearly (steps in filing a claim in the small-claims court, symptoms of anemia).

Types of Visual Aids

OBJECTS AND MODELS Sometimes the most effective visual aid is the actual thing you are talking about. This is true when the thing you are talking about is portable enough to carry and simple enough to use during a demonstration before an audience: a piece of sports equipment such as a jai-alai racket or a small piece of weight-training equipment. **Models** are scaled representations of the object you are discussing and are used when that object is too large (the new medical center) or too small (a DNA molecule) or simply doesn't exist anymore (a *Tyrannosaurus rex*).

PHOTOGRAPHS When blown up large enough for the entire audience to see, photographs can be particularly striking. Photographs have the advantage over

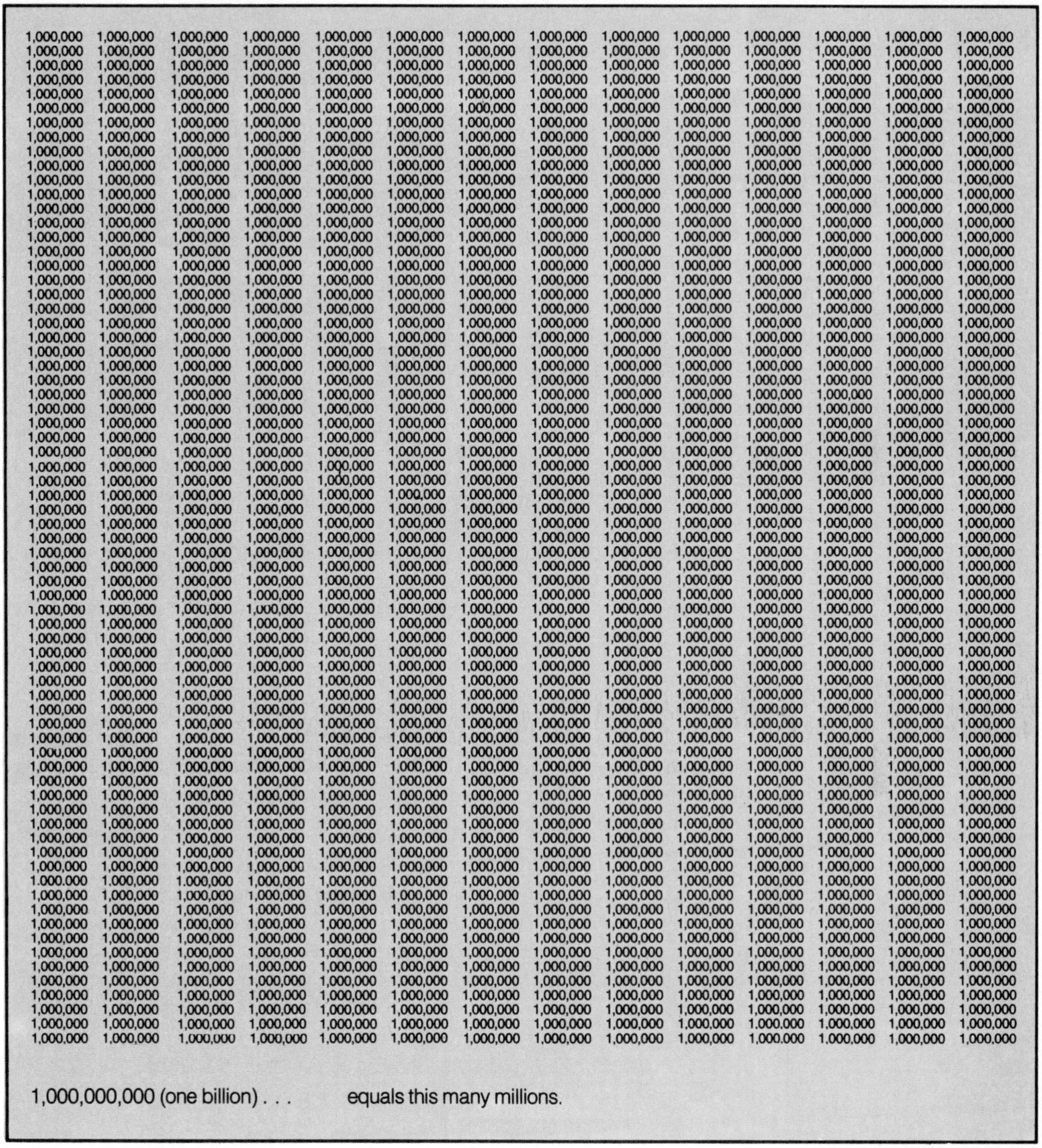

1,000,000,000 (one billion) . . .　　　equals this many millions.

FIGURE 12–6
Visual Aids Often Have More Impact than Words

actual objects when those objects might be dangerous to an audience as in a speech about poisonous plants or wild animals. They can also add an artistic touch to a speech as when you show the portrait of the person you are discussing.

315

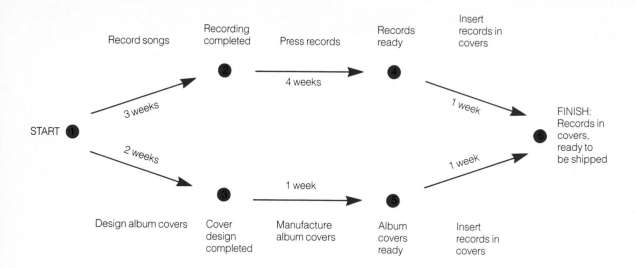

FIGURE 12–7
Flowchart: Production of a
Record Album

DIAGRAMS A **diagram** is any kind of line drawing that shows the most important properties of an object. Diagrams do not try to show everything but just those parts of a thing that the audience most needs to be aware of and understand. Blueprints and architectural plans are common types of diagrams as are maps and organizational charts. A diagram is most appropriate when you need to simplify a complex object and make it more understandable to the audience. The diagram in Figure 12–7 is a flow chart showing the steps in producing a record album.

WORD AND NUMBER CHARTS **Word charts** and **number charts** are visual depictions of key facts or statistics. Shown visually, these facts and numbers will be understood and retained better than if you just talked about them. Many speakers arrange the main points of their speech, often in outline form, as a word chart. (See Figure 12–8.) Many other speakers list their main statistics.

PIE CHARTS AND PICTOGRAPHS **Pie charts** are shaped as circles with wedges cut into them. They are used to show divisions of any whole: where your tax dollars go, the percentage of the population involved in various occupations, and so on. Pie charts are always made up of percentages that add up to

FIGURE 12–8
Word Chart

Computer Keyboard Shortcuts for PC–DOS	
Key	**Description**
\<F1\>	Repeats previous command character by character
\<F2\>	Repeats previous command up to a specified character
\<F3\>	Repeats last command in entirety
\<F4\>	Skips over characters in previous command
\<F5\>	Saves currently displayed line, advances to next line

FIGURE 12–9
Pie Chart

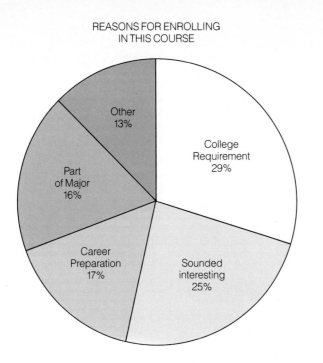

REASONS FOR ENROLLING
IN THIS COURSE

100 percent. Usually, the wedges of the pie are organized from largest to small-est, with the largest beginning top center at twelve o'clock. The pie chart in Figure 12–9 represents the reasons a sample of students gave for enrolling in a communication course.

Pictographs are artistic modifications of graphs or charts, designed to make information interesting. Figure 12–10 is a pictograph representing how a typical broadcast hour is divided at a radio station.

BAR AND COLUMN CHARTS **Bar charts,** such as the one shown in Figure 12–11, compare two or more values by stretching them out in the form of hori-zontal rectangles. **Column charts,** such as the ones shown in Figure 12–12 and 12–13, perform the same function as bar charts but use vertical rectangles. These charts can be simple (like the column chart in Figure 12–12, which com-

FIGURE 12–10
Pictograph Division of Radio Hour

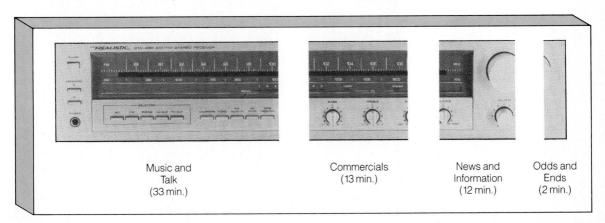

Music and
Talk
(33 min.)

Commercials
(13 min.)

News and
Information
(12 min.)

Odds and
Ends
(2 min.)

FIGURE 12–11
Bar Chart

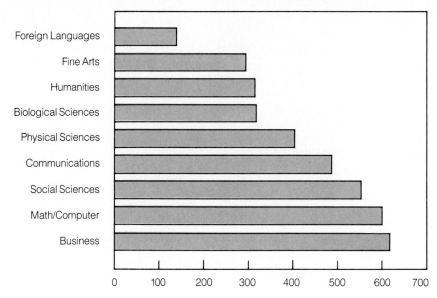

NUMBER OF 1988 GRADUATES
BY ACADEMIC DIVISION

FIGURE 12–12
Simple Column Chart

ANNUAL PROFITS DIVIDED
BY SOURCE OF INCOME

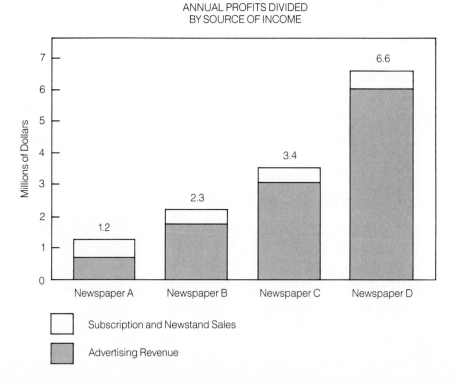

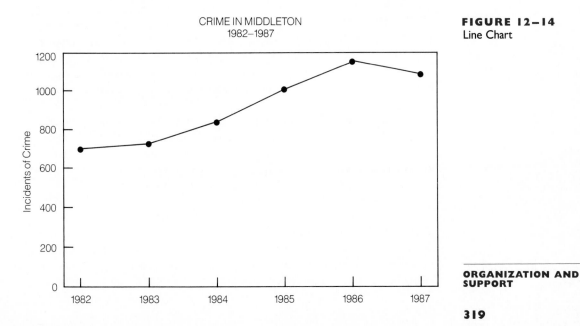

ANNUAL PROFITS
OF FOUR NEWSPAPERS

Millions of Dollars

6.6

3.4

2.3

1.2

Newspaper A   Newspaper B   Newspaper C   Newspaper D

FIGURE 12–13
Divided Column Chart

pares the annual profits of four newspapers), or subdivided (like the column chart in Figure 12–13, which compares the annual profits of four newspapers, divided by their source of income.

LINE CHARTS A **line chart** maps out the direction of a moving point; it is ideally suited for showing changes over time. The time element is usually placed on the horizontal axis so that the line visually represents the trend over time. A soaring increase in crime in a community, for example, could be represented in the line chart in Figure 12–14.

CRIME IN MIDDLETON
1982–1987

Incidents of Crime

1982   1983   1984   1985   1986   1987

FIGURE 12–14
Line Chart

Media for the Presentation of Visual Aids

CHALKBOARD   The major advantages of chalkboards are availability and spontaneity: They can be found in any classroom, and with them you can create your visual aid as you go, including items generated from audience responses. The major disadvantages of chalkboards (in addition to that squeaking sound that hurts your teeth) is the difficulty of preparing visual aids on them in advance, especially if several speeches are scheduled in the same room at the same hour.

POLYMER MARKING SURFACES   Available in most bookstores and art supply shops, polymer marking surfaces can be brought in and applied to any wall. These can be written on with special colored markers that wipe off easily with a dry cloth, and they can also be used as a projector screen.

FLIP PADS AND POSTER BOARD   Flip pads are like oversized writing tablets attached to a portable easel. As the name suggests, you reveal visuals on a flip pad one at a time by turning pages. Flip pads enable you to combine the spontaneity of the chalkboard (you can write on them as you go) with the portability that enables you to prepare them in advance. If you plan to use your visuals more than once or if you don't need to write on them, you can prepare them in advance on rigid poster board, and display them on the same type of easel.

OVERHEAD PROJECTORS AND OPAQUE PROJECTORS   Overhead projectors use transparencies—large, clear sheets of acetate—to cast an image on a screen. Opaque projectors are the same general type of device except that with them you can use sheets of paper, including pages from books, as your image to be projected. These types of projectors can be used with an audience that is too large to see a flip pad all at once.

HANDOUTS   The major advantage of handouts is that the audience takes these visuals with them. They are, therefore, excellent memory and reference aids. The major disadvantage is that they are distracting when handed out during a speech; first, there is the distraction of passing them around, and then there is the distraction of having them in front of the audience members while you have gone on to something else. It's best, therefore, to pass them out at the end of the speech.

Aids that extend senses other than sight are also effective in some circumstances. If you were speaking about perfume, skunks, or the effects of a chemical plant on a community, actually producing the appropriate smells might help explain your point. It you were talking about baking brownies, or brewing beer, a taste probably wouldn't hurt. And you could incorporate something to touch if you were speaking about the texture of a substance or how it feels.

Audio aids such as tape recordings and records can supply information that could not be presented any other way (comparing musical styles, for example, or demonstrating the differences in the sounds of gas and diesel engines), but in most cases you should use them sparingly. Remember that your presentation already relies heavily on your audience's sense of hearing; it's better to use a visual aid, if possible, than to overwork the audio. Of course, there are audio-visual aids, including films, videotapes, and sound-on-slide. These should also be used sparingly, however, because they allow the audience members to receive information passively, thus relieving them of the responsibility of becoming active participants in the presentation.

Rules for Using Visual Aids

It's easy to see that each type of visual aid and each medium for its presentation have their own unique advantages and disadvantages. No matter which type you use, however, there are a few rules that you should keep in mind.

SIMPLICITY Keep your visual aids simple. Your goal is to clarify, not confuse. Use only key words or phrases, not sentences. Use eight or fewer lines of text, each with twenty-five or fewer characters. Keep all printing horizontal. Omit all nonessential details.

SIZE Visual aids should be large enough for your entire audience to see them at one time but portable enough so you can get them out of the way when they no longer pertain to the point you are making.

ATTRACTIVENESS Visual aids should be visually interesting and as neat as possible. If you don't have the necessary skills, try to get help from a friend or at the audiovisual center on your campus.

APPROPRIATENESS Visuals must be appropriate to all the components of the speaking situation—you, the audience, and your topic—and they must emphasize the point you are trying to make. Often a speaker will grab a visual aid that

"It's just something the kids scratched out, but for some reason I feel good when I look at it."

has *something* to do with the topic and use it even though it is not directly related—such as showing a map of a city transit system while talking about the condition of the individual cars.

RELIABILITY You must be in control of your visual aid at all times. Wild animals, chemical reactions, and gimmicks meant to shock a crowd are often too likely to backfire.

When it comes time for you to *use* the visual aid, remember one more point: Talk to your audience, not to your visual aid. Some speakers become so wrapped up in their props that they turn their backs on their audience and sacrifice all their eye contact.

▶ SAMPLE SPEECH

The sample speech for this chapter was presented by Kellie Sanders, a student at Kansas State University. Kellie was one of the semifinalists in the 1984 Interstate Oratorical Association Annual Contest. Comments on the organization and supporting material appear in the margin; an outline of the speech follows it.

Scientific Fiction[17]

Kelley Sanders, Kansas State University, Kansas

The introduction begins with an attention-getting joke that is appropriate and effective. This joke also qualifies as an anecdote because it is a "brief story with a point."

There's a story going around about an engineer, a philosopher, and a research scientist who were all asked a very simple question: What is 2 + 2? The engineer calculated it to be 4.0000 to the fourth decimal place accuracy. The philosopher thought the answer was somewhere greater than 3 but less than 5, probably 4. The research scientist's answer: "What do you want it to be?"

Statement of thesis; setting tone of speech

Unfortunately, the scientific community has been giving this answer far too often. Scientists, victims of the publish or perish syndrome, are resorting to fabricating evidence.

First main point of body

We don't like to think of our scientists as being less than perfect. However, recently, over a dozen major cases of biomedical scientific fraud have come to light at such prestigious institutions as Harvard and Yale. Says University of Georgia ecologist Frank Golley, "I suspect that there are many more attempts at deception that are not publicized. *Science* magazine reports the sensational cases, but these are the tip of an iceberg."

Quantification

Quotation/Testimony

Preview of main points

In order to make you more aware of the extent of this "science fiction" in both the academic and commercial lab, I'd like first to discuss what causes scientific fraud to occur; how this fraud can affect us; and, finally, recommend some solutions to the problem.

Testimony/Quantification

Unfortunately, the question of how common fraud in science is doesn't permit a precise answer. Yet William Broad and Nicolas Wade, authors of *Betrayers of the Truth,* estimate that every major case of fraud discovered is representative of 100,000 others that are never detected.

Description

Broad and Wade believe scientific fraud may remain undetected because experiments are seldom replicated by other scientists. Besides this lack of replication, the carelessness found in many labs makes the atmosphere ripe for fraud. Scientists too busy to oversee the fine details rely on lab technicians to collect data. If the scientist is careless by not double-checking the data, fraud can occur.

Careerism and the race to get funding are also possible causes. Dr. William Raub, grant director for the National Institute of Health, notes that "today, only 30 percent of the applicants for NIH grants get them, as compared with 70 percent in the 1950s." So, the pressure on scientists to produce is greater now than ever before.

Testimony/Statistics/Analogy

This pressure has led to what *Science* magazine calls the "LPU" or Least Publishable Unit. This euphemism means fragmentation of writing up data. For example, a researcher slices one long paper into four short papers. This trend toward "salami science" has significantly increased the number of papers a scientist has on his résumé, but, too often, at the expense of quality. Likewise, the increase in the number of journals makes it easier for researchers to fabricate data or plagiarize without getting caught. For example, Elias Alsbeti was able to publish sixty plagiarized papers and secure positions at such prestigious institutions as the MD Anderson Hospital in Houston before he was caught.

Operational definition

Example/Quantification

As you can see, cheating in science does occur. But whatever the cause, this chicanery can have profound effects. And that is what I would like to discuss next—how scientific fraud actually can and does affect us.

Transition to second main point/Internal preview

A case in point is Industrial Bio-Test Laboatories of Illinois, or IBT. During IBT's twenty-six-year existence, they conducted over 1,000 studies, which were used to obtain government approval for hundreds of drugs, pesticides, and food additives on the market. But five years ago, fraudulent data destroyed their credibility when it was discovered that 97 percent of their cancer studies on pesticides and herbicides were faulty. One of these herbicides tested by IBT was paraquat. These tests were the basis for approving paraquat. But later it was found that IBT had grossly manipulated their data. Paraquat can kill if even small amounts are swallowed, inhaled, or spilled on the skin. *Science Digest* estimated that already over 1,000 people have died because of this misuse of paraquat.

Example/Statistics

Statistics

Testimony/Statistics

Perhaps more immediate to most of us are problems with IBT's fraudulent studies on more commonly used products. Their studies on TCC, an antibacterial agent used in many deodorant soaps and on Naprosyn, an arthritis drug, have been questioned because of faulty data. So, even though IBT has been shut down, the products they tested still remain on the market.

Example

Another case with potential widespread impact on our lives is that of Dr. John Darsee of Harvard. He claimed to have produced drugs that limited the damage done by heart attacks. When he was asked to produce research to back up this claim, Darsee went back to his lab and manufactured two weeks of data in only an hour while his co-workers watched. Darsee dismissed this as an isolated event because of the academic pressure he was under. Harvard allowed him to continue with his research until it was discovered that Darsee had faked research throughout most of his academic career. Currently, Darsee is practicing critical care medicine in New York, but if his patients knew his background, I'm sure they would question his fitness to practice medicine at all.

Example

Description

Although fraudulent research can destroy scientists' careers, endanger lives, and cost the taxpayers and industry millions, the greatest cost in the long run is the perpetuation of a wrong idea. In the 1950s, respected British psychologist Cyril Burt published studies of identical twins reared separately. These studies supported his theory that heredity is the major determinant of intelligence. His

Transition to third main point/Internal review
Example

work heavily influenced education. It wasn't until the 1970s that his data were discovered to be fabricated.

The implications of the thousands of other Burts who have not been discovered are clear: Many of the basic scientific beliefs we hold may be based on fraudulent data. Think about the seriousness of this if something, such as our theories dealing with nuclear warfare, were faked by a pressured scientist anxious to find a solution to World War II.

Now that we've discussed what causes scientific fraud to flourish and seen how this fraud can affect us through examining some actual cases, what can be done to alleviate this problem? The solution lies in two areas: what scientists can do and what the government can do.

There are three things scientists can do. One potential solution is for senior scientists to double-check data that seem too good to be true. Secondly, promotions and grants shouldn't be handed out on the sole basis of a long résumé. Institutions should implement the more sophisticated means of reading and evaluating a scientist's research record that are now available, such as citation analysis. This is where the influence of a scientist is measured by the number of times his work is cited by others rather than by the sheer number of times he has been published. Though it's not perfect, it is a beginning toward solving the problem.

Other experts who have analyzed the problem believe journals should be more selective in what they print. Many of these journals serve as little more than a "vanity press," with the taxpayer supporting the vanity through government grants given to researchers.

There is also something the government can do to reduce fraud and that is to force scientists to repay misspent funds. The National Institute of Health ordered the hospital where Darsee did his research on heart medication to repay most of the $122,000 grant he spent. Unfortunately, this is the only instance in which the NIH has demanded repayment of misspent funds. Experts in the May *Science 83* magazine believe that this threat of financial retribution is the most persuasive way to ensure that senior scientists will tighten up what goes on in their labs. Says Seymour Perry of the American Association of Medical Colleges, "There are few ways of influencing people and institutions. One of them is to strike at the pocketbook."

At a time when initiatives against waste and fraud are being pursued in all areas, the area of scientific fraud can no longer be ignored. Remember the story about the engineer, the philosopher, and the research scientist who were asked the sum of 2 + 2? Although it is humorous, it does point out the need for change. If scientists are more careful in supervising subordinates and wary of inflated résumés and if the government forces misspent moneys to be repaid, then scientific fraud can significantly be reduced. And no longer will research scientists be tempted to answer research problems by asking "What do you want it to be?"

Analogy/Hypothetical example

Transition to fourth main point/Internal review, internal preview

Description

Comparison

Comparison

Description/Example

Testimony

Description

Conclusion refers back to introduction for memory aid and review of main ideas.

ORGANIZATION AND SUPPORT

Speech Outline

One of the reasons Kelley's speech is effective is because of its tight organization. In outline form, the speech could be represented as follows:

I. Introduction
    A. Opening joke: The engineer, the philosopher, and the research scientist.
    B. Statement of startling fact: Scientists are resorting to fabricating evidence.
        Quotation/Testimony, Frank Golley: "The Tip of the Iceberg"
    C. Preview of main points.

II. Body
    A. How common is scientific fraud?
        Testimony, Broad and Wade: Every discovered case is representative of 100,000 others.
    B. What are the causes of scientific fraud?
        1. Experiments are not replicated.
        2. Careless atmosphere exists in labs.
        3. Scientists are too busy to double-check.
        4. Careerism and the race for funding are factors.
           Quotation/Testimony: Raub, NIH grants
           Definition: Least Publishable Unit
           Example: Elias Alsbeti
    C. What are the effects of scientific fraud?
        1. Lives may be placed in danger through improper testing of drugs, pesticides, and food additives.
           Example: IBT Laboratories
           a. Paraquat
              Statistics: 1,000 deaths
           b. TCC
           c. Naprosyn
           Example: Darsee's drug research
        2. Important scientific beliefs may be based on fradulent data.
           Example: Cyril Burt
    D. What can be done to alleviate scientific fraud?
        1. Scientists can do three things.
           a. Senior scientists should double-check data.
           b. Promotions and grants shouldn't be handed out on the basis of a long résumé.
              Comparison: citation analysis
           c. Scientific journals should be more selective in what they print.
        2. The government can force scientists to repay misspent funds.
        Example: NIH on Darsee research
        Quotation: Seymour Perry

III. Conclusion
    A. Review of main points.
    B. Memory aid: refer to introductory joke.

This chapter dealt with speech organization and supporting material. Speech organization is a process that begins with the formulation of a thesis statement to express the central idea of a speech. The thesis is established in the introduction, developed in the body, and reviewed in the conclusion of a structured speech. The introduction will also gain the audience's attention, set the mood and tone of the speech, and demonstrate the importance of the topic to the audience.

Organizing the body of the speech will begin with a list of points you might want to make in your speech. These points are then organized according to the principles of outlining. They are divided, coordinated, and placed in a logical order. Transitions from point to point help make this order apparent to your audience.

Organization follows a pattern such as that of time, space, topic, problem-solution, cause-effect, and climax arrangements. Along with reviewing your thesis or main points or both, the conclusion also supplies the audience with a memory aid.

Supporting materials are the facts and information you use to back up what you say. Supporting material has four purposes: to clarify, to make interesting, to make memorable, and to prove. Any piece of support could perform any or all of these functions, and any of the functions could be fulfilled by any of the types of support.

Types of support include *definitions,* which can be either *traditional* or *operational; detailed descriptions,* which create word pictures that enable an audience to visualize an idea; *analogies,* which compare or contrast (or both) an unknown or unfamiliar concept with a known or familiar one; *anecdotes,* which add a lively, personal touch; *examples,* which can be either real or hypothetical; *quantification,* which makes an idea more specific; *statistics,* which show that a fact or principle is true for a large number of cases; *quotations,* which are used for memorable wording as well as testimony from a well-known or authoritative source; and *visual aids,* which help clarify complicated points and keep an audience informed on where you are in the general scheme of things. Any piece of support might combine two or more of these types.

► **ACTIVITIES**

1. For practice in dividing ideas, divide each of the following into subcategories that are exhaustive and focused:
   a. Transportation
   b. Careers
   c. U.S. Government
   d. The National Park System
   e. Balanced diets
   f. Television programs
   g. Houseplants

ORGANIZATION AND SUPPORT

2. To practice coordinating points, write out the following "steps in studying" in parallel wording:
   a. Preview quickly
   b. Read slowly
   c. Take notes
   d. Review notes
   e. Test yourself

3. For practice in formulating definitions, see if you can come up with both a traditional and an operational definition for each of the following terms:
   a. politician
   b. living room
   c. automobile
   d. college student

4. For practice in recognizing the functions of support, identify three instances of support in each of the speeches at the end of Chapters 14 and 15. Explain the function of each instance of support. (Keep in mind that any instance of support *could* perform more than one function.)

5. One of the best ways to practice description is to paint a word picture of something you're so familiar with that you don't normally take the time to observe it carefully. Consider the room you're in right now—how would you describe it in one written paragraph? What details would you include so that someone else could visualize it from your description?

6. For practice in formulating analogies, provide one for each of the following: deficit spending, inflation, shopping, studying, infatuation, true love, and a job interview. Once again these particular terms are not essential to the exercise. Use any terms you like, but try to make them original. It was a good use of analogy when Vince Lombardi said that tying a football game was like "kissing your sister," but just to dredge up an analogy like that from your memory is less useful in this exercise than making up one of your own.

7. For practice in using anecdotes, try the following list: first, identify an anecdote to prove a point of your choice ("college is a rewarding experience," for example, or "power corrupts" or "love is blind"). Whatever point you choose, make sure you start with the point first and then think up the anecdote to support it. Then reverse the exercise: Think of one of your favorite stories or personal experiences, and then identify a point that the story could be used to support.

8. For practice in using examples to support points, team up with someone else, and take turns supplying examples for points each of you identify. These points could be well-established truisms ("cheaters never prosper," "better safe than sorry") or more specific ideas ("Robert DeNiro is a great actor," "the Bermuda Triangle is a dangerous place"). Take note of those examples that combine with other forms of support.

9. For practice in quantifying vague statements, try supporting statements such as the following with specific numbers:
   "Servicing your own car saves money."
   "It takes a lot of time to write a good speech."
   "Local housing is very expensive."

10. To practice using statistics, dig up a copy of this year's *Information Please Almanac, Statistical Abstract of the United States, World Almanac and Book of*

Facts, or any other statistical yearbook or almanac. Then support or refute these statements statistically:

a. There are a lot of people out of work today.

b. The United States imports a lot of oil.

c. A lot of people die of heart attacks.

d. Crime is on the rise.

e. More and more people are getting divorced these days.

f. There are a lot of people on welfare these days.

11. This exercise will give you practice with the different forms of support. It can be done individually or in a group.

a. Choose one of the following situations:

(1) You have just received a lower grade on a term paper than you think you deserve because the instructor thinks your topic was inappropriate. You would like to convince your instructor to change your grade.

(2) You finally summon the courage to ask out a person to whom you have been strongly attracted for months. The person thinks about it and says, "Convince me."

(3) Someone you really don't care for has just asked you out. You need to explain to that person why it isn't a good idea.

(4) You've just found a classified ad for the ideal job. Answer it, explaining why they should hire you.

(5) Your best friend, a varsity athlete, has broken a leg the night before the opening game. You go to the hospital to cheer up your friend.

b. Fill in the missing details of the situation you chose, such as the topic in (1), the people in (2) and (3), the job in (4), and the type of sport in (5).

c. Come up with one example of each type of support for the chosen situation.

12. For practice in designing visual aids, describe three different visual aids that could be used to clarify the following ideas:

a. Unemployment.

b. Inflation.

c. The difference between cheaply made and good-quality clothing.

d. The operation of an internal combustion engine (or some other piece of machinery).

e. How to juggle.

▶ NOTES

1. Research into this effect is summarized in G. Cronkhite, *Persuasion: Speech and Behavioral Change* (Indianapolis: Bobbs-Merrill, 1969), pp. 195–196.

2. Kate L. Turabian, *Student's Guide for Writing College Papers* (Chicago: University of Chicago Press, 1976).

3. See, for example, George A. Miller, "The Magical Number Seven, Plus or Minus Two: Some Limits on Our Capacity for Processing Information," in Richard C. Anderson and David P. Ausubel (eds.), *Readings in the Psychology of Cognition* (New York: Holt, Rinehart and Winston, 1965), pp. 242–267.

4. Alan H. Monroe, *Principles and Types of Speech* (Glenview, Ill.: Scott, Foresman, 1935).

5. Katherine Graham, "The Press and Its Responsibilities," *Vital Speeches of the Day* 42 (April 15, 1976).

6. From Red Cross fund-raising material.

7. Katherine Graham, op. cit.

8. Martin Luther King, Jr., "I Have a Dream," speech at civil rights rally, Washington, D.C., August 28, 1963. See James C. McCroskey, *An Introduction to Rhetorical Communication* (Englewood Cliffs, N.J.: Prentice-Hall, 1968), pp. 248–249, for transcript.

9. Carl Sagan, *The Dragons of Eden: Speculations on the Evolution of Human Intelligence* (New York: Ballantine, 1978), pp. 13–17.

10. Bob Burgess, "Hiking/Biking," *Santa Barbara News Press* (February 25, 1978).

11. Edmund Fuller, *2500 Anecdotes for All Occasions* (New York: Avenel Books, 1970), p. 275. Copyright © 1970 by Crown Publishers, Inc. Reprinted by permission.

12. Lori VanOverbeke, "Nutrasweet," *Winning Orations 1986* (Interstate Oratorical Association, 1986), p. 56.

13. Tracy Tomasino, "Censorship in Public School Libraries," *Winning Orations, 1986* (Interstate Oratorical Association, 1986), p. 18.

14. G. C. Wiegand, "Inflation," *Vital Speeches of the Day* 43 (June 15, 1978).

15. Bert E. Bradley, *Fundamentals of Speech Communication: The Credibility of Ideas* (Dubuque, Iowa: William C. Brown, 1974), p. 157.

16. Theresa Clinkenbeard, "The Loss of Childhood," *Winning Orations, 1984* (Interstate Oratorical Association, 1984), p. 4.

17. Kelley Sanders, "Scientific Fiction," *Winning Orations, 1984* (Interstate Oratorical Association, 1984), pp. 30–33.

►CHAPTER 13

KEY TERMS

addition

articulation

debilitative stage fright

deletion

extemporaneous speeches

facilitative stage fright

fallacy of approval

fallacy of catastrophic failure

fallacy of overgeneralization

fallacy of perfection

imaging

impromptu speeches

irrational thinking

manuscript speeches

memorized speeches

pitch

rate

slurring

substitution

visualization

PRESENTING YOUR MESSAGE

After reading this chapter, you should understand the following:

1. The differences among the various types of delivery.

2. The visual and auditory aspects of delivery that help you choose the best type of delivery for a particular speech.

3. The difference between facilitative and debilitative stage fright.

4. The sources of debilitative stage fright.

You should be able to do the following:

1. Choose the most effective type of delivery for a particular speech.

2. Follow the guidelines for effective extemporaneous, impromptu, manuscript, and memorized speeches.

3. Overcome debilitative stage fright.

4. Offer constructive criticism of others' presentations.

"So far, so good," you may be thinking to yourself. You've developed a purpose; you've chosen and researched a topic that suits your own interests, your audience, and the occasion. You feel confident about your ability to organize your ideas in a logical, effective way, and you've built up a healthy reserve of supporting material.

But then comes a problem: When you think about the actual act of standing before a group, your self-confidence begins to erode. How will you act? Should you be formal or casual? Should you memorize your remarks, read from a script, or use notes? How loudly should you speak, and·how quickly? And what about your nerves? The prospect of talking to an audience probably seems much more threatening than expressing yourself in a blue book or even mixing chemicals in a laboratory.

Because the act of speaking before a group of listeners may be a relatively new one for you, we'll look at the process now. The purpose of this chapter is to make you feel more confident about yourself as a speaker and to give you a clearer idea of how to behave before an audience. The first thing to consider in this area is the style of delivery you choose.

▶ TYPES OF DELIVERY

There are four basic types of delivery—extemporaneous, impromptu, manuscript, and memorized. Each type creates a different impression and is appropriate under different conditions. Any speech may incorporate more than one of these types of delivery. For purposes of discussion, however, it is best to consider them separately.

Extemporaneous Speeches

An **extemporaneous speech** is planned in advance but presented in a direct, spontaneous manner. Extemporaneous speeches are conversational in tone, which means that they give the audience members the impression that you are talking to them, directly and honestly, without the artificiality that an obvious "prepared statement" has. Don't misunderstand: Extemporaneous speeches *are* carefully prepared, but they are prepared in such a way that they create what actors call "the illusion of the first time"—in other words, the audience hears your remarks as though they were brand-new. This style of speaking is generally accepted to be the most effective, especially for a college class. In a classroom you generally speak before a small audience (five to fifty people) made up of people with diverse backgrounds. Spontaneity is essential with this type of audience, but so is careful message planning. Extemporaneous speaking allows you to benefit from both careful planning and spontaneous delivery. A speech presented extemporaneously will be focused, organized, and planned out in advance, but the exact wording of the entire speech will not be memorized or otherwise predetermined. Because you speak from only brief, unobtrusive notes, you are able to move and maintain eye contact with your audience.

Extemporaneous speaking is not only the most effective type of delivery for a classroom speech, but it is also the most common type of delivery in the "outside" world. Most of those involved in communication-oriented careers find that the majority of their public speaking is done before audiences that, in terms of size and diversity of interests represented, resemble those found in a college classroom. Professional public speakers recognize the advisability of both careful planning and spontaneity with such an audience.

The extemporaneous speech does have some disadvantages. It is difficult to keep exact time limits, to be exact in wording, or to be grammatically perfect with an extemporaneous speech. Therefore, if you are speaking as part of a radio or television broadcast or if your speech will be reproduced "for the record," you might want to use a manuscript or to memorize your speech. Also, an extemporaneous speech requires time to prepare. If you don't have that time, an impromptu speech might be more appropriate.

Impromptu Speeches

An **impromptu speech** is given off the top of one's head, without preparation. An impromptu speech is often given in an emergency, such as when a scheduled speaker becomes ill and you are suddenly called upon:

> Grunt Johnson couldn't make it this evening, folks, but I notice in our audience another Sioux U student leader who I am sure would be glad to say a few words ...

Impromptu speeches are sometimes given when speakers forget they are scheduled for extemporaneous speeches. In fact, a certain amount of confusion exists between the terms *extemporaneous* and *impromptu*.

The problem with an impromptu speech is that it is given on the spur of the moment and, as more than one expert has point out, "Too often the 'moment' arrives without the necessary informed and inspired 'spur.' "[1] There are, however, advantages to impromptu speaking. For one thing, an impromptu speech is by definition spontaneous. It is the delivery style necessary for informal talks, group discussions, and comments on others' speeches. It also can be an effective training aid; it can teach you to think on your feet and organize your thoughts quickly. To take full advantage of an impromptu speaking opportunity, remember the following points:

1. Take advantage of the time between being called on to speak and actually speaking. Even if you have only a minute, you can still scribble a few brief notes to protect against mental blocks.

2. Don't be afraid to be original; you don't have to remember what every other expert says about your topic—what do *you* say about it? Review your personal experiences and use them. If nothing else, consider questions such as "Who? What? When? Where? How?" and formulate a plan to answer one or more of them.

3. Observe what is going on around you, and respond to it. If there were other speakers, you might agree or disagree with what they said. You can comment on the audience and the occasion, too, as well as on your topic.

4. Keep a positive attitude. Remember that audience expectations are low. They know you haven't prepared in advance, and they don't expect you to be Patrick Henry.

5. Finally, and perhaps most important, keep your comments brief. Especially, do not prolong your conclusion. If you have said everything you want to say or everything you can remember, wrap it up as neatly as possible and sit down. If you forgot something, it probably wasn't important anyway. If it was, the audience will ask you about it afterward.

Manuscript Speeches

Manuscript speeches are read "word for word" from a prepared text. They are necessary when you are speaking "for the record," as at legal proceedings or when presenting scientific findings. The greatest disadvantage of a manuscript speech is the lack of spontaneity that may result. Manuscript readers have even been known to read their directions by mistake: "And so, let me say in conclusion, look at the audience with great sincerity . . . oops!" Needless to say, this can lead to extreme embarrassment.

Manuscript speeches are difficult and cumbersome, but they are sometimes necessary. If you find occasion to use one, here are some guidelines:

1. When writing the speech, recognize the differences between written essays and speeches. Speeches are usually less formal, more repetitive, and more personal than written messages.[2] They use more adverbs, adjectives, and cir-

cumlocutions such as "well" and "as you can see." As one expert points out, "Speeches use more words per square thought than well-written essays or reports."[3]

2. Use short paragraphs. They are easier to return to after establishing eye contact with your audience.
3. Type the manuscript triple-spaced, in all caps, with a dark ribbon. Underline the words you want to emphasize. (See Figure 13–1.)
4. Use stiff paper so that it won't fold up or fly away during the speech. Type on only one side, and number the pages by hand with large, circled numbers.
5. Rehearse until you can "read" whole lines without looking at the manuscript.
6. Take your time, vary your speed, and try to concentrate on ideas rather than words.

FIGURE 13–1
Sample Page from Manuscript Speech

⑧

TO SUMMARIZE, WE ARE IN THE EARLY STAGE OF DEVELOPMENTS IN THE SCIENCE AND TECHNOLOGY OF INFORMATION PROCESSING THAT WILL TRULY REVOLUTIONIZE OUR SOCIETY. ADVANCES ARE OCCURRING AT SUCH A FAST PACE THAT RECENT EXPERIENCE IS NOT ALWAYS A GOOD GUIDE TO THE FUTURE. IN THE PAST 30 YEARS, COMPUTER COMPUTATIONS HAVE GONE FROM A FEW INSTRUCTIONS PER SECOND AT A COST OF SEVERAL DOLLARS TO MILLIONS OF INSTRUCTIONS PER SECOND AT A COST OF LESS THAN 1 CENT. BUT SUCH DRAMATIC INDICATORS OF PROGRESS DO NOT MEASURE THE FULL IMPACT OF WHAT IS TAKING PLACE OR WHAT IS LIKELY TO OCCUR IN THE NEXT 30 YEARS. THERE CAN BE LITTLE DOUBT THAT THESE CHANGES WILL ALTER THE WAY PEOPLE LIVE AND EARN A LIVING, AND THE WAY THEY PERCEIVE THEMSELVES AND RELATE TO ONE ANOTHER.

Memorized Speeches

Memorized speeches—those that are learned "by heart"—are the most difficult and often the least effective. They usually seem excessively formal. They tend to make you think of words rather than ideas. However, like manuscript speeches, they are sometimes necessary. They are used in oratory contests and on very formal occasions such as eulogies or church rituals. They are used as training devices for memory. They are also used in some political situations. For example, in the 1984 presidential debates, Walter Mondale and Ronald Reagan were allowed to make prepared speeches, but they were not allowed to use notes. Thus, they had to memorize precise, "for-the-record" wording.

There is only one guideline for a memorized speech: Practice. The speech won't be effective until you have practiced it so you can present it with that "illusion of the first time" that we mentioned previously.

▶ PRACTICING THE SPEECH

Once you choose the appropriate delivery style for the type of speech you are giving, the best way to make sure that you are on your way to an effective delivery is to practice your speech repeatedly and systematically. One way to do that is to go through as many of the following five steps as possible:

1. First, present the speech to yourself. "Talk through" the entire speech, including your examples and forms of support. In other words, don't just say, "This is where I present my statistics" or "This is where I explain about photosynthesis."
2. Tape-record the speech, and listen to it. Because we hear our own voices partially though our cranial bone structure, we are sometimes surprised at what we sound like to others.
3. Present the speech in front of the mirror, and watch your physical mannerisms.
4. Present the speech in front of a small group of friends or relatives or both.
5. Present the speech to at least one listener in the same room (or, if that room is not available, a similar room) that you will present the final speech in.

▶ GUIDELINES FOR DELIVERY

The best way to consider guidelines for delivery is through an examination of the nonverbal aspects of presenting a speech. As you read in Chapter 5, nonverbal messages can change the meaning assigned to the spoken word and, in some cases, can contradict that meaning entirely. In fact, if the audience wants to interpret how you *feel* about something, they are likely to trust your nonverbal communication more than the words you speak. If you tell an audience, "It's good to be here today," but you stand before them slouched over with your hands in your pockets and an expression on your face as if you were about to be

---

shot, they are likely to discount what you say. This might cause your audience to react negatively to your speech, and their negative reaction might make you even more nervous. This cycle of speaker and audience reinforcing each other's feelings can work *for* you, though, if you approach a subject with genuine enthusiasm. Enthusiasm is shown through both the visual and auditory aspects of your delivery.

Visual Aspects of Delivery

Visual aspects of delivery include such things as appearance, movement, posture, facial expressions, and eye contact.

APPEARANCE   Appearance is not a presentation variable as much as a preparation variable. Some communication consultants suggest new clothes, new glasses, and new hairstyles for their clients. In case you consider any of these, be forewarned that you should be attractive to your audience but not flashy. Research suggests that audiences like speakers who are similar to them, but they prefer the similarity to be shown conservatively. For example, studies run in 1972, when long hair on males was becoming popular, showed that even long-haired listeners considered long-haired speakers less credible than shorter-haired speakers.[4]

MOVEMENT   Movement is an important visual aspect of delivery. The way you walk to the front of your audience, for example, will express your confidence and enthusiasm. And once you begin speaking, nervous energy can cause your body to shake and twitch, and that can be distressing both to you and to your audience. One way to control involuntary movement is to move voluntarily when you feel the need to move. Don't feel that you have to stand in one spot or that all your gestures need to be carefully planned. Simply get involved in your message, and let your involvement create the motivation for your movement. That way, when you move, you will emphasize what you are saying in the same way you would emphasize it if you were talking to a group of friends. If you move voluntarily, you will use up the same energy that would otherwise cause you to move involuntarily.

Movement can help you maintain contact with *all* members of your audience. Those closest to you will feel the greatest contact with you whereas the people who are less interested will have a tendency to sit farther away to begin with.

► Ornaments of style are the very eyes of eloquence; but I should not wish eyes to be spread over the whole body.

Quintilian

▶ Gesture, but do not *make* gestures. Let your gestures spring from the impulse common to all expression through action.

James A. Winans

This creates what is known as the "action zone" of audience members sitting in the front and center of the room. Movement enables you to extend this action zone, to include in it people who would otherwise remain uninvolved. Without overdoing it, you should feel free to move toward, away, or from side to side in front of your audience.

Remember: Move with the understanding that it will add to the meaning of the words you use. It is difficult to bang your fist on a podium or to take a step without conveying emphasis. Make the emphasis natural by allowing your message to create your motivation to move.

POSTURE   Generally speaking, good posture means standing with your spine relatively straight, your shoulders relatively squared off, and your feel angled out to keep your body from falling over sideways. In other words, rather than standing at military attention, you should be comfortably erect.

Of course, you shouldn't get *too* comfortable. There are speakers who are effective in spite of the fact that they sprawl on tabletops and slouch against blackboards, but their effectiveness is usually in spite of their posture rather than because of it. Sometimes speakers are so awesome in stature or reputation that they need an informal posture to encourage their audience to relax. In that case, sloppy posture is more or less justified. But because awesomeness is not usually a problem for beginning speakers, good posture should be the rule.

Good posture can help you control nervousness by allowing your breathing apparatus to work properly; when your brain receives enough oxygen, it's easier for you to think clearly and dispel irrational fears. Good posture will also help you get a positive audience reaction because standing up straight makes you more visible. It also increases your audience contact because the audience members will feel that you are interested enough in them to stand formally, yet relaxed enough to be at ease with them.

FACIAL EXPRESSIONS   The expression on your face can be more meaningful to an audience than the words you say. Try it yourself with a mirror. Say, "College is neat," with a smirk, with a warm smile, deadpan, and then with a scowl. It just doesn't mean the same thing. When speaking, keep in mind that your face might be saying something in front of your back. Remember also that it is just about impossible to control facial expressions from the outside. Like your movement, your facial expressions will reflect your involvement with your message. Don't try to fake it. Just get involved in your message, and your face will take care of itself.

EYE CONTACT   Eye contact is perhaps the most important nonverbal facet of delivery. Eye contact not only increases your direct contact with your audience; it also should increase their interest in you by making you more attractive. Eyes are beautiful things; much more beautiful than eyelids, foreheads, or scalps. Furthermore, and contrary to popular opinion, eye contact can be used to help you control your nervousness. Direct eye contact is a form of reality testing. The most frightening aspect of speaking is the unknown. How will the audience react? What will they think? Direct eye contact allows you to test your perception of your audience as you speak. Usually, especially in a college class, you will find that your audience is more "with" you than you think. We found that out ourselves through personal experience; when we first began teaching, we were terrified of the students who would slither down in their chairs, doodle, and generally seem bored. These students upset us so thoroughly that we usually would try *not* to look at them. And that made matters worse. Eventually, by deliberately establishing eye contact with the apparently bored students, we found that they often *were* interested; they just weren't showing that interest because they didn't think anyone was looking. Once these bored-looking students realized that someone was actually looking at them, noticing their existence, they made their attention more obvious by sitting up and looking back at us. The more eye contact they received, the more interested they became. Because of this tendency, eye contact could be viewed as a form of "audience control."

To maintain eye contact, you might try to meet the eyes of each member of your audience squarely at least once during any given presentation. Once you have made definite contact, move on to another audience member. You can learn to do this quickly, so you can visually latch onto every member of a good-sized class in a relatively short time.

The characteristics of appearance, movement, posture, facial expression, and eye contact are visual, nonverbal facets of delivery. Now consider the auditory, nonverbal messages that you might send during a presentation.

Auditory Aspects of Delivery

As you read in Chapter 5, the way you use your voice—your paralanguage—says a great deal about you—most notably about your sincerity and enthusiasm. In addition, using your voice well can help you control your nervousness. It's another cycle: Controlling your vocal characteristics will decrease your nervousness, which will enable you to control your voice even more. But this cycle can also work in the opposite direction. If your voice is out of control, your nerves will probably be in the same state. Controlling your voice is mostly a matter of recognizing and using appropriate *volume, rate, pitch,* and *articulation.*

VOLUME Volume—the loudness of your voice—is determined by the amount of air you push past the vocal folds in your throat. The key to controlling volume, then, is controlling the amount of air you use. The key to determining the *right* volume is audience contact. Your delivery should be loud enough so that your audience can hear everything you say but not so loud that they feel you are talking to someone in the next room. Too much volume is seldom the problem for beginning speakers. Usually, they either are not loud enough or have a tendency to fade off at the end of a thought. Sometimes, when they lose faith in an idea in midsentence, they compromise by mumbling the end of the sentence so that it isn't quite coherent. That's an unfortunate compromise, rather like changing your mind in the middle of a broad jump.

One contemporary speaker who has been criticized for inappropriate volume is Senator Edward M. Kennedy. One researcher recently pointed out that

▶ I walked to the lectern. I hemmed. Then I hawed. I cleared my throat. then I said:

"I shall give an illustrated lecture on the interior of the human mouth—the teeth, the tongue, the upper palate, the lower palate and other points of interest."

Then, to illustrate my lecture, I stuck my finger in my mouth, as if to point out the various things I was talking about, and for five solid minutes I spoke totally unintelligible gibberish, never removing the finger from my mouth and sometimes inserting my entire fist.

Alan Sherman
A Gift of Laughter

"Kennedy tended to shout when an audience was small or uninterested or when he sensed he was losing them. Thus, his volume was often inappropriate to the time and place."[5] *Newsweek's* John Walcott observed, "When he had an unresponsive audience—300 Iowa farmers who were not jumping up on their chairs—he tended to shout more and it became more and more incongruous."[6]

RATE **Rate** is your speed in speaking. There is a range of personal differences in speaking rate. Daniel Webster, for example, is said to have spoken at around 90 words per minute whereas the actor who does the fast-talking Federal Express commercials speaks at about 250. Normal speaking speed, however, is between 120 and 150 words per minute. If you talk much more slowly than that, you may tend to lull your audience to sleep. Faster speaking rates are stereotypically associated with speaker competence,[7] but if you talk too rapidly, you will tend to be unintelligible. Once again, your involvement in your message is the key to achieving an effective rate.

PITCH **Pitch**—the highness or lowness of your voice—is controlled by the frequency at which your vocal folds vibrate as you push air through them. Because taut vocal folds vibrate at a greater frequency, pitch is influenced by muscular tension. This explains why nervous speakers have a tendency occasionally to "squeak" whereas relaxed speakers seem to be more in control. Pitch will tend to follow rate and volume. As you speed up or become louder, your pitch will have a tendency to rise. If your range in pitch is too narrow, your voice will have a singsong quality. If it is too wide, you may sound overly dramatic. You should control your pitch so that your listeners believe you are talking *with* them rather than performing in front of them. Once again, your involvement in your message should take care of this naturally for you.

When considering volume, rate, and pitch, keep *emphasis* in mind. You have to use a variety of vocal characteristics to maintain audience interest, but remember that a change in volume, pitch, or rate will result in emphasis. If you pause or speed up, your rate will suggest emphasis. Words you whisper or scream will be emphasized by their volume. One of our students once provided an example of how volume can be used to emphasize an idea. He was speaking on how possessions like cars communicate things about their owners. "For example," he said, with normal volume, "a Cadillac says, 'I've got money!' But a Rolls-Royce says, *'I'VE GOT MONEY!'* " He blared out those last three words with such force the podium shook.

ARTICULATION   The final auditory nonverbal behavior, articulation, is perhaps the most important. For our purposes here, **articulation** means pronouncing all the parts of all the necessary words and nothing else.

It is not our purpose to condemn regional or ethnic dialects within this discussion. Native New Yorkers can continue to have their "hot dawgs" with their "cawfee," and Southerners can drawl as much as they-all please. You *should* know, however, that a considerable amount of research suggests that regional dialects can cause negative impressions.[8] But it is also true that an honest regional accent can work in your favor. For example, when Paul Volcker was president of the Federal Reserve Bank of New York, he used his accent to his benefit when he began a speech this way:

> Fellow New Yorkers: I am emboldened to use that simple salutation tonight for more than one reason. At the most personal level, I was reminded the other day where my own roots lay. I heard a tape recording of some remarks I had made. After spending three quarters of the past 16 years in Washington, I confess to being startled by what I heard—the full, rounded tones of a home-grown New York accent.[9]

The purpose of this discussion is to suggest *careful,* not standardized, articulation. Incorrect articulation is nothing more than careless articulation. It usually results in (1) leaving off parts of words (deletion), (2) replacing part of a word (substitution), (3) adding parts to words (addition), or (4) overlapping two or more words (slurring).

Deletion   The most common mistake in articulation is **deletion,** or leaving off part of a word. As you are thinking the complete word, it is often difficult to recognize that you are only saying part of it. The most common deletions occur at the end of words, especially *-ing* words. *Going, doing,* and *stopping* become *goin' doin',* and *stoppin'.* Parts of words can be left off in the middle, too, as in *natully* for *naturally* and *reg'lar* for *regular.*

Substitution   **Substitution** takes place when you replace part of a word with an incorrect sound. The ending *-th* is often replaced at the end of a word with a single *t,* as when *with* becomes *wit.* (This tendency is especially prevalent in many parts of the northeastern United States.) The *th-* sound is also a problem at the beginning of words, as *this, that,* and *those* have a tendency to become *dis, dat,* and *dose.*

Addition   The articulation problem of **addition** is caused by adding extra parts to words that are already perfectly adequate, such as *incentative* for *incentive, athalete* instead of *athlete,* and *orientated* instead of *oriented.* Sometimes this type of addition is caused by incorrect word choice, such as when *irregardless* (which is not a word) is used for *regardless.*

Another type of addition is the use of "tag questions," such as "you know?" or "you see?" or "right?" at the end of sentences. To have every other sentence punctuated with one of these barely audible superfluous phrases can be maddening.

Probably the worst type of addition, or at least the most common, is the use of *uh* and *anda* between words. *Anda* is often stuck between two words when

For Better or For Worse®　　　　　　　　　　　　**by Lynn Johnston**

and isn't even needed. If you find yourself doing that, you might want just to pause or swallow instead.

Slurring　　**Slurring** is caused, in effect, by trying to say two or more words at once—or at least overlapping the end of one word with the beginning of the next. Word pairs ending with *of* are the worst offenders in this category. *Sort of* becomes *sorta, kind of* becomes *kinda,* and *because of* becomes *becausa.* Word combinations ending with *to* are often slurred, as when *want to* becomes *wanna.* Sometimes even more than two words are blended together, as when "that is the way" becomes "thatsaway." Careful articulation means using your lips, teeth, tongue, and jaw to bite off your words, cleanly and separately, one at a time.

　　The general rule for articulation in extemporaneous speaking is to be both natural and clear. Be yourself, but be an understandable, intelligent-sounding version of yourself. The best way to achieve this goal is to accept your instructor's evaluation of whether you add, substitute, drop, or slur word sounds. Then you can, as Shakespeare had King Lear suggest, "Mend your speech a little, lest you may mar your fortune."
　　One cause of poor articulation is stage fright, a topic we will now attack in some detail.

▶ SPEAKING WITH CONFIDENCE

▶ I have a slight inferiority complex still. I go into a room and have to talk myself into going up to people . . . If I'm the epitome of a women who is always confident and in control, don't ever believe it of anyone.

Barbara Walters

The terror that strikes into the hearts of so many beginning speakers is called communication apprehension or speech anxiety by communication scholars, but it is more commonly known to those who experience it as stage fright.

Facilitative and Debilitative Stage Fright

Although stage fright is a very real problem for many speakers, it is a problem that can be overcome. Interestingly enough, the first step in feeling less apprehensive about speaking is to realize that a certain amount of nervousness is not only natural but facilitative. That is, **facilitative stage fright** is a factor that can

BAWLAMER, Sept. 20—Following is a brief glossary of "Bawlamerese" compiled as a traveler's guide to the local patois by the Citizens Planning and Housing Association of this city, which outsiders often mispronounce "BALT-i-more" and local residents pronounce "BAWL-uh-mer." The excerpts from the association's list are reproduced with its permission from its handbook. "Bawlamer":

AIG   The thing with a yoke.

ARSH   People from Arlin.

AWL   Goes into the crankcase.

ARN   What you do on an arnin board.

BLOW   Opposite of above.

COLE RACE BEEF   A favorite sandwich.

CALF LICK   Protestant, Jewish and . . .

DRAFF   Animal with the longest neck.

DRUCKSTEWER   Drugstore.

DUDDNEY   Doesn't he.

ELFIN   Animal with a trunk.

ERF   Planet on which we live.

FARN GIN   Used for fighting fars.

FARST FARS   Smokey Bear fights them.

GRANITE   What you don't want to be taken for.

HOSKULL   Where you went before cahwidge.

IGGLE   Our national symbol.

JEET?   Did you eat? Usually answered by "no, jew?"

LOBBLE   Responsible for.

MERLIN   The Free State.

MACELY   Mostly.

MORALITY   The race for mayor.

MEER   What you look at in the morning.

MURIEL   A large painting on a large wall.

NAPLIS   The state capital.

OLTNO   I don't know.

OLL   What you walk down when you get married.

OLLIN   A piece of land surrounded by water.

PO-LEECE   A single police officer.

PLEECE   Two or more po-leece.

PARAMOUR   What your neighbor uses at 8 A.M. Sundays.

PHANE   What you answer when it rings.

QUARR   Sings in Church.

ROSTRUM   Where the ladies go after dinner.

SORE   Drainage area under streets.

TORST   Tourist.

WARSHNIN   Our nation's capital.

WRENCH   Rinse, as in "wrench your hands in the zinc."

WOODER   What you wrench your hands with.

YERP   Europe.

ZOLLAFANE   Xylophone.

help improve your performance. Just as totally relaxed athletes or musicians aren't likely to perform at the top of their potential, speakers think more rapidly and express themselves more energetically when their level of tension is moderate.

It is only when the level of anxiety is intense that it becomes **debilitative,** inhibiting effective self-expression. Intense fear causes trouble in two ways. First, the strong emotion keeps you from thinking clearly. Second, intense fear leads to an urge to do something, anything, to make the problem go away. This urge to escape often causes a speaker to speed up delivery, which results in a rapid, almost machine-gun style. As you can imagine, this boost in speaking rate leads to even more mistakes, which only adds to the speaker's anxiety. Thus, a relatively small amount of nervousness can begin to feed on itself until it grows into a serious problem.

PRESENTING YOUR
MESSAGE

Sources of Debilitative Stage Fright

Before we describe how to manage **debilitative stage fright,** it might be helpful to look at some reasons people are afflicted with the problem.[10]

PREVIOUS EXPERIENCE   One reason people feel apprehensive about speech giving is because of unpleasant past experiences. Most of us are uncomfortable doing *anything* in public, especially if it is a form of performance that puts our talents and abilities "on the line." An unpleasant experience in one type of performance can cause you to expect that a future similar situation will also be unpleasant. These expectations can be realized through the self-fulfilling prophecies discussed in Chapter 2.[11] A traumatic failure at an earlier speech or low self-esteem from critical parents during childhood are common examples of experiences that can cause later stage fright.

You might object to the idea that past experiences cause stage fright. After all, not everyone who has bungled a speech or had critical parents is debilitated in the future. To understand why some people are affected more strongly than others by past experiences, we need to consider another cause of speech anxiety.

IRRATIONAL THINKING   Cognitive psychologists argue that it is not events that cause people to feel nervous but rather the beliefs they have about those events.[12] Certain irrational beliefs leave people feeling unnecessarily apprehensive. Psychologist Albert Ellis lists several such beliefs, or examples of **irrational thinking,** which we will call "fallacies" because of their illogical nature.[13]

1. **Catastrophic Failure.** People who succumb to the **fallacy of catastrophic failure** operate on the assumption that if something bad can happen, it probably will. Their thoughts before and during a speech resemble these:

   "As soon as I stand up to speak, I'll forget everything I wanted to say."

   "Everyone will think my ideas are stupid."

   "Somebody will probably laugh at me."

   Although it is naive to imagine that all your speeches will be totally successful, it is equally wrong to assume they will all fail miserably. One way to escape from the fallacy of catastrophic failure is to take a more realistic look at the situation. Would your audience really hoot you off the stage? Will they really think your ideas are stupid? Even if you did forget your remarks for a moment, would the results be a genuine disaster?

2. **Perfection.** Speakers who succumb to the **fallacy of perfection** expect themselves to behave flawlessly. Whereas such a standard of perfection might serve as a target and a source of inspiration (rather like making a hole-in-one for a golfer), it is totally unrealistic to expect that you will write and deliver a perfect speech—especially as a beginner.

3. **Approval.** The mistaken belief called the **fallacy of approval** is based on the idea that it is vital—not just desirable—to gain the approval of everyone in the audience. It is rare that even the best speakers please everyone,

▶ A man is hurt not so much by what happens as by his opinion of what happens.

Montaigne

▶ I never was what you would call a fancy skater— and while I seldom actually fell, it might have been more impressive if I had. A good resounding fall is no disgrace. It is the fantastic writhing to avoid a fall which destroys any illusion of being a gentleman. How like life that is, after all!

Robert Benchley

especially on topics that are at all controversial. To paraphrase Abraham Lincoln, you can't please all the people all the time...and it is irrational to expect you will.

4. **Overgeneralization.** The **fallacy of overgeneralization** might also be labeled the fallacy of exaggeration, for it occurs when a person blows one poor experience out of proportion. Consider these examples:

"I'm so stupid! I mispronounced that word."

"I completely blew it—I forgot one of my supporting points."

"My hands were shaking. The audience must have thought I was a complete idiot."

A second type of exaggeration occurs when a speaker treats occasional lapses as if they were the rule rather than the exception. This sort of mistake usually involves extreme labels such as "always" and "never."

"I *always* forget what I want to say."

"I can *never* come up with a good topic."

"I can't do *anything* right."

Overcoming Stage Fright

There are four fairly simple ways to overcome debilitative stage fright. The first, as suggested earlier, is to be rational about the beliefs that cause your stage fright. The other three are to be receiver-oriented, positive, and prepared.

1. **Be Rational.** Listen to your thought processes, your internal voice, and try to figure out if the basis for your stage fright is rational. Then dispute any irrational beliefs. Use the list of fallacies given earlier to discover which of your internal statements are based on mistaken thinking.

2. **Be Receiver-oriented.** Concentrate on your audience rather than on yourself. Worry about whether they are interested, about whether they understand, and about whether or not you are maintaining human contact with them.

3. **Be Positive.** It is important to build and maintain a positive attitude toward your audience, your speech, and yourself as a speaker. Some communication consultants suggest that public speakers should concentrate on three statements immediately before speaking. The three statements are:

"I'm glad I'm here."

"I know my topic."

"I care about you" ("you," of course, being the audience).

Keeping these ideas in mind is supposed to help you maintain a positive attitude.

Another technique for building a positive attitude is known as **imaging** or **visualization.** This technique has been used successfully with athletes. It requires you to visualize the successful completion of a specific speech

▶ I believe that courage is all too often mistakenly seen as the absence of fear. If you descend by rope from a cliff and are not fearful to some degree, you are either crazy or unaware. Courage is seeing your fear in a realistic perspective, defining it, considering the alternatives and choosing to function in spite of the risk.

Leonard Zunin
Contact: The First Four Minutes

> ▶ In speaking to the Winnipeg Rotary Club, I arrived a little early for the meeting and was greeted by an attractive lady who asked, "What are you doing here?"
>
> She looked a little familiar. I thought perhaps I had met her at a convention two years earlier. "I'm here to give a speech to the Rotary Club," I replied.
>
> "Do you do this often?" she asked.
>
> "Quite often," I said.
>
> "Are you nervous before you talk?" she demanded.
>
> "I don't think so," I replied.
>
> She retorted, "Then what are you doing in the ladies' washroom?"

Ross Smyth

---

assignment.[14] Visualization can help the "self-fulfilling prophecy" mentioned earlier work in your favor.

4. **Be Prepared.** If you are fully prepared, your speech will represent less of a threat. Devote enough time to each step of message preparation so that you can feel secure. Devote an extra amount of time and effort to the introduction so that you can "break the ice" and develop audience rapport early. Be sure to leave enough time to *practice* your presentation thoroughly. As a guide, you might consult the checklist for delivery presented in Table 13–1. And when it comes time to give your presentation, keep in mind that ner-

TABLE 13–1 Checklist for Delivery

——Choose Best Style of Delivery
    ——extemporaneous
    ——impromptu
    ——manuscript
    ——memorized
——Practice the Speech
    ——alone
    ——tape-recorded
    ——in front of a mirror
    ——in front of a small group of friends
    ——in the room where the final speech will take place
——Analyze Effectiveness of Delivery
    ——visual aspects
        ——appearance
        ——movement
        ——posture
        ——facial expressions
        ——eye contact
    ——auditory aspects
        ——volume
        ——rate
        ——pitch
        ——articulation

vousness is normal. Expect it, and remember that its symptoms—even shaky knees and trembling hands—are more obvious to you than they are to the audience. Beginning public speakers, when congratulated for their poise during a speech, are apt to make such remarks as "Are you kidding? I was *dying* up there."

Remember also some of the tips mentioned earlier: Stand with good posture so that you can breathe well. In fact, it usually helps to take one or two deep breaths before you begin. And use one or two effective visual aids; they give you something to do with your hands, and they distract attention away from yourself.

These four guidelines will enable most speakers to control their stage fright to the point where it will be facilitative rather than debilitative. Speakers who find these methods inadequate have two other options: They might enlist the help of a professional counselor (these services are often provided free by colleges), or they could research a more extensive procedure for themselves, such as systematic desensitization. Ron Adler's book *Confidence in Communication: A Guide to Assertive and Social Skills*[15] outlines several procedures for managing communication anxiety.

OFFERING CONSTRUCTIVE CRITICISM ◄

As we hinted earlier, one of the most important examples of impromptu speaking is your criticism of a classmate's speech. It is important to make this criticism constructive, which means that it will be designed to help the speaker improve. To be constructive, your criticism has to be *substantive*.

1. **Be Complete.** The first element of substantive criticism is to criticize *what* was said as well as *how* it was said; in other words, to not concentrate on delivery traits to the point where you lose track of the speaker's ideas.[16]
2. **Be Specific.** The second aspect of substance is to be specific: Rather than just saying, "I liked this" or "I didn't like that," you should provide a detailed explanation of your reasons for liking or disliking parts of the speech.
3. **Be Positive.** Perhaps the most important guideline in offering criticism, however, is to point out what is *right* with the speech as well as what is *wrong* with it. Otherwise, you run the risk of extinguishing the *positive* aspects of the speaker's behavior. In fact, negative criticism unaccompanied by positive criticism is often useless because the speaker might become defensive and block out your criticism completely. It is a good idea, therefore, to offer your positive criticism first and then tactfully offer your suggestions for improvement. For example, rather than saying, "Your ideas about the psychological aspects of diabetes were completely unclear and unsupported," you might say, "I found your explanation of the physical aspects of diabetes to be clearly stated and well backed up with details and examples. However, your explanation of the psychological aspects of the disease left me a little confused. It might be my own fault, but it just did not seem to be as well supported as the rest of your speech."

"Must you use those three-by-five cards every time we have a discussion?"

To encourage this type of criticism, many instructors have their students use a speech evaluation form like the ones in Chapters 14 and 15 (pp. 366 and 396). Notice especially the first two open-ended questions on these forms: "What did you especially like?" comes before "In your opinion, how could the speech be improved?"

Your instructor might prefer a different evaluation form, or you might want to amend the one in Chapter 14 or 15 to your own liking. Whatever type of form you choose, make sure it allows for substantive, positive criticism.

▶ SUMMARY

There are four types of delivery: extemporaneous, impromptu, manuscript, and memorized. In each type, the speaker must be concerned with both visual and auditory aspects of the presentation. Visual aspects include appearance, movement, posture, facial expressions, and eye contact. Auditory aspects include volume, rate, pitch, and articulation. The four most common articulation problems are deletion, substitution, addition, and slurring of word sounds.

One of the most serious delivery problems is debilitative (as opposed to facilitative) stage fright. Sources of debilitative stage fright include irrational thinking, which might include a belief in one or more of the following fallacies: the fallacy of perfection (a good speaker never does anything wrong), the fallacy of absolute approval (*everyone* has to like you), the fallacy of overgeneralization (you *always* mess up speeches), the fallacy of helplessness (there's nothing you can do about it), and the fallacy of catastrophic failure (all is lost if this speech bombs).

There are several methods of overcoming speech anxiety. The first is to refute the irrational fallacies just listed. The others include being receiver-oriented, positive, and prepared.

Effective delivery is aided through the constructive criticism of speeches presented in class. Your criticism should be substantive, which means that it should address what was said as well as how it was said, it should be specific, and it should include positive as well as negative aspects of the speaker's behavior.

ACTIVITIES ◄

1. You can analyze speech delivery problems either by examining yourself or other speakers. Try one of the following:
   a. Make a list of your own problems in speech delivery. See if you can either (1) add to that list or (2) list some possible solutions to your problems from what you read in this chapter.
   b. Name two good and two bad speakers you have heard. Identify the good and bad features of each style, and suggest an alternative style, if appropriate.
2. For practice in analyzing visual aspects of delivery, pick a favorite celebrity (comedian, actor, newscaster, or talk-show host) whose delivery you find effective. What are the visual aspects of his or her delivery that help make it effective?
3. This chapter suggested that you practice your speech by talking into a tape recorder. You might also try recording the following classic articulation exercises:
   a. Nonsense syllables: Run through all the consonants of the alphabet, pronouncing them with the five vowels: *Ba, be, bi, bo, bu* (pronounced bay, be, buy, beau, boo); *ca, ce, ci, co, cu; da, de, di, do, du,* and so on. As you do so, try to overarticulate; that is, move the tongue, jaw, and lips in an exaggerated manner. (There will be some duplication of consonant sounds with *c/s, x/z, or k/q.* However, all others—such as *f/v*—should be distinctly different.)
   b. Tongue twisters: Repeat the following several times as quickly as possible:

      "She sells seashells on the seashore."

      "Rubber baby buggy bumpers."

      "Saw some sleek, slim, slender saplings."

      You probably know more of these, or you can make them up. Feel free to do so.
   c. Poetry: Recite the following clearly and dramatically:

      To sit in solemn silence in a dull, dark dock
      In a pestilential prison, with a lifelong lock,
      Awaiting the sensation of a short, sharp shock,
      From a cheap and chippy chopper on a big black block!
      (Gilbert and Sullivan)

PRESENTING YOUR MESSAGE

349

d. Prose selection: Read the following in the grand style its author obviously intended:

> Shakespeare was an intellectual ocean whose waves touched all the shores of thought; within which were all the tides and waves of destiny and will; over which swept all the storms of fate, ambition, and revenge; upon which fell the gloom and darkness of despair and death, and all the sunlight of content and love, and within which was the inverted sky lit with the eternal stars—an intellectual ocean—toward which all rivers ran, and from which now the isles and continents of thought receive their dew and rain.
> (Robert G. Ingersoll, Lecture on Shakespeare, 1894)

e. Get an idea of how you sound in normal conversation by leaving a tape recorder running in everyday situations: at the dinner table, while you're using the telephone, when studying with friends, and so on. The results can be surprising!

4. For practice in recognizing the symptoms of stage fright, identify a speech you either gave or witnessed someone else give. This speech might be something as ordinary as a classroom response or as eventful as a presidential debate. In your opinion, what was the effect of stage fright in this speech? Was it facilitative or debilitative?

5. To become better at understanding how your thoughts shape your feelings about speechmaking, think about the following situations, and list two opposite ways you could interpret each situation. Take note of the feelings that would follow from each interpretation.
   a. While researching your topic you find it difficult to find material.
   b. While organizing your ideas, you come to one that all the experts agree on but that you're not too sure about.
   c. When you get up to give your speech, someone giggles.
   d. In the middle of an important point you're making, one audience member yawns emphatically.
   e. Toward the end of your presentation, you notice an attractive person staring at you and smiling.

6. To analyze your own reaction to stage fright, think back to your last public speech, and rate yourself on how "rational, receiver-oriented, positive, and prepared" you were. How did these attributes affect your anxiety level?

▶ NOTES

1. Alan H. Monroe and Douglas Ehninger, *Principles and Types of Speech Communication,* 7th ed. (Glenview, Ill.: Scott, Foresman, 1974), p. 142.
2. For a synthesis of findings on these differences, see F. Niyi Akinnaso, "On the Differences Between Spoken and Written Language," *Language and Speech* 25 (March–June 1982): 97–125.
3. Jerry Tarver, "Can't Nobody Here Use This Language? Function and Quality in Choosing Words," *Vital Speeches of the Day* (May 1, 1979): 420–423.
4. These studies are reviewed in Lawrence R. Rosenfeld and Jean M. Civikly, *With Words Unspoken* (New York: Holt, Rinehart and Winston, 1976), p. 62. Also see Shelly Chaiken, "Communicator Physical Attractiveness and Persuasion," *Journal of Personality and Social Psychology* 37 (1979): 1387–1397.
5. L. Patric Devlin, "An Analysis of Kennedy's Communication in the 1980 Campaign," *Quarterly Journal of Speech* 68 (November 1982): 397–417.

6. Ibid.

7. A study demonstrating this stereotype is Richard L. Street, Jr., and Robert M. Brady, "Speech Rate Acceptance Ranges as a Function of Evaluative Domain, Listener Speech Rate, and Communication Context," *Speech Monographs* 49 (December 1982): 290–308.

8. See, for example, Anthony Mulac and Mary Jo Rudd, "Effects of Selected American Regional Dialects upon Regional Audience Members," *Communication Monographs* 44 (1977): 184–195. Some research, however, suggests that nonstandard dialects do not have the detrimental effects on listeners that were once believed. See, for example, Fern L. Johnson and Richard Buttny, "White Listener's Responses to 'Sounding Black' and 'Sounding White': The Effects of Message Content on Judgments about Language," *Communication Monographs* 49 (March 1982): 33–39.

9. Paul A. Volcker, "The Dilemmas of Monetary Policy," *Vital Speeches of the Day* 42 (January 15, 1976).

10. A substantial body of research literature on communication apprehension and anxiety has accumulated. See James C. McCroskey, "Oral Communication Apprehension: A Summary of Recent Theory and Research," *Human Communication Research* 4 (1977): 78–96. Or see James C. McCroskey, "Oral Communication Apprehension: A Reconceptalization," in Michael Burgoon (ed.), *Communication Yearbook 6* (Beverly Hills, Calif.: Sage, 1982), pp. 136–170.

11. Expectations are a significant predictor of communication apprehension. See, for example, John O. Greene and Glenn G. Sparks, "The Role of Outcome Expectations in the Experience of a State of Communication Apprehension," *Communication Quarterly* 31 (Summer 1983): 212–219.

12. See John O. Greene and Glenn G. Sparks, "Explication and Test of a Cognitive Model of Communication Apprehension: A New Look at an Old Construct," *Human Communication Research* 9 (Summer 1983): 349–366. See also Ralph R. Behnke and Michael J. Beatty, "A Cognitive-Physiological Model of Speech Anxiety," *Communication Monographs* 48 (June 1981): pp. 158–163.

13. Adapted from Albert Ellis, *A New Guide to Rational Living* (North Hollywood, Calif.: Wilshire Books, 1977).

14. Joe Ayres and Theodore S. Hop, "Visualization: A Means of Reducing Speech Anxiety," *Communication Education* 34:4 (October 1985): 318–323.

15. Ronald B. Adler, *Confidence in Communication: A Guide to Assertive and Social Skills* (New York: Holt, Rinehart and Winston, 1977).

16. We will not, at this point, get into the age-old argument of the relative importance of substance (what you say) and style (how you say it). Suffice it to say that this question is as old as the study of public speaking. See, for example, Barbara Warnick, "The Quarrel Between the Ancients and the Moderns," *Communication Monographs* 49 (December 1982): 263–276. One recent study pointed out that media commentators viewed substance as *less* important than delivery, appearance, and manner in the 1980 presidential debates. See Goodwin F. Berquist and James L. Goldin, "Media Rhetoric, Criticism, and the Public Perception of the 1980 Presidential Debates," *Quarterly Journal of Speech* 67 (May 1981): 125–137.

▶CHAPTER 14

KEY TERMS

audience involvement
audience participation
general needs
information hunger
informative purpose
   statement
signpost
specific needs

INFORMATIVE SPEAKING

After reading this chapter, you should understand the following:

1. The importance of having a specific informative purpose.

2. The importance of creating information hunger.

3. The importance of using clear language.

4. The importance of generating audience involvement.

You should be able to do the following:

1. Formulate an effective informative purpose statement.

2. Create "information hunger" by stressing the relevance of your material to your listeners' needs.

3. Emphasize important points in your speech.

4. Generate audience involvement.

Informative speaking is especially important in the dawning "age of information," in which transmitting knowledge will account for most of the work we do and, in a large part, for the quality of our lives. Although much of the information of the future will be transmitted by machines—computers and electronic media—the spoken word will continue to be the best way to reach small audiences with messages tailored specifically for them. At least some of these messages will be designed to help people make sense of the glut of information that surrounds them.

Informative speaking seeks to increase the knowledge and understanding of an audience. This type of speaking goes on all around you: in your professors' lectures, in news reports on radio and TV, in a mechanic's explanation of how to keep your car from breaking down. All demonstrations and explanations are forms of informative speaking. You engage in this type of speaking often whether you realize it or not. Sometimes it is formal as when you are giving a report in class. At other times, it is more casual, as when you are telling a friend how to prepare your favorite dish. It is often this everyday, informal type of informative speaking that we find most frustrating. One of the objectives of this chapter is to give you the skills that can help relieve that frustration. Another objective is to apply some general principles from earlier chapters to the specific task of informative speaking.

▶ TECHNIQUES OF INFORMATIVE SPEAKING

Define a Specific Informative Purpose

As Chapter 12 explained, any speech must be based on a purpose statement that is audience-oriented, precise, and attainable. When you are preparing an informative speech, it is especially important to define in advance, for yourself, a clear informative purpose. An **informative purpose statement** will generally be worded to stress audience knowledge or ability or both:

> After listening to my speech, the audience will be able to name three types of witchcraft practiced today.

> After listening to my speech, the audience will be able to list the three main causes of World War II.

> After listening to my speech, the audience will be able to recall the four major components of an internal combustion engine.

Notice that in each of these purpose statements a specific verb such as *to name, to list,* or *to recall* points out the kind of thing the audience will be able to do after hearing the speech. Other key verbs for informative purpose statements include these:

analyze	contrast	explain	recognize
apply	describe	identify	summarize
compare	discuss	integrate	support

Setting a clear informative purpose will help keep you focused as you prepare and present your speech. Now that you have a purpose in speaking, you must give your audience a purpose in listening:

Create "Information Hunger"

In informative speaking, you must create **information hunger:** a reason for your audience to want to listen to and learn from your speech. The most effective way to do that is to respond in some way to their needs—either general needs that all human beings feel or specific needs that are unique to your audience.

GENERAL NEEDS To relate your speech to **general needs,** you can use Maslow's analysis, discussed in Chapter 1, as a guide. You could tap *physical needs* by relating your topic to your audience's survival or to the improvement of their living conditions. If you gave a speech on food (eating it, cooking it, or shopping for it), you would probably be dealing with that basic need. If you gave a speech on water pollution, you could relate it to physical needs by listing the pollutants in one of your local lakes and explaining what each one could do to a human body. In the same way, you could meet *safety needs* by relating your topic to your audience's security; you could touch on *esteem needs* by showing your audience how to be respected—or simply by showing them that *you* respect them. You can appeal to *self-actualization needs,* those based on the need to accomplish as much as possible with our lives, by showing your audience some way to improve themselves.

One speaker tapped a variety of audience needs in his speech "Waking Up the Right Lobe":

> My text is drawn from an exciting book by Julian Jaynes, called *The Origin of Consciousness in the Breakdown of the Bicameral Mind.* You must read it or else you will not be aware of some of the most exciting stuff that's going on in the scientific and academic search for how we came to be, who we are now, and what we are becoming.

> We don't have to generalize about these discoveries or speak in the abstract. You can apply these ideas right now, right here.

> The ultimate goal is to be fully alive—to your family, your work, and to yourself—to use your full brain! You will never possess anything in your life that is more valuable to you or will give you more thrills and excitement and pleasure than your mind![1]

This speaker is creating information hunger mostly by touching on self-actualization needs, but he also taps all the other needs Maslow outlined. Being "fully alive" is a physiological need, "family" is a social need, and the world of "work" involves both security and esteem needs.

SPECIFIC NEEDS Maslow's analysis of needs should be kept in mind for all audiences, for all human beings share them. Yet the closer you can come to the **specific needs** of your audience, the more information hunger you will generate. For example, sleeping problems are universal. Everyone has a physiological need for sleep, but you could adapt this problem for a particular audience:

▶ Because information can change society, and because the amount of information doubles every fifteen years, our culture, if it is to become enriched and improved by its information, needs speakers to digest and assimilate this information and present it with clarity.

Otis Walter
Speaking to Inform and Persuade

Tonight, 50 million American adults will crawl into bed, draw up the covers, lay their heads down on their pillows, and then, try as they might, they will not be able to find restful sleep. You may very well be one of them. In fact, many college students suffer from sleep disorders that are particularly harmful to their academic and social success. And the chances are very good that the disorder will hit the night before a big test, just when you need your sleep more than ever. In just one month, we will all be involved in final exams. How many of us will get lower grades than we might have, simply because we couldn't get to sleep the night before?

Emphasize Important Points

Along with defining a specific informative purpose and creating information hunger, you should stress the important points in your speech through *repetition* and "*signposts.*"

REPETITION   Chapter 12 discusses ways that you can emphasize material through clear organization: limiting your speech to three to five main points; dividing, coordinating, and ordering those main points; using a strong introduction that previews your ideas; using a conclusion that reviews them and makes them memorable; and using lots of transitions, internal summaries, and internal previews. Strong organization, in effect, provides your listeners with a repetition of important points, and that repetition will help them understand and remember those points.

You can also be repetitive stylistically by saying the same thing in more than one way, by restating an important idea:

> It is a known fact that jogging is good for your heart; medical research is unequivocal in supporting the fact that jogging builds up heart muscle by increasing the flow of blood that nourishes the muscular tissue of the heart itself.

This is the type of repetition that one speaker used when she wanted to emphasize, without *sounding* redundant, the number of people killed by drunk drivers:

> Each year in the U.S., about 25,000 people are killed in alcohol-related crashes. In the past 10 years more than 250,000 have been killed nationwide and millions have been injured—many crippled or impaired for life.[2]

Twenty-five thousand a year is the same as 250,000 every ten years, but, stated in this way, the point does not sound redundant. Notice also that this speaker adds new information to her repetition of this important point. This expansion is another technique for making the second statement of a point "fresh."

Redundancy is no fault when you are using it to emphasize important points; it is only a fault when (1) you are redundant with obvious, trivial, or boring points; or (2) you run an important point into the ground. There is no sure rule for making certain you have not overemphasized a point. You just have to use your own best judgment to make sure that you have stated the point enough that your audience "gets" it without repeating it so often that they want to give it back.

SIGNPOSTS Another way to emphasize important material is by using "**signposts**": words or phrases that emphasize the importance of what you are about to say. You can state, simply enough, "What I'm about to say is important"; or you can use some variation of that statement: "But listen to this...," or "The most important thing to remember is...," or "The three keys to this situation are...," and so on.

Use Clear Informative Organization and Structure

The following principles of organization from Chapter 12 become especially important in the *introduction* of an informative speech:

1. Establish the importance of your topic to your audience.
2. Preview the thesis, the one central idea you want your audience to remember.
3. If possible, preview your main points.

This is the way Kim Perry, a student at the University of Northern Iowa, organized the introduction of her speech on "Effortless Exercise":

> It matters not whether one is young or old, male or female, black or white. The victim is obsessed with single-minded purpose and will do almost anything to reach his [or her] goal. I know, I've suffered from this affliction, and I'm sure that you have or know of someone who has, also.
>
> I'm talking about the new American obsession—becoming "fit and trim." Yes, it's great that we're more aware of the importance of exercise and fitness, but, unfortunately, we're also seeking lazy alternatives for our overweight and out-of-shape bodies.

Passive exercise is one of the fastest-growing gimmicks offering quick fixes to our body bulges. The main promotion involving passive exercise is EMS, electrical muscle stimulators.... I'd like to explain what EMS is, the potential dangers associated with it, why little is currently being done, and what measures should be taken to forestall further problems.[3]

In the *body* of an informative speech, the following organizational principles take on special importance:

1. Use only three to five main points.
2. Limit your division of main points to three to five subpoints.
3. Use transitions, internal summaries, and internal previews.
4. Order your points in the way that they will be most easy to understand and remember.

Kim Perry followed these rules to organize the body of her speech on "Effortless Exercise" (see Figure 14–1).

Organizational principles are also important in the *conclusion* of an informative speech:

1. Review your main points.
2. Remind your audience of the importance of your topic to them.
3. Provide your audience with a memory aid.

For example, here is the way Kim Perry concluded her speech on "Effortless Exercise":

I hope you now have a clearer understanding of what EMS is, its definitive hazards, and steps which the FDA, the state legislators, and we can take to stop such hazards from arising. Most of you know the only way you can fit back into your size 9 dress or your favorite blue jeans is by proper diet and exercise. Yet it's clear that the problems we've seen to date are merely "early warning signals" and will multiply with the growth in use of EMS. So if you're tempted to be an armchair jogger, maybe it's time to get out of your chair and into your jogging suit, or even your swimsuit. Who knows, you may find it "stimulating!"[4]

Use Supporting Material Effectively

The fifth technique for effective informative speaking has to do with the supporting material discussed in Chapter 12. Three of the purposes of support (to clarify, to make interesting, and to make memorable) are essential to informative speaking. Therefore, you should be careful to support your thesis in every way possible.

Use *examples,* lots of them. Often, if you cannot think of an example to support your idea, then there is something wrong with the idea. It might be a little misstated or undeveloped. Either way it is going to be confusing to your audience. Susan Martinez, a student at Bethany College in West Virginia, used examples to good effect when she began her speech on the importance of learning a foreign language with three of them:

FIGURE 14–1
Body of Informative Speech

A. Electrical Muscle Stimulators (EMS) are devices that contract muscles involuntarily by delivering an electrical current through electrodes attached to the skin.

 1. They can be used as physical therapy under proper medical supervision.

 2. Individuals are turning to EMS to replace exercise.

 Internal preview   So what are the complications associated with EMS? At least three can be identified: no significant muscle improvement, no cardiovascular benefits, and health hazards caused by improper use.

B. Electrical Muscle Stimulators are potentially dangerous.

 1. The "muscle toning effects" from EMS devices are basically worthless.

 Transition   Not only does EMS fail to strengthen muscles; it may also indirectly contribute to reduced cardiovascular fitness.

 2. People are being lulled into a false sense of fitness, which could stop them from performing the muscle-strengthening types of exercise required in a balanced exercise routine.

 Internal Summary and Preview   And aside from the fact that EMS does not really improve muscle strength or promote cardiovascular fitness, many hazards are associated with its misuse.

 3. Improper use results in electrical shocks and burns.

 Transition   So in consideration of the intended uses and actual abuses of EMS, why isn't something being done to stop these multimillion-dollar industries from flourishing at the expense of our pocketbooks and our health?

C. Why isn't more being done to control EMS?

 1. The Food and Drug Administration (FDA) has limited authority.
  a. FDA has the authority to seize but not to ban.
  b. FDA funding is limited.
  c. FDA authority is fraught with legal loopholes.
 2. Uninformed consumers are lulled into accepting EMS devices.
  a. Advertisements offer "money-back guarantees."
  b. Consumers avoid expensive lawsuits.
  c. Some consumers see an improvement because of a "placebo effect."

 Internal Summary and Preview   Tens of thousands of untrained consumers are continually buying EMS devices. How can we stop this growing epidemic?

D. Measures should be taken to control EMS.
 1. Sales to the general public should be forbidden.
 2. Operation should be restricted to licensed practitioners.

—When General Motors advertised its "Body by Fisher" car in Belgium, the slogan was described in Flemish as "corpse by Fisher."

—In Spanish-speaking countries, car buyers avoided the Chevrolet Nova because "No va" in Spanish means "It doesn't go."

—And at the 1981 economic summit meeting held in Canada, President Reagan had to ask Canadian Prime Minister Pierre Trudeau for a translation when world leaders began chatting informally in French.[5]

Provide *detailed descriptions* to increase audience involvement in the information you are presenting. Here is the description Vic Vieth, a student at Winona State University in Minnesota, used to begin his speech on "Prisoners of Conscience":

> Tenzin Chodrak lived on nine ounces of grain a day as he was forced to work a rock-hard soil beneath a beating sun. In time, his hair fell out and his eyebrows fell off. Tortured by his hunger he ate rats and worms and, eventually, his leather jacket. Hector Martinez was blindfolded and then beaten. His head was repeatedly submerged in buckets of vomit and urine. His head was then placed inside a suffocating plastic bag and banged against a wall. Ashraf Mahmoudi, four months pregnant at the time, was seized on a street corner and then beaten with the rifle butts of her captors. She awoke in a prison cell bleeding from her abdomen. Yet her cries for assistance went mocked, and she lost her baby....[6]

Define your key terms if there is any chance that the audience might be confused by them. Here is the way Vic Vieth defined his key term in "Prisoners of Conscience":

> Prisoners of conscience, according to *Newsweek*, are simply those who have been jailed for their beliefs, those whose convictions often directly challenge their governments. Prisoners of conscience do not advocate violence, and they have no hope of overthrowing their governments. Yet oftentimes they do speak out against tyranny.[7]

Use *analogies* to enable your audience to view your information from a different perspective. One student's speech on the false testing of medicines was built around the analogy of poison:

> The falsifying of tests in laboratories does exist, and the harm that can and does come of it has turned it into a deadly poison. There are antidotes, but they're useless unless they're injected into the system....[8]

Use *quantification and statistics* to make your information more authoritative and accurate. One student used quantification and statistics when explaining the dangers of boxing:

> Since 1945, 339 professional fighters have died in the ring, 53 of those deaths since 1970.... This figure includes only professional fighters, so you must include injury and death among the estimated 10,000 10- to 15-year-old amateurs, the estimated 12,500 golden-glove boxers, and innumerable contestants in "tough-man" contests.[9]

Use *anecdotes* to make your information more interesting and memorable. Here is how one student used an anecdote in her speech about the importance of speech education in public schools:

As I was working my way through the public school system, I, like my peers, believed that I was receiving a fine education. I could read and write, and add and sub-tract—yes, all of the essentials were there. At least that's what I thought. And then, the boom lowered: "Attention class—your next assignment is to present an oral report of your paper in front of the class next week." My heart stopped. Panic began to rise up inside. Me? In front of thirty other fourth-graders giving a speech? For the next five days I lived in dreaded anticipation of the forthcoming event. When the day finally arrived, I stayed home. It seemed at the time to be the perfect solution to a very scary and very real problem. Up to that time, I had never been asked to say a word in front of anyone, and, more importantly, had never been taught anything about verbal communication skills.[10]

Any time you can make your ideas visual in an informative speech, do so. Sometimes one *visual aid* displays all your main points and therefore, keeps your audience constantly attuned to your topic. See Chapter 12 for reminders on how to use visuals.

Demonstrations can be particularly effective in creating impact and understanding. One physics major wanted to give a speech with the following purpose:

After listening to my speech, my audience will understand the total independence of contiguous motions that are directed along mutually perpendicular axes.

When he gave his speech, the class did not know what he was talking about; so he tried clarifying his purpose somewhat and including a demonstration. (See Figure 14–2.) This time, his purpose was the following:

After listening to my speech, my audience will understand that to predict trajectory, you have to take two different perpendicular motions into consideration.

Believe it or not, his speech fulfilled his purpose because it included the fol-lowing demonstration:

Apparatus:
toy crossbow, teddy bear

Procedure:
1. Hang teddy from coatrack.
2. Secure crossbow, and aim directly at teddy.
3. Explain that both y motion and x motion must be taken into consideration to shoot teddy out of tree (place diagram on board).
4. With help of volunteer, release arrow and teddy simultaneously.
5. Because of the interaction of x motion and y motion, arrow will drop at the same rate as teddy, and you will score a bull's-eye every time!

DIAGRAM

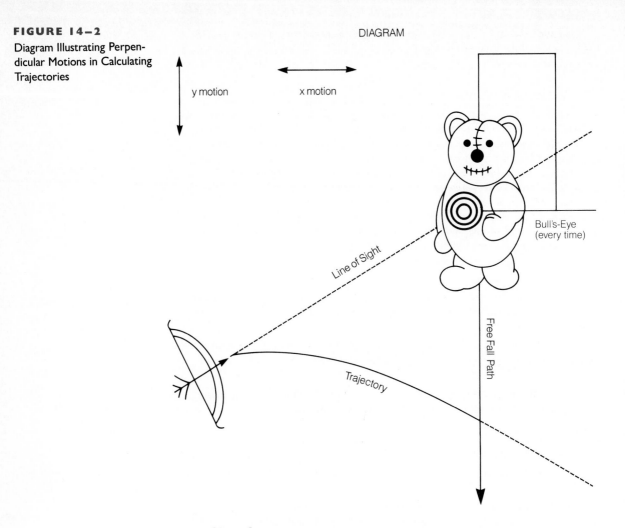

y motion

x motion

Line of Sight

Bull's-Eye
(every time)

Free Fall Path

Trajectory

Use Clear Language

Another technique for effective informative speaking is to use clear language—
which means using precise, vivid, simple wording and providing definitions for
obscure but necessary terms.

PRECISE VOCABULARY   When planning an informative speech, you have to be
a wordsmith, an artisan just like a silversmith or a watchsmith, only with words
as your raw materials and dictionaries (or even a thesaurus, which is really just a
dictionary of synonyms) as your tools. You should use these tools to find the
most precise word to say what you want to say. If you have any doubt about the
clarity of something you are saying, then you should devise several different
ways of saying it and choose the best way. Most of the memorable phrases that
are so familiar to us now started off in some different form and were then
refined by the speaker. Consider the following expressions and see if they ring a
bell:

"Friends, Romans, Countrymen: May I have your attention, please?"

"Eighty-seven years ago, our fathers brought forth on this continent..."

"Don't fire until they get right up next to you."

"Old soldiers don't die; they just leave."

"Why, I'd sooner die than not have liberty."

"You should ask what services you can perform for your country rather than asking what it can do for you."

Notice the way Porter Crow used precise language to explain the difference between the perceptions produced in the two lobes of the brain:

> What, then, are the differences in these perceptions, Right and Left? Now, please note, the following generalizations are reversed if you are left-handed! Isn't that rich?
>
> To begin, then: The Left Lobe is often viewed as more masculine. It's more logical, sequential, and orderly. It is most interested in problem-solving and that which is pragmatic—the "business" mind.
>
> Now, on the other hand—rather, on the other side—the Right Lobe is often perceived as more feminine. It's more inclined toward the whole picture, the spatial, the artistic, the musical. It's more intuitive and humanistic—the "home" mind.[11]

VIVID LANGUAGE   You should make your language "come alive" through devices such as action-oriented vocabulary and varied sentence structure. Crow continued his description of the two lobes of the brain vividly:

> But! And this is where it all starts to get really exciting! More and more, we are recognizing these differences are not a matter of sex identification but a matter of training and culture. You all can use both sides of your brain more effectively and more creatively. Whichever lobe you are inclined to use, the other can be turned on! Never forget that! You have a whole brain, a whole mind! We are inclined to use only part of our greatest piece of equipment. It's like having a computer with two drives and using only one.[12]

Of course, the last part of that description is an analogy, giving us another example of how these principles combine in practice.

SIMPLE VOCABULARY   Using the right word, the most precise word, seldom means using a word that is difficult to find. In fact, just the opposite is true. Important ideas do not have to sound complicated. Consider the following passage:

> Objective considerations of contemporary phenomena compel the conclusion that success or failure in competitive activities exhibits no tendency to be commensurate with innate capacity, but that a considerable element of the unpredictable must invariably be taken into account.[13]

That is George Orwell's satirical idea of how a biblical passage would be written in twentieth-century jargon. The original verse, from the King James translation of Ecclesiastes, reads:

The race is not to the swift, nor the battle to the strong, neither yet bread to the wise, nor yet riches to men of understanding, nor yet favor to men of skill; but time and chance happeneth to them all.

DEFINE OBSCURE BUT NECESSARY TERMS It is a good idea to define key terms that you use; it is also a good idea to define any words that might be obscure or misunderstood in the context in which they are used. This is especially necessary if the word you're using qualifies as jargon, which is a word of a specialized nature that is used, and therefore understood, only by specific groups of people. Educators, for example, talk of "empirically validated learning" and "multimode curricula" and rather than saying that a child can do better, they say that "academic achievement is not commensurate with abilities." Doctors and military strategists are famous for their use of jargon also. A heart attack is a "coronary thrombosis" or a "cardiovascular accident" for doctors whereas air raids are "routine limited duration protective reactions" for military folks. Business people, religious groups, sports enthusiasts, lawyers, and many other groups have semiprivate vocabularies that are clearly understood only by those who use them regularly. When speaking to an outsider, jargon should probably be avoided; if it turns out to be absolutely necessary, it should be defined.

Generate Audience Involvement

The final technique for effective informative speaking is to get your audience involved in your speech. Educational psychologists have long known that the best way to *teach* people something is to have them *do* it; social psychologists have added to this rule by proving, in many studies, that involvement in a message increases audience comprehension of, and agreement with, that message.

There are many ways to encourage **audience involvement** in your speech. One way is by following the rules for good delivery by maintaining enthusiasm, energy, eye contact, and so on. Other techniques include audience participation, the use of volunteers, and a question-and-answer period.

AUDIENCE PARTICIPATION One way to increase audience involvement is to have the audience members actually *do* something during your speech, that is, bring about **audience participation.** For example, if you were giving a demonstration on isometric exercises (which don't require too much room for movement), you could have the entire audience stand up and do one or two sample exercises. (Exercise not only involves them psychologically; it also keeps them more alert physically by increasing the flow of blood and adrenalin in their systems.) If you were explaining how to fill out a federal income-tax long form, you could give each class member a sample form to fill out as you explain it. Outlines and checklists could be used in a similar manner for just about *any* speech.

VOLUNTEERS If the action you are demonstrating is too expensive or intricate to allow all the class members to take part in it, you can select one or two volunteers from the audience to help you out. You will increase the psychological involvement of all the members, because they will tend to identify with the volunteers.

QUESTION-AND-ANSWER PERIOD   One way to increase audience involvement that is nearly *always* appropriate if time allows is to answer questions at the end of your speech. You should encourage your audience to ask questions. Solicit questions and be patient waiting for the first one. Often no one wants to ask the first question. When the questions do start coming, the following suggestions might increase your effectiveness in answering them:

1. **Listen to the Substance of the Question.** Don't zero in on irrelevant details; listen for the big picture—the basic, overall question that is being asked. If you're not really sure *what* the substance of a question is, ask the questioner to paraphrase it. Don't be afraid to let the questioners do their share of the work.
2. **Paraphrase Confusing Questions.** Use the active listening skills described in Chapter 4. You can paraphrase the question in just a few words: "If I understand your question, you are asking _____. Is that right?"
3. **Avoid Defensive Reactions to Questions.** Even if the questioner seems to be calling you a liar or stupid or biased, try to listen to the substance of the question and not to the possible personality attack.

CATHY, by Cathy Guisewite. Copyright,1986, Universal Press Syndicate. Reprinted with permission. All rights reserved.

365

4. Answer the Question as Briefly as Possible. Then check the questioner's comprehension of your answer. Sometimes you can simply check his or her nonverbal response—if he or she seems at all confused, you can ask, "Does that answer your question?"

The importance of audience involvement, as well as the other techniques mentioned earlier, is reflected in the sample speech evaluation form in Figure 14–3.

FIGURE 14–3
Evaluation Form for an Informative Speech

SPEECH EVALUATION FORM

Informative Speech

Name_____ Topic_____

Assignment #_____ Date_____

What did you especially like?_____

_____

In your opinion, how could the speech be improved?_____

_____

Please comment on the following areas:

Did the speaker seem to have a clear informative purpose?

Was "information hunger" created?

Were important points emphasized?

Was the speech clearly organized and structured?

   Did the introduction—
      establish importance of topic to audience?
      preview thesis?
      preview main points?
   Did the body of the speech—
      contain three to five main points?
      contain three to five subpoints per main point?
      contain transitions, internal summaries, internal previews?
      contain points ordered to be easy to understand and remember?
   Did the conclusion of the speech—
      review main points?
      remind audience of the importance of the topic to them?
      provide audience with a memory aid?

Was supporting material used effectively?

Was the language clear?

Did the speaker seek to involve the audience?

The following speech was given by Amy Gillespie, a student at St. Olaf College in Minnesota. Amy, who was coached by Deborah Ballard-Reisch, was one of the semifinalists in the 1985 Interstate Oratorical Association Annual Contest.[15]

Listen Up!

Amy Gillespie, St. Olaf College, Minnesota

Good evening, and welcome to ABC Newsbrief. Top stories in the news include the hijacking of a Swiss airliner late Thursday evening by armed Iranian extremists. The terrorists are holding 23 hostages in Paris. Also in the news, Congress votes down defense spending cuts, but not before 5,000 protest in front of the Pentagon. And the weather outlook for tomorrow indicates warmer temperatures, with a slight chance of precipitation in the early morning hours. This has been Newsbrief. Now these words.

The simulated news report stimulates audience interest...

We hear news reports like this one every day. But how carefully do we listen to them? Let's find out. See if you can answer the following questions. Number one, what country did the hijacked airplane belong to? Number two, when was it hijacked? And three, where did people protest?

...and the "quiz" heightens audience participation and involvement.

I ask these questions to illustrate something we usually take for granted—listening. What is listening? That may sound like an elementary question, but too often we confuse listening with simply hearing. Hearing involves the vibration of sound waves on our eardrums. But listening is the interpretation and evaluation of what we hear.

Definition of key term.

Today I'd like to talk about listening. First, I'll establish its importance in our society and show the problems that can arise when it breaks down. Then I'll examine the causes of our bad listening habits and, finally, offer some solutions for them, which can be implemented in our nation's school systems and in our daily lives.

Preview of main points.

First of all, we need to understand how important listening really is. Says Robert Montgomery, author of *Listening Made Easy,* "We listen more than we do any other human activity except breathe." And the *American School Board Journal* of September 1981 reports that the average adult spends 80 percent of his or her time communicating—45 percent of that time is spent listening. As for college students, we spend 70 percent of our class time listening.

Supporting material includes quotation, testimony, and statistics.

Unfortunately, despite the fact that we spend so much time doing it, we are atrocious listeners. According to the *Executive Health Newsletter* of December 1981, "Immediately after listening to a ten-minute presentation, the average listener had heard, correctly understood, properly evaluated and retained approximately half of what was said." Fifty percent is lost forever. After forty-eight hours, that figure jumps to 75 percent. How about you? Did you know the answers to my questions? Here they are. The hijacked plane was Swiss. It was attacked late Thursday evening. And 5,000 people protested in front of the Pentagon. If you got one or more of these wrong, you're not alone. The *Executive Health Newsletter* estimates [that] "most people make more than one listening mistake every day."

Audience involvement is encouraged by returning to the "quiz" answers.

The problems that arise from our poor listening affect every aspect of our

A University of Minnesota study reports that "in the business world, nearly 60 percent of misunderstandings can be traced to poor listening." Listening expert Dr. Lyman Steil notes, "Because of listening mistakes, letters have to be retyped, appointments rescheduled, shipments rerouted. Productivity is affected and profits suffer." Another listening expert, Dr. Ralph Nichols, says that if ineffective listening "could be tallied in terms of dollars and cents," [it would] "undoubtedly cost our nation's industry millions of dollars a year."

Not only is good listening essential in the corporate world, but it is vital in our personal lives as well. In the home, says Montgomery, "Poor listening leads the list of causes of marital conflict." The Family Service Association of America asked husbands and wives, "What are the major conflicts in your married life?" Eighty-seven percent responded, "Poor communication... My spouse doesn't listen to me." How many times have we complained about that boyfriend or girlfriend who simply doesn't listen! The day-to-day friction between roommates and families that is caused by poor listening makes its personal cost very great.

Before I explain what we can do to improve our listening, it will be helpful to understand the cause of poor listening. The main reason we are bad listeners is the attitude in our society that takes listening for granted. After all, we've been listening since we were born! Unfortunately, most educators wrongly believe that, just because we know how to listen, we are good at it. Thus, listening is not taught in schools the way other communication skills like speaking, reading, and writing are. In fact, of those four skills, listening is used the most, but it is taught the least.

To make matters worse, our educators actually go out of their way to make listening easy for us. "Teachers routinely repeat instructions and directions, so students come to expect it and don't listen the first time," says Dr. Nichols. This coddling is continued throughout our lives, with radio and TV announcements that are simplified and repeated. The result is lazy listeners with poor listening habits.

Although our bad habits are ingrained from the outset, there is a cure for poor listening, and that is instruction and practice. Good listening won't come about by itself; it must be taught and worked on. First of all, it must be begun with our nation's school children. According to Dr. Nichols, "Our best listeners... [are] primary school children. [But] as the grade level increases, the caliber of listening performance... falls." If we can teach people good listening habits when they're young, they will retain their natural listening abilities all their lives.

The January 1985 issue of the *International Listening Association Newsletter* encourages teachers to incorporate listening in their regular school curricula by coordinating subjects like English or social studies to focus on listening skills.

The results of school listening programs are tremendous. Says Dr. Steil, "In schools where listening is taught, listening comprehension has as much as doubled in a few months." In one study reported by the *Journal of Educational Research,* fifth-graders were given specific training in listening for main ideas, details, and inferences: "Not only were gains in these skills significant; but other

---

She addresses two major concerns of her audience to build "information hunger": the business world...

...and the personal world.

Transition statement previews next points.

Repetition—combined with new information—emphasizes this important point.

Preview of next points.

Supporting material used to prove...

...and to clarify.

INFORMATIVE SPEAKING

skills, such as getting word meaning and following directions, also showed improvement."

Clearly, then, a listening program is well worth the time and effort on the part of our nation's schools.

Even though the rest of us are beyond our grade school days, Dr. Steil tells us there are three ways in which we too can improve our listening. The first way is to try to find some personal benefit in what we hear. Often when a seemingly irrelevant topic is introduced, we automatically shut our ears. For example, how many of us really listen to the safety instructions on an airplane anymore? After our first few flights, we tend to just tune out the flight attendant's instructions. But think if there were an emergency. Could you properly use the safety equipment? If we try to find this kind of value in what is floating into our ears, we will pay better attention and thus be better listeners.

Another preview

A second tip Steil clues us in on is to make use of the fact that thought is faster than speech. Now I'm speaking at a rate of about 125 words per minute. You are thinking four times that fast. This discrepancy, known as a time lag, leaves a lot of time for spare thinking. But what do we do with that time? Too often we become bored or distracted by our own thoughts. So Steil proposes that, instead of daydreaming, we use that extra time to our advantage: to summarize mentally what the speaker has said, to weigh the facts and evidence presented, or to anticipate the upcoming ideas or arguments. This will keep us from drifting off and also give us a better understanding of what is being said.

Signpost: A second tip . . .

Notice the clarity of language here.

A third way to improve our listening is actually to practice it by consciously pursuing difficult listening material. Two examples would be presidential debates or programs like "Meet the Press," which have a lot of facts to be digested and judgments to be made. We'll find that, with practice, we will all become better, more effective listeners.

Signpost: A third way . . .

When we see what can and does go wrong every day is due to our own listening errors, it becomes clear that our listening is an area in which we need to work. Implementation of programs in our schools will go far to achieve better listening, as will practical measures we can start right now. Remember the questions I asked at the beginning of my speech? You know how many answers you got right. If you're not satisfied with your tally, I challenge you to start today, to find something of personal benefit in even the dullest conversations. Use the time lag effectively, and refrain from tuning out if subject matter becomes a bit difficult or technical. Force yourself to listen.

A review . . .

. . . combined with a memory aid and one last encouragement of audience interest.

SUMMARY ◀

This chapter suggested techniques for effective informative speaking. These suggestions include the use of a specific informative purpose, the creation of "information hunger" by tapping both general and specific audience needs, the emphasis of important points through repetition and "signposts," the use of clear informative organization and structure, the use of effective supporting material, the use of clear language (language that incorporates precise, vivid, simple vocabulary), and the involvement of the audience.

1. For practice in defining informative speech purposes, reword the following statements so they specifically point out what the audience will be able to do after hearing the speech.

   a. My purpose is to tell my audience about Hitler's rise to power.

   b. I am going to talk about internal combustion engines.

   c. My speech is about the causes and cures of premature baldness.

2. Consider your classmates as an audience. How does Maslow's analysis of needs relate to these people? What other, more specific needs do they have? How could you relate the following speech topics to these needs?

   a. The Changing Climate of the United States

   b. Civil Rights

   c. Gun Control

   d. U.S. Foreign Policy

3. For practice in using clear language, select an article from any issue of a professional journal in your major field. Using the suggestions in this chapter, rewrite a paragraph from the article so that it will be clear and interesting to the layperson.

4. To analyze an informative speech, you go through it and point out where the speaker used effective techniques; if necessary, you point out places where effective techniques are still needed, making specific suggestions for improvement. To hone your skills in recognizing effective informative speaking, try one of the following analyses:

   a. Go over the analysis of the sample speech on pages 367–369. See which points you agree or disagree with, or both, and tell why. What would you add to the analysis?

   b. Select an informative speech from *Vital Speeches of the Day, Representative American Speeches,* a newspaper, or any other source. Analyze this speech in terms of its effectiveness as an informative message. Use our analysis of the sample speech as a model.

   c. Perform your analysis on your own informative speech, as delivered or to be delivered in class.

► **NOTES**

1. Porter Crow, "Waking Up the Right Lobe," *Vital Speeches of the Day,* (July 15, 1984), pp. 600–601.

2. Candy Lightner, "Mothers Against Drunk Drivers," in George Rodman, *Public Speaking,* 3d ed. (New York: Holt, Rinehart and Winston, 1986), p. 10.

3. Kim Perry, "Effortless Exercise," *Winning Orations, 1984* (Interstate Oratorical Association, 1984), pp. 27–28.

4. Ibid., p. 30.

5. Susan Martinez, "Sorry...We Only Speak English," *Winning Orations, 1983* (Interstate Oratorical Association, 1983), p. 82.

6. Vic Vieth, "Prisoners of Conscience," *Winning Orations, 1984* (Interstate Oratorical Association, 1984), p. 46.

7. Ibid., pp. 46–47.

8. Veda M. Backman, "Science's Internal Poison," *Winning Orations, 1984* (Interstate Oratorical Association, 1984), p. 21.

9. Keith Murphy, "The Shadows of Boxing," *Winning Orations, 1984* (Interstate Oratorical Association, 1984), p. 34.

10. Marcie Groover, "Learning to Communicate: The Importance of Speech Education in Public Schools," *Winning Orations, 1984* (Interstate Oratorical Association, 1984), p. 7.

11. Porter Crow, op. cit.

12. Ibid.

13. George Orwell, "Politics and the English Language," in *Shooting an Elephant and Other Essays* (New York: Harcourt Brace Jovanovich, 1945).

14. Hecklers can be helpful. See "A Politician's Guide to Success on the Stump: Hire a Heckler," *Psychology Today*, April 1971.

15. Amy Gillespie, "Listen Up!" *Winning Orations, 1985* (Interstate Oratorical Association, 1985), pp. 48–51.

▶ CHAPTER 15

KEY TERMS

actuating
causal reasoning
character
charisma
competence
convincing
credibility
deduction
direct persuasion
emotional appeal
enthymeme
ethical persuasion
evasion of argument
indirect persuasion
induction
insufficient evidence
logical appeals
logical fallacy
non sequitur fallacies

persuasion
question of fact
question of policy
question of value
reasoning by analogy
sign reasoning
strategy to actuate
strategy to convince
syllogisms
target audience

PERSUASIVE SPEAKING

After reading this chapter, you should understand the following:

1. That persuasion can be worthwhile and ethical.

2. The difference between questions of fact, value, and policy.

3. The difference between the goals of convincing and actuating.

4. The difference between direct and indirect approaches.

5. The basic idea of a persuasive strategy.

6. The functions of three types of persuasive appeals.

7. The importance of analyzing and adapting to your audience.

You should be able to do the following:

1. Formulate an effective persuasive strategy to convince or actuate an audience.

2. Bolster your credibility as a speaker by enhancing your competence, character, and charisma.

3. Use effective logical and emotional appeals to achieve your persuasive goal.

4. Detect logical fallacies in a persuasive message.

5. Use the techniques for effective persuasive speaking that are discussed on pages 394–397.

Persuasion is the act of motivating someone, through communication, to change a particular belief, attitude, or behavior. You can appreciate the importance of this skill by imaging how your life would be without the ability to persuade others. Your choice would be limited either to accepting people as they were or to coercing them to comply.

This last point is worth further comment, for persuasion is not the same thing as coercion. If you held a gun to someone's head and said, "Do this or I'll shoot," you would be acting coercively. Besides being illegal, this approach would be ineffective. Once you took the gun away, the person would probably stop following your demands.

The failure of coercion to achieve lasting results is apparent in less dramatic circumstances. Children whose parents are coercive often rebel as soon as they can; students who perform from fear of an instructor's threats rarely appreciate the subject matter; and employees who work for abusive and demanding employers are often unproductive and eager to switch jobs as soon as possible. Persuasion, on the other hand, makes a listener *want* to think or act differently.

Even when they understand the difference between persuasion and coercion, some students are still uncomfortable with the idea of persuasive speaking. They see it as the work of high-pressure hucksters: salespeople with their feet stuck in the door, unscrupulous politicians taking advantage of beleaguered taxpayers, and so on. Indeed, many of the principles we are about to discuss have been used by unethical speakers for unethical purposes, but that is not what all—or even most—persuasion is about. Ethical persuasion plays a necessary and worthwhile role in everyone's life.

Persuasion Can Be Worthwhile

It is through persuasion that we influence others' lives in worthwhile ways. The person who says, "I do not want to influence other people," is really saying. "I do not want to get involved with other people," and that is an abandoning of one's responsibilities as a human being. Look at the good you can accomplish through persuasion: You can convince a loved one to give up smoking or to give up some other destructive habit; you can get members of your community to conserve energy or to join together in some other beneficial action; you can persuade an employer to hire you for a job where your own talents, interests, and abilities will be put to their best use.

Persuasion Can Be Ethical

Persuasion is considered ethical if it conforms to accepted standards. What standards are accepted today? Whose opinion should you accept for what is good or bad? If your plan is selfish and not in the best interest of your audience—but you are honest about your motives—is that ethical? If your plan *is* in the best interest of your audience, yet you lie to them to get them to accept the plan, is *that* ethical?[1]

▶ He that complies against his will
Is of his own opinion still.

Samuel Butler

▶ The heart of the wise teaches his mouth, and adds persuasiveness to his lips.

Proverbs 16:23

▶ Honesty is one part of eloquence. We persuade others by being in earnest ourselves.

William Hazlitt

These questions are thorny. Eventually, the answer will depend on a set of moral values you decide to live by. For our purposes, however, a simple general definition is sufficient: **Ethical persuasion** is communication in the best interest of the audience that does not depend on false or misleading information to induce attitude change in that audience.

As Table 15–1 shows, not all persuasion is ethical, even by this simple standard. Some messages are unethical because they border on deception, such as "Enter the state lottery and win a million dollars a year for the rest of your life" or "You may have already won a vacation in the grand magazine sweepstakes." Those appeals make it sound as though just entering the sweepstakes makes you an automatic winner, when your chances are actually slim.

Other messages are unethical because they are absolutely false. They purposely seek to mislead the audience. An example of this type of message might be: "Congratulations! You have won a free one-year subscription to six of your favorite magazines, and all you need to pay is the cost of postage and handling!"

▶ The credit goes to the person who convinces the world, not to the one to whom the idea first occurs.

Sir Francis Darwin

TABLE 15–1 Unethical Communication Behaviors

  I. Failing to Prepare Adequately
    A. Insufficient research (speaker does not know what he or she is talking about)
    B. Not meeting logical standards of proof
  II. Sacrificing Convictions in Adapting to an Audience
    A. In propositions endorsed
    B. In style of presentation (for example, clothing)
  III. Appearing to Be What One Is Not; Insincerity
    A. In words, saying what one does not mean or believe
    B. In delivery (for example, feigning enthusiasm)
  IV. Withholding Information; Suppression
    A. About self (speaker); not disclosing private motives or special interests
    B. About speech purpose
    C. About sources (not revealing sources; plagiarism)
    D. About evidence; omission of certain evidence (card-stacking)
    E. About opposing arguments; presenting only one side
  V. Relaying False Information
    A. Deliberate lying
    B. Ignorant misstatement
    C. Deliberate distortion and suppression of material
    D. Using fallacious reasoning to misrepresent truth
  VI. Using Motivational Appeals to Hinder Truth
    A. Using emotional appeals as a substitute or cover up for a lack of sound reasoning and valid evidence
    B. Failing to use balanced appeals

Adapted from Mary Klaaren Andersen, "An Analysis of the Treatment of Ethos in Selected Speech Communication Textbooks" (unpublished dissertation, University of Michigan, 1979), pp. 244–247.

This strategy is used in door-to-door magazine con games. After people sign for the "free magazines" they wind up paying more for the "postage and handling" than they would for a regular subscription.

▶ TYPES OF PERSUASION

There are several ways to categorize the kinds of persuasive attempts you will make as a speaker. What kinds of subjects will you focus on? What results will you be seeking? How will you go about getting those results? In the following pages we will look at each of these questions.

Types of Questions

All persuasive topics fall into one of three categories: questions of fact, questions of value, and questions of policy.

QUESTIONS OF FACT   Some persuasive messages focus on **questions of fact:** issues in which there are two or more sides with conflicting evidence, where listeners are required to choose the truth for themselves. Some questions of fact are these:

A "nuclear winter" is likely (unlikely) after even a small nuclear war.

Experience shows that rent control will (will not) make housing more available for tenants.

The present administration is fighting an illegal (a legal) war in Central America.*

These examples show that many questions of fact can't be settled with a simple yes or no or with an objective piece of information. Rather, they are open to debate, and answering them requires careful examination and interpretation of evidence, usually collected from a variety of sources. That's why it's possible to debate questions of fact, and that's why these questions form the basis of persuasive speeches, and not of informative ones.

QUESTIONS OF VALUE   **Questions of value** go beyond issues of truth or falsity and explore the worth of some idea, person, or object. Questions of value include the following:

The use of laboratory animals for many scientific experiments is (is not) cruel and immoral.

Abortion is (is not) justified in certain cases.

Magazines such as *Playboy* and *Cosmopolitan* are (are not) sexist.

*Despite their label, the "questions" of fact, value, and policy described in the following pages are usually phrased as statements in a speech in order to strengthen the speaker's argument. They are called "questions" because they can be answered in more than one way. For example, the three questions in this example could be worded thus:

"Is a 'nuclear winter' likely after even a small nuclear war?"

"Will rent control make housing more available for tenants?"

"Is the present administration fighting an illegal war in Central America?"

In order to answer most questions of value, you will first need to answer one or more questions of fact. For example, you won't be able to debate whether the experimental use of animals in research is often immoral—a question of value—until you have dealt with several fundamental questions of fact such as whether lab animals suffer during experiments and whether such experiments are necessary.

QUESTIONS OF POLICY **Questions of policy** go one step beyond questions of fact or value; they recommend a specific course of action (a "policy") for the audience. Some questions of policy are these:

The United States should (should not) withdraw its support from any government that uses torture.

College athletes should (should not) be paid in cash for their talents.

Capital punishment should (should not) be made mandatory for certain criminal offenses.

One student attacked the trend of frivolous lawsuits with the following suggestions for his audience:

First of all, we must define the term *frivolous case* so that judges can rule immediately on whether or not a case is justified.... Another solution lies in awarding adequate compensation to victims of frivolous lawsuits.... Finally, we must try to settle our minor problems outside the courtroom.[2]

Looking at persuasion according to "type of question" is a convenient way to generate topics for a persuasive speech. However, fully developed persuasive speeches are likely to develop all three types of questions within their arguments. For example, one student outlined his persuasive argument against high insurance premiums this way:

To insure ourselves against this out-of-control industry, I am filing a claim that, first, these rising premiums are a problem for all of us; and, second, I will investigate who is liable for this dilemma; and, finally, I will offer a protection plan to safeguard us from further and future damage.[3]

This speaker dealt first with a question of value, then with a question of fact, and finally with a question of policy.

Desired Outcome

We can also divide persuasion according to two major outcomes: **convincing** and **actuating.**

CONVINCING When you set about to convince an audience, you want to change the way they think. When we say that convincing an audience changes the way they think, we do not mean that you have to swing them from one belief or attitude to a completely different one. Sometimes an audience will already think the way you want them to, but they will not be firmly enough committed to that way of thinking. When that is the case, you *reinforce,* or strengthen, their opinions. For example, if your audience already believed that

the federal budget should be balanced but did not consider the idea important, your job would be to reinforce their current beliefs. Reinforcing is still a type of change, however, because you are causing an audience to adhere more strongly to a belief or attitude. In other cases, convincing will *begin* to shift attitudes without bringing about a total change of thinking. For example, an effective speech to convince might get a group of skeptics to *consider the possibility* that bilingual education is (isn't) a good idea.

ACTUATING   When you set about to actuate an audience, you want to move them to a specific behavior. Whereas a speech to convince might move an audience to action based on the ideas you've convinced them about, it won't be any specific action that you've recommended. In a speech to actuate, you do recommend that specific action.

There are two types of action you can ask for—*adoption* or *discontinuance.* The former asks an audience to engage in a new behavior; the latter asks them to stop behaving in an established way. If you gave a speech for a political candidate and then asked for contributions to that candidate's campaign, you would be asking your audience to adopt a new behavior. If you gave a speech against smoking and then asked your audience to sign a pledge to quit or to throw away the cigarettes they were carrying, you would be asking them to discontinue an established behavior.

Examples of both types of persuasive speech—to convince and to actuate—can be found at the end of this chapter.

Direct and Indirect Persuasion

We can also categorize persuasion according to the directness of approach employed by the speaker.

DIRECT PERSUASION   **Direct persuasion** is that which does not try to disguise the speaker's persuasive purpose in any way. In direct persuasion the speaker will make his or her purpose clear, usually by stating it outright early in the speech. This is the best strategy to use with a friendly audience, especially when you are asking for a response that the audience is reasonably likely to give you:

> I'm here to day to let you know why you should take part in the Red Cross blood drive....

> Have you ever wished that students had more rights and power? They can, if they organize effectively. I'm here today to show you how to do just that....

> I'm going to try to convince you today that Candy Tate is the best choice for city council and that she needs your vote....

Direct persuasion is the kind we hear in most academic situations. One student, speaking on the FDA's proposal to allow the irradiation of food and vegetables, announced her intent to persuade:

> Today I would like to urge you to recognize the startling lack of safety of this proposal and to help you see how unnecessary the "Federal Food Irradiation Development and Control Act" is.[4]

Another student chose a direct approach in her speech on the importance of wills:

> My purpose today is to convince each of you that having a will is important by discussing why people avoid writing a will; what a will is and why we need one; and, finally, how we can obtain a will.[5]

First Lady Nancy Reagan also chose a direct approach in one of her speeches on drug abuse. After the customary introductory remarks, she began this way:

> I want to talk about the battle against drugs.
> Now before any of you can think to yourself, "Well, drug abuse really doesn't concern me," let me say it does concern you. It concerns you if you have a family because drugs can unexpectedly tear a family to pieces—even the most loving families.

It concerns you as an employer because drugs cost billions in illness, accidents, lost productivity, and corruption.

It concerns you as a citizen because there's a direct and undeniable link between crime and drugs. Law enforcement officers are being murdered in their effort to protect our society from those who would destroy it with drugs.

And, furthermore, it concerns you as an individual of conscience because the tragedy and pain drugs cause are staggering.

Ladies and gentlemen, there's a drug and alcohol epidemic in this country and no one is safe from its consequences—not you, not me, and certainly not our children. Drugs are a very powerful force in America, and we cannot ignore them.[6]

INDIRECT PERSUASION **Indirect persuasion** disguises or de-emphasizes the speaker's persuasive purpose in some way. The question "Is a season ticket to the symphony worth the money?" (when you intend to prove that it is) is based on indirect persuasion, as is any strategy that does not express the speaker's purpose at the outset.

Indirect persuasion is sometimes easy to spot. A television commercial that shows us a handsome young man and a beautiful young woman romping in the surf on a beautiful day and then flashes the product name on the screen is pretty indisputably indirect persuasion. Political oratory is sometimes indirect persuasion, also, and it is sometimes more difficult to identify as such. A political hopeful might be ostensibly speaking on some great social issue when the real persuasive message is "Please—remember my name, and vote for me in the next election."

Indirect persuasion is the type of approach that is perhaps best exemplified in Shakespeare's version of Marc Antony's funeral oration for Julius Caesar.[7] Brutus, one of Caesar's assassins, has just finished speaking, convincing the crowd that Caesar's murder was just and honorable. Antony has to appear cordial toward the assassins so they will allow him to speak over Caesar's body in the forum. Antony begins by saying that he has "come to bury Caesar, not to praise him," but he slowly works his crowd back to an appreciation of their murdered leader and rage against those who killed them.

Indirect persuasion is the approach to use when your audience is hostile to either you or your topic. It is also often necessary to use the indirect approach to get a hearing from listeners who would tune you out if you took a more direct approach. Under such circumstances, you might want to ease into your speech slowly.[8] You might take some time to make your audience feel good about you or the social action you are advocating. If you are speaking in favor of Candy Tate for city council, but Tate is in favor of a tax increase and your audience is not, you might talk for a while about the benefits of that increase. You might even want to change your desired audience response. Rather than trying to get them to rush out to vote for Tate, you might want them simply to read a recent newspaper article about her or attend a speech she will be giving. The one thing you cannot do in this instance is to begin by saying, "I'm not here to speak in support of Candy Tate"—that would be a false statement. It is more than indirect; it is unethical.

Indirect persuasion *can* be ethical, however. The test of the ethicality of an indirect approach would be whether you *would* express your persuasive purpose directly if asked to do so. In other words, if someone in the audience stopped you and asked, "Aren't you supporting Candy Tate for city council?" if you were ethical, you would admit to it rather than deny your true purpose.

As one example of a situation in which indirect persuasion might be ethical and fruitful, imagine that certain books—books like *Huckleberry Finn, To Kill a Mockingbird,* or *Romeo and Juliet* are being removed from the shelves of your local library because of pressure from groups who believe that these books promote "un-American" values.[9] If you chose to speak to the citizens of your town about this matter, you would be well advised to begin your speech by assuring them that you share most of the same values they do: You want the children of your town to grow up honest and healthy; you want them to be levelheaded about drugs, sex, and alternative life-styles. You want them to be civilized and humane, and you want them to be active members of American democracy. You would agree with your listeners that obscenity and pornography degrade humanity, that they are devoid of human sentiments and ideals.

Only after you have established these mutual values would you try to persuade them that the censorship of works of literature is not the best way to achieve their objectives. You might then point out the dangers of artistic repression and the impracticality of trying to "legislate morality." You might then point out that works of literature are not instruction manuals, and readers are not destined to imitate the events portrayed in the book. You might wind up with the idea that, as one speaker pointed out, the censorship of books undermines the more vital function of education, which is to help students cope with life by exploring with them the realities and ambiguities expressed in recognized literary works.[10]

PERSUASIVE STRATEGY ◀

Whether you choose a direct or an indirect approach to reaching your goal, your approach when persuading an audience should follow the same basic strategy, outlined in Table 15–2. In many ways, this strategy is similar to the approach

TABLE 15–2 Strategy for a Persuasive Speech

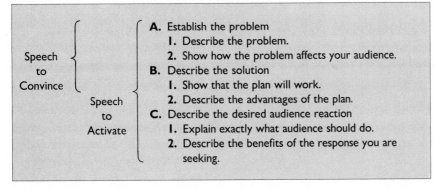

Speech to Convince / Speech to Activate

A. Establish the problem
  1. Describe the problem.
  2. Show how the problem affects your audience.
B. Describe the solution
  1. Show that the plan will work.
  2. Describe the advantages of the plan.
C. Describe the desired audience reaction
  1. Explain exactly what audience should do.
  2. Describe the benefits of the response you are seeking.

you would use in an informative speech because you have to explain your topic to your audience before you persuade them. In fact, a persuasive speech will actually contain two or three different informative ones. First, you will have to explain the problem. Next, you will describe the solution. Finally, if your goal is to actuate the audience, you will inform the audience about the part they can play in bringing about the solution. Let's look at each of these steps more closely.

Define the Problem

In order to convince an audience that something needs to be changed, you have to show them that a problem exists. After all, if your listeners don't recognize the problem, they won't find your arguments for a solution very important. An effective definition of the problem will answer two questions, either directly or indirectly.

WHAT IS THE NATURE OF THE PROBLEM? Your audience might not recognize that the topic you are discussing is a problem at all, so your first task is to convince them that there is something wrong with the present state of affairs. For example, if your thesis was "This town needs a shelter for homeless families," you would need to show that there are, indeed, homeless families and that the plight of these homeless families is serious.

If your prespeech analysis shows that your audience may not feel sympathetic to your topic, you will need to explain why your topic is, indeed, a problem in a manner that the listeners will accept. In your homeless speech, you might need to explain that not all homeless people are lazy, able-bodied drifters who choose to panhandle and steal instead of working. You could cite respected authorities, give examples, and maybe even show photographs to demonstrate that some homeless people are hardworking but unlucky parents and innocent children who lack shelter owing to forces beyond their control.

HOW DOES THE PROBLEM AFFECT YOUR AUDIENCE? It's not enough to prove that a problem exists. Your next challenge is to show your listeners that the problem affects them in some way. This is relatively easy in some cases: the high cost of tuition, the lack of convenient parking near campus, and so on. In other cases, you will need to spell out the impact to your listeners more clearly. If you are trying to show the audience that the drinking water or air in your community is contaminated, you will need to explain how that contamination will affect their health. If you want to show them that having even a few drinks before driving can lead to tragic accidents, you'll need to show cases in which these accidents have affected people like them.

The most challenging goals are ones in which there seems to be no connection between your audience and the problem you are describing. Take the plight of homeless families, for example. Their dilemma probably has no clear impact on the health, safety, or comfort of the people who will be listening to your speech. In cases like these, you need to appeal to less obvious needs. You might link your topic to values the audience claims to hold by pointing out that no decent person would ignore the plight of unfortunate parents and children who are on the street without food or shelter.

Define the Solution

Your next step in persuading your audience is to convince them that there is an answer to the problem you have just introduced. In other words, you need to propose a solution—a plan to correct this problem. Just describing your solution isn't enough. You have to answer two questions about this solution before your audience is likely to accept it.

WILL THE PLAN WORK? A skeptical audience might agree with the desirability of your solution but still not believe that it has a chance of succeeding. Suppose your thesis is "The United States should immediately begin reducing the number of nuclear weapons, in order to encourage the USSR to do likewise." As many of your listeners might brush off this idea as too idealistic to work, you'll need to offer some evidence that unilateral disarmament has a chance of succeeding. In the homeless speech we have been discussing, you would need to prove that establishment of a shelter can help unlucky families get back on their feet—especially if your audience analysis shows that some listeners might view such a shelter as a way of coddling people who are too lazy to work.

WHAT ADVANTAGES WILL RESULT FROM YOUR PLAN? You need to describe in specific terms how your plan will lead to desired changes. This is the step where you will paint a vivid picture of the benefits of your proposal. In the speech proposing a shelter for homeless families, the benefits you describe would probably include these:

1. Families will have a safe place to stay, free of the dangers of living on the street.
2. Parents will have the resources that will help them find jobs: an address, telephone, clothes washers, and showers.
3. The police won't have to apply antivagrancy laws (such as prohibitions against sleeping in cars) to people who aren't the intended target of those laws.
4. The community (including your listeners) won't need to feel guilty about ignoring the plight of unfortunate citizens.

Describe the Desired Audience Response

You should follow the previous steps of describing the problem and outlining your solution in all persuasive speeches. When you want to go beyond simply a **strategy to convince** your audience and use a **strategy to actuate** them to follow your plan, you need to describe exactly what you want them to do (see Table 15–2). This action step, like the previous ones, should answer two questions.

WHAT CAN THE AUDIENCE DO TO PUT YOUR PLAN INTO ACTION? Make the behavior you are asking your audience to adopt as clear and simple as possible for them. If you want them to vote in a referendum, tell them when and where to go to vote and how to go about registering, if necessary. (Some activists even provide transportation.) If you're asking them to support a legislative change, don't expect them to write their congressional representative. *You* write the letter or draft a petition, and ask them to sign it. If you're asking for donations, pass the hat at the conclusion of your speech, or give each audience member a stamped, addressed envelope and simple forms that they can return easily.

WHAT ARE THE DIRECT REWARDS OF THIS RESPONSE? Your solution might be important to society, but your audience will be most likely to adopt it if you can show that they will get a personal payoff. Show that supporting legislation to reduce acid rain will produce a wide range of benefits from reduced lung damage to healthier forests to longer life for their car's paint. Explain that saying no to a second drink before driving will not only save lives but also help your listeners avoid expensive court costs, keep their insurance rates low, and prevent personal humiliation. Show how helping to establish and staff a homeless shelter can lead to personal feelings of satisfaction and provide an impressive demonstration of community service on a job-seeking résumé.

▶ TYPES OF PERSUASIVE APPEALS

A persuasive strategy is put into effect through the use of persuasive appeals. These appeals supply your audience with reasons to say yes to a plan. In other words, they make an audience *want* to agree with you and adopt your plan.

The early Greeks first outlined a set of devices through which reasons could be given convincingly. Aristotle labeled them *ethos, logos,* and *pathos.* These categories correspond roughly to appeals based on credibility, logic, and emotion.

Credibility-based Appeals

Credibility refers to the believability of a speaker. Credibility isn't an objective quality; rather, it is a *perception* in the minds of the audience. A speaker might deserve the trust of an audience and yet, owing to an ineffective style of speaking, not get it. Likewise, a talented but immoral, incompetent speaker might fool an audience and gain credibility he or she does not deserve.

Credibility is perhaps the most important ingredient in persuading an audience. Without it you won't be able to convince your listeners that your ideas are worth accepting even if your material is outstanding. On the other hand, if you can develop a high degree of credibility in the eyes of your listeners, they will be likely to open up to ideas they wouldn't otherwise accept.

An audience forms judgments about the credibility of a speaker based on their perception of many characteristics, the most important of which might be called the "Three C's" of credibility: *competence, character,* and *charisma.*[11]

COMPETENCE **Competence** refers to the speaker's expertise on the topic. Sometimes this competence can come from *personal experience* that will lead your audience to regard you as an authority on the topic you are discussing. If everyone in the audience knows you've earned big profits in the stock market, they'll probably take your investment advice seriously. If you tell them you lost twenty-five pounds from a diet-and-exercise program, they'll almost certainly respect your opinions on weight loss.

In other cases, however, you won't have the personal qualifications to persuade an audience. If you have no background in nuclear power, listeners probably wouldn't accept a thesis like "nuclear power plants are unsafe" just because you said so. In cases like this, you can still boost your credibility by *citing experts* whom the audience will believe. It's important to use sources that your listeners will recognize as authorities to get the maximum credibility. For instance, you might give a carefully worded statement to demonstrate the qualifications of the expert you cite:

> According to Professor A. Thom-Kerschmacher, winner of the Nobel Prize and highly respected for his work in nuclear safety, nuclear power plants are unsafe.

Besides demonstrating personal expertise and citing recognized authorities, a third way to demonstrate expertise is by *effective delivery.* Although the way you present material doesn't have any logical relationship to the quality of that information, audiences do tend to believe people who speak with confidence and skill. Chapter 13 contains guidelines for delivering a speech effectively. The key elements are looking good (being well dressed and well groomed), standing and moving effectively, and using your voice well. The best way to develop an effective style of delivery—and thereby increase your perceived competence—is to practice your speech until you can deliver it smoothly without the stumbles that come from lack of preparation.

CHARACTER All the expertise in the world won't generate enough credibility unless your audience trusts you enough to believe what you are saying. **Character** involves the audience's perception of at least two ingredients: honesty and impartiality. When speaking to an audience who already know you, it's probably too late to try to gain their trust, for your past actions will have already spoken more eloquently about the kind of person you are than anything you can say. With unfamiliar audiences, you can try to find ways to talk about yourself (without boasting, of course) that demonstrate your integrity. You might describe how much time you spent researching the subject or demonstrate your open-mindedness by telling them that you changed your mind after your investigation. For example, if you were giving a speech arguing against a proposed tax cut in your community, you might begin this way:

> You might say I'm an expert in the municipal services of this town. As a lifelong resident, I owe a debt to its schools and recreation programs. I've been protected by its police and fire fighters and served by its hospitals, roads, and sanitation crews.
>
> As I'm also a taxpayer who's on a tight budget, when I first heard about the tax cut that's been proposed, I liked the idea. But then I did some in-depth investigation into the possible effects. I looked into our municipal expenses and into the expenses of similar communities where tax cuts have been mandated by law . . .

In addition to demonstrating your sincerity, you can also boost your credibility by proving that you are impartial. One way to do so is to mention both sides of the issue you are discussing if the audience will consider the opposing position and then show why you support your position instead of the other one. Another way to demonstrate your lack of bias is to cite impartial authorities that the audience will respect. For example, in praising the merits of a certain product, you might quote an endorsement from *Consumer Reports* magazine. Likewise, if you favor legislation to control the use of handguns, your audience will be impressed with quotes from police officials who support this position. The best sources to quote to show your impartiality are ones who would be expected to oppose the issue you're advocating. A Republican's praise for the local Democratic candidate would be more effective than a fellow Democrat's, for instance.

CHARISMA **Charisma** is a combination of a speaker's enthusiasm and likability. Audiences are more likely to be persuaded by a charismatic speaker than by a less charismatic one who delivers the same information.

The first ingredient of charisma is enthusiasm, sometimes termed "dynamism" by communication scholars. Your enthusiasm will mostly be perceived from *how* you deliver your remarks, not from *what* you say. The nonverbal parts of your speech will show that you believe in what you are saying far better than your words. Is your voice animated and sincere? Do your gestures reflect your enthu-

"I should like to depart from my prepared text and speak as a human being."

Drawing by Richter; © 1986 The New Yorker Magazine, Inc.

siasm? Do your facial expression and eye contact show you care about your audience?

Trying to *act* enthusiastic when you don't feel that way is almost always a mistake. There are too many nonverbal tip-offs that will show you're being insincere. Besides detracting from your dynamism, that perceived insincerity will cast doubts on your trustworthiness. "After all," your audience might think, "if this person is faking concern, what *else* is phony about the speech?" It's far better to choose a topic that you believe in and then rehearse your speech enough so that you can minimize any nervousness that might be mistaken for a lack of sincerity. Be yourself (as we suggested in Chapter 13), but be an articulate, well-prepared version of yourself.

You can boost your likability in two ways. First, you can *show that you like and respect your audience.* Insincere flattery will boomerang, of course, but if you can find a way to give your listeners a genuine compliment, they'll be more receptive to your ideas.

You can also increase your likability by *emphasizing the similarities between you and your listeners.* If you're asking for contributions, tell them that you're on a tight budget just as they are . . . and then show them why their donation will still be worth making. If you're encouraging them to stay away from drugs, let them know that you like to have a good time too . . . and then show them that there are safer ways to have fun. It isn't necessary to pretend that you are *exactly* like your audience, but finding key areas of common ground will bridge the gap between you and your listeners.

Logical Appeals

FORMS OF REASONING   In the purest form **logical appeals** supply an audience with a series of statements that lead to the conclusion the speaker is trying to establish. The most common forms of logical reasoning are *deduction* and *induction.*

Deduction   **Deduction** is reasoning from a generality to a specific; in other words, you present general evidence that leads to a specific conclusion. Deductive reasoning can be demonstrated in **syllogisms,** which are arguments made up of two premises (a major premise and a minor premise) and a conclusion. The classic syllogism is:

> All men are mortal.
> Socrates is a man.
> Therefore, Socrates is mortal.

This is the way one student used deduction to argue one of her points in a speech on the problem of illiteracy:

> We come into the picture as taxpayers, especially in welfare and unemployment costs. According to *U.S. News and World Report,* 75 percent of the unemployed lack the skills necessary in reading and communication. Welfare is the answer for those illiterates who can't work. This costs us $6 billion per year.[12]

This argument might be phrased in the following syllogism:

Unemployment costs us plenty.
Illiteracy causes unemployment.
Therefore, illiteracy costs us plenty.

If all logical appeals were expressed as complete syllogisms, people could examine the major and minor premises and decide if the conclusions drawn from those premises were valid. This method would make most arguments cumbersome, so we generally use *enthymemes* for logical appeals.[13] An **enthymeme** is a compressed version of a syllogism in which the underlying premises are concealed, as in:

Because Socrates is a man, he is mortal.

Enthymemes become dangerous when they disguise faulty premises. Some of the best examples of this type of enthymeme are provided in the form of arbitrary rules. For example, take the rule enforced by some college-town landlords: "Because Joe Schmidlap is a college student, he will have to pay a damage deposit before he can rent an apartment." This rule is based on an enthymeme that is based on the following syllogism:

All college students wreck apartments.
Joe Schmidlap is a college student.
Therefore, Joe Schmidlap will wreck this apartment.

The conclusion, "Joe Schmidlap will wreck this apartment," is based on an untrue, unstated premise: "All college students wreck apartments."

College students often run up against this type of reasoning from landlords and utility companies. Even if they can supply letters of reference from former landlords and receipts for utility bills paid on time, they are still told, "I'm sorry, we don't rent to college students. It's a rule we have," or "I'm sorry, we require a deposit of $75 to turn on your electricity. It's a rule," or "There's no sense arguing. We don't need to give you a *reason*. It's a rule."

The frustration you feel when you are subjected to illogical rules is the same frustration that an audience feels when it is subjected to an argument that does not supply valid reasons. That is why we take this close look at deductive reasoning: To make sure that the reasons we use in deduction are valid, we examine the underlying premises of our argument.

Of course, formal logic does not explain all of human reasoning.[14] Humans are not inherently logical or illogical; they are instead "psychological," which means that their reasoning processes are far more complex than any set of rules, no matter how elaborate, could encompass. However, formal logic does have at least one specific use besides being a standard for testing arguments. People who reason fallaciously are generally able to recognize their reasoning as fallacious when confronted with their errors through formal proofs. Therefore, we use formal logic to point out errors in reasoning.[15]

INDUCTION **Induction** is reasoning from specific evidence to a general conclusion. In induction we observe that something is true for a specific sample. From this evidence we reason that it is *generally* true.

The student speaking against illiteracy used induction to argue that it is a serious problem:

> Nonreading adults have innumerable problems because of their handicap.... Illiterates can't read maps or signs, bills or bank statements. They have problems telling the difference between, for example, dog food and beef stew because they can't read the labels.... In one case, an illiterate worker at a construction company was killed because he couldn't read a warning sign.... In another case, a forty-two-year-old mother from Syracuse who can't read or write unintentionally poisoned her young daughter because she confused pink dishwashing soap with Pepto-Bismol.[16]

Induction would be the appropriate type of reasoning to use with a skeptical or hostile audience when you do not want to state an unpopular claim right away. If you are seeking to prove that your local government is generally corrupt, for example, you might build your case with specific examples: The mayor has been convicted of bribery, the building inspector has resigned after being charged with extortion, the fire chief has been indicted for running the station's Dalmation at the track, and the chief of police has admitted to keeping his infant nephew on the police department's payroll. If you used these specific instances to conclude that most of your local officials are corrupt, you would be using induction.

Although induction and deduction are the most common types of logical reasoning, there are other forms. These forms include reasoning by sign, causal reasoning, and reasoning by analogy. Often these forms are combined with induction and deduction.

Reasoning by Sign **Sign reasoning** is reasoning from specific evidence to a specific conclusion without explaining how the evidence and conclusion are related. The classic example of sign reasoning is, "It is snowing outside, therefore it must be winter." Sign reasoning is used when the argument will be easily accepted by the audience. For example, an audience would probably accept the claim that an increase in bank robberies is a sign that a community is becoming more dangerous to live in. We would not need to go into a long, logical explanation of our reasoning in that case, and the time we save could be used to develop more important aspects of the argument. For example, we might want to go on to claim a particular *cause* for the rash of bank robberies. That would require causal reasoning.

Causal Reasoning **Causal reasoning,** like sign reasoning, is reasoning from one specific to another specific. However, in causal reasoning you go on to prove that something happened or will happen *because* of something else. If you claimed that the increase in bank robberies in your community was caused by a decrease in police personnel, you would be involved in causal reasoning. In fact, you would be using effect-to-cause reasoning, which is based on the organizational pattern of the same name discussed in Chapter 12. Effect-to-cause reasoning is used when you are talking about something that has already happened. If you were arguing about something that *will* happen (for example, the probability of future bank robberies because the police have cut the size of their force or the hours they patrol), you would be using cause-to-effect reasoning.

Reasoning by Analogy   **Reasoning by analogy** is reasoning from specific evidence to a specific conclusion by claiming that something is *like* something else. Although this type of reasoning could not be used for legal proof, it can help prove a point to an audience. For example, if you were arguing that the methods of law enforcement that curbed bank robbery in a nearby city would also work in your city, you would have to argue that your city is similar to that nearby city in all the respects that are important to your argument—number of banks, size of banks, size of police department, and so on. Thus, if you could argue that the two cities are alike except in one respect—for example, the size of their police forces—you could argue that this is what makes the difference in the incidence of bank robbery. If you did so, you would be arguing by analogy.

There are two types of analogy—*literal* and *figurative.* The analogy of the two cities is a literal analogy because it compares two things that are really (literally) alike. A figurative analogy compares two things that are essentially different. If you argued that bank robberies are like a disease that must be treated to keep it from spreading, you would be using a figurative analogy.

No matter which type of reasoning you are using (deduction, induction, sign, causation, or analogy), you can check the validity of your arguments by checking them against the basic logical fallacies.

LOGICAL FALLACIES   Scholars have devoted lives and volumes to the description of various types of **logical fallacies.**[17] The three most common types seem to be insufficient evidence, non sequitur, and evasion of argument. Most fallacies can be included under one of those categories.

Insufficient Evidence   The fallacy of **insufficient evidence** is sometimes difficult to recognize, especially when it is caused by *ignored causes* or *ignored effects.*

Examples of *ignored causes* run rampant through everyday conversations. Take a typical discussion about college sports:

> State U. beat State Tech.
> State Tech creamed State Teachers.
> Therefore, State U. will murder State Teachers.

This argument might ignore previously injured players who are now back in action, stars who are now injured, or a host of other variables.

Logical fallacies based on *ignored effects* are even worse:

> If other nations overcharge for oil that is needed for American consumers, an invasion of those countries is warranted.

That argument ignores undesirable effects of war, such as drafting college students who would rather be studying communication.

You might not recognize that an argument is based on insufficient evidence because the argument *sounds* so reasonable. One cause of this deception is reasoning according to slogan, which occurs when we use some folksy, familiar expression as proof. Max Black provides two excellent examples:

We hear all too often that "the exception proves the rule." Probably not one person in a thousand who dishes up this ancient morsel of wisdom realizes that "prove" is here used in its older sense of "probe" or "test." What was originally intended was that the exception tests the rule—shows whether the rule is correct or not. The contemporary interpretation, that a rule is confirmed by having an exception, is absurd. This tabloid formula has the advantage of allowing a person to glory in the fact that his general principle does *not* square with the facts.

"It's all right in theory, but it won't do in practice," is another popular way of reveling in logical absurdity. The philosopher Schopenhauer said all that needs to be said about this sophism: "The assertion is based upon an impossibility: what is right in theory *must* work in practice; and if it does not, there is a mistake in theory; something has been overlooked and not allowed for; and consequently, what is wrong in practice is wrong in theory too."[18]

Non Sequiturs   Fallacies of insufficient evidence are caused by not telling enough. **Non sequitur fallacies** are those in which the conclusion does not relate to (literally, "does not follow from") the evidence. Unreasonable syllogisms such as those we described as being used by landlords and utility companies are non sequiturs based on faulty premises. Non sequiturs based on true premises can be just as dangerous. Take, for example, the non sequitur fallacy known as *post hoc*, which is short for *post hoc, ergo propter hoc.* Translated from the Latin, that phrase means "after this, therefore because of this." This fallacy occurs when it is assumed that an action was caused by something that happened before it. Post hoc arguments are often applied to politics:

> Obviously, Ronald Reagan caused the space shuttle disaster. It happened, after all, during his administration.

Spurious research is often post hoc.

> Nearly all heroin users started with marijuana. Marijuana obviously leads to the use of harder drugs.

Nearly all marijuana users started with aspirin, too, but aspirin does not necessarily lead to the abuse of drugs.

Another type of non sequitur is an *unwarranted extrapolation,* which is a statement that suggests that because something happened before, it will happen again, or that because something is true for a part, it is true for a whole.

> State U. has massacred State Teachers every year for the past five years. They'll do it again this year.

Then there is the *circular argument,* in which the evidence is dependent on the truth of the argument:

> Of course the administration is concerned with student welfare. It says so right in the college catalog.

Evasion of Argument   In the fallacy of **evasion of argument,** the speaker dodges the question at hand by arguing over some other, unrelated point. One such evasion is the *ad hominem* argument, which is the fallacy of attacking the person who brought up the issue rather than the issue itself:

> Of course Louis thinks marijuana should be legalized. Louis is an idiot.

The most common type of evasion of argument is the *red herring*. This fallacy, which derives its name from the practice of dragging an odoriferous fish across a trail when running away from bloodhounds, consists of evading an issue by concentrating on another, more volatile one:

> Should school children be allowed to read *Das Kapital*? The real question here is, "Who would like to see this happen?" And the obvious answer to that question is, *the Communists*. The threat of the Communist conspiracy is as real today as it was…

No argument is perfect. If all the evidence were available and it related perfectly to the argument, there probably would not *be* an argument in the first place. You should recognize the major fallacies, though, and watch for them in your own reasoning. If an audience is able to discount your arguments as illogical, you probably will not persuade them.

Emotional Appeals

▶ To say that it is possible to persuade without speaking to the passions is but at best a kind of specious nonsense.

George Campbell

An **emotional appeal** uses a feeling like love, hate, fear, guilt, anger, loneliness, envy, or pity to entice an audience to change its attitude. An emotional appeal is not necessarily unethical although it does allow the most room for an unethical speaker to operate. It is not necessarily illogical either. Because emotional appeals are *psychological,* they can be particularly powerful.[19] Clarence Darrow once pointed out, "You don't have to give reasons to the jury. Make them *want* to acquit your client, and they'll find their own reasons."

It would be a good idea to accept half of Darrow's advice. Give your audience reasons, *and* make them want to accept your plan. Instead of just giving reasons from expert authorities why nuclear power plants are unsafe, you might also describe a nuclear holocaust or explain the details of radiation illness. On the other hand, if you were arguing in favor of nuclear power, you might describe what life would be like without any energy sources—slowly freezing to death. Let us take a look at four emotions on which emotional appeals are sometimes based: *fear, anger, pride,* and *pity.*

FEAR Appropriate fear appeals are sometimes effective persuaders. Modern advertising—especially the TV variety—commonly appeals to audience fears. In fact, television advertising has done more than its share of originating new fears. The fear of body odor, one of the classics of prime-time advertising, has recently been fragmented into more specific fears, like the fear of foot odor (one commercial featured a hapless father driving his entire family from the house by taking off his shoes), the fear of personal-hygiene odor, and the fear of soap odor. ("But I used a deodorant soap!" cries the sweet young thing in the kissing booth. "That's just it," explains the reticent young stranger in front of her. "You *smell* like a deodorant soap.")

Fear appeals can be detrimental if they go too far. In a classic study high school students were presented several persuasive messages about toothbrushing.[20] The high-fear appeal showed grotesque pictures of dental diseases, rotting gums, and black stumps of teeth. The moderate-fear appeal merely mentioned tooth decay in passing, but the researchers found it to be more effective. This study, like many that have come after it, suggests that if you tap audience fears, you should do so with moderation.

ANGER   If an audience is angry (or can be *made* angry) about something, you should show them that you are angry about the same thing. This stance will do two things: (1) It will show that you are similar to them, increasing your persuasiveness; (2) It will also allow you to offer your solution as a cure for whatever is causing the anger. For example, a bandwagon full of political hopefuls is telling people how angry they are about high taxes. Fear not, the audience is told. There is a way to change this situation: Vote for Candidate X.

Appeals based on anger can be successful, but in order to be ethical, you have to *feel* the anger honestly. According to our definition of ethics, you should not say you are angry if you are not.

PRIDE   The satisfaction audience members feel in their achievements or worth can be a rich vein to tap. Audience members might be proud of their work, their family, their community, their country, or any one of a thousand other things they identify with. If they are not proud to begin with, they can be made

▶ Rev. Samuel J. May: Mr. Garrison, you are too excited—you are on fire!

William Lloyd Garrison: I have need to be on fire, for I have icebergs around me to melt.

to feel proud by being reminded of the pride they *should* feel. A British professor who happened to be speaking before an American audience tapped their pride in this way:

> Let me start with a banal and embarrassing confession, such as is seldom nowadays made, either by Americans or by their allies. I love America. You are a truly amazing people: rich, ingenious, generous, entertaining, powerful, and deeply human. You are the leaders in every branch of science and technology, every field of scholarship and the arts.... There may still be Europeans who feel culturally superior, but I am certainly not one of them. I view the United States with admiration and gratitude for all it has done for mankind and is still doing.... [21]

PITY Pity is the emotion that allows us to feel sorrow for the suffering of others. You can use pity as an emotional appeal by reminding your audience that someone, somewhere, is suffering. Pity is an especially potent emotion if the sufferer comes from a group toward which we already feel sympathetic, such as children or animals. One effective antiabortion message was delivered from the point of view of an unborn fetus, who claimed that it was able to feel pain from the beginning of its development. Therefore, to allow abortion to remain legal was to allow this fetus to suffer. The listeners were thus told that a *child* was suffering; and worse yet, that they were partially responsible.

The key to an emotional appeal is sincerity. Most audiences will be able to recognize false emotions and reject appeals based on them.

Emotional appeals, as well as logical reasoning and credibility, are important to keep in mind when planning a persuasive strategy. Although any one type of appeal might dominate a particular argument, different appeals can also be *combined* to good effect.

▶ TECHNIQUES FOR EFFECTIVE PERSUASIVE SPEAKING

The preceding discussion suggested several techniques for effective persuasion. Let us focus on a few important techniques.

Analyze and Adapt to Your Audience

▶ People are not against you; they are merely for themselves.

Gene Fowler

It is important to know as much as possible about your audience for a persuasive speech. For one thing, you should appeal to the values of your audience whenever possible even if they are not *your* strongest values. This advice does not mean you should pretend to believe in something. According to our definition of ethical persuasion, pretense is against the rules. It does mean, however, that you have to stress those values that are felt most forcefully by the members of your audience.[22]

Also, you should analyze your audience carefully to predict the type of response you will get. Sometimes you have to pick out one part of your audience—**a target audience,** the subgroup you MUST persuade to reach your goal—and aim your speech mostly at them. Some of your audience members might be so opposed to what you are advocating that you have no hope of reaching them. Still others might already agree with you, so they do not need to be persuaded. A middle portion of your audience might be undecided or uncommitted, and they would be the most productive target for your appeals.

Of course, you need not ignore that portion of your audience that does not fit your target. For example, if you were giving a speech against smoking, your target audience might be the smokers in your class. Your main purpose would be to get them to quit, but at the same time, you could convince the non-smokers not to start.

All the methods of audience analysis described in Chapter 11—surveys, observation, interviews, and research—are valuable in collecting information about your audience for a persuasive speech.

Set a Clear Persuasive Purpose

Remember that your objective in a persuasive speech is to move the audience to a specific, attainable attitude or behavior. In a speech to convince, the purpose statement will probably stress an attitude:

> After listening to my speech, my audience members will agree that steps should be taken to save whales from extinction.

In a speech to actuate, the purpose statement will stress a behavior:

> After listening to my speech, the audience members will sign my petition to the United Nations.

As we explained in Chapter 11, your purpose statement should always be specific, attainable, and worded from the audience's point of view. "The purpose of my speech is to save the whales" is not a well-thought-out purpose statement.

Establish "Common Ground"

It helps to stress as many similarities as possible between yourself and your audience. This technique helps prove that you understand them: if not, why should they listen to you? Also, if you share a lot of common ground, it shows you agree on many things; therefore, it should be easy to settle one disagreement—the one related to the attitude or behavior you would like them to change.

The manager of public affairs for *Playboy* magazine gave a good demonstration of establishing common ground when he reminded a group of Southern Baptists that they shared some important values with him:

> I am sure we are all aware of the seeming incongruity of a representative of *Playboy* magazine speaking to an assemblage of representatives of the Southern Baptist Convention. I was intrigued by the invitation when it came last fall, though I was not surprised. I am grateful for your genuine and warm hospitality, and I am flattered (although again not surprised) by the implication that I would have something to say that could have meaning to you people. Both *Playboy* and the Baptists have indeed been considering many of the same issues and ethical problems; and even if we have not arrived at the same conclusions, I am impressed and gratified by your openness and willingness to listen to our views.[23]

Organize According to the Expected Response

It is much easier to get an audience to agree with you if they have already agreed with you on a previous point. Therefore, you should arrange your points in a persuasive speech so you develop a "yes" response. In effect, you get your audience into the habit of agreeing with you. For example, one of the sample speeches that follow is on the donation of body organs. The speaker begins by asking the audience if they would like to be able to get a kidney if they needed one. Then he asks them if they would like to have "a major role in curbing . . . tragic and needless dying. . . ." The presumed answer to both questions is yes. It is only when he has built a pattern of "yes" responses that the speaker asks his audience to sign organ donor cards.

Another example of a speaker who was careful to organize material according to expected audience response was the late Robert Kennedy. Kennedy,

FIGURE 15–1
Speech Evaluation Form

SPEECH EVALUATION FORM

Persuasive Speech

Name_____   Topic_____

Assignment #_____   Date_____

What did you especially like?_____

_____

In your opinion, how could the speech be improved?_____

_____

Please comment on any of the following areas:

Did speaker formulate an effective persuasive strategy?

Did speaker establish own credibility?

Did speaker establish credibility of material used?

Were logical appeals well reasoned?

Were emotional appeals effective?

Did speaker analyze and adapt to audience?

Did speaker appear to have a clear persuasive purpose?

Did speaker establish "common ground"?

Did speaker organize according to expected response?

Did speaker use a variety of appeals and supporting materials effectively?

This evaluation form—or some adaptation of it—might be handy as a guide for your own persuasive speeches, as well as for your evaluation of others' speeches.

when speaking on civil rights before a group of South Africans who believed in racial discrimination, arranged his ideas so that he spoke first on values that he and his audience shared—values like independence and freedom.[24]

If an audience is already basically in agreement with you, you can organize your material to reinforce their attitudes quickly and then spend most of your time convincing them to take a specific course of action. If, on the other hand, they are hostile to your ideas, you have to spend more time getting the first "yes" out of them.

Use a Variety of Appeals and Supporting Materials

You should examine each of your points and ask, "Is there another appeal I could use here?" If you are using only a logical appeal, you could consider emotional appeals or credibility appeals also. The same test applies to supporting material—ask, "Is there any other support I could offer to help prove this point?"

Speech to Convince

Our first sample speech was given by Roger Aden, a student at the University of Nebraska-Lincoln. With it, Roger won first place in the 1984 Interstate Oratorical Association annual tournament.[25] He was coached by Jack Kay. His purpose was to convince his audience that "atomic veterans" are being treated unfairly by the Veteran's Administration. Some comments on his persuasive strategy are in the margin.

The Forgotten Victims

Roger Aden, University of Nebraska-Lincoln

The motto of the Veteran's Administration is simple—"to care for him who shall have borne the battle and for his widow and orphans." Certainly this is a very noble creed. Unfortunately, forcing the VA to carry through on this promise is another matter entirely.

Approximately 250,000 veterans from the different services can attest to the difficulty of this task. They participated in 235 atomic test explosions between the end of World War II and the signing of the Partial Test Ban Treaty in 1963. Like veterans of many other tests, they were told little about the possible dangers of their forced participation in the experiments. But unlike most veterans, atomic veterans have not received VA care for injuries resulting from their test participation. Atomic veterans suffer higher rates of radiation-caused diseases than the general public, yet the VA has refused to provide health care benefits for these men. In exploring the plight of this nation's atomic veterans, we must undertake an examination of the problems faced by these men, discover the three barriers between them and health care, and demand a solution to this problem.

Strategy

Immediate statement of the speaker's thesis. He uses the VA's own words as testimony against them. This technique recurs, to good effect, several times.

He begins development of the problem: he sets up the logic of his main argument and previews his main points.

PERSUASIVE SPEAKING

397

Deductive reasoning serves to define and specify the problem.

Problems addressed today will be limited to the veterans themselves and not their relatives or people living near the atomic test sites. Those are civil questions for the courts to handle. We are dealing with the Veteran's Administration. By law the VA is required to provide health care and compensation to veterans for service-related disability and death. Veterans of our foreign wars have received care in VA hospitals. Vietnam veterans exposed to Agent Orange have collected relief. But *atomic veterans remain the forgotten victims*—victims of ionizing radiation and a careless VA. We need to discover the problems they encounter.

Testimony supports his basic premise.

In a study published in the Journal of the American Medical Association last August, Dr. Glyn Caldwell of the Center for Disease Control found that atomic veterans suffer leukemia at a rate three times the national average. A study conducted by the National Association of Atomic Veterans discovered that fully 70 percent of its membership was victimized by some form of cancer, heart disease, or degenerative muscle disease.

Example, with description and testimony.

John Smitherman was one of those men. He was a subject in two atomic test explosions in 1946 while serving in the navy. According to the *Atlanta Constitution* of May 23, 1983, doctors diagnosed his case as only a lymph system gone haywire. Both his legs were amputated. A chunk of flesh was removed from his back. His left hand swelled to the size of a cataloupe. After going through this living hell, John Smitherman eventually died. Dr. Karl Morgan, director of Health Physics at Oak Ridge National Laboratory, says there is no doubt that Smitherman's death resulted from his participation in atomic test explosions. Yet incredibly the VA denied Smitherman's claim for health care benefits six times.

Statistics, testimony, and a transition to subpoints.

He is not alone. The VA reviewed the cases of nearly 2,000 atomic veterans and found that about 40 percent were suffering various malignancies. But South Dakota Congressman Thomas Daschle reports that the VA has denied an astounding 98 percent of atomic veteran claims. Behind this twisted logic stand three barriers which are nearly insurmountable to atomic veterans seeking health care.

Each argument *against* health care for atomic veterans is analyzed and refuted; testimony and description are entered in evidence.

First, the VA claims that radiation doses received by atomic veterans weren't large enough to cause serious problems. But there is a fundamental flaw in that contention. Any radiation dose, no matter how minute, produces adverse health effects. In 1978, the Nuclear Regulatory Commission issued a document admitting that there is no known safe dose of ionizing radiation. In 1975, the American *Journal of Epidemiology* reported that physicians exposed to X rays suffered higher rates of cancer and leukemia. When you consider the difference between an X ray and a nuclear explosion, the absurdity of the VA's position becomes apparent, especially in light of the appalling safety procedures followed at the tests. In its September 26, 1982, edition, *The New York Times* printed a story about one serviceman who received an X ray of sorts during a 1953 test explosion in the Nevada desert. Joseph Rovenski was told to cover his eyes with his hands when the bomb exploded. It didn't do much good. Rovenski said the blast was so bright he could see the bones through his hands.

In two test explosions near Bikini Atoll in the South Pacific, the International Radiation Research and Training Institute found tolerance levels to be 5,000 times the limit set by the Nuclear Regulatory Commission for nuclear power plant operators. John Smitherman participated in those tests. He was told it was safe to escape the South Pacific heat by cooling off in the Bikini Lagoon, even though dead fish were floating in the lagoon. Dr. Karl Morgan of Oak Ridge National Laboratory says Bikini Atoll is unsafe to inhabit today, but the VA maintains the island was perfectly safe over thirty years ago when the nuclear devices were first detonated. The logic of this statement is similar to my telling you that the sun doesn't set in the west.

Besides ignoring the obvious, the VA also ignores federal law, the second barrier faced by atomic veterans. Public Law 97-72, signed in November 1981, was intended to give any atomic veteran suffering any disability free health care at VA institutions, even if, according to the law, "there is insufficient evidence to conclude that such disability may be associated with exposure to radiation." But in drawing up its guidelines, the VA twisted the intent of Congress. Dr. D. Earl Brown, associate deputy chief medical director of the VA, told a House subcommittee last May that any veteran with a history of radiation exposure would be treated, provided that "they have a condition for which there is no ready explanation." As VA officials see it, leukemia, cancers, and other well-known diseases suffered by atomic veterans have ready explanations which don't include radiation and don't qualify for health care. A partial explanation of the VA's actions can be found in an examination of the third barrier faced by atomic veterans—the attitude of the VA.

Put simply, the VA does not want to deal with this problem. VA spokesperson John Hickman says, "There's no way, medically or scientifically, that these veterans can prove a link between their cancers and the low level of radiation. Many have reached an age now where people tend to develop these problems." At times this blind attitude toward evidence reaches ridiculous porportions. The VA defended the Bikini Atoll tests, saying they were one of the safest operations radiologically in the atmospheric nuclear testing program.

It would seem that the VA does not want to consider the possibility of dealing with 250,000 veterans who may be suffering fatal diseases because of their service. In holding this attitude, VA officials are sacrificing human lives at the expense of dollars. They are also committing one of the gravest injustices this nation has ever witnessed. Clearly, we have a problem begging for a solution.

When considering a solution to this problem, we must keep in mind that the fatal diseases suffered by these men cannot be reversed. The solution, therefore, lies not in curing their ills, but in establishing a sense of justice. Health care will reduce the physical pain, plus give atomic veterans a feeling that their government cares. The morality of the situation can be restored with a three-step approach.

First, an advisory committee must be established outside the VA composed of atomic veterans, representatives of the International Radiation Research and Training Institute, and officials of the VA's Department of Medicine and Surgery.

Second, this committee will be responsible for rewriting the VA guidelines for health care for atomic veterans in accordance with the intent of Public Law 97-72. Congress assumed that all atomic veterans suffering disabilities were harmed by radiation exposure. The guidelines should reflect that assumption.

Third, the committee will serve as an appeals board for VA decisions relating

A logical fallacy is pointed out to refute another argument; then comes more testimony and an analogy.

Testimony backs up a deductive argument.

Another fallacy is pointed out; the VA's own words, once again, are used as testimony against it.

Emotion-laden language.

The solution is previewed.

The three-part solution is developed.

to the health care of atomic veterans now and in the future. If the VA refuses to recognize its responsibility to atomic veterans by denying them health care, the veterans can take their case to the committee.

Unfortunately, this three-step solution will probably not save the life of a single atomic veteran. The diseases they suffer cannot be corrected. But the injustice done them by the Veteran's Administration can be corrected. Shifting the burden of proof to the VA and establishing an avenue of appeal will allow atomic veterans to receive the health care they deserve. That care may not save their lives, but it will preserve the justice and morality in a situation that has for far too long been unjust and immoral. Certainly, that is not too much to ask.

This speaker spends most of his time establishing the problem; only when the problem is fully developed does he introduce the solution. He relies heavily on logical appeals bolstered by testimony. Compare both his strategy and his use of appeals with the second sample speech that follows.

Speech to Actuate

The following speech was given by Philip Doughtie, a student at the University of New Hampshire, Merrimack Valley Branch.[26] His purpose was to persuade his classmates to sign and carry an organ donor card. Some comments on his persuasive strategy are noted in the margin.

The Gift of Life

Strategy

His introduction suggests that this will be a direct persuasive strategy.

He begins with a moderate fear appeal. He previews his thesis.

His next statement suggests that both he and his information are credible.

He begins establishing the problem by explaining that the kidneys are essential organs.

Philip Doughtie, University of New Hampshire, Merrimack Valley Branch

If any of you needed a kidney or other vital organ to live, would you be able to get one? Would you know where to begin searching for information which would lead to obtaining this needed organ?

These are questions many of us have never even considered. Yet, each year, in America alone, many people die with kidney disease because donated kidneys are not available. Now wouldn't it be nice—no; *fantastic*—to have a major role in curbing some of this tragic and needless dying? You can do just that. I'd like to show you how, today.

In researching and preparing for this speech, I had the opportunity to conduct an interview with the state secretary for the Kidney Foundation, Mrs. Florence Murray, at her home. She related some basic background information about kidneys, kidney disease, and kidney donation, and I would like to relay this information to you.

Kidneys are vital to human life. They are the "twin organs" that perform the following vital life-maintaining functions:

1. They clean waste materials and excess fluids from the blood.
2. They filter the blood, retaining some compounds while excreting others.
3. They help regulate blood pressure and red blood cell count.

The human body cannot function without kidneys, and kidney disease is the fourth leading health problem in this country today. Over 8,000,000 Americans suffer from some type of kidney disease. Approximately 60,000 people die of it each year. In addition, over 4,000 children between the ages of one to six are stricken annually with "childhood nephrosis," which is simply medical jargon for kidney disease.

Perhaps your first question might be, "What is being done to combat this disease?" The National Kidney Foundation has many objectives, including the following:

1. It offers advice and assistance on important topics like kidney disease detection (warning signals), diagnosis (tests, X rays, and so on), and drugs needed to treat this disease.
2. It provides assistance in obtaining artificial kidney machines, which are also called dialysis machines.
3. But most important, it coordinates the kidney donation and transplantation program, whereby donors may give one kidney while living or two kidneys posthumously in order to save another person's life.

Since the first kidney transplant back in 1954, over 5,000 of these operations have been performed. Thanks to improved medical techniques, better blood testing, and new tissue-typing processes, doctors are now reducing the risk of organ rejection. If rejection does occur, the patient can go back on dialysis to await a second, third, or even a fourth transplant until one is successful.

To accelerate organ donations, the Kidney Foundation is also responsible for the widespread distribution of these uniform donor cards.

These cards enable you to donate a vital organ after your death. In order to illustrate how this program works, let me use as an example one of our neighbors, whose life was recently saved by a transplant.

I refer to a sixteen-year-old New Hampshire boy, John Warner, Jr., whose body had already rejected his father's kidney transplant. Now a second transplant was essential to save the boy, whose parents could not afford the costly dialysis machine—$150 per treatment, three treatments per week. Luckily, on December 9 of this year, a matching tissue donor posthumously gave his kidney to Johnny, and the transplantation was performed and determined a success. The original transplant from his father came three years earlier, and the boy had waited since then for a matching kidney. Now, thanks to this wonderful donation, no further wait was necessary. Instances like these really touch us when we stop to realize that the next victim could be someone close to us.

I had the opportunity to speak with Dr. John Steinmuller, a well-known New Hampshire nephrologist and head of the "organ-retrieval team" whose job it is to go out and retrieve the organs that donors have pledged.

Dr. Steinmuller told me that skeptics always have excuses for not giving a vital organ, and he asked me to say a few words about some of those excuses:

1. The first excuse is usually a lack of knowledge about the donation procedures. People do not know where to go or whom to contact. This is a problem I hope to solve for you in just a minute.

He explains next that kidney disease is prevalent, using an inductive argument.

He begins to set up his solution.

(Here he picks up one of the cards as an illustration.)

He offers some evidence that the solution is a good one. He uses an emotional appeal.

He misses a transition here, which is a little confusing.

He builds up credibility for his next point.

He answers some potential arguments.

2. **Apathy and lack of time.** Some people are indifferent to the needs of others—they just do not care, or they claim to be too busy to waste time on such endeavors. Actually, there is little or no time involved, and I know from personal experience that you are not apathetic people.

3. **Inconvenience.** Some people fear a delay in funeral and burial arrangements. However, since the operation has to be performed immediately after death, no delay is ever caused in funeral arrangements.

4. **Usefulness.** Some people assume that their gift will not be used. So far, however, the overwhelming problem has been a lack of donors—not recipients.

Consider now two reasons why each of us should give of ourselves in this worthwhile way:

1. **The gift of life itself.** The act of giving this organ will very probably save someone's life in the future. Isn't that a nice thought—to think that you had a part in saving another human's life?

2. **Personal pride and satisfaction.** How can anyone be prouder or more satisfied with himself or herself than when he or she has contributed to an effort that saves lives? No emotions can compare with those associated with a generous donation for the sake of others.

Perhaps one last question in your mind might be: If I sign up at this time, can I change my mind later? The answer to this question is yes. Since the only way authorities will know you are a donor is by the donor card in your possession, you could simply tear up the card at any time, and no one will be the wiser.

Now that all of you are more informed about this vital and worthy program, I would like to conclude my speech by setting the example—signing the first donor card myself. Then I will circulate the other cards to each of you.

Please search your innermost being, and conclude that such a gift would be an unselfish and generous sacrifice on your part, and then sign the donor card. Thank you very much.

This speaker used many persuasive techniques in ways that are relatively easy to point out. Your own speech might not be as direct, and it might not follow persuasive strategy in quite so lockstep a fashion. However, your speech will almost certainly be improved by a consideration of the techniques discussed in this chapter.

He provides his own arguments in favor of the action he wants them to take.

He answers a final argument.

He asks for a specific response, and he makes it as easy as possible.

▶ SUMMARY

Persuasion—the act of moving someone, through communication, toward some particular belief, attitude, or behavior—can be both worthwhile and ethical. It is different from coercion in that it makes an audience *want* to do what you want them to do.

Persuasion can be categorized according to the type of question (fact, value, and policy), approach (direct or indirect), or its outcome (convincing or actuating). A typical strategy for a speech to convince requires you to establish a problem and a solution. For a speech to actuate, you also have to establish a desired audience response. For each of these components, you need to analyze the arguments your audience will have against accepting what you say and then answer those arguments.

A persuasive strategy is put into effect through the use of persuasive appeals, which include credibility appeals (based on the competence, character, and charisma of the source of information), logical appeals (based on reasoning), and emotional appeals (based on emotions like fear, anger, pride, or pity). Logical appeals must be checked for fallacies such as insufficient evidence, non sequiturs, or evasions of argument.

Techniques for effective persuasive speaking include the formulation of a clear persuasive purpose, establishing common ground, organizing material according to an expected "yes" response, and using a variety of appeals and supporting material.

ACTIVITIES ◄

1. Find a current political speech in *Vital Speeches of the Day, The New York Times* on microfilm, or some other source. Which type of persuasive strategy is used in the speech, direct or indirect? Is the strategy used effectively? Why or why not?

2. Identify an advertisement, editorial, or sales pitch with which you are familiar. Is this message, in your opinion, ethical or unethical? Does it conform to the definition of ethical persuasion given in this chapter?

3. For practice in analyzing different types of persuasive appeals, try one or both of the following:
   a. What appeals (logical, emotional, credibility-based) might be used for each of the following:

   Teacher to student: "Study diligently in this course."
   Parent to kids: "Don't drink and drive."
   Charity to potential donors: "Give us your money and time."

   b. Examine an everyday appeal of your own choosing. This appeal might be one made by a child to a parent, by one friend to another, by a student to a teacher, or by anyone else who is trying to change someone else's attitude or behavior or both. Decide which elements of this appeal are based on logic, which elements are based on emotion, and which are based on credibility.

4. For practice in formulating persuasive strategies, choose one of the following topics, and analyze it according to the checklist in Table 15–2 (p. 381).
   a. Parole should (should not) be abolished.
   b. Standardized tests should (should not) be used as the main criteria for college admissions.
   c. The capital of the United States should (should not) be moved to a more central location.

d. Police should (should not) be required to carry nonlethal weapons only.

e. Capital punishment should (should not) be abolished.

f. Bilingual education should (should not) be required for all schools serving bilingual students.

5. The chapter points out that one common shortcoming in the use of logical appeals is "disguised faulty premises." In your experiences with landlords, banks, loan companies, registrars, deans, and other people, what "disguised faulty premises" and "illogical rules" have you encountered? Explain why you think the logic is faulty.

6. Consider the topic you have selected for your next speech. List four or five emotional appeals that you could employ. Which appeals might be successful when you speak to your classmates? Why?

7. From your experiences hearing or reading persuasive messages about social or political issues, how well do you think the advice for planning a strategy to convince is followed? If you think such advice is *not* heeded, what steps or components of the process are most often ignored or slighted?

8. Study the sample speech to actuate. Has the speaker explained the problem, the solution, and the audience's role in the solution adequately? Can you suggest any changes that might have improved his presentation?

▶ **NOTES**

1. For an incisive look into the problem of deception, see Robert Hopper and Robert H. Bell, "Broadening the Deception Construct," *Quarterly Journal of Speech* 67:3 (August 1984): 288–302. These authors found six different types of deception: fictions, playings, lies, crimes, masks, and unlies. Another recent analysis is Michael Osborne, "The Abuses of Argument," *Southern Speech Communication Journal* 49:1 (Fall 1983), 1–11. Osborne lists six major abuses.

2. Greg Robinson, "The Frivolous Fever," *Winning Orations, 1986* (Interstate Oratorical Association, 1986), p. 65.

3. Matthew J. Solomon, "A Case of Liable," *Winning Orations, 1986* (Interstate Oratorical Association, 1986), p. 23.

4. Samantha L. Hubbard, "Irradiation of Food," *Winning Orations, 1986* (Interstate Oratorical Association, 1986), p. 1.

5. Laurel Johnson, "Where There's a Will There's a Way," *Winning Orations, 1986* (Interstate Oratorical Association, 1986), p. 59.

6. Nancy Reagan, "The Battle Against Drugs: What Can You Do?" *Vital Speeches of the Day* (August 15, 1986), p. 645.

7. William Shakespeare, *Julius Caesar,* Act III, Scene ii.

8. Some research findings suggest that audiences may perceive a direct strategy as a threat to their "freedom" to form their own opinions. This perception hampers persuasion. See J. W. Brehm, *A Theory of Psychological Reactance* (New York: Academic Press, 1966). There also exists considerable evidence to suggest that announcing an intent to persuade in the introduction can reduce a message's effectiveness. Sample studies on this matter include J. Allyn and L. Festinger, "The Effectiveness of Unanticipated Persuasive Communications," *Journal of Abnormal and Social Psychology* 62 (1961): 35–40; C. A. Kiesler and S. B. Kiesler, "Role of Forewarning in Persuasive Communications," *Journal of Abnormal and Social Psychology* 18 (1971): 210–221.

9. Censorship of this type is, in fact, on the rise. See, for example, Fred M. Hechinger, "Censorship Found on the Increase," *The New York Times* (September 16, 1986), p. C1.

10. Jerzy Kosinsky, "Against Book Censorship," in George Rodman (ed.) *Mass Media Issues: Analysis and Debate* (Chicago: SRA, 1984), p. 21.

11. Joseph A. DeVito, *The Communication Handbook: A Dictionary* (New York: Harper & Row, 1986), pp. 84–86.

12. Joan Braaten, "It's English," *Winning Orations, 1984* (Interstate Oratorical Association, 1984), p. 64.

13. Aristotle once stated, "Everyone who persuades by proof in fact uses either enthymemes or examples. There is no other way," (*The Rhetoric,* op. cit., 1.2, 1356b 5–7). An excellent modern look at the enthymeme and the nature of argument is Thomas M. Conley, "The Enthymeme in Perspective," *Quarterly Journal of Speech* 70:2 (May 1984): 168.

14. An explanation of two theories of why reasoning breaks down is provided in Sally Jackson, "Two Methods of Syllogistic Reasoning: An Empirical Comparison," *Communication Monographs* 49 (September 1982).

15. P. C. Wason and P. N. Johnson-Laird, *Psychology of Reasoning: Structure and Content* (Cambridge, Mass.: Harvard University, 1972), p. 2.

16. Joan Braaten, op. cit.

17. See, for example, Vincent E. Barry, *Practical Logic* (New York: Holt, Rinehart and Winston, 1976).

18. Max Black, "Fallacies," in Jerry M. Anderson and Paul J. Dovre (eds.), *Readings in Argumentation* (Boston: Allyn and Bacon, 1968), pp. 301–311.

19. Emotional proof is sometimes necessary because people will cling to unwarranted, untrue beliefs even if those beliefs have been disproved empirically. See, for example, Mary John Smith, "Cognitive Schema Theory and the Perseverance and Attenuation of Unwarranted Empirical Beliefs," *Communication Monographs* 49 (June 1982): 115–126. For an article exploring the nature, function, and scope of emotional appeals, see Michael J. Hyde, "Emotion and Human Communication: A Rhetorical, Scientific, and Philosophical Picture." *Communication Quarterly* 32:2 (Spring 1984): 120–132.

20. Irving L. Janis and Seymour Feshbach, "Effects of Fear-Arousing Communications," *Journal of Abnormal and Social Psychology* 48 (1953): 78–92.

21. Michael Eliot Howard, "America and the Wider World." *Vital Speeches of the Day,* (July 1, 1984), p. 557.

22. For an examination of how one politician adapted to his audience's attitudes, see David Zarefsky, "Subordinating the Civil Rights Issue: Lyndon Johnson in 1964," *Southern Speech Communication Journal* 48 (Winter 1983): 103–118.

23. Anson Mount, speech before Southern Baptist Convention, in Wil A. Linkugel, R. R. Allen, and Richard Johannessen (eds), *Contemporary American Speeches,* 3d ed. (Belmont, Calif.: Wadsworth, 1973).

24. Harriet J. Rudolf, "Robert F. Kennedy at Stellenbosch University," *Communication Quarterly* 31 (Summer 1983): 205–211.

25. Roger Aden, "The Forgotten Victims," *Winning Orations, 1984* (Interstate Oratorical Association, 1984), p. 55.

26. Classroom speech presented December 14, 1976.

GLOSSARY

Abstract language   Language that lacks specificity, that fails to refer to observable behavior or other sense data. *See also* Behavioral description.

Abstraction ladder   A range of more-to-less abstract terms describing an event or object.

Actuating   *See* Strategy to actuate.

Addition   The articulation error that involves adding extra parts to words.

Advising response   A helping response in which the receiver offers suggestions about how the speaker should deal with a problem.

Affect blend   The combination of two or more expressions, each showing a different emotion.

Affection   The social need to care for others and know that one is cared for.

Ambiguous response   A disconfirming response with more than one meaning, leaving the other party unsure of the responder's position.

Ambushing   A style in which the receiver listens carefully to gather information to use in an attack on the speaker.

Analogy   An extended comparison that can be used as supporting material in a speech.

Analyzing response   A helping style in which the listener offers an interpretation of a speaker's message.

Anecdote   A brief personal story, used to illustrate or support a point in a speech.

Articulation   The process of pronouncing all the necessary parts of a word.

Assertion   A direct expression of the sender's needs, thoughts, or feelings, delivered in a way that does not attack the receiver's dignity.

Attitude   A predisposition to respond to an idea, person, or thing favorably or unfavorably.

Attending   The process of focusing on certain stimuli from the environment. *See also* Selection.

Audience analysis   A consideration of characteristics including the type, goals, demographics, beliefs, attitudes, and values of your listeners.

Authoritarian leadership style   A leadership style in which the designated leader uses legitimate, coercive, and reward power to dictate the group's actions.

Bar chart   A visual aid that compares two or more values by showing them as elongated horizontal rectangles.

Basic speech structure   The division of a speech into introduction, body, and conclusion.

Behavioral description   An account that refers only to observable phenomena.

Belief   An underlying conviction about the truth of an idea, often based on cultural training.

Brainstorming   A method for creatively generating ideas in groups by minimizing criticism and encouraging a large quantity of ideas without regard to their workability or ownership by individual members.

Causal reasoning   *See* Cause-effect pattern.

Cause-effect pattern   Organizing plan for a speech that demonstrates how one or more events result in another event or events.

Certainty   Messages that dogmatically imply that the speaker's position is correct and that the other person's ideas are not worth considering. Likely to generate a defensive response.

Channel   The medium through which a message passes from sender to receiver.

Charisma   The dimension of credibility that is a combination of a speaker's enthusiasm and likability.

Climax pattern   Organizing plan for a speech that builds ideas to the point of maximum interest or tension.

Closed question   Interview question that can be answered in a few words.

Coercive power   The power to influence others by the threat or imposition of unpleasant consequences.

Cohesiveness   The totality of forces that causes members to feel themselves part of a group and makes them want to remain in that group.

Column chart   Visual aid that compares two or more values by showing them as elongated vertical rectangles.

Communication   A continuous, irreversible, transactive process involving communicators who occupy different but overlapping environments and are simultaneously senders and receivers of messages, many of which are distorted by physical and psychological noise.

Communication climate   The emotional tone of a relationship as it is expressed in the messages that the partners send and receive.

Conclusion (of a speech)   The final structural unit of a speech, in which the main points are reviewed and final remarks are made to motivate the audience to act or help listeners remember key ideas.

Confirming response   A message that expresses caring or respect for another person.

Conflict   An expressed struggle between at least two interdependent parties who perceive incompatible goals, scarce rewards, and interference from the other party in achieving their goals.

Connotation   The emotional associations of a term.

Consensus   Agreement between group members about a decision.

Content message   A message that communicates information about the subject being discussed. *See also* Relational message.

Control   The social need to influence others.

Controlling communication   Messages in which the sender tries to impose some sort of outcome on the receiver, usually resulting in a defensive reaction.

Coordination   The state of being equal in rank, quality, or significance. In outlining, the principle of coordination requires that all main points be of similar importance and that they be logically related to one another.

Crazymaking   An indirect expression of aggression, delivered in a way that allows the sender to maintain a facade of kindness.

Credibility   The believability of a speaker or other source of information.

Debilitative stage fright   Intense level of anxiety about speaking before an audience, resulting in poor performance.

Decoding   The process in which a receiver attaches meaning to a message.

Deduction   Reasoning from a generality to a specific conclusion.

Defensive listening   A response style in which the receiver perceives a speaker's comments as an attack.

Democratic leadership style   A style in which the nominal leader invites the group's participation in decision making.

Demographics   Audience characteristics that can be analyzed statistically, such as age, gender, education, group membership, and so on.

Denotation   The objective, emotion-free meaning of a term. *See also* Connotation.

Descriptive communication   Messages that describe the speaker's position without evaluating others. Synonymous with "I" language.

Diagram   A line drawing that shows the most important components of an object.

Direct aggression   An expression of the sender's thoughts or feelings or both that attacks the position and dignity of the receiver.

Direct persuasion   Persuasion that does not try to hide or disguise the speaker's persuasive purpose.

Direct question   Interview question that makes a straightforward request for information.

Disconfirming response   A message that expresses a lack of caring or respect for another person.

Disfluency   A nonlinguistic verbalization, for example, *um, er, ah.*

Dysfunctional roles   Individual roles played by group members that inhibit the group's effective operation. *See also* Functional roles.

Emblems   Deliberate nonverbal behaviors with precise meanings, known to virtually all members of a cultural group.

Emotional appeal   An argument that uses feelings like love, hate, fear, guilt, anger, loneliness, envy, or pity to entice an audience to change its attitude or behavior.

Emotive language   Language that conveys the sender's attitude rather than simply offering an objective description.

Empathic listening   Listening in which the goal is to help the speaker solve a problem.

Empathy   The ability to project oneself into another person's point of view, so as to experience the other's thoughts and feelings.

Encoding   The process of putting thoughts into symbols, most commonly words.

Enthymeme   Compressed version of a syllogism in which the underlying premises are not stated.

Environment   Both the physical setting in which communication occurs and the personal perspectives of the parties involved.

Equality   A type of supportive communication described by Gibb, suggesting that the sender regards the receiver as worthy of respect.

Equivocal words   Words that have more than one dictionary definition.

Ethical persuasion   Persuasion in an audience's best interest that does not depend on false or misleading information to induce change in that audience.

Euphemism A pleasant-sounding term used in place of a more direct but less pleasant one.

Evaluative communication Messages in which the sender judges the receiver in some way, usually resulting in a defensive response.

Evaluative listening Listening in which the goal is to judge the quality or accuracy of the speaker's remarks.

Evasion of argument Communication in which the speaker dodges the question at hand by arguing over some other, unrelated point.

Example A specific case that is used to demonstrate a general idea.

Exhaustiveness (in outlining) The quality of including all the necessary information in the organizational plan.

Expert power The ability to influence others by virtue of one's perceived expertise on the subject in question. *See also* Information power.

Explicit norms Norms that are publicly defined. *See also* Implicit norms.

Extemporaneous speech A speech that is planned in advance but presented in a direct, conversational manner.

External noise Factors outside the receiver that interfere with the accurate reception of a message.

Facilitative stage fright A moderate level of anxiety about speaking before an audience that helps improve the speaker's performance.

Factual question Interview question that investigates matters of fact. *See also* Opinion question.

Factual statement A statement based on direct observation of sense data.

Fallacy of approval The irrational belief that it is vital to win the approval of virtually every person a communicator deals with.

Fallacy of catastrophic expectations The irrational belief that the worst possible outcome will probably occur.

Fallacy of overgeneralization Irrational beliefs in which (1) conclusions (usually negative) are based on limited evidence or (2) communicators exaggerate their shortcomings.

Fallacy of perfection The irrational belief that a worthwhile communicator should be able to handle every situation with complete confidence and skill.

Focus The quality of having each division of an idea contain only one point.

Force field analysis A method of problem analysis that identifies the forces contributing to resolution of the problem and the forces that inhibit its resolution.

Formal outline A consistent format and set of symbols used to identify the structure of ideas. *See also* Speech structure.

Forum A discussion format in which audience members are invited to add their comments to those of the official discussants.

Functional roles Member roles (usually unstated) that must be carried out if the group is to accomplish its task-related goals. *See also* Task functions; Maintenance functions.

General needs Needs that are shared by all humans. *See also* Maslow's needs.

General purpose One of three basic ways a speaker seeks to affect an audience: to entertain, inform, or persuade.

Gibb categories Six sets of contrasting styles of verbal and nonverbal behavior. Each set describes a communication style that is likely to arouse defensiveness and a contrasting style that is likely to prevent or reduce it. Developed by Jack Gibb.

Group A small collection of people who interact with each other, usually face-to-face, over time in order to reach goals.

Group goals Goals that a group collectively seeks to accomplish. *See also* Individual goals.

Growth group A group whose goal is to help members learn more about themselves.

Hearing The process wherein sound waves strike the eardrum and cause vibrations that are transmitted to the brain.

Hidden agendas Individual goals that group members are unwilling to reveal.

Hypothetical example Example that asks an audience to imagine an object or event.

"I" language Language that describes the speaker's position without evaluating others. Synonymous with *description*.

Illustrators Nonverbal behaviors that accompany and support verbal messages.

Imaging Technique for behavior rehearsal (for example, for a speech) that involves visualization of the successful completion of the task.

Impersonal communication Behavior that treats others as objects rather than as individuals. *See also* Interpersonal communication.

Impersonal response   A disconfirming response that is superficial or trite.

Impervious response   A disconfirming response that ignores another person's attempt to communicate.

Implicit norms   Norms that are not publicly discussed. *See also* Explicit norms.

Impromptu speech   A speech given "off the top of one's head," without preparation.

Inclusion   The social need to feel a sense of belonging in some relationship with others.

Incongruous response   A disconfirming response in which two messages, one of which is usually nonverbal, contradict one another.

Indirect aggression   A concealed attack on another person. *See also* Crazymaking.

Indirect question   Interview question that does not directly request the information being sought. *See also* Direct question.

Individual goals   The motives of individual members that influence their behavior in groups. *See also* Group goals.

Induction   Reasoning from specific evidence to a general conclusion.

Inferential statement   A statement based on interpretation of sense data.

Information hunger   An audience's desire to learn information. Created by a speaker.

Information power   The ability to influence others by virtue of the otherwise obscure information one possesses. *See also* Expert power.

Informational listening   Listening in which the goal is to receive accurately the same thoughts the speaker is trying to convey.

Insensitive listening   Failure to recognize the thoughts or feelings that are not directly expressed by a speaker, instead accepting the speaker's words at face value.

Insufficient evidence   A fallacy in which not enough proof is offered to support an argument.

Insulated listening   A style in which the receiver ignores undesirable information.

Interactive communication model   A characterization of communication as a two-way event in which sender and receiver exchange messages in response to one another.

Interpersonal communication   Communication in which the parties consider one another as unique individuals rather than as objects. It is characterized by minimal use of stereotyped labels; unique, idiosyncratic social rules; and a high degree of information exchange.

Interpersonal relationship   An association in which the parties meet each other's social needs to some degree.

Interpretation   The act of attaching meaning to a set of stimuli.

Interrupting response   A disconfirming response in which one communicator interrupts another.

Interview   A form of oral communication involving two parties, at least one of whom has a preconceived and serious purpose and both of whom speak and listen from time to time.

Intimate distance   One of Hall's four distance zones, ranging from skin contact to eighteen inches.

Introduction (of a speech)   The first structural unit of a speech, in which the speaker captures the audience's attention and previews the main points to be covered.

Irrational thinking   Beliefs that have no basis in reality or logic; one source of debilitative stage fright.

Irrelevant response   A disconfirming response in which one communicator's comments bear no relationship to the previous speaker's ideas.

Johari Window   A model that describes the relationship between self-disclosure and self-awareness.

Judging response   A reaction in which the receiver evaluates the sender's message either favorably or unfavorably.

Kinesics   The study of body motion.

Laissez-faire leadership style   A style in which the designated leader gives up his or her formal role, transforming the group into a leaderless collection of individuals.

Language   A system of symbols that follows semantic and syntactic rules to convey meaning.

Leader   *See* Nominal leader.

Leadership   The ability to influence the behavior of others in a group.

Learning group   A group whose goal is to expand their knowledge about some topic other than itself or its individual members. *See also* Growth group.

Legitimate power   The ability to influence a group owing to one's position in a group. *See also* Nominal leader.

Line chart   A visual aid consisting of a grid that maps out the direction of a trend by plotting a series of points.

Linear communication model   A characterization of communication as a one-way event in which a message flows from sender to receiver.

Listening   The process wherein the brain reconstructs electrochemical impulses generated by hearing into representations of the original sound and gives them meaning.

Logical appeal   A series of statements that leads, through the use of reason, to the conclusion that the speaker is trying to establish.

Logical fallacy   A statement that at first may appear logical but that under closer scrutiny fails to satisfy the conditions of valid inference.

Lose-lose problem solving   An approach to conflict resolution in which neither party achieves its goals.

Maintenance functions   Functional roles concerned with maintaining smooth personal relationships among group members. Also termed "Social functions." *See also* Task functions.

Managerial Grid   A two-dimensional model that describes the various combinations of a leader's concern with task-related and relational goals.

Manipulators   Movements in which one part of the body grooms, massages, rubs, holds, fidgets, pinches, picks, or otherwise manipulates another part.

Manuscript speech   A speech that is read word-for-word from a prepared text.

Maslow's needs   A hierarchy of needs that motivate humans, that is, physical, safety, social, self-esteem, and self-actualization needs in that order.

Memorized speech   A speech that is learned and delivered by rote without a written text.

Message   A sender's planned and unplanned words and nonverbal behaviors.

Metacommunication   Messages (usually relational) that refer to other messages: Communication about communication.

Mixed messages   Contradiction between a verbal message and one or more nonverbal cues.

Model   A simplified representation of some process or object.

Negotiation   A process in which two or more parties discuss specific proposals in order to find a mutually acceptable agreement.

Networks   Patterns that individual channels of communication form between group members.

Neutrality   A defense-arousing behavior described by Gibb in which the sender expresses indifference toward a receiver.

Noise   External, physiological, and psychological distractions that interfere with the accurate transmission and reception of a message.

Nominal leader   The person who is identified by title as the leader of a group.

Nonassertion   The inability to express one's thoughts or feelings when necessary. Nonassertion may be due to a lack of confidence or communication skill or both.

Non sequitur fallacy   An argument in which the conclusion is unrelated to the proof offered.

Nonverbal communication   Messages expressed by other than linguistic means.

Norms   Rules that govern the behavior of group members.

Number chart   Visual aid that lists numbers in tabular form in order to clarify information.

One-way communication   Communication in which a receiver provides no feedback to a sender.

Open question   Interview question that requires the interviewee to respond in detail. *See also* Closed question.

Opinion question   Interview question seeking the interviewee's opinion. *See also* Factual question.

Organization   The act of arranging perceived data in some manner.

Organizational chart   A graphic representation of the authority relationships in an organization.

Panel discussion   A discussion format in which participants consider a topic more or less conversationally, without formal procedural rules. Panel discussions may be facilitated by a moderator.

Paralanguage   Nonlinguistic means of vocal expression: rate, pitch, tone, and so on.

Parallel relationship   One in which the balance of power shifts from one party to the other according to the situation.

Paraphrasing   Feedback in which the receiver rewords the speaker's thoughts and feelings. Can be used to verify understanding, demonstrate empathy, and help others solve their problems.

Parliamentary procedure   A problem-solving method in which specific rules govern the way issues may be discussed and decisions made.

Participative decision making   Development of solutions with input by the people who will be affected.

Perception checking   A three-part method for verifying the accuracy of interpretations, including a description of the sense data, two possible interpretations, and a request for confirmation of the interpretations.

Personal distance   One of Hall's four distance zones, ranging from eighteen inches to four feet.

Persuasion   The act of motivating a listener, through communication, to change a particular belief, attitude, value, or behavior.

Physical need   Identified by Maslow as the most fundamental type of human need. Includes sufficient food, air, rest, and the ability to reproduce as a species.

Physiological noise   Biological factors in the receiver that interfere with accurate reception of a message.

Pictograph   A visual aid that artistically modifies a chart or graph in order to make it more interesting.

Pie chart   A visual aid that divides a circle into wedges, representing percentages of the whole.

Pitch   The highness of lowness of one's voice.

Primary question   The first question asked to elicit information on an interview topic. See also Secondary question.

Probative question   An open question used to analyze a problem by encouraging exploratory thinking.

Probe   See Secondary question.

Problem orientation   A supportive style of communication described by Gibb in which the communicators focus on working together to solve their problems instead of trying to impose their own solutions on one another.

Problem-solution pattern   Organizing pattern for a speech that describes an unsatisfactory state of affairs and then proposes a plan to remedy the problem.

Problem-solving group   A task-related group whose goal is to resolve a mutual concern of its members.

Procedural norms   Norms that describe rules for the group's operation. See also Task norms; Social norms.

Prod   Word or phrase that encourages a speaker to continue talking.

Provisionalism   A supportive style of communication described by Gibb in which the sender expresses a willingness to consider the other person's position.

Proxemics   The study of how people and animals use space.

Pseudolistening   An imitation of true listening in which the receiver's mind is elsewhere.

Psychological noise   Forces within a communicator that interfere with the ability to express or understand a message accurately.

Public distance   One of Hall's four distance zones, extending outward from twelve feet.

Purpose statement   A complete sentence that describes precisely what a speaker wants to accomplish.

Quantification   The use of numbers to clarify a concept.

Question of fact   Issue in which there are two or more sides of conflicting factual evidence.

Question of policy   Issue that involves adopting or rejecting a specific course of action.

Question of value   Issue involving the worth of some idea, person, or object.

Questioning   Feedback that usually requests the speaker to supply additional information in order to clarify or expand the receiver's understanding. Also, a style of helping in which the receiver seeks additional information from the sender. Some questioning responses are really disguised advice.

Rate   The speed at which a speaker utters words.

Reasoning by analogy   An argument based on the similarity between two ideas.

Receiver   One who notices and attends to a message.

Referent power   The ability to influence others by virtue of the degree to which one is liked or respected.

Reflected appraisal   The theory that a person's self-concept matches the way the person believes others regard him or her.

Relational message   A message that expresses the social relationship between two or more individuals.

Relationship   See Interpersonal relationship.

Relative words   Words that gain their meaning by comparison.

Remembering   The act of recalling previously introduced information. Recall drops off in two phases: short- and long-term.

Residual message   The part of a message a receiver can recall after short- and long-term memory loss.

Reward power   The ability to influence others by the granting or promise of desirable consequences.

Roles   The patterns of behavior expected of group members.

Safety need   Identified by Maslow as protection from threats to an individual's well-being.

Secondary question   Follow-up question used in an interview to elicit information not revealed by a primary question.

Selection   The act of attending to stimuli from the environment.

Selective listening   A listening style in which the receiver responds only to messages that interest him or her.

Self-actualization   One of five of Maslow's needs. The desire to reach one's maximum potential.

Self-concept   The relatively stable set of perceptions each individual holds of himself or herself.

Self-disclosure   The process of deliberately revealing information about oneself that is significant and that would not normally be known by others.

Self-esteem   The degree of regard a person holds for himself or herself.

Self-fulfilling prophecy A prediction or expectation of an event that makes the outcome more likely to occur than would otherwise have been the case.

Semantic rules Rules that govern the meaning of language as opposed to its structure. See *also* Syntactic rules.

Sender The creator of a message.

Sign reasoning Reasoning from specific evidence to a specific conclusion without explaining how the evidence and conclusion are related.

Significant other A person whose opinion is important enough to affect one's self-concept strongly.

Signpost A phrase that emphasizes the importance of upcoming material in a speech.

Situational leadership A theory that argues that the most effective leadership style varies according to leader-member relations, the nominal leader's power, and the task structure.

Slurring The articulation error that involves overlapping the end of one word with the beginning of the next.

Social distance One of Hall's distance zones, ranging from four to twelve feet.

Social goals Motives of individual group members related to satisfying their social needs, for example, inclusion, control, affection. See *also* Task-related goals.

Social group A group whose goal is to meet the social needs of its members rather than to meet task-related goals.

Social needs Identified by Maslow as needs associated with one's interpersonal relationships. See *also* Inclusion; Control; Affection.

Social norms Norms that govern the relationship of group members to each other. See *also* Task norms; Procedural norms.

Spatial pattern Organizing plan in a speech that arranges points according to their physical location.

Specific needs The needs of a particular audience as opposed to "general needs."

Specific purpose The precise effect that the speaker wants to have on an audience. Expressed in the form of a *purpose statement.*

Spontaneity A supportive communication behavior described by Gibb in which the sender expresses a message without any attempt to manipulate the receiver.

Stage hogging A listening style in which the receiver is more concerned with making his or her own point than in understanding the speaker.

Statistic Numbers arranged or organized to show how a fact or principle is true for a large number of cases.

Strategy A defense-arousing style of communication described by Gibb in which the sender tries to manipulate or trick a receiver; also the general term for any type of plan, as in the plan for a persuasive speech.

Strategy to actuate Persuasive plan that seeks to move an audience to immediate action.

Strategy to convince Persuasive strategy that seeks to change the way an audience thinks. See *also* Actuating.

Substitution The articulation error that involves replacing part of a word with an incorrect sound.

Superiority A defense-arousing style of communication described by Gibb in which the sender states or implies that the receiver is not worthy of respect.

Supporting response A response style in which the receiver reassures, comforts, or distracts the person seeking help.

Survey research Information gathering in which the responses of a sample of a population are collected to disclose information about the larger group.

Syllogism Arguments made up of two premises and a conclusion.

Symbol An arbitrary sign used to represent a thing, person, idea, event, or relationship in ways that make communication possible.

Symposium A discussion format in which participants divide the topic in a manner that allows each member to deliver in-depth information without interruption.

Syntactic rules Rules that govern the ways symbols can be arranged as opposed to the meanings of those symbols. See *also* Semantic rules.

Tangential response A disconfirming response that uses the speaker's remark as a starting point for a shift to a new topic.

Target audience That part of an audience that must be influenced in order to achieve a persuasive goal.

Task functions Functional roles of group members concerned with accomplishing the group's stated task. See *also* Maintenance functions.

Task norms Norms that focus on how a group should achieve its goal. See *also* Social norms; Procedural norms.

Task-related goals Goals related to accomplishing the group's stated purpose for operating.

Territory Fixed space that an individual assumes some right to occupy.

Testimony Supporting material that proves or illustrates a point by citing an authoritative source.

Thesis statement A complete sentence describing the central idea of a speech.

Topic pattern Organizing scheme for a speech that arranges points according to logical types or categories.

Trait theories of leadership The belief that it is

possible to identify leaders by personal traits, such as intelligence, appearance, or sociability.

Transactional communication model   A characterization of communication as the simultaneous sending and receiving of messages in an ongoing, irreversible process.

Transition   Phrase that connects ideas in a speech by showing how one relates to the other.

Two-way communication   An exchange of information in which the receiver deliberately provides feedback to a sender.

Understanding   The act of interpreting a message by following grammatical and semantic rules.

Value   A deeply rooted belief about a concept's inherent worth.

Visual aid   Graphic devices used in a speech to illustrate or support ideas.

Visualization   The technique for self-improvement that involves one's imagining the successful completion of a task.

Word chart   Visual aid that lists words or terms in tabular form in order to clarify information.

Whorf-Sapir hypothesis   The theory that the structure of a language shapes the worldview of its users.

Win-lose problem solving   An approach to conflict resolution in which one party reaches its goal at the expense of the other.

Win-win problem solving   An approach to conflict resolution in which the parties work together to satisfy all their goals.

"You" language   Language that judges another person, increasing the likelihood of a defensive reaction. *See also* Evaluative communication.

INDEX

A

Abstraction ladder, 65
Abstract language, 65–69
   vs. behavioral descriptions, 67–69
Active listening, 76–78
Actuating, 378–379, 383–384; *see also* Persuasion
Aden, Roger, 397
Addition of speech sounds, 341–342
Ad hominen arguments, 391–392
Advising, 92
Affect blends, 115
Affection, 9, 107, 137
Agenda, 200
Age of audience members, 274
Aggression, 172–173
Alexander, Shana, 264–265
Altman, Irwin, 148
Ambiguity, 164
   in nonverbal communication, 105, 108–109
Ambushing, 83
Amplification, in interviews, 199
Analogies, 309–310, 360
   reasoning by, 390
Analyzing response, 93–94
Anecdotes, 301, 310–311, 360–361
Anger, appeals to, 393
Animal communication, 6
Anticlimatic organization, 300
Anxiety, speech. *See* Stage fright
Appearance, 253, 337
Appraisal interview, 207
Apprehension, speech. *See* Stage fright
Approval, fallacy of, 344–345
Architectural symbolism, 125
Articulation, 341–343
Asch, Solomon, 255–256
Assertive behavior, 173; *see also* Win-win resolutions
Assimilation to prior input, 82
Assumptions, 28, 31–32, 120
Attending, 79–80

Attitudes, 275–277
   and language, 53–61
Attraction, 60–61
Attractiveness, 249
Audience
   adaptation, 394
   analysis, 272–277, 394–395
   expectation, 279
   involvement, 364–365
   participation, 364
   response, 383–384
   types of, 273
Audio aids, 320–321
Audiovisual aids. *See* Visual aids
Auditory aspects of delivery, 339–342
Authoritarian leadership, 253
Authority rule, 230–231
Avoiding stage, 146

B

Bach, George, 156–157, 172–182
Background noise, 79
Balance, in interviews, 190
Bar charts, 317–318
Barker, Larry, 79
"Bawlamerese," 343
Behavioral descriptions, 67–68, 179
Beliefs, 275–276
Bergman, Ingmar, 310
Bias, lack of, 385–386
Bibliography, for speech, 295
Black, Max, 390–391
Blake, Robert R., 254–255
Body language. *See* Proxemics
Bonding stage, 144
Brainstorming, 244, 256
Businessman vs. businesswoman, 64
Buzz phrase, 67

C

Captive audiences, 272
Card catalog, 280
Causal reasoning, 389

Cause-effect patterns, 299–300
Certainty vs. provisionalism, 170
Chalkboards, use of, 320
Channels, 11, 108
Character, 385–386
Charisma, 386–387
Chronological patterns of organization, 298
Circular argument, 391
Circumscribing stage, 145
Clichés, 149
Climate. *See* Communication climate
Climax patterns, 300
Closed questions, 192–193
Clothing, 119–121
Coercion, 374
Coercive power, 250, 253
Cohesiveness, in groups, 246–249
Column charts, 317–318
Combs, Arthur, and Donald Snygg, 24
Commitment, 35
Common ground, 387, 395
Communication
   characteristics of, 5–6
   defined, 4–5
   functions of, 6–9
   misconceptions about, 15–17
   model of, 10–15
   perception and, 26–35
   see also Relationships; Language; Listening
Communication anxiety. *See* Stage fright
Communication climate, 162–170
   development of, 164–166
Communication networks, 229–230
Comparisons, 309–310
Competence, 142, 385
Complementary communication, 60
Complementary relationships, 140–141
Compromise, 175–176
Conclusions, speech, 300, 304–305
Confirming responses, 162–163
Conflict, 170–182

(Credits continued from page iv.)

PHOTO CREDITS